DEFINING SPORT COMMUNICATION

Defining Sport Communication is a comprehensive resource addressing core topics and issues, including humanistic, organizational, relational, and mediated approaches to the study of sport communication. It provides foundational work in sport communication for students and scholars, reflecting the abundance of research published in recent years and the ever-increasing interest in this area of study.

Bringing together scholars from various epistemological viewpoints within communication, this volume provides a unique opportunity for defining the breadth and depth of sport communication research. It will serve as a seminal reference for existing scholarship as well as provide an agenda for future research.

Andrew C. Billings is the Director of the Alabama Program in Sports Communication and Ronald Reagan Chair of Broadcasting in the Department of Journalism & Creative Media at the University of Alabama. His research interests lie in the intersection of sport, mass media, consumption habits, and identity-laden content. With twelve books and over 130 journal articles and book chapters, he is one of the most published sports media scholars in the world. His books include *Olympic Media: Inside the Biggest Show on Television* (Routledge, 2008) and *The Fantasy Sport Industry: Games within Games* (Routledge, 2014) and his journal outlets include the *Journal of Communication, Journalism & Mass Communication Quarterly, Mass Communication & Society*, and the *Journal of Broadcasting & Electronic Media*. His writings have been translated into five languages. He also serves on many editorial boards, including as an Associate Editor of the journals *Communication & Sport* and *Journal of Global Sport Management*. Billings' work has won numerous awards from organizations such as the International Communication Association, National Communication Association, Broadcast Education Association, and the Association for Education in Mass Communication and Journalism. He is the current chair of the Communication & Sport Division of the National Communication Association, and a former chair of the Sport Communication Interest Group of the International Communication Association. He has lectured in nations around the world, from Spain to China to Austria. His work in the classroom has also earned him many teaching awards. He has been interviewed over 500 times by media outlets ranging from *The New York Times* to *The Los Angeles Times* to ESPN. Billings has also consulted with many sports media agencies and is a past holder of the Invited Chair of Olympism at the Autonomous University of Barcelona.

DEFINING SPORT COMMUNICATION

Edited by Andrew C. Billings

ASSISTANT EDITOR: FEI QIAO

Routledge
Taylor & Francis Group

NEW YORK AND LONDON

First published 2017
by Routledge
711 Third Avenue, New York, NY 10017

and by Routledge
2 Park Square, Milton Park, Abingdon, Oxon, OX14 4RN

Routledge is an imprint of the Taylor & Francis Group, an informa business

Library of Congress Cataloging in Publication Data
Names: Billings, Andrew C., editor.
Title: Defining sport communication / edited by Andrew C. Billings.
Description: New York : Routledge, 2017. | Includes bibliographical
    references and index.
Identifiers: LCCN 2016022558 (print) | LCCN 2016042596 (ebook) |
    ISBN 9781138909595 (hardback) | ISBN 9781138909601 (paperback) |
    ISBN 9781315693910 (ebook)
Subjects: LCSH: Communication in sports.
Classification: LCC GV567.5 .D43 2017 (print) | LCC GV567.5 (ebook) |
    DDC 070.4/49796—dc23
LC record available at https://lccn.loc.gov/2016022558

ISBN: 978-1-138-90959-5 (hbk)
ISBN: 978-1-138-90960-1 (pbk)
ISBN: 978-1-315-69391-0 (ebk)

Typeset in Bembo Std
by Swales & Willis Ltd, Exeter, Devon, UK

Printed and bound in the United States of America by
Edwards Brothers Malloy on sustainably sourced paper

CONTENTS

ACKNOWLEDGMENTS

Edited books require the support and cooperation of so many people; the sheer number of moving pieces and coordinating communications are too numerous to count. However, the creation of *Defining Sport Communication* represents the work of so many people not only meeting deadlines, but also doing so with an exceedingly high level of skill and dedication. I was (and am) honored to be shepherding work that I believe will truly advance the subdiscipline of sport communication in a substantial manner.

The primary appreciation has to be extended to the 32 people who contributed to the project as sole or co-authors of these chapters. The book necessitated some stricter requirements on structures for their writing, yet all found ways to work within these parameters to still be creative, articulate, and visionary.

Thanks must also be extended to Taylor & Francis/Routledge and specifically to Linda Bathgate, who never wavered in her support for the project. She also brings an institutional knowledge to the field of communication that is invaluable, brainstorming units and chapters while still allowing me flexibility in final decisions.

Next, I must thank Fei Qiao for serving the oft-thankless task of being an assistant editor. From checking reference matches to emailing scholars for different pieces of information, she exemplified what it means to be an engaged doctoral student and research assistant.

I also must note the support I receive from the College of Communication & Information Sciences at the University of Alabama as they allow me the academic space and flexibility to pursue book projects with this type of scope. Truly, the work also could not be accomplished without the support provided via my endowed chair as the Ronald Reagan Chair of Broadcasting, for which I am very thankful.

Finally, I must thank my family for their unwavering support that allows me to pursue these types of larger projects. My wife, Angela, and sons, Nathan and Noah, somehow find a way to allow me the time to get the work done while then making me smile at moments when parts of the work seem stressful.

CONTRIBUTORS

Steve Bien-Aimé (PhD, Pennsylvania State University, 2016) is an assistant professor in the Manship School of Mass Communication at Louisiana State University. His research interests concentrate on race and gender portrayals in news and sports media.

Andrew C. Billings (PhD, Indiana University, 1999) is the Ronald Reagan Chair of Broadcasting and Director of the Alabama Program in Sports Communication at the University of Alabama. His research interests lie in the intersection of sport, media, and society.

Kim Bissell (PhD, Syracuse University, 1999) is a professor in the Department of Journalism and the Director of Undergraduate Research at the University of Alabama. Her research interests lie in the intersection of health, sport, media, and children.

Nicholas D. Bowman (PhD, Michigan State University, 2010) is an associate professor with the Department of Communication Studies at West Virginia University, where he is also the founding research associate of their Interaction Lab (#ixlab). His research looks at the uses and effects of interactive media as related to users' thoughts, emotions, and behaviors.

Andy Boyan (PhD, Michigan State University, 2012) is an assistant professor with the Communication Studies Department at Albion College. His research and teaching examine the role that patterns of rule systems impact digital game play and learning, sport spectatorship, and the communication process.

Kenon A. Brown (PhD, University of Alabama, 2012) is an assistant professor of public relations at the University of Alabama and a fellow for the Plank Center for Leadership in Public Relations and the Alabama Program in Sport Communication. His sport-related research interests include athlete image repair and the effects of mediated coverage of international sporting events.

Michael L. Butterworth (PhD, Indiana University, 2006) is Director and Associate Professor in the School of Communication Studies at Ohio University. His research investigates the relationships between rhetoric, democracy, and sport, with particular interests in national identity, militarism, and public memory.

R. Glenn Cummins (PhD, University of Alabama, 2005) is Associate Professor in the College of Media and Communication and Director of the Center for Communication Research at Texas Tech University. His research examines the impact of message content and structural properties on individual processing of and response to media messages.

Michael B. Devlin (PhD, University of Alabama, 2013) is an assistant professor of advertising in the College of Communications at DePaul University. His research interests examine the intersection of advertising and sport – focusing on the cognitive, affective, and behavioral effects of fan identification, and its impact on sponsorships, endorsements, branding, and campaigns.

Walter Gantz (PhD, Michigan State University, 1975) is Professor and Chair of Communication Science in the Media School at Indiana University. His current research focuses on the arc of sport fanship.

Howard Giles (PhD, DSc, University of Bristol, 1971, 1996) is Distinguished Professor of Communication at the University of California, Santa Barbara and Honorary Professor in the School of Psychology, University of Queensland, Australia. His research focuses on many areas of intergroup communication, including police–community encounters, interethnic, and intergenerational relations.

Daniel A. Grano (PhD, Louisiana State University, 2003) is an associate professor in the Department of Communication Studies at the University of North Carolina at Charlotte. His research focuses on intersections between popular morality and power in mediated sport contexts.

Marie Hardin (PhD, University of Georgia, 1998) is the Dean of the College of Communications at Penn State University. Her research interests concentrate on diversity, ethics, and professional practices in mediated sport.

Davis W. Houck (PhD, Pennsylvania State University, 1995) is Fannie Lou Hamer Professor of Rhetorical Studies at Florida State University. His scholarship on sports and media engages themes of race, masculinity, gender, and nationality.

Thomas E. Isaacson (PhD, Michigan State University, 2012) is Assistant Professor of Public Relations at Northern Michigan University. His research interests include sport public relations and international public relations education.

Jeffrey W. Kassing (PhD, Kent State University, 1997) is Professor of Communication Studies at Arizona State University. He has published organizational communication research focusing largely on employee dissent and sport research that considers coach–athlete communication, fan–athlete interaction, social media, and sport media.

Abraham I. Khan (PhD, University of Minnesota, 2010) is Assistant Professor of African American Studies and Communication Arts and Sciences at Pennsylvania State University. He is a rhetorical scholar whose research centers on the intersection of sport and black political culture and is the author of a book about baseball player Curt Flood, and essays on black athletes such as Jackie Robinson, Michael Sam, and Richard Sherman.

Edward (Ted) M. Kian (PhD, Florida State University, 2006) is the Welch-Bridgewater Endowed Chair of Sports Media in the School of Media and Strategic Communications at Oklahoma State University. His research focuses on sport media, specifically examining the framing of gender, sex, and LGBTQ in content, social media, and Web 2.0, attitudes and experiences of sport media members, and sport marketing.

Robert L. Krizek (PhD, Arizona State University, 1995) is Emeritus Associate Professor in the Department of Communication at Saint Louis University with a secondary appointment in aviation science. He conducts research in the areas of organizational communication, sport communication, storytelling/narrative, identity performance, and ethnographic methodologies.

Nicky Lewis (PhD, Indiana University, 2015) is an assistant professor in the School of Communication at the University of Miami. Her research interests center on social psychological perspectives in the processing and effects of entertainment media.

Simon Ličen (PhD, University of Ljubljana, 2011) is an assistant professor in the College of Education at Washington State University. His research interests include the management of sport, media, and identity, most notably in international contexts.

Robyn Matthews (MA, Communication Studies, 2016) is a graduate student at Arizona State University. Her research interests are within the context of sport looking at communication between coaches, athletes, parents and fans.

Lindsey J. Meân (PhD, University of Sheffield, 1995) is an associate professor at Arizona State University. Her research interests involve the intersections of sport, identities, discourses, ideology, culture, power, language, and representational practices with a focus on gender, sexuality, race, media, and youth sport.

Jon F. Nussbaum (PhD, Purdue University, 1981) is Professor of Communication Arts and Sciences and Human Development and Family Studies at Pennsylvania State University. His research interests lie in lifespan communication, health communication, and family communication.

Arthur A. Raney (PhD, University of Alabama, 1998) is the James E. Kirk Professor of Communication at Florida State University. In general terms, his research and writings explore the psychology of media entertainment, with specific interests in the nature of enjoyment and the role of morality in the reception process.

Jimmy Sanderson (PhD, Arizona State University, 2012) is a Visiting Assistant Professor of Communication at Arizona State University. His research centers on the influence of social media in sport and he also maintains research interests in sport and health.

Michael Stohl (PhD, Northwestern University, 1974) is Professor of Communication and Director of the Orfalea Center for Global and International Studies at the University of California, Santa Barbara. His research focuses on political communication with special reference to terrorism and human rights, including issues of intergroup identity and violence.

Paul D. Turman (PhD, University of Nebraska-Lincoln, 2000) is the System Vice President for Academic Affairs with the South Dakota Board of Regents. His research interests lie in the intersection of sport and interpersonal/ instructional relationships.

Lawrence A. Wenner (PhD, University of Iowa, 1977) is Von der Ahe Professor of Communication and Ethics in the College of Communication and Fine Arts and the School of Film and Television at Loyola Marymount University. His research on communication and sport focuses on critical and ethical assessments of sport spectacle, commodification, and the intersection of gender and race.

Erin Whiteside (PhD, Pennsylvania State University, 2010) is Associate Professor of Journalism and Electronic Media at the University of Tennessee. Her research, which focuses on sociopolitical issues in communication and sport, has appeared in *Mass Communication & Society*, *Journalism*, *Sociology of Sport Journal*, and *International Journal of Sport Communication*, among others.

Amber K. Worthington (MA, Pennsylvania State University, 2013) is a doctoral candidate in the Department of Communication Arts and Sciences at Pennsylvania State University. Her research interests lie in lifespan/family communication, health communication, and message design.

DEFINING SPORT COMMUNICATION

An Introduction to a Nuanced Field

Andrew C. Billings

UNIVERSITY OF ALABAMA

The late renowned novelist David Foster Wallace (2008) once offered an intriguing story:

> There are these two young fish swimming along, and they happen to meet an older fish swimming the other way, who nods at them and says, "Morning, boys, how's the water?" And the two young fish swim on for a bit, and then eventually one of them looks over at the other and goes, "What the hell is water?"
>
> *(para. 1)*

Wallace uses the parable to explain that many of our most difficult conceptions are the most ubiquitous, and, upon reflection, the most permeating—the most obvious. In sum, when a concept becomes so immersive, one often neglects to critique and consider it as that ubiquity is equated as context for other events rather than a core element itself.

How does this story fit the core elements of this book? Because sport is the context for so many elements of modern life. For humans, sport is part and parcel of the 'water' in which we navigate our own lives. The mere fact that a book such as this can offer relationships between sport and 22 unique subfields of communication alone underscores just how pervasive sport often is. The fact that one could do the same types of sports-related applications within other disciplinary subfields adds veracity to this claim.

When making the decision as to whether to author or edit a book, one core question should be primary: Can any single person or even pair of people adequately cover the issues the volume hopes to traverse? If the answer is yes, one writes the book—sometimes with a coauthor. If the answer is no, one seeks an edited volume, carefully culling together voices and intellects that can, collectively, accomplish the end goal. With this book, that core question was relatively easy to answer, as no person (most certainly including myself) has the breadth and depth of knowledge to cover the vast reach encompassed when sport and communication are central touchstones. Thus, this book is edited, knowing that even in the scope of 22 chapters, there is considerable terrain left unsynthesized.

At the outset, the title for this book, *Defining Sport Communication*, was potentially troubling. Such an attempt at definition seemingly inherently represents an attempt to limit the scope of the field. And yet, after decades of robust research under the umbrella designation of 'sport communication' or 'communication and sport', there had been relatively little attempt to pinpoint what that uniquely is or how it unfolds within given communicative subdisciplines. Indeed, the argument of 'which comes first' (see Wenner, 2015) continues to be a subject of considerable debate, as 'communication and sport' places the disciplinary grounding before the context of investigation; conversely, 'sport communication' offers the context in which the discipline and theoretical underpinnings should be deciphered. Moreover, one camp could claim that 'communication and sport' offers a label with two nouns that could be argued to be of equal value (albeit with one listed in front of the other), while another camp could claim 'sport communication' places communication more centrally, offering 'sport' as a mere adjective modifying the central element to scholarly investigation: communication. In my coauthored textbook (Billings, Butterworth, & Turman, 2014), communication is listed before sport, making the case that doing so emphasizes study over practice. However, as one will discover over the course of reading this book, the interplay of study and practice is differentially applied, sometimes privileging one over the other while, more often than not, having the two inevitably overlap and inform each other. Ultimately, this volume could have been titled *Defining Communication and Sport* and still been structured in a similar manner, with the current title being offered as a slightly more concise attempt at defining an omnipresent and rapidly ascending field.

More than a decade after Kassing et al. (2004) offered a landmark glimpse not only at what the field of communication and sport was through the lens of community, the four-pronged approach offered with the *Communication Yearbook* piece still largely holds. Kassing and colleagues offered communication and sport through the quad-partite structure of enacting, (re)producing, consuming, and organizing sport; each of those elements now percolates within a body of sport-related scholarship that is shaping substantial understanding of communication as a holistic discipline. The result is the ability to explore sport within 22 separate subdisciplines within this book, jointly telling not merely how sport informs communication, but how communication informs sport.

Communication, as a field, has often usefully embraced the lack of formal disciplinary boundaries to offer relevance to a wide range of scholarly pursuits;

Communication-Across-the-Curriculum (CAC) initiatives are at least partly the result of such willingness for communication scholarship and pedagogy to share understandings with other ancillary disciplines. Nevertheless, there is value in definition, as doing so necessitates critical contemplation of what communication—or in this case, sport communication—uniquely brings to the table. D.H. Lawrence once said that, "It is never freedom until you find something you really positively want to be. And people in America have always been shouting about the things they are not." In defining sport communication, some of these boundaries will likely appear limiting to some, yet such concreteness appears to be what is needed at this stage of formally developing sport communication as a subdiscipline. Otherwise, if the approach is 'everyone in the winner's circle', one could astutely counter: 'Then why have a circle?' Thus, I wholeheartedly concede that a great book could be constructed focusing on what non-communication-oriented fields bring to the sport communication equation. I also readily maintain that a volume focusing on issues beyond American borders could considerably advance the conversation. However, as a U.S.-based communication scholar, I am likely not the one to facilitate those discussions.

The chapters offered in this book do more than just define 22 different subdisciplines as they relate to sport, as each author was asked to (a) indicate how a given communication subdiscipline ties to sport, (b) delineate communication-based theories relevant to sport within the subdiscipline, (c) overview published seminal works offering connections between sport and the communication subdiscipline, and (d) articulate directions for future research within sport and the communication subdiscipline. In an attempt to achieve these lofty aims, only scholars with a formal communication background were asked to participate. This is not to discount the tremendous work in fields that could be labeled communication-adjacent (e.g., sociology, management, kinesiology), but, instead, to bolster a best attempt at rendering what communication as a discipline can uniquely offer to any work wishing to embrace the joint concepts of sport and communication in a variety of relevant contexts.

One of the strengths of sport communication work is the global embodiment of the sport, with megasporting events (see Eastman, Newton, & Pack, 1996) such as the Olympics and World Cup serving as touchstones for understanding communication beyond strict national boundaries. Nevertheless, the majority of sport unfolds within specific—and usually unique—national circumstances. Core elements of sport, ranging from the games played to the value society places within the athletic complex to the differential mediating aims of a multitude of multimedia platforms, all differ greatly from nation to nation. As such, this book also focuses rather exclusively on American sport and how it unfolds within the national culture. Certainly chapters such as Ličen's contribution (see Chapter 14) on international communication pertain to issues beyond the geographic boundaries of the United States, yet Anderson's (1983) notion of the "imagined political community" (p. 6) nonetheless underscores that these seemingly arbitrary boundaries are nonetheless formalized under national governmental structures. Exploring international sport as it unfolds within communication processes and structures is a very worthy endeavor, yet ultimately falls beyond the scope of the parameters of this book.

Instead, what this book does is explore three main thrusts of current scholarship that each have robust potential areas for expansion. Unit structures arguably work from the individual to the masses, beginning with humanistic approaches to sport communication (Part I) before then moving to organizational/relational approaches (Part II) and then, finally, media-based approaches (Part III). Chapter authors are truly experts within communication—some with established records of producing sport communication scholarship, some others with considerable prestige in a given subarea yet exploring the relationships specifically with sport for the first time. All have an excellent sense of where intellectual conversations reside within a communicative subarea, making them ideal resources for synthesizing past research with an eye on how research can be more innovative and integrative in the coming years.

The book is also designed in a manner that one can easily seek out a single chapter and, hopefully, determine the key scholars, contributions, and streams of thought/argument that are currently prominent in that area. As such, one can treat this as a reference book. However, that is not the manner in which it is hoped you opt to consume it because, when read as a collective, single contribution, one should be able to decipher where 22 different subdisciplines intersect, blend, and, potentially, could yield more robust scholarship in the future. When taking the book as a whole, one discovers a plethora of ideas that are typically not in opposition, but rather, more likely, issues of micro vs. macro as well as epistemological difference.

Indeed, the key questions are answered in ways that offer many future debates and potential refinement. For instance, many authors attempt to specifically offer their own definition of sport communication. For instance, in Chapter 4, Krizek offers an astute definition of the field being defined in the broader volume, arguing that:

> Sport communication is the process of creating and sharing meanings by individuals participating in the embodied (combining physical and mental exertion and execution) activity of sport. Sport communication also includes the meaning making of individuals observing that activity; governing, directing or commenting on that activity; and/or discussing the influence of sport on individuals and on society.

Using such concepts in tandem with previous definitions from the likes of J. Bowyer Bell, who argues that sport is "a repeatable, regulated, physical contest producing a clear winner" (in Rowe, 2004, pp. 12–13), or Guttmann (1978), who differentiates between play, games, contests, and sports in noteworthy manners, can help aid the understanding of where communication fits within a broader landscape of sport culture. One could adopt the thinking of the wisdom of crowds to find the points of contact and mutual collaboration between definitions, building a useful heuristic which sport communication scholars could adopt in future work.

As such, one can find various warrants and claims throughout the book that can be used to counter any notion that sport communication merely involves fun and games without any serious connotation. In Chapter 3, Wenner notes that "the role of communication is essential as sport comes to have social force and cultural meaning through its communication." How complex and pervasive are these concepts? Turman, in Chapter 11, claims that "sport represents a complex, multilayered, and pervasive institution composed of athletes, coaches, and parents/families working collectively to shape experiences for those involved." From a mediated point of view, Gantz and Lewis claim in Chapter 16 that

> Sport audiences matter in ways similar to the audiences for all other content. They are bought and sold, coveted, lured and triumphantly trumpeted, cared for and cared about. Sport audiences are not a province or breed apart from the rest: those who follow sport work, play, and study; have families, colleagues, and friends; and turn to a variety of media platforms and content domains.

Humanistic approaches are certainly central to understanding these layers of meaning undergirding the modern sport complex; Butterworth, in Chapter 1, claims that "rhetoric, sport, and democracy are connected—and have been connected historically—in substantial ways". In each chapter, one will discover some sense of staking a claim, with scholars such as Nussbaum and Worthington noting in Chapter 12 that "the very core of both of our family's identities is grounded in sport." These are not uncommon tales. In virtually every sphere, the case can be made for substantial, deep interrogation of sport communication because the book collectively claims, as Raney specifically states in Chapter 17, that "sport is much more than *just* entertainment."

Thus, you are invited to delve deeply into the world of sport communication as defined by 32 authors, coauthors, and editors that collectively render this volume. The book is specifically divided into three units of understanding, although those could certainly be argued as being artificial distinctions. Nevertheless, the design works somewhat from micro to macro, or, perhaps, from the specific to the general, with a greater emphasis on critical/cultural scholarship in the opening, more qualitative work represented in the middle, and more quantitative empirical work being represented in the concluding chapters. The goal is to no longer place these approaches in opposition to one another; rather, they are, at least within core elements, in concert with one another.

Within Part I one gains a glimpse at humanistic approaches to the field of sport communication. The first two chapters represent approaches that are typically quite complementary to one another, with Michael Butterworth (Ohio University) offering understandings in the rhetorical domain and Daniel Grano (University of North Carolina-Charlotte) offering critical–cultural insights. Chapter 3 features perhaps the most established sport communication scholar in the world, Lawrence Wenner (Loyola Marymount University), offering an exposition of the role of ethics through the lens of dirt theory and other hybrid approaches for exacting meaning from context and social structures. Chapter 4 is offered by Robert Krizek (Saint Louis University), exploring a part of the field that has largely gone unexplored except for him and a small cadre of others: sport as ethnographic examination. The next chapter is offered by Davis Houck (Florida State University), who focuses on political communication in its many forms from the language to enactment of sport within formalized structures. The final three chapters in this part offer humanistic approaches regarding issues of identity, certainly a core element of any sophisticated investigation of the impact of sport on society—and society on sport. Lindsey Meân (Arizona State University) offers insights regarding gender and feminist studies, Abraham Khan (Pennsylvania State University) focuses on issues of race and ethnicity, and Edward Kian (Oklahoma State University) reviews impacts in and on sport regarding GLBTQ issues.

The chapters in Part II function as a quintet of works related to organizational and relational approaches to sport communication. Arguably many of these chapters represent areas in need of a greater number of studies, as some, specifically intergroup and family communication, are largely neglected from a sport-specific perspective even while acknowledging tremendous impact of sport surrounding these types of relationships. Chapter 9 is written by Jeffrey Kassing and Robyn Matthews (Arizona State University), who focus on sport as organizations and the communication built within them using a sporting lens. Next, Howard Giles and Michael Stohl (University of California-Santa Barbara) offer a very useful set of guide points to advance work in the area of intergroup communication. Paul Turman (South Dakota Board of Regents) explores the intriguing dynamics involved within interpersonal messages in sport, ranging from coach/athlete to parent/child dyads in Chapter 11. Nussbaum and Worthington (Pennsylvania State University) offer a personalized Chapter 12, using some specific instances from their own upbringings to underscore key issues involved in sport as family communication. Finally, this part concludes with an extensive review in Chapter 13, as Kim Bissell (University of Alabama) highlights the critical role sport plays within all elements of how we study health.

The final set of chapters explores sport communication within the mediated realm. Simon Ličen (Washington State University) opens with a unique examination of how sport is often studied when mediation crosses national borders.

Chapter 15 thoroughly debunks conceptions of sport journalism being the 'toy store' of media entities, as Steve Bien-Aimé (Louisiana State University), Erin Whiteside (University of Tennessee), and Marie Hardin (Pennsylvania State University) collectively review sport in and as journalism. Next, Walter Gantz (Indiana University) and Nicky Lewis (University of Miami) offer a sophisticated discussion of how audiences respond to and about sport in mediated contexts within Chapter 16, specifically offering very fruitful potential areas for future investigation. Building directly from some of the core tenets of the previous chapter, Arthur Raney (Florida State University) then explores entertainment studies within media in Chapter 17, while Glenn Cummins (Texas Tech University) specifically delves into the world of broadcast studies in Chapter 18, usefully delineating between visual and aural aspects. Next are two chapters representing burgeoning new areas of study within sport communication, with Jimmy Sanderson (Clemson University) exploring social media networking studies in Chapter 19 and the pair of Nicholas Bowman (West Virginia University) and Andy Boyan (Albion College) attempting to initiate the uninitiated into the world of sport and gaming in Chapter 20. This final part concludes with two industry-specific offerings that each have useful implications not only for scholars but for practitioners within these applied fields. Michael Devlin (DePaul University) offers a review of how sport permeates the realm of advertising in Chapter 21, while Kenon Brown (University of Alabama) and Thomas Isaacson (Northern Michigan University) offer a concluding chapter focusing on public relations, specifically focusing on issues of crisis communication and image repair in Chapter 22.

Of course, even a book like this could have had more subdisciplines represented with more approaches to the study of sport communication appearing in scholarship in seemingly greater number each year. Sport is in the water of modern American culture, with this book offering a deep dive into the mechanisms, structures, discourses, cognitions, and behaviors that likely will keep scholars fascinated for decades to come.

References

Anderson, B. (1983). *Imagined communities*. New York: Verso.

Billings, A.C., Butterworth, M.L., & Turman, P.D. (2014). *Communication and sport: Surveying the field* (2nd ed.). Thousand Oaks, CA: Sage.

Eastman, S.T., Newton, G.D., & Pack, L. (1996). Promoting primetime programs in megasporting events. *Journal of Broadcasting & Electronic Media, 40*, 366–388.

Guttmann, A. (1978). *From ritual to record: The nature of modern sports*. New York: Columbia University Press.

Kassing, J.W., Billings, A.C., Brown, R.S., Halone, K.K., Harrison, K., Krizek, B., Meân, L., & Turman, P.D. (2004). Communication in the community of sport: The process of enacting, (re)producing, consuming, and organizing sport. *Communication Yearbook, 28*, 373–410.

Rowe, D. (2004). *Sport, culture, and media.* Buckingham, UK: Open University Press.

Wallace, D.F. (September 20, 2008). Plain old untrendy troubles and emotions. *The Guardian.* Retrieved June 6, 2016, from http://www.theguardian.com/books/2008/sep/20/fiction.

Wenner, L.A. (2015). Where art thou? *Communication & Sport, 3*(3), 247–260.

PART I

Humanistic Approaches to Sport

1

SPORT AS RHETORICAL ARTIFACT

Michael L. Butterworth

OHIO UNIVERSITY

Arguably the oldest of academic disciplines, rhetoric's origins date back to the 6th century BCE (Ricouer, 1997). It truly came of age in ancient Greece and was later institutionalized as part of the original three liberal arts, along with grammar and dialectic, known together as the *trivium* (Booth, 2004). In the 21st century, rhetoric maintains a strong disciplinary identity in both communication studies, featuring a tradition grounded in public address, and English, featuring a tradition grounded in composition. Yet, despite this rich history and continued currency, rhetorical scholars have only very recently begun to take sport seriously as a site of inquiry.

On the one hand, this is of little surprise, given that the development of rhetorical criticism as a method in the 20th century was animated by a focus on political speakers and speeches. From this view, scholarship largely appropriated the vocabulary of Aristotle and, to a lesser degree, Cicero, in the effort to evaluate "rhetorical discourse in terms of its effects on its immediate audience" (Black, 1978, p. 31). Such an approach necessarily privileges more formal political arenas and discourse, often at the expense of communicative forms residing within the popular or vernacular.

On the other hand, the bifurcation of the political and the popular neglects the various ways they implicate one another, something evident when the subject is sport. Indeed, from its emergence as a form of persuasive discourse in antiquity, rhetoric was linked overtly with sport. Rhetoric's earliest practitioners, the Sophists, engaged in a project characterized by the *dissoi logoi*, a principle that spotlights the "double argument" entailed in any discourse. As Crick (2014, p. 187) explains, "*Dissoi logoi* is not simply a statement that people disagree; it emphasizes that productive action must be preceded by thoughtful debate, criticism, and advocacy that draw on the wealth of available knowledge to produce warranted assertions." In other words, rhetoric is defined by an *agonistic* attitude that can be understood as a kind of contest or competition. Poulakos (1995) connects this attitude explicitly to the sporting context of the time:

> Normalized and internalized through the organization of the Olympic Games, this institutionalized form of cultural activity shaped sophistical rhetoric in its image, making public discourse a matter of competition. In turn, sophistical rhetoric pushed competition beyond the boundaries of the stadium and into the rhetorical forums of the court and the Assembly.
>
> *(pp. 32–33)*

Hawhee (2005) expands on this connection, again stressing that rhetoric and sport—in her terms, athletics—are mutually invested in *agonism*:

> Concerning the contest between rhetoric and athletics, a comment by Gorgias underscores my point about the importance of the encounter of the *agōn*. In an extant fragment of a speech delivered at the Olympic Games, Gorgias explicitly places athletics and rhetoric next to each other: "A contest (*agōnisma*) such as we have requires double excellence (*dittōn areitōn*): daring (*tolmēs*) and skill (*sophia*). Daring is needed to withstand danger, and skill to understand how to trip the opponent (*pligma*). For surely speech, like the summons at the Olympic Games, calls the willing but crowns the capable."
>
> *(pp. 29–30)*

Importantly, Hawhee observes that competition is not an end in and of itself. Rather, agonism privileges the sense of community cultivated by the contest. As she notes, "The Olympic Games . . . depended on the gathering of athletes, judges, and spectators alike. *Agora*, the marketplace, shares the same derivative and a strikingly similar force of meaning as *agōn*, and, as is commonly known, functioned as the ancient gathering place par excellence" (Hawhee, 2005, p. 15). Later, Roman emperors Nero and Domitian included oratorical contests in athletic festivals inspired by the Greek Olympic Games (Kyle, 2014).

Both rhetoric and sport developed in the same era as a third significant contribution from ancient Greek society: democracy. Timmerman and McDorman (2008, p. xiii) assert the relationship between rhetoric and democracy is "a necessary one, in the sense that democracy is impossible without the practice of public discourse and dialogue among citizens." Moreover, defining democracy in rhetorical terms once again implies the presence of contestation and competition. All of which is to say that rhetoric, sport, and democracy are connected—and have been connected historically—in substantial ways.

The shared agonism of rhetoric, sport, and democracy has implications for contemporary rhetorical studies. No longer restrained by academic conventions limiting subject matter to speakers and speeches, rhetorical critics now attend to a range of discursive forms, from social movements, to films, to monuments and memorials. Increasingly in the past decade or so, sport can be added to this list. With this in mind, it is useful to outline the general commitments of contemporary rhetorical theory, especially as they hail the classical practices I have detailed above. In doing so, we can begin to chart the trajectory of recent scholarship that views sport as a rhetorical artifact.

In their book, *Contemporary Rhetorical Theory*, Lucaites and Condit (1998) suggest that contemporary rhetorical scholars borrow from the classical tradition in four important ways. First, rhetoric is understood as *persuasive* discourse. In contrast to ancient philosophers, who viewed 'truth' as an inherent property for which words were merely a vehicle of communication, classical rhetoricians believed "especially in the context of social and political affairs, the manner and form of discourse was integral to the 'truth' of the thing being described and played a central role in shaping collective identity and action" (Lucaites & Condit, 1998, p. 3). In other words, rhetoric acknowledges that symbols are manipulated for a particular effect. Second, rhetoric takes place in *public*. Given the democratic context of ancient Greek society, citizens needed a means through which they could deliberate and make decisions. Thus, the "emphasis on public discourse focused attention on communicative acts that affected the entire community" (Lucaites & Condit, 1998, p. 3). Third, rhetoric operates in situations of *contingency*. Given the imperfections of both people and language, rhetoric allows for an assessment of the probable over the certain. As Lucaites and Condit (1998, p. 2) conclude, "The best we can do is to make reasoned decisions based upon our knowledge of the past and the likelihood of future possibilities." Fourth, rhetoric is *contextual*, meaning that what is persuasive for one audience at a given point in time may not be persuasive for another audience at a different point in time. Accordingly, "The capacity for meaning in any linguistic usage is almost always subject to change and adaption" (Lucaties & Condit, 1998, p. 4).

Although few contemporary rhetorical critics frame their scholarship explicitly in the four characteristics I've identified above, they nevertheless are likely influenced by these core concepts. With these principles in mind, then, I want to attend to the ways scholars have conceptualized sport as a rhetorical phenomenon. I cannot claim to be exhaustive here, but I maintain that rhetorical studies of sport can be organized around four primary themes: (1) public address in sport, especially through instances of image repair; (2) sport as metaphor and the use of metaphor in sport; (3) rhetorical approaches to mediated representations in sport; and (4) rhetorical interpretations of the myths communicated by sport.

Public Address in Sport

Studies of public address may no longer be the dominant form of rhetorical inquiry, but they nevertheless retain a prominent place in the field. For scholars interested in sport, public address is most commonly studied in terms of apologia and image repair (see Chapter 22). Apologia is a rhetorical genre defined as "a public speech of self-defense" (Ware & Linkugel, 1973). Early studies (Kruse, 1981; Nelson, 1984) focused on high-profile athletes attempting to recover from public relations mistakes. The context for those studies—the 1970s and 1980s—shares much in common with the contemporary era. The claim that sport "has such a pervasive effect upon the lives of so many" (Kruse, 1981, p. 283), for example, remains one of the primary reasons for the communicative study of sport. The significance of this statement, however, is also found in the ways that today's sporting context is exponentially larger, louder, and more pervasive. Accordingly, we find ourselves in an era of intense scrutiny of athletic figures, both within their respective sports and their larger communities. Thus, recent years have seen a growing interest in this area of scholarship, especially as it intersects with the theory of image repair.

Image repair, previously known as image restoration, is an approach to apologetic discourse largely attributed to the work of Benoit (1997, 2015). Benoit's framework builds on the theory of apologia and establishes a set of possible responses for crisis situations. As he defines it, "Image repair discourse is a persuasive message or group of messages that respond(s) to attacks or suspicions that promote a negative attitude about the source of image repair" (Benoit, 2015, p. 10). His approach has been highly generative, including for scholars in communication and sport. This is best exemplified by a full collection of essays, *Repairing the Athlete's Image* (Blaney, Lippert, & Smith, 2013). As Blaney (2013) details, image restoration can occur across five broad strategies: deny wrongdoing, evade responsibility, reduce the seriousness of the offense, offer corrective action, or ask for forgiveness. In recent years, a range of high-profile athletes—Lance Armstrong, Kobe Bryant, Hope Solo, Serena Williams, Tiger Woods, and so forth—have been involved in actions or events that have prompted a need to repair their image.

Brazeal's (2013) study of Serena Williams offers a good example of how a rhetorical critic might approach image repair. Williams found herself needing to apologize after an "on-court meltdown" during the 2009 U.S. Open, during which she berated a line judge so forcefully that she received a point penalty that ultimately gave her semifinal opponent, Kim Clijsters, the victory (Brazeal, 2013, p. 239). The ferocity of Williams' outburst warranted an apology, but she was reluctant to take accountability when questioned in the post-match press conference. It took two written statements for Williams to offer an apology, by which time she had faced considerable criticism. Based on this case of inadequate image repair, Brazeal (2013, pp. 249–250) concludes that "the timing of the apology is critical to its success," "athletes must understand the culture of their particular sport and be willing to embrace its values," and "athletes should be firm in their stand against rehashing their failings for the press."

Image repair scholarship largely follows a traditional model of rhetorical criticism primarily interested in single speakers, speeches (or formal statements), and potential influence on a specific audience. To that extent, it is appropriate to place image repair in the context of this chapter. At the same time, image repair studies might align more strongly with public relations scholarship, which is generally less interested in rhetoric's democratic commitments and more in its *instrumental* capacities. Thus, more commonly, contemporary theorists are invested in rhetoric's *constitutive* capacities. This approach, most often associated with the work of Charland (1987), views rhetoric's effects as less direct and more ideological. Scholarship about sport from this perspective commonly addresses use of metaphor, issues of representation, and articulations with common mythologies. These themes necessarily intersect and overlap with other areas, including many of those addressed in this volume. My aim here, then, is to spotlight these themes in the cases when they are specifically understood in rhetorical terms, with the open recognition that no one approach can claim ownership of these complicated and important issues.

Metaphor in Sport/Sport as Metaphor

Nietzsche (1989, p. 250) famously declared, "What is truth? A mobile army of metaphors, metonyms, anthropomorphisms, in short, a sum of human relations which were poetically and rhetorically heightened, transferred, and adorned, and after long use seem solid, canonical, and binding to a nation." This passage, itself built from metaphor—"a mobile army"—reminds us that human language evolves from ambiguity to a sense of certainty over time. Metaphor, one of Burke's four "master tropes," is therefore a powerful rhetorical resource, for the repeated use of metaphorical language can lead to its naturalization, a belief that meaning is fixed in the term itself. On the one hand, metaphor is a relatively simple concept. Burke (1941, p. 421) defines it as "a device for seeing something in terms of something else." This understanding is helpful, especially to the degree that metaphor is used to make language more interesting and vibrant. In addition, metaphor's creativity assists in the construction of arguments (Foss, 2009).

Thinking of metaphor as a rhetorical device of argumentation returns us to rhetoric's constitutive function. In American culture, this is especially true with respect to metaphors that feature sport. As Segrave (2000) notes, "The idea of sport as a metaphor for life . . . is so common in America and American literature that it has become part of our conventional wisdom." In particular, he identifies sports such as baseball, boxing, and football as the most familiar vehicles for describing arenas such as "warfare, politics, business and sexual relations" (p. 48).

His study is both descriptive and evaluative. For instance, he identifies common phrases used in business or sex—"take the bull by the horns," "get to first, second, or third base"—that are designed to add variety or provide a way of talking about subjects that might be frowned upon in polite company. Moving beyond this initial level, Segrave (2000) also acknowledges the limits of metaphor, noting that the sport/war intersection can "sanitize the cruelties of war" (p. 50) or that reducing sex to sport transforms "a profound and delicate human relations issue into a problem of strategy" (p. 56).

Other rhetorical studies have provided extended analyses of these metaphorical limits in areas such as politics. Anderson (2011, p. 329) notes that the "most common procedural frame for political campaigns is the game or strategy frame, which structures campaign news using metaphors of competition, particularly those invoking games, sports, and war." More specifically, one longitudinal analysis of *New York Times* coverage reveals the metaphorical horse race to be "the most common topic of newspaper coverage of the presidential campaign" (Benoit, Stein, & Hansen, 2005, p. 359). Although this metaphor may capture the attention of citizens, helping them make sense of long presidential campaigns, there are concerns with such a perspective. In particular, critics worry that thinking of elections as sporting contests reduces citizens to spectators. As Jamieson (1992, p. 165) concludes, "So enmeshed is the vocabulary of horse race and war in our thoughts about politics that we are not conscious that the 'race' is a metaphor and 'spectatorship' an inappropriate role for the electorate. Press reliance on the language of strategy reduces candidate and public accountability."

War is another arena where metaphor may diminish critical reflection. Herbeck (2004) examines the use of football metaphors by public officials and major media outlets during the Desert Storm military campaign in 1991. He concludes that sport metaphors went well beyond clever terminology to describe the conflict. As he observes, "Rather than simply claiming that war can be understood as football, a complex set of football metaphors was employed to characterize all aspects of Desert Storm" (Herbeck, 2004, p. 125). For example, each nation was commonly portrayed as a 'team,' and military strategies were frequently compared with football plays. Perhaps most importantly, much as the 'horse race' diminishes critical engagement, using football to describe war "discouraged substantive discussion of alternatives by casting the American public in the subservient role of the fans" (Herbeck, 2004, p. 129). In the years since 9/11, the persistent and ubiquitous presence of the military at sporting events has so normalized the metaphor that the effect has been to "normalize a culture of war and discourage democratic dissent" (Butterworth, 2014, p. 206).

If such moments occurred in isolation, they perhaps would not have such resonance. However, sport and national politics are so frequently linked that, in some cases, it is difficult to imagine how anyone could claim them to be separate. Consider, for example, the reliance on international sport as a metaphor for the Cold War as evidenced by five decades' worth of Olympic Games and media coverage (Wagg & Andrews, 2007). Even after the Cold War ended in the early 1990s, international events such as the World Cup are widely celebrated as expressions of goodwill and common purpose. Yet, as Delgado (2003) details in his study of the 1998 match between the United States and Iran, media efforts to frame the event as a metaphor for global politics fail to account for the ideological commitments of individual nations and the complexity of international relations. This is similarly the case in Butterworth's (2007a) critique of the 2004 U.S. presidential election, during which the George W. Bush campaign took credit for the ability of the Iraqi National Soccer Team to compete in the Summer Olympics. Despite resistance from many of the players on the Iraqi team, Bush nevertheless exploited the idea that the very presence of the team in the Olympic Games was a metaphor for the presumed success of the U.S.-led war effort in Iraq.

As these examples demonstrate, metaphor is often used for political or ideological purposes. Indeed, it is for these reasons that rhetorical critics should take sport seriously as a site for constituting and contesting political culture. A similar point can be made, as well, with respect to the rhetorical study of representation.

Rhetorical Representations

The communication studies discipline typically compartmentalizes areas of study, including marking a distinction between rhetoric and media studies. Yet, given the degree to which commercialized sport is made available and intelligible through media sources, it can be helpful to think of these two approaches in concert with one another. To the extent that media productions are public messages that can affect attitudes, values, and actions, they can be understood as rhetorical texts. Thus, although subsequent chapters in this book will attend to matters such as gender (Chapter 6) and race (Chapter 7), I will briefly address here the ways rhetorical scholars attend to media representation.

Fuller (2006, p. 7) observes that "as a predominantly male discourse, sporttalk tends to be militaristic, sexual, even violent." Thus, rhetorical studies of gender and sport often attempt to deconstruct these language choices as a means to reimagine how nonheterosexual men are portrayed in the sporting community. Shugart (2003), for example, demonstrates that media coverage of the 1999 Women's World Cup champion soccer team defaulted to the "appropriation of feminist sensibilities" (Shugart, 2003, p. 28), whereby themes of empowerment and female athletic achievement become mechanisms for actually minimizing the role of women in the broader culture. Elsewhere, Lavelle (2015) turns her attention to the presence, or the relative lack thereof, of women in ESPN's highly regarded *30 for 30* documentary series. Her study reveals that, in the cases of Marion Jones, Chris Evert, and Martina Navratilova, the documentaries overvalued characteristics of femininity, family relations, and displays of emotion. By doing so, even efforts to present female athletes in positive terms easily default to common stereotypes about womanhood. As Lavelle (2015, p. 137) concludes, "By focusing on how these accomplished female athletes conform to conventional notions of femininity, it suggests that successful female athletes must uphold these norms to be successful." Other studies (Butterworth, 2006; Cherney & Lindemann, 2010; Mozisek, 2014) confirm that athletes who disrupt gendered norms—by questioning heterosexuality, challenging notions of ableism, or intruding into traditional masculine spaces—are often represented as threats to cultural order.

Similar themes are found in rhetorical studies of race in sport, which is a particularly robust area of study. Khan's (2012) book, *Curt Flood in the Media*, for example, provides an excellent baseline to assess rhetorical studies of sport media (see more in Chapter 7). In it, he contextualizes the moment in 1969 when African-American baseball star Curt Flood refused to accept a trade and initiated a legal challenge to Major League Baseball that ultimately led to free agency in contemporary sports. Flood himself never reaped the benefits of his efforts, however, and the mainstream media of his day largely portrayed him as disrespectful to the game and its fans. Khan maps the articulations between Flood and Jackie Robinson, drawing distinctions between the Black press and the mainstream media, and questioning the logic of contemporary commentators who invoke Flood's memory in order to chasten today's athletes who appear hesitant to speak politically. Through this discussion, Khan is able to demonstrate that African-American athletes are often caught in a double bind, wherein they are expected to honor the pioneers who came before them while simultaneously celebrating the status quo of sport culture and capitalism. As he summarizes (2012), "Instead of demanding more from the framework of our political culture, we take our shots at Michael [Jordan] and Tiger [Woods] for their refusal to be Jackie [Robinson] and Curt [Flood], when perhaps who they are is exactly who liberalism hoped they would be" (p. 25).

Because African-American athletes are so often celebrated and highly compensated, it can be difficult to understand why some still feel that the playing field is far from level. Sociological studies have done much to reveal the imbalance of non-Whites in leadership positions, both on the field and in terms of management. Rhetorical studies provide evidence of a different sort, identifying the symbolic choices made to reinforce particular racial expectations, underscoring why it is important to assess why terms such as 'character,' for example, are so commonly used to praise White athletes and condemn African-American athletes (Butterworth, 2013; Grano, 2010). Here, Griffin and Calafell (2011) provide a helpful example, through their study of the National Basketball Association's (NBA) controversial dress code policy that was introduced in 2005. For these authors, the dress code could largely be understood as a response to the infamous fight that took place in 2004 between members of the Indiana Pacers and Detroit Pistons, as well as some of the fans in attendance at the game. The incident rattled both the NBA and sport media, and critics of the players involved less than subtly implied that the players were symbols of violence attributed to stereotypes of African-Americans. Griffin and Calafell (2011) highlight an important tension, noting that the spectacular aggression characteristic of sports such as basketball and football is one of the characteristics used to appeal to White, middle-class audiences. In their words, "These sports arenas include predominantly white fans and black players, which inevitably produces cultural clashes in a society organized in part by racial hierarchies" (p. 126).

Grano's analysis (2007) reinforces this point, contending that the fight (known colloquially as the "Malice at the Palace") disrupts an implied social contract between fans and players. That contract, however, implicitly reinforces cultural norms based on race and class, which made the violence in the arena all the more threatening. In his words, "While the perceived violation of boundaries in the NBA brawl was particularly revealing of nonideal distinctions between savage and civilized space and people, the incident was also understood as a sign of greater cultural decay because there was disorder on both sides of the boundary" (Grano, 2007, p. 462). Elsewhere, Grano (2014; see also Grano & Zagacki, 2011) has demonstrated how African-American communities are too easily hailed as deviant or criminal. Thus, when an athlete such as football's Michael Vick faces public backlash for actual criminal behavior, his subsequent pleas for forgiveness must "naturalize racial and other inequities through languages of sincerity, therapy, and redemption" (Grano, 2014, p. 95). This is not to suggest that Vick should not have faced the consequences of his criminal activity connected with dogfighting, but rather to suggest that the standards by which he was able to reconcile with the public were filtered through a racialized lens.

One risk of focusing so much attention on the distinctions between representations of White and African-American athletes is that it risks reducing understandings of race to a simple White/non-White binary. Nevertheless, these rhetorical studies tell us much about contemporary race relations in sport and also offer parallel examples for making sense of other identity positions. Moreover, much as scholars in cultural studies of sport (Birrell & McDonald, 2000) have insisted that critical analyses attend to the intersectionality of identities, rhetorical scholars can also help make sense of the ways that race, gender, sexuality, and class are implicated in one another.

It is often the case that these representations are situated within broader cultural narratives seeking to explain collective identities and purpose. These narratives commonly take a mythic form, providing the final subject for this chapter.

Sporting Mythology

Despite the colloquial tendency to place 'myth' in opposition to 'reality,' rhetorical scholars adopt the view that myths are important symbolic resources for a community. Real (1975, p. 36) asserts that myths "reflect and sacrilize the dominant tendencies of a culture, thereby sustaining social institutions and lifestyles."

Thus, myths need not be 'true' to be effective; rather, they must be true to experience and help people make sense of their place in the world. With respect to the United States specifically, myths are commonly rooted in themes of American exceptionalism, the American dream, and the adventure of the frontier. These themes become actualized by sport, which enacts American mythology through its emphasis on "performance, the ability to conquer uncharted territory, and the prominence of individual acts of greatness" (Butterworth, 2007b, p. 232). O'Rourke (2003, p. 68) adds, "Heroic tales and scapegoating myths persist in the unending conversation of our collective lives. . . . It is in this rich mythic ground that sports narratives can flourish."

The centrality of heroes in mythic narratives captures the attention of rhetorical critics, in particular because these figures become "enactments of their nations' mythologies" (Milford, 2012, p. 486). Milford demonstrates that iconic athletes such as Jesse Owens—best remembered for winning four gold medals at the 1936 Berlin Olympics, thereby undermining Adolf Hitler's claims to Aryan superiority—are upheld by the public because his achievement symbolizes the triumph of American values of liberal democracy. As he observes, "By framing an individual as a communal hero, the community is able to imbue the hero's activities with ideological significance. The hero becomes the representative for the community's ideals, and with each appearance functions to reinforce ideology and/or refute opposition" (Milford, 2012, p. 499). On the one hand, this rhetorical process provides a means by which a community can affirm values and cultivate positive identifications with one another. Unfortunately, such identifications often coalesce not merely around virtuous individuals but also through constructions of 'others' who do not share the community's values. When this happens, sport risks exacerbating discourses of 'us' and 'them' and transforms shared mythologies into troubling discourses of nationalism (Butterworth, 2010).

With some regularity, these national myths also invoke selective forms of memory that rely on nostalgic rhetoric. For example, Aden (1995) views the 1991 documentary, *When It Was a Game*, as a rhetorical text that returns the audience to a "secure place of opposition" (p. 23). This nostalgic longing "allows viewers to feel as if they have left behind the social pressures of contemporary culture" (Aden, 1995, p. 26). However, nostalgia for a so-called 'golden age' of baseball offers no means to redress contemporary material shortcomings and, at the same time, risks idealizing a past that exploited labor and marginalized racial and ethnic minorities. Similarly, Von Burg and Johnson (2009) identify the strands of nostalgia during the contemporary era in which the use of performance-enhancing drugs has threatened the myth of American exceptionalism. In this case, sport media coverage attempted to scapegoat the 'steroid era' in order to recover a pure interpretation of the national pastime. As the authors conclude, "The ability to scapegoat the performance-enhancement era gives comfort that the nostalgic sentiments of the past can reconnect with the nostalgic longings we will experience again in the future. Yet the fundamental contradictions in the American exceptionalism that baseball embodies and nostalgia ignores remains unexamined" (Von Burg & Johnson, 2009, p. 367).

Studies of sport mythology need not focus only on national narratives. As Hartman (2015) demonstrates, other cultural myths are enacted by sport. In her study of ESPN's coverage of the 40th anniversary of Title IX, for example, she notes that the network's special coverage "mythologizes the law and diminishes the legal and social realities facing women in sport." She adds that "the mythologizing of Title IX is a rhetorical strategy that evades any serious discussion of the law and its consequences" (Hartman, 2015, p. 98). Hartman's study, therefore, allows us to see that the emphasis on a presumably shared value—equality— serves to distract viewers from remaining structural barriers and discriminatory practices faced by female athletes. Instead, media coverage misses the opportunity to engage an ongoing problem in favor of a mythology of equality that portrays Title IX "as established, non-controversial, and fully implemented" (Hartman, 2015, p. 108), demonstrating that mythologies not only function at multiple levels, but also have the capacity to shape broader public understandings of crucial issues.

Expanding the Rhetorical Study of Sport

Rhetorical studies have made a significant contribution to the study of communication and sport. Studies of public address have invoked the rhetorical tradition's emphasis on instrumental persuasive discourse, while those focusing on metaphor and mythology turn more toward an assessment of sport's democratic possibilities and limitations. Scholars interested in representation, meanwhile, articulate rhetorical principles with media texts to provide insights about the nature of identity and the work yet to be done with respect to equality and inclusion. In short, it is an area of scholarship that is flourishing and will likely continue to grow.

Nevertheless, there are opportunities for rhetorical scholars to expand the scope of their work. Across these areas of inquiry, there are three ways in particular that scholars can continue to explore the rhetorical dimensions of sport. First, as I have noted above, much of the work understood as public address is focused on instances of image repair. Additional studies in this area are certainly appropriate, but it would be equally valuable to advance studies of other forms of public address. Sport provides an almost endless supply of ceremonial occasions for example—retirement announcements, trophy presentations, Hall of Fame acceptance speeches, and more. These speeches often draw upon what rhetoricians refer to as epideictic address, speech identifying shared values of a community. Clearly, such speech also intersects with metaphor, representation, and mythology, as well, which invites more efforts to cross the boundaries that I have (somewhat artificially) created in this chapter. Second, echoing the advice of Birrell and McDonald (2000), rhetorical scholars should provide more studies of the intersectionality of identity. In recent years, for example, categories of race, gender, and sexuality have been challenged and reimagined within the sport community, with subsequent implications for our culture beyond sport. While continuing to address the mythologies and representations of gender and race, rhetorical scholarship can also better account for the multiple and varied identity positions in and around sport. Third, rhetorical critics can adopt a more global attitude. The majority of the current scholarship is grounded in North American sport, a product both of the influence of the United States on the sporting landscape and the U.S.-centric discipline of rhetorical studies. Yet borders of time and space are increasingly fluid and a corresponding global perspective would add much to rhetorical studies of sport.

Finally, rhetorical criticism cannot be thought of simply as a tool or 'method.' Yes, it is methodological, but it is rooted in classical principles suggesting the study of rhetoric must be accompanied by a critical disposition—what Burke (1984) refers to as an *attitude*. Such an attitude requires that scholars acknowledge rhetoric's role in shaping the world in which we live for the better. It also suggests that rhetorical study aims to add complexity and nuance, especially with respect to the simplicity often assigned to sport. With that in mind, a final suggestion for the future is that both fields—that is, sport communication and rhetorical studies—would benefit from more in-depth, book-length projects. At present, there have been only a handful of scholarly books about sport written through the lens of rhetoric (e.g., Butterworth, 2010; Khan, 2012; Grano, forthcoming). Books are important not merely because they require more work, but because they offer depth and sophistication that cannot be achieved in even the best journal articles. Moreover, they help advance the disciplinary conversations and develop theoretical approaches that are uniquely informed by sport, a substantial area for potential growth. Certainly, though, rhetorical approaches to communication and sport represent a robust area of study. As we draw from a rich historical tradition, there is still much yet to learn about sport as a rhetorical artifact.

References

Aden, R.C. (1995). Nostalgic communication as temporal escape: *When It Was a Game*'s reconstruction of a baseball/work community. *Western Journal of Communication, 59*, 20–38.

Anderson, K.V. (2011). "Rhymes with blunt": Pornification and U.S. political culture. *Rhetoric & Public Affairs, 14*, 327–368.

Benoit, W.L. (1997). Image restoration discourse and crisis communication. *Public Relations Review, 23*, 177–186.

Benoit, W.L. (2015). *Accounts, excuses, apologies: Image repair theory and research* (2nd ed.). Albany, NY: State University of New York Press.

Benoit, W.L., Stein, K.A., & Hansen, G.J. (2005). *New York Times* coverage of presidential campaigns. *Journalism & Mass Communication Quarterly, 82*, 356–376.

Birrell, S., & McDonald, M.G. (2000). Reading sport, articulating power lines: An introduction. In S. Birrell & M.G. McDonald (Eds.), *Reading sport: Critical essays on power and representation* (pp. 3–13). Boston, MA: Northeastern University Press.

Black, E. (1978). *Rhetorical criticism: A study in method*. Madison, WI: University of Wisconsin Press.

Blaney, J.R. (2013). Introduction: Why sports image restoration and how shall we proceed? In J.R. Blaney, L. Lippert, & J.S. Smith (Eds.), *Repairing the athlete's image: Studies in sports image restoration* (pp. 1–8). Lanham, MD: Lexington.

Blaney, J.R., Lippert, L., & Smith, J.S. (Eds.). (2013). *Repairing the athlete's image: Studies in sports image restoration*. Lanham, MD: Lexington.

Booth, W.C. (2004). *The rhetoric of rhetoric: The quest for effective communication*. Malden, MA: Blackwell.

Brazeal, L.M. (2013). Belated remorse: Serena Williams' image repair rhetoric at the 2009 U.S. Open. In J.R. Blaney, L. Lippert, & J.S. Smith (Eds.), *Repairing the athlete's image: Studies in sports image restoration* (pp. 239–252). Lanham, MD: Lexington.

Burke, K. (1941). Four master tropes. *Kenyon Review, 3*, 421–438.

Burke, K. (1984). *Attitudes toward history* (3rd ed.). Berkeley, CA: University of California Press.

Butterworth, M.L. (2006). Pitchers and catchers: Mike Piazza and the discourse of gay identity in the national pastime. *Journal of Sport & Social Issues, 30*, 138–157.

Butterworth, M.L. (2007a). The politics of the pitch: Claiming and contesting democracy through the Iraqi national soccer team. *Communication and Critical/Cultural Studies, 4*, 184–203.

Butterworth, M.L. (2007b). Race in "the race": Mark McGwire, Sammy Sosa, and heroic constructions of whiteness. *Critical Studies in Media Communication, 24*, 228–244.

Butterworth, M.L. (2010). *Baseball and rhetorics of purity: The national pastime and American identity during the war on terror*. Tuscaloosa, AL: University of Alabama Press.

Butterworth, M.L. (2013). The passion of the Tebow: Sports media and heroic language in the tragic frame. *Critical Studies in Media Communication, 30*, 17–33.

Butterworth, M.L. (2014). Public memorializing in the stadium: Mediated sport, the 10th anniversary of 9/11, and the illusion of democracy. *Communication & Sport, 2*, 203–224.

Charland, M. (1987). Constitutive rhetoric: The case of the Peuple Québécois. *Quarterly Journal of Speech, 73*, 133–150.

Cherney, J.L., & Lindemann, K. (2010). Sporting images of disability: Murderball and the rehabilitation of masculine identity. In H.L. Hundley & A.C. Billings (Eds.), *Examining identity in sports media* (pp. 195–215). Los Angeles, CA: Sage.

Crick, N. (2014). Rhetoric and Dewey's experimental pedagogy. In B. Jackson & G. Clark (Eds.), *Trained capacities: John Dewey, rhetoric, and democratic practice* (pp. 177–193). Columbia, SC: University of South Carolina Press.

Delgado, F. (2003). The fusing of sport and politics: Media constructions of U.S. versus Iran at France '98. *Journal of Sport & Social Issues, 27*, 293–307.

Foss, S. (2009). *Rhetorical criticism: Exploration & practice* (4th ed.). Long Grove, IL: Waveland.

Fuller, L.K. (2006). Introduction. In L.K. Fuller (Ed.), *Sport, rhetoric, and gender: Historical perspectives and media representations* (pp. 1–16). New York: Palgrave Macmillan.

Grano, D.A. (2007). Ritual disorder and the contractual morality of sport: A case study in race, class, and agreement. *Rhetoric & Public Affairs, 10*, 445–474.

Grano, D.A. (2010). Risky dispositions: Thick moral description and character-talk in sports culture. *Southern Communication Journal, 75*, 255–276.

Grano, D.A. (2014). Michael Vick's "genuine remorse" and problems of public forgiveness. *Quarterly Journal of Speech, 100*, 81–104.

Grano, D.A. (Forthcoming). *The eternal present of sport: Athletic bodies, movement, and memory.* Philadelphia, PA: Temple University Press.

Grano, D.A., & Zagacki, K.S. (2011). Cleansing the Superdome: The paradox of purity and post-Katrina guilt. *Quarterly Journal of Speech, 97*, 201–223.

Griffin, R.A., & Calafell, B.M. (2011). Control, discipline, and punish: Black masculinity and (in)visible whiteness in the NBA. In M.G. Lacy & K.A. Ono (Eds.), *Critical rhetorics of race* (pp. 117–136). New York: New York University Press.

Hartman, K.L. (2015). ESPN's mythological rhetoric of Title IX. In J. McGuire, G.G. Armfield, & A. Earnheardt (Eds.), *The ESPN effect: Exploring the worldwide leader in sports.* New York: Peter Lang.

Hawhee, D. (2005). *Bodily arts: Rhetoric and athletics in ancient Greece.* Austin, TX: University of Texas Press.

Herbeck, D.A. (2004). Sports metaphors and public policy: The football theme in Desert Storm discourse. In F.A. Beer & C.D. Landtsheer (Eds.), *Metaphorical World Politics* (pp. 121–139). East Lansing, MI: Michigan State University Press.

Jamieson, K.H. (1992). *Dirty politics: Deception, distraction, and democracy.* New York: Oxford University Press.

Khan, A.I. (2012). *Curt Flood in the media: Baseball, race, and the demise of the activist-athlete.* Jackson, MS: University Press of Mississippi.

Kruse, N. (1981). Apologia in team sport. *Quarterly Journal of Speech, 67*, 270–283.

Kyle, D.G. (2014). *Sport and spectacle in the ancient world.* Malden, MA: John Wiley & Sons.

Lavelle, K.L. (2015). The ESPN effect: Representation of women in *30 for 30* films. In J. McGuire, G.G. Armfield, & A. Earnheardt (Eds.), *The ESPN effect: Exploring the worldwide leader in sports* (pp. 127–138). New York: Peter Lang.

Lucaites, J.L., & Condit, C.M. (1998). Introduction. In J.L. Lucaites, C.M. Condit, & S. Caudill (Eds.), *Contemporary rhetorical theory: A reader* (pp. 1–18). New York: Guilford.

Milford, M. (2012). The Olympics, Jesse Owens, Burke, and the implications of media framing in symbolic boasting. *Mass Communication and Society, 15*, 485–505.

Mozisek, K.D. (2014). Female ballplayers as feminine tomboys and citizens: A progressive concordance in American culture. In B. Brummett & A.W. Ishak (Eds.), *Sports and identity: New agendas in communication* (pp. 129–147). New York: Routledge.

Nelson, J. (1984). The defense of Billie Jean King. *Western Journal of Communication, 48*, 92–102.

Nietzsche, F. (1989). On truth and lying in the extra-moral sense. In S.L. Gilman, C. Blair, & D.J. Parent (Eds.), *Friedrich Nietzsche on rhetoric and language* (pp. 246–257). New York: Oxford University Press.

O'Rourke, D.J. (2003). The talk of the town: A rhetorical analysis of the Browns' departure from and return to Cleveland. In R.S. Brown & D.J. O'Rourke (Eds.), *Case studies in sport communication* (pp. 63–79). Westport, CT: Praeger.

Poulakos, J. (1995). *Sophistical rhetoric in classical Greece.* Columbia, SC: University of South Carolina Press.

Real, M. (1975). Super Bowl: Mythic spectacle. *Journal of Communication, 25*, 31–43.

Ricouer, P. (1997). Rhetoric—poetics—hermeneutics. In W. Jost & M.L. Hyde (Eds.), *Rhetoric and hermeneutics: A reader* (pp. 60–72). New Haven, CT: Yale University Press.

Segrave, J.O. (2000). The sports metaphor in American cultural discourse. *Culture, Sport, Society, 3,* 48–60.

Shugart, H.A. (2003). She shoots, she scores: Mediated constructions of contemporary female athletes in coverage of the 1999 US women's soccer team. *Western Journal of Communication, 67,* 1–31.

Timmerman, D.M., & McDorman, T.F. (2008). Introduction: Rhetoric and democracy. In T.F. McDorman & D.M. Timmerman (Eds.), *Rhetoric & democracy: Pedagogical and political practices* (pp. xi–xxxv). East Lansing, MI: Michigan State University Press.

Von Burg, R., & Johnson, P.E. (2009). Yearning for a past that never was: Baseball, steroids, and the anxiety of the American dream. *Critical Studies in Media Communication, 26,* 351–371.

Wagg, S., & Andrews, D.L. (Eds.). (2007). *East plays West: Sport and the Cold War.* Abingdon: Routledge.

Ware, B.L., & Linkugel, W.A. (1973). They spoke in defense of themselves: On the generic criticism of apologia. *Quarterly Journal of Speech, 59,* 273–283.

2

SPORT AS CRITICAL/CULTURAL STUDIES

Daniel A. Grano

UNIVERSITY OF NORTH CAROLINA-CHARLOTTE

One of the earliest spaces (with much early resistance) for emerging work in U.S. cultural studies (Grossberg, 1993) can be found in communication studies. Yet, critical studies, cultural studies, and communication studies have separate—and at times conflicting—histories often glossed by the slash between critical/cultural now common in our discipline (Hay, 2013a). These histories are ongoing, and have been covered in thoughtful detail elsewhere.[1] I mention them very briefly to make the point that any definitions of these three intersecting strands—critical, cultural, communication—is, by necessity, both selective and perhaps exclusive of other definitions important within the discipline. 'Critical/cultural' represents efforts to negotiate a big tent within communication studies (Hay, 2013a), and it is underneath that tent I will take some liberties.

With that caveat in mind, I will characterize a critical/cultural studies perspective of sport communication around what Lawrence Grossberg (2010a) calls "radical contextualism." That characterization represents, I think, several of the themes central to critically/culturally informed sport scholarship among U.S. communication scholars, helping to set out a concrete set of next steps for such work. This chapter is broken into two parts: first, I define 'radical contextualism' and the related idea of 'articulation,' illustrating the importance of these ideas through selected critical/cultural studies of sport communication; second, I offer some thoughts about justifying sport as an area for critical inquiry and political change around the idea of 'conjuncture.'

Critical/Cultural Approaches to Sport Communication

Radical Contextualism

Critical/cultural approaches are not unified by any particular method. Within communication studies 'critical' might imply reference to various approaches to *criticism* (e.g., rhetorical criticism, media criticism, Marxist criticism, psychoanalytic criticism), but cultural studies practitioners have argued frequently against reducing their approaches to specific "interpretive strategies" (Hay, 2013a, p. 3). This is not to say that critical/cultural studies are free of method, but that methods are not determined ahead of time; they are chosen based upon the analytical and political commitments of a specific project. As Cary Nelson, Paula Treichler, and Grossberg (1992) write, methodology is a strategic decision:

> cultural studies . . . has no distinct methodology, no unique statistical, ethnomethodological, or textual analysis to call its own. Its methodology, ambiguous from the beginning, could best be seen as a bricolage. . . . The choice of research practices depends upon the questions that are asked, and the questions depend on their context.
>
> *(p. 2)*

Context also establishes standards for analytical rigor. Grossberg noted in an interview that he was in favor of any method "that helps you gather more and better information, descriptions, resources, and interpretations" so long as it is applied "rigorously" and "suspiciously," with an awareness that methods are themselves "discursive constructions" and are "interwoven with all sorts of theoretical assumptions" (Wright, 2001, pp. 144–145). Though cultural studies is often criticized for not having a specific methodology, Grossberg (2010a) views this as a strength, maintaining that a concern over method for its own sake is more likely to affirm sanctioned forms of disciplinary knowledge than surprising or meaningful insights about the complex social relations under investigation.

Critical/cultural studies are also not unified by an aim to develop, advance, or apply any particular theory; theory is, like method, viewed as a strategic resource selected for particular problems and contexts, a "wager about what will work" for understanding complex forms of social relation (Grossberg, 2010a, p. 27). As Stuart Hall (1997a) said of his own work, "I don't regard myself as a theorist . . . I am not interested in the production of theory as an object in its own right." Aware that he was opening himself to charges of "eclecticism and lack of rigor," Hall chose to borrow ideas from different and sometimes contradictory paradigms based on what made sense for a specific context (p. 152).

While cultural studies cannot be unified in terms of method or theory, Grossberg (2010a) argues that it *can* be defined by its practice, which he summarizes as "radical contextualism." He writes that cultural studies assumes:

> that the identity, significance, and effects of any practice or event . . . are defined only by the complex set of relations that surround, interpenetrate, and shape it, and make it what it is. No element can be isolated from its relations, although those relationships can be changed, and are constantly changing. Any event can only be understood relationally, as a condensation of multiple determinations and effects. Cultural studies thus embodies the commitment to the openness and contingency of social reality, where change is the given or norm. This radical contextualism is the heart of cultural studies.
>
> *(p. 20)*

So, any study focusing on a specific object or problem (e.g., African-American male athletes as criminal types) cannot perform the work of cultural studies by simply "reading social power off of texts" in isolation (Grossberg, 2010a, p. 8). The larger relations between social forces intersecting through that object or problem—for example, racial pseudosciences, mass imprisonment, reality TV, policing, drug policies, league disciplinary structures—must be accounted for and treated as historically unique.

Calls for such contextualism trace back to seminal works within the emerging field of sport communication,[2] especially early efforts to map what became known variously as "MediaSport" (Wenner, 1998, pp. 3–13), "the media sports cultural complex" (Rowe, 2004, pp. 1–21), or the "media sport content economy" (Hutchins & Rowe, 2009, p. 355). Michael Real's (1975) foundational essay "Super Bowl: Mythic spectacle" was especially important in moving communication and sport studies beyond analyses of "content alone" by considering "the media sports production complex in the context of American society" (Wenner, 1989, p. 34). Wenner (1989) developed an influential agenda for sport communication by mapping the "media sports production complex," as an intersection of forces that included sport journalists, media conglomerates, leagues, the court system, fans, and commercial content (pp. 34–41). And, in his important essay on the "sports/media complex," Jhally (1989) turned to British cultural studies to address limitations of "critical" sport scholarship, which at the time predominantly treated sport as an opiate. Jhally analyzed an "interlocking" structure of relations involving the commodity value of sport media content, the economics of player values (their ability to sell specialized labor to teams, and celebrity to fans), and state regulation (e.g. antitrust exemptions and tax shelters granted to sport leagues) (p. 80). These and other foundational mappings of the "sport-media complex" called for a study of sport where no single figure, artifact, or problem could be analyzed in isolation. The focus was to be on sport *as context*.

This early attention to context shaped sport studies in communication. For instance, in his influential essay on hegemonic masculinity and Major League pitcher Nolan Ryan, Trujillo (1991) argued that "[p]erhaps no single institution in American culture has influenced our sense of masculinity more than sport" (p. 292). Accordingly, baseball has served as an important site for mapping the complex relations of American power condensed in the "national pastime." More recently, Butterworth (2005) has demonstrated, for example, how baseball serves as an institution deeply implicated with post-9/11 politics. Ballpark rituals and nostalgic associations with pre-industrial American innocence were appropriated by the George W. Bush administration to justify the 'war on terror,' suppressing democratic dissent while elevating militaristic patriotism (Butterworth, 2010). Moreover, 'steroid era' baseball offenses signified a larger national contamination against which the body politic had to be inoculated in the name of national security, and through Bush-era economic and military policies (Butterworth, 2008, 2010). Beyond serving as a mere 'diversion,' or offering a facile image of national healing, Butterworth (2005) persuasively argues that baseball indexes a larger structure of relations shaping "democratic practice in public culture" and the suppressive potential of national 'unity' in times of war (p. 109). These implications for democracy and dissent are best understood within the larger context of sport discourses that "link American identity with militarism" within and beyond baseball (Butterworth, 2012, p. 242; also see Butterworth, 2007; Butterworth & Moskal, 2009).

Baseball also condenses Americans' idealizations of sport as a site that uniquely facilitates progressive and harmonious race relations. Khan (2012) examines such public memories of athlete-heroes in his book *Curt Flood in the Media*, situating Flood's opposition to baseball's Reserve Clause against the backdrop of the 'social agreement' regarding race that had founded baseball's cultural significance since Jackie Robinson's first year with the Brooklyn Dodgers in 1947. After Flood violated that agreement by referring to himself as a "well-paid slave," various civil rights advocates moved to appropriate his rhetoric, so that "[b]etween 1970 and 1972, Flood found himself positioned fatally on the fault line between liberal and radical modes of black political speech" (pp. 14–15). Khan's re-reading of Flood's story contributes to how we understand race and the (presumed) decline of athlete-activists today because of the *concreteness* of the cultural and historical moment he analyzes.

The word 'critical' in critical/cultural studies often signifies a focus on the politics of identity (e.g., race, class, gender, sexuality, nationality, ethnicity, disability), which in sport are typically inscribed upon particular bodies, and within specific relations of power. Consider, for example, the complex ways in which Blackness is both envied and pathologized in sport. Presumptions persist about 'natural' (genetic, biological) athletic endowment track with a familiar White brains/Black brawn dichotomy, which types African-American male athletes as both 'superendowed' and unstable (prone to criminality and loss of rational control) (Grano, 2010). Understanding how these presumptions are sustained requires mapping African-American athletes' ever-changing positions within the complex structures that maintain Whiteness in sport culture. Black male athletes are, for example, frequently positioned as objects of the erotic gaze, mobilizing a set of economic and sexual relationships wherein mostly White, male, heterosexual consumers compensate for their (perceived) genetic inferiority to Black men by visually touring and openly admiring prospects' bodies, while at the same time casting those bodies as primitive (beastly, animalistic), physical commodities (Oates, 2007; also see Lavelle, 2010). Male athletes of color are commonly granted and/or lose status within media sport institutions according to performances of post-racial identity, control over appetites (sexual, violent), and carefully crafted narratives about family values (Houck, 2013). Women athletes of color are variously elevated or marginalized according to how they perform race, sexuality, femininity, and family dependency, all of which either accord with or grate against the predominantly White, heterosexual predispositions of U.S. sport journalism (Meân, 2013). When women athletes struggle against sexist, homophobic, and racist responses to their participation in elite sport, they negotiate a complex set of relations condensed within categories including social class, linking problems of bodily performance (of racial, sexual, and economic identity) with structural socioeconomic inequities (Bagley, 2009). So, a contextualist approach to race and sport is never about race alone, but considers race as an anchoring point around and through which complex social forces are at work.

As Grossberg (2010a) argues, a contextualist approach accounts not only for relationships between cultural elements, but also for the changeability of those relations. As a final example of contextualism, then, one can consider how communication scholars have understood ongoing changes to elite sport as a predominantly male, heterosexual domain. Those changes are occurring on multiple, overlapping fronts, including women's increased participation in traditionally masculine sports (Poniatowski & Hardin, 2012), the troubling of gender- and sex-segregated competition by transgender and intersex athletes (Sloop, 2012; Winslow, 2012), and women's struggles for status and opportunity within sport media institutions (Hardin & Shain, 2006). As sport communication scholars consider possible changes to the gender and sexual politics of journalism, network coverage, and competitive eligibility, they provide insight into the specific cultural forces that might facilitate or limit such change. Hardin, Dodd, and Lauffer (2006) argue, for example, that changing the structural inequities of sport newsrooms requires a critical assessment of patriarchy in college-level journalism instruction, especially at a time when a new generation of students might "bring more progressive ethics and values to the practice" (p. 430). And Whiteside and Hardin (2011) warn against premature enthusiasm over an expanding, post-Title IX audience for women's sport, which will not materialize without changes to still-durable presumptions about gender, leisure time, domestic labor, and emotion labor. Such attention to conditions for potential change is vital for critical/cultural studies of sport and relates directly to the productive forces of articulation.

Articulation

Grossberg (2010a) writes that "radical contextualism is embodied in the concept of articulation," which is perhaps the closest thing that cultural studies has to a consistent method (pp. 21, 52). For Hall, "articulation" names the "specific linkage" or "form of connection" creating unity out of different cultural elements. As Hall notes in an interview, that unity appears to be natural—"determined, absolute and essential for all time"—but it is, in fact, based upon contingent, historically specific relations of power that have no "necessary 'belongingness'" (Grossberg, 1986, p. 53). So, we can analyze how particular articulations take shape and how they might be disarticulated and rearticulated to create alternative futures (Grossberg, 2010a).

Certain articulations are uniquely powerful within sport culture; recognizing this would enhance justifications for critical/cultural studies of sport in communication. There likely are not any cultural linkages belonging *exclusively* to sport. Yet, even if sport alone does not produce relations, say, between Black bodies and genetic determinism, or between disability and gender, these articulations take *particular shape* within, through, and around sport, such that a contextualist approach to their various forms of connection *absent* sport might be fundamentally incomplete. Such incompleteness could entail a partial understanding (or even misunderstanding) of how specific relationships of power came to be, or a failure to recognize openings for possible rearticulations.

To provide one particularly good example, consider the centrality of sport in articulating and disarticulating relations between gender and the body. As Butler (1998) argues, women's sports uniquely "call into question what we take for granted as idealized feminine morphologies" and contain the "power to rearticulate gender ideals such that . . . our ordinary sense of what constitutes a gendered body is itself dramatically contested and transformed" (p. 104). Certainly gender and sexual binaries are troubled in popular contexts outside of sport, but they are persistently and conspicuously policed, redrawn, and challenged in elite athletic competition. This is especially true because governing bodies have long tested for—and publicly failed to identify—scientific markers upon which gender/sexual binaries could be posed as stable determinants for competitive eligibility (Sullivan, 2011). As Sloop (2012) argues, major controversies over gender and competitive advantage—as in the well-known case of intersex track athlete Caster Semenya—stage public discussions "over the meaning of gender and bodies" (p. 89) previously exclusive to academic and activist circles. Calling such discussions 'revolutionary' would be an overstatement. The desire to base eligibility standards on conceptions of 'natural' male advantage persists, and public acceptability is often based on an athlete conforming to heteronormative standards (Sloop, 2012; Winslow, 2012). Nevertheless, meaningful changes to gender configurations have been, and will continue to be, pushed by elite sport, where a combination of "incommensurable discourses" about gender, "international conflict, and sprawling media access, leads to a fascinating site for conflict and change" (Sloop, 2012, pp. 89–92).

Questions of competitive regulation also constitute powerful linkages between gender, sexuality, disability, and technology. These linkages—which become conspicuous, for example, in disability sport (particularly through the use of prostheses and assistive technologies), or through transgender and intersex athletes' struggles for competitive eligibility—exist along a continuum of threats to the myth that sport "is about the 'natural ability' of 'normal' people" (Cherney & Lindemann, 2014, p. 3). There are no guarantees that these threats will produce radical change. In their analysis of wheelchair rugby, for example, Lindemann and Cherney (2008) argue that images of quadriplegic athletes violently colliding and sacrificing their bodies issue a challenge to ableist assumptions about what disabled persons can do. At the same time that challenge reifies "heterosexist and ableist notions of what it means to be a 'man,'" thus circumscribing the participation of women and gay men (p. 110). The wheelchairs themselves (intimidatingly decorated and modified for collisions) contribute to these problems of progressive and regressive resistance, articulating with athletes' bodies to form a thoroughly gendered human/machine interface. This is but one example of sport's broader importance as a site for post-human body politics (the changing meanings of gender and sexuality as bodies merge with various technologies). In a similar vein, the participation of women drivers in motor sports is conditioned by "historical articulations made between and among gender, automobiles and stock car racing" and also by the ways in which drivers' (gendered) bodies are articulated to cars as (gendered) prosthetics (Sloop, 2005, pp. 192–193). Again, these articulations between gender, sexuality, ability/disability, and technology appear in several other contexts (e.g., military or medical) but, as they work within and through sport, they are made uniquely explicit around concerns over competitive fairness and the 'natural' (non-technological, categorically gendered) capacities of the human body.

Articulation, Discourse, and a Cultural Approach to Sport Communication

Articulation is, according to Grossberg (2010a), "cultural studies' version of what is generally called constructionism," the idea that reality is socially made rather than predetermined. Cultural studies' constructionism refuses, however, to "assume there are two modes of being: the real and the discursive or symbolic," which exist separately "and can only be bridged by distinctly human acts of consciousness" (p. 23). Debates over the relative status of symbolic/material realities run throughout critical/cultural studies of communication, especially surrounding the subject of ideology.[3] Such debates cannot be comprehensively covered here; suffice to say that material realities are no less real because we make meaning out of them communicatively and, at the same time, that material, "brute facts" cannot be separated from "social facts" (Grossberg, 2010a, p. 23). As Hall (2006, pp. 166–167) puts it: "Reality exists outside of language, but is constantly mediated by and through language." So, the "*problem* of ideology is," according to Hall (1986), to figure out how different ideas "grip the minds of masses, and thereby become a 'material force.'" Accordingly, Hall advances a conception of ideology aimed at analyzing how "concepts and . . . languages" come to "stabilize a particular form of power" that reconciles "people to their subordinate place in the social formation," and how "new forms of consciousness . . . arise, which move" people "into historical action against the prevailing system" (p. 29).

Discursive practices matter because they contribute to that stabilization; they help us to construct and occupy a world of our own making (Grossberg, 2010a). This was at the heart of Carey's (1992) understanding of culture:

> The particular miracle we perform daily and hourly—the miracle of producing reality and then living within and under the fact of our own productions—rests upon a particular quality of symbols: their ability to be both representations "of" and "for" reality . . . as "symbols of" they present reality; as "symbols for" they create the very reality they represent . . . All human activity is such an exercise . . . in squaring the circle. We first produce the world by symbolic work and then take up residence in the world we have produced.
>
> *(pp. 29–30)*

More than simply celebrating discourse, Carey calls here for the analytical and ethical work of understanding how cultures are made and remade (Grossberg, 2010b). For Carey (1992), the challenge of a cultural approach to communication is "to grasp the meanings people build into their words and behavior and to make these meanings . . . explicit and articulate so that we might fairly judge them." Those meanings are publicly available as interpretations of experience, and our job "is to interpret the interpretations" (pp. 59–60). This is where I think communication studies scholars offer particularly valuable contributions to the larger project(s) of critical/cultural sport studies. Interpreting other people's interpretations implies a commitment to treating discourse as an entry point into broader contextual relations, and more specifically to thoughtful, rigorous analysis of the *referential* and *figurative* qualities of social experience. As Butterworth (2014) argues, communication studies scholars are well positioned to "intervene in sporting discourses" because of our "shared interest in symbols—in the idea that words, images, and representations *matter*" (pp. 3–4) not merely as descriptions of exchange (e.g., information-sharing), but as keys to understanding how sport cultures *work*. Per Carey's (1992) seminal argument for a "ritual view of communication," the "highest manifestation of communication" does not appear "in the transmission of intelligent information but in the construction and maintenance of an ordered, meaningful cultural world that can serve as a control and container for human action" (pp. 18–19). Certainly we can find thoughtful analyses of meaning-making in scholarship across the interdisciplinary spectrum of sport studies, but a transmission view of communication is often implied in work outside our discipline (and unfortunately, sometimes within it); messages are exchanged, information is shared, media are 'used,' yet we learn little about how these practices relate to the production of cultures.

By way of contrast, a cultural approach to communication involves "a process of making large claims from small matters: studying particular rituals, poems, plays, conversations, songs, dances, theories, and myths, and *gingerly reaching out to the full relations within a culture or a total way of life*" (Carey, 1992, p. 64, emphasis added). As Hall (1997b) suggests "[o]ne way of thinking about 'culture' . . . is in terms of . . . shared conceptual maps, shared language systems and the *codes which govern the relationships of translation between them*" (p. 21, emphasis in original). The "trick," Carey (1992) notes, is to read texts "in relation to [a] concrete social structure without reducing them to that structure," nor to some "extrinsic and arbitrary" method or theory (p. 61). So, a critical/cultural studies of sport *communication* might be organized around the assumption that discursive practices (e.g., inscriptions of gender, sex, race, or disability relations on athletic bodies) are particularly good entry points into the broader material/symbolic relations shaping sport. The value of our contribution to *critical/cultural sport* should be ultimately based, however, on the uniqueness and quality of our insights about sport culture contexts, and not from our ability to claim any methodological or theoretical property that 'belongs' to communication studies.

Conclusion: Working within Sport Cultural Conjunctures

I want to close by proposing a set of next steps for critical/cultural studies of sport communication around the idea of conjuncture. Hall defines conjuncture as "a period in which the contradictions and problems and antagonisms, which are always present in different domains in a society, begin to . . . accumulate" around a point of rupture. Conjuncture includes the aftermath of that rupture, relevant processes of social change, and "challenges to the existing historical project or social order" (Hay, 2013b, pp. 16–17). Conjunctures do not guarantee progressive change. They do, however, open spaces for potentially new and productive conceptions of historical reality (Hall, 1986). Accordingly, a critical/cultural studies of sport communication might proceed as an analysis of conjunctures within which sport exerts unique force. This would follow from Striphas's (2013) recent suggestion that communication scholars pursue a "clinical" understanding of the word *critical*, an understanding related to decisive turning points (as in the medical phrase "critical condition"), an attunement to coming historical and cultural changes (p. 325).[4] Contemporary sport is at the center of any number of such 'critical' turning points, including: (a) the increasing disruptiveness of queer athletic bodies (transgender fighters, intersex Olympians, cyborg runners); (b) rearticulations of race and labor relations in men's college basketball and football; (c) alternative essentializations of violent, hypermasculine bodies through 'steroid era' and brain injury controversies; or (d) agitated class consciousness over public funding for stadiums. These and countless other opportunities are apparent, but we have to acknowledge and respond to at least two problems within our discipline.

The first problem is that critical/cultural studies of sport communication are typically compartmentalized by communication studies editors, reviewers, and readers as ultimately, merely *about sport*. Thus, an essay analyzing complex interrelationships between masculinity, Whiteness, nationalism, religion, sexuality, and citizenship through the case of a major sport figure will likely be read and categorized as a 'sport' essay, published separately from works covering similar problems of identity (Butterworth, 2014). Categorized in this way, it is difficult to perform a contextualist analysis of sport culture that is recognized *as contextualist*. The practical result is that communication scholars conducting critical/cultural work on sport are unlikely to be cited by colleagues within the discipline who have clearly parallel and overlapping interests (in, for example, identity politics or body theory). Just as problematic, communication scholars who only tread occasionally into sport are more likely to cite a cherry-picked list of studies (usually from sociology) than to engage with directly relevant sport scholarship published within disciplinary journals and book series. So, we have an in-house version of our discipline's import/export problem: much non-reciprocal borrowing.

We cannot respond to this first problem by justifying sport as *yet another* site for struggles over problems that communication studies scholars already care about (race, class, sexuality, gender, nationalism, religion, and so on). If that is our strategy, we lose by way of comparison: if I can learn everything I need to know about these problems by interrogating a site with more status in the discipline (say electoral politics, social movements, even other popular cultural forms like film, music, or reality TV), why bother with sport? Why not just leave engagements with sport to the 'sport' people? Instead, we need to advance sport as a context within, through, and around which certain articulations and disarticulations of power *take unique shape*, so that gerrymandering sport from a cultural configuration where it implicitly or explicitly matters stands as an analytical failure. That failure resonates singularly, however. We need to direct explicit attention to it by way of justification, argument, and analysis.

Here, we run into our second problem. If conjuncture is to serve as a focal point for critical/cultural studies of sport communication, there needs to be an attending account of political change, an argument for imagining alternative futures (Grossberg, 2010a). Yet sport is commonly perceived as fundamentally incompatible with politics, a form of activity that is not just "apolitical" but "actively *anti*-political" (Carrington, 2009, pp. 20–21; Butterworth, 2012). Just as with critical/cultural work more generally, sport scholars operate under a "logic of 'no guarantees'" (Grossberg, 2010a, p. 22). Yet, given the still-developing status of sport within our discipline, we need to be realistic that our standards for proof regarding potential political change are particularly high. Again, a focus on conjuncture might prove valuable. Because sport is inherently central to current antagonisms over gender and sexual binarism, queer visibilities, race and labor relations, public health, domestic violence, global institutional corruption, and other crises, we have an opportunity to work the politics of disciplinary status *through* the performance of work that carefully and thoughtfully delineates lines of force and change unique to sport cultures. In short, we need to make a contextualist case for sport.

Notes

1 See, for example: Hay, 2013a, 2013c; Steiner & Christians, 2010; Hardt, 1992, 2008.
2 To be clear, Grossberg's (2010a) definition of cultural studies as 'radical contextualism' is meant to define what cultural studies is, but also what it is *not*. I am aware that some of the studies I cite throughout this chapter (including much of my own work) might not qualify strictly as 'cultural studies' works under this definition—thus my opening qualifications related to the 'big tent' of critical/cultural studies.
3 I am thinking in particular about debates in rhetorical theory. See, for example: McGee, 1980; Wander, 1983; Cloud, 1994, 1997, 2006; Cloud & Gunn, 2011.
4 Striphas (2013) borrows this clinical definition of 'critical' from Raymond Williams's (1983) book *Keywords*, as well as from Williams's (1977) concept "structure of feeling," which describes a latent cultural consciousness that is lived though not yet fully articulated.

References

Bagley, M.M. (2009). Performing social class: The case of Rutgers basketball versus Don Imus. In B. Brummett (Ed.), *Sporting rhetoric: Performance, games and politics* (pp. 235–258). New York: Peter Lang.

Butler, J. (1998). Athletic genders: Hyperbolic instance and/or the overcoming of sexual binarism. *Stanford Humanities Review, 6*(2), 103–111.

Butterworth, M.L. (2005). Ritual in the "church of baseball": Suppressing the discourse of democracy after 9/11. *Communication and Critical/Cultural Studies, 2*(2), 107–129.

Butterworth, M.L. (2007). The politics of the pitch: Claiming and contesting democracy through the Iraqi national soccer team. *Communication and Critical/Cultural Studies, 4*(2), 184–203.

Butterworth, M.L. (2008). Purifying the body politic: Steroids, Raphael Palmeiro, and the rhetorical cleansing of Major League Baseball. *Western Journal of Communication, 72*(2), 145–161.

Butterworth, M.L. (2010). *Baseball and rhetorics of purity: The national pastime and American identity during the war on terror.* Tuscaloosa, AL: University of Alabama Press.

Butterworth, M.L. (2012). Militarism and memorializing at the Pro Football Hall of Fame. *Communication and Critical/Cultural Studies, 9*(3), 241–258.

Butterworth, M.L. (2014). Introduction: Communication and sport identity scholarship, and the identity of communication and sport scholars. In B. Brummett & A.W. Ishak (Eds.), *Sports and identity: New agendas in communication* (pp. 1–16). New York: Routledge.

Butterworth, M.L., & Moskal, S.D. (2009). American football, flags, and "fun": The Bell Helicopter Armed Forces Bowl and the rhetorical production of militarism. *Communication, Culture & Critique, 2*(4), 411–433.

Carey, J.W. (1992). *Communication as culture: Essays on media and society.* New York: Routledge.

Carrington, B. (2009). Sport without final guarantees: Cultural studies/Marxism/sport. In B. Carrington & I. McDonald (Eds.), *Marxism, cultural studies and sport* (pp. 15–31). New York: Routledge.

Cherney, J.L. & Lindemann, K. (2014). Queering Street: Homosociality, masculinity, and disability in *Friday Night Lights. Western Journal of Communication, 78*(1), 1–21.

Cloud, D.L. (1994). The materiality of discourse as oxymoron: A challenge to critical rhetoric. *Western Journal of Communication, 58*(3), 141–163.

Cloud, D.L. (1997). Concordance, complexity, and conservatism: Rejoinder to Condit. *Critical Studies in Mass Communication, 14*, 193–200.

Cloud, D.L. (2006). The *Matrix* and critical theory's desertion of the real. *Communication and Critical/Cultural Studies, 3*, 329–354.

Cloud, D.L., & Gunn, J. (2011). Introduction: W(h)ither ideology? *Western Journal of Communication, 75*, 407–420.

Grano, D.A. (2010). Risky dispositions: Thick moral description and character-talk in sports culture. *Southern Communication Journal, 75*(3), 255–276.

Grossberg, L. (1986). On postmodernism and articulation: An interview with Stuart Hall. *Journal of Communication Inquiry, 10*(2), 45–60.

Grossberg, L. (1993). Can cultural studies find true happiness in communication? *Journal of Communication, 43*(4), 89–97.

Grossberg, L. (2010a). *Cultural studies in the future tense.* Durham, NC: Duke University Press.

Grossberg, L. (2010b). James W. Carey and the conversation of culture. In L. Steiner & C. Christians (Eds.), *Key concepts in critical cultural studies* (pp. 73–87). Champaign, IL: University of Illinois Press.

Hall, S. (1986). The problem of ideology: Marxism without guarantees. *Journal of Communication Inquiry, 10*(2), 28–44.

Hall, S. (1997a). Politics, contingency, strategy. *Small Axe, 1*, 141–159.

Hall, S. (1997b). The work of representation. In S. Hall (Ed.), *Representation: Cultural representations and signifying practices* (pp. 13–74). London: Sage.

Hall, S. (2006). Encoding/decoding. In M.G. Durham & D.M. Kellner (Eds.), *Media and cultural studies: KeyWorks* (pp. 163–173). Malden, MA: Blackwell.

Hardin, M., Dodd, J.E., & Lauffer, K. (2006). Passing it on: The reinforcement of male hegemony in sports journalism textbooks. *Mass Communication & Society, 9*(4), 429–446.

Hardin, M., & Shain, S. (2006) "Feeling much smaller than you know you are": The fragmented professional identity of female sports journalists. *Critical Studies in Media Communication, 23*(4), 322–338.

Hardt, H. (1992). *Critical communication studies: Communication, history, and theory in America.* New York: Routledge.

Hardt, H. (2008). Foreword. In D.W. Park & J. Pooley (Eds.), *The history of media and communication research: Contested memories* (pp. xi–xvii). New York: Peter Lang.

Hay, J. (2013a). Introduction. *Communication and Critical/Cultural Studies, 10,* 1–9.

Hay, J. (2013b). Interview with Stuart Hall, June 12, 2012. *Communication and Critical/Cultural Studies, 10,* 10–33.

Hay, J. (2013c). Interview with Lawrence Grossberg, November 14, 2012. *Communication and Critical/Cultural Studies, 10,* 59–97.

Houck, D.W. (2013). "Earl's loins—Or, inventing Tiger Woods". In D.L. Andrews & B. Carrington (Eds.), *A companion to sport* (pp. 564–581). Malden, MA: Wiley-Blackwell.

Hutchins, B., & Rowe, D. (2009). From broadcast scarcity to digital plentitude: The changing dynamics of the media sport content economy. *Television & New Media, 10*(4), 354–370.

Jhally, S. (1989). Cultural studies and the sports/media complex. In L.A. Wenner (Ed.), *Media, sports & society* (pp. 70–93). Newbury Park, CA: Sage.

Khan, A.I. (2012). *Curt Flood in the media: Baseball, race, and the demise of the activist athlete.* Jackson, MS: University Press of Mississippi.

Lavelle, K.L. (2010). A critical discourse analysis of black masculinity in NBA game commentary. *The Howard Journal of Communications, 21*(3), 294–314.

Lindemann, K., & Cherney, J.L. (2008). Communicating in and through "Murderball": Masculinity and disability in wheelchair rugby. *Western Journal of Communication, 72*(2), 107–125.

McGee, M.C. (1980). The "ideograph": A link between rhetoric and ideology. *Quarterly Journal of Speech, 66*(1), 1–16.

Meân, L. (2013). On track, off track, on Oprah: The framing of Marion Jones as golden girl and American fraud. In L. Wenner (Ed.), *Fallen sports heroes, media, & celebrity culture* (pp. 77–91). New York: Peter Lang.

Nelson, C., Treichler, P., & Grossberg, L. (1992). Cultural studies: An introduction. In L. Grossberg, C. Nelson, & P. Treichler (Eds.), *Cultural studies* (pp. 1–16). New York: Routledge.

Oates, T.P. (2007). The erotic gaze in the NFL draft. *Communication and Critical/Cultural Studies, 4*(1), 74–90.

Poniatowski, K., & Hardin, M. (2012). "The more things change, the more they . . .": Commentary during women's ice hockey at the 2010 Olympic Games. *Mass Communication & Society, 15*(4), 622–641.

Real, M. (1975). Super Bowl: Mythic spectacle. *Journal of Communication, 25*(1), 31–43.

Rowe, D. (2004). Introduction: Mapping the media sports cultural complex. In D. Rowe (Ed.), *Critical readings: Sport, culture and the media* (pp. 1–22). Berkshire, UK: Open University Press.

Sloop, J. (2005). Riding in cars between men. *Communication and Critical/Cultural Studies, 2*(3), 191–213.

Sloop, J. (2012). "This is not natural": Caster Semenya's gender threats. *Critical Studies in Media Communication, 29*(2), 81–96.

Steiner, L., & Christians, C. (Eds.). (2010). *Key concepts in critical cultural studies.* Champaign, IL: University of Illinois Press.

Striphas, T. (2013). Keyword: Critical. *Communication and Critical/Cultural Studies, 10*(2–3), 324–328.

Sullivan, C.F. (2011). Gender verification and gender policies in elite sport: Eligibility and "fair play". *Journal of Sport and Social Issues, 35*(4), 400–419.

Trujillo, N. (1991). Hegemonic masculinity on the mound: Media representations of Nolan Ryan and American sports culture. *Critical Studies in Mass Communication, 8*(3), 290–308.

Wander, P.C. (1983). The ideological turn in modern criticism. *Central States Speech Journal, 34*(1), 1–18.

Wenner, L.A. (1989). Media, sports, and society: The research agenda. In L.A. Wenner (Ed.), *Media, sports & society* (pp. 13–48). Newbury Park, CA: Sage.

Wenner, L.A. (Ed.). (1998). *MediaSport.* New York: Routledge.

Whiteside, E., & Hardin, M. (2011). Women (not) watching women: Leisure time, television, and implications for televised coverage of women's sports. *Communication, Culture & Critique, 4*(2), 122–143.

Williams, R. (1977). *Marxism and Literature.* New York: Oxford University Press.

Williams, R. (1983). *Keywords: A vocabulary of culture and society* (Rev. ed.). New York: Oxford University Press.

Winslow, L. (2012). Colonizing Caster Semenya: Gender transformation and the makeover genre. *Western Journal of Communication, 76*(3), 298–313.

Wright, H.K. (2001). "What's going on?" Larry Grossberg on the status quo of cultural studies: An interview. *Cultural Values, 5*(2), 133–162.

3

SPORT AND THE COMMUNICATION OF ETHICS

Lawrence A. Wenner

LOYOLA MARYMOUNT UNIVERSITY

As moral and ethical breaches in sport have become increasingly commonplace, sport has become a visible cultural site for the communication of ethics in the public sphere. A surprising range of improper actions and lapses in judgment have raised questions about the ethical climate in a sporting world that many look to for heroic leadership and values that can be celebrated and emulated. These include (see Mather, 2013; Wenner, 2013a) substance (from performance-enhancing and recreational drugs) and alcohol abuse, sexual 'improprieties' (from bad sexual manners to sexual assault to sex addiction to homophobia to questions over verification of sex), routine thuggery (from 'cheap shots' to brawls to gun play and even dogfighting), ill-directed politics (from overly loyal 'bad' nationalism to racist and otherwise prejudicial remarks), and plain old cheating on the field and off (from deflating footballs to stealing and videotaping signals to hacking into a competing team's information network to using nondisabled athletes in disability sport and overage athletes in youth sport).

The constant ethical breaches in sport have caused sport sociologists to sometimes joke "we know that sport builds character but we're just not sure what kind." The pressures to gain competitive advantage, to 'unlevel' the playing field, often puts sport at odds with what is frequently seen as its most beneficial social function: teaching and appreciating fair play. Because sport can be a compelling cultural enterprise with high financial stakes, there is temptation to look away or minimize ethical lapses less well tolerated in other quarters. Fervent fanship can facilitate moral "blindness" (Bird, 2002) or "myopia" (Drumwright & Murphy, 2004) and the sport press, often called the 'toy department' of journalism, is more concerned with stimulating appreciation of sport and its communication than in 'soiling the sell' of sport with ethical considerations.

Thus, scholars of sport and its communication can provide important service by using critical faculties and theories of ethical reasoning to interrogate the ethical climate of a cultural enterprise so often celebrated. The role of communication is essential as sport comes to have social force and cultural meaning through its communication. Towards stimulating ethical analysis of sport and its communication, this chapter considers ethical inquiry, using ethical theories in analysis, the scholarly terrain, and priorities for future research.

Ethics, Sport Ethics, and Communication Ethics

The long study of ethics stems from core concerns in moral philosophy about how best to live. Ethical analysis engages essential, ongoing, and sometimes irresolvable debates. Views even about the nature of ethical inquiry and its purposes can be diverse. What follows is a brief characterization of ethics and ethical inquiry and their applicability to the study of sport and communication.

Ethics

While ethics has been defined in many ways, most helpful is Josephson's (2002) characterization that "ethics refers to standards of conduct, standards that indicate how one should behave based on moral duties and virtues, which themselves are derived from principles of right and wrong" (p. 5). Debates over standards, essential moral duties and virtues, and the principles that should be at play are inherent in assessing ethical action. Considering such debates and understanding ethical dynamics, rather than offering moral prescription, are integral to scholarly ethical inquiry. Here, media ethicist John Merrill's (1999) definition of ethics as "the *study* of what we ought to do" (p. 1, emphasis added) characterizes the posture of scholarly ethical analysis. Ethical inquiry requires assessing varied ethical priorities and moral dispositions in the course of rendering evaluation or judgment about what is right and good and what ought to be, has, or should have been done.

Thus, bringing an ethical lens to sport explores what ought to and should be done by actors in sporting contexts. In thinking about communication in and about sport, such issues remain essential, but interrogation further considers the ethical dimensions of communication with sport entailments. Inquiry considers not only the ethical propriety of communicative acts, but also the casting or absence of ethical considerations in relation to sport. In the case of both sport and its communication, we see familiar concerns endemic to normative, social, and professional ethics. Here are basic questions about consequence and creating a greater good, over duties, loyalties, and the right thing to do, about finding a 'righteous' middle ground through exercising character and temperance, over acting with compassion and care to avoid causing harm, and about being fair to all and providing justice.

Such concerns are at the heart of ethical inquiry, not only about sport or communication, but in assessing the character and appropriateness of virtually all human action. While not exhaustive of the possibilities for ethical analysis, they undergird the major ethical theories and processes of ethical reasoning considered later.

Sport Ethics

Sport can do many good things (see Hurka, 2007). Participation facilitates fitness and skill. Team sport teaches cooperation. Rules and codes of conduct remind us of what is fair. Competition stimulates giving one's best. Spectatorship can bring enjoyment from the aesthetics and excellence of play. Fanship brings stimulation and joy with 'winning.' Sport can bring communities and nations together and serve as 'social glue.'

Yet not all in sport is good. In tandem with an emerging "media-commodification-marketing complex" (McNamee, 2010, p. 1) in the 1970s and 1980s, sport ethics, as a field of inquiry distinct from a larger philosophy of sport, was driven by an evident escalation of ethical problems in the sporting world. It recognized that opportunities to participate may not be egalitarian. Participation brings risks and preventable harms. Celebration of sport stars may encourage selfishness over cooperation. Pressures to win may naturalize cheating to gain unfair advantage. Spectatorship and fanship can go awry in hooliganism and hatred of opponents. The aesthetics of fine form may take a back seat to end results. National and local group cohesion that comes from supporting one's team may fuel distrust and even hate of those outside the group. Here too are social justice inequities, ranging from equal pay for male and female athletes, to access to participation for disabled athletes, to obstacles to opportunity stemming from race, ethnicity, gender, sexual orientation, and economics; deviance such as cheating, doping, homophobia, sexual harassment and abuse, and even child abuse may be condoned in sport subcultures.

In a celebrated and enriched sport marketplace, the privileging of elite and 'star' athletes risks compromising moral sensibilities, engendering expectations that they can act inappropriately with little consequence. This raises questions about the propriety of and our relationship with athletic role models who have ethically problematic off-the-field involvement with domestic violence, bar brawls and drunk driving, prostitutes and wayward sexual escapades, drug use, gunplay, and other breaches. Compromised ethical action extends far beyond athletes to coaches who are abusive and duplicitous to others such as those in command of professional leagues or in charge of sporting bodies, such as FIFA and the IOC, who have leveraged power in ethically improper ways to personal advantage over public benefit.

Because sport is so celebrated by the sport press, marketers and fans, inquiry about sport ethics provides important counterpoint and a twofold opportunity for communication of sport scholars. First, they can benefit from engagement in the considerable scholarly literature of sport ethics, seen in key works (McNamee, 2010; McNamee & Parry, 1998; Morgan, 2007; Shogan, 2007; Simon, 2010) and scholarly journals such as the *Journal of the Philosophy of Sport* and *Sport, Ethics and Philosophy*. Second, recognizing the role that the sport press and marketing have on fans and public sensibilities, communication scholars can broaden the focus of sport ethicists by focusing on how ethical dimensions of sport play out in the public sphere.

Communication Ethics

The study of ethics in communication is broad, traceable to foundations in philosophy and rhetoric (Aristotle, 1953). Inquiry ranges from the overtly theoretical and philosophical to the practical and applied. The field of communication ethics may be seen as bifurcated in other ways.

On one hand, there is what appears to be a broad-based field of communication ethics. Grounded in a larger philosophy of communication, it is driven by concerns over the ethos of rhetoric, discourse, and power in communication. Here, the ethical character of communicative intent, formulation, delivery, reception, effects, transactions, and situations are considered. Inquiry may be situated in familiar disciplinary areas such as rhetoric and public address, interpersonal, group, organizational and mediated communication, as well as intercultural, gender, family, health, political and other communicative contexts (Cheney, May, & Munshi, 2011; Jensen, 1997; Johannesen, Valde, & Whedbe, 2007; Neher & Sandin, 2007). All of these communicative contexts—and the challenges they bring to ethical propriety and action—have ready relevance for communication and sport.

Yet, even recognizing such breadth in communicative contexts as relevant to ethical assessment, there has been a chief concern with the public sphere. Indeed, in both the study of communication and sport and in communication ethics, media and media ethics respectively have dominated inquiry. Thus, the 'other side' of communication ethics receiving focused attention, and often detached from the broader field of communication ethics (while at the same time subsumed by it), has been the study of media ethics (Wilkins & Christians, 2009). Here, assessments of journalism ethics dominate with focus also on the ethics of persuasion in public relations and advertising (Bivins, 2009; Christians, Fackler, Richardson, Kreshel, & Woods, 2015; Parsons, 2008; Patterson & Wilkins, 2013; Spence & Van Heerkeren, 2004). While much study of media ethics has centered on the ethics of practice and the practitioner, assessments of the ethical climate of media industries and their structures, regulation, policy, pressures, and conventions have importance in ethical inquiry (Spence, Alexandra, Quinn, & Dunn, 2011).

The study of media ethics is driven by questions of what ought to be done in professional practice and the media marketplace. Consideration is given to 'duties' and 'loyalties' that come with professional practice, establishing what is responsible, fair, limits harm, and facilitates greater good. Common issues involve questions of transparency, truthfulness, deception, fairness, conflicts of interest, confidentiality, privacy, the casting of antisocial behavior, morally offensive content, the portrayal and stereotyping of individuals and groups, and larger issues of social justice. As issues such as these are readily universalized to other domains, such as sport, scholars will find ample opportunities to assess ethical propriety in communication and sport contexts. The next section considers some basic tactics for approaching ethical inquiry.

Approaching Sport and the Communication of Ethics

Engaging ethics in the study of communication and sport calls on interdisciplinary knowledge. Scholars need to build on understandings of sport in social and cultural contexts and have facility with a range of ethical theories and their application in moral reasoning. What follows is a brief characterization of some foundational ethical lenses and how ethical inquiry may illuminate the communication and sport nexus.

Ethical Theories and Moral Reasoning

Theoretical approaches to ethics are diverse and plentiful. From hedonism to humanism, from natural law to nihilism, from communitarianism to objectivism, unending debates over standpoints take place at distinct levels of meta-, normative, and applied ethical concern (Baggini & Fosi, 2007). Although the intricacies of debates consuming ethicists are considerable and a myriad of standpoints have been engaged in ethical analysis of communication and media, five approaches to ethical theory dominate ethical inquiry. An essentialist characterization of these follows.

Utility

Anchored in the 18th-century ideas of British philosophers Jeremy Bentham (1948) and John Stuart Mill (1861), utilitarianism is today's most common ethical yardstick, used regularly to guide public policy. In assessments, utility focuses on outcomes. Called 'consequentialism' or 'ends-based' thinking, this 'teleological' disposition relies on the 'utility principle,' which, when facing an ethical dilemma, aims to create 'the greatest good' for the 'greatest number.' In finding ethical pathways, one explores all possible outcomes of all possible actions on all parties and seeks to minimize harm.

Duty

In avoiding utilitarianism's potential 'ends justifies the means' problem, 'duty-based' or 'deontological' theories invoke 'nonconsequentialism.' Focusing on ethical action, duties, and loyalties, rather than possible outcomes, advocates invoke 18th-century German philosopher Immanuel Kant's (1959) conception of the 'categorical imperative,' which commands people to 'act so your choices could be universal law.' Kant sees this imperative and moral laws being unconditionally binding on rational beings, growing from higher truths or 'noumena,' seen as born in each person and to be obeyed. Simply put, we should act according to precepts we would like everyone else to follow in similar circumstances. Here, focus is on righteous actions, including truth-telling, benevolence, freedom, and respect for others and life, and wrongful actions, such as cheating, lying, stealing, dishonesty, deception, or creating harm.

Virtue

Focused on *phronesis*, or the development of practical wisdom, the building of character is central to virtue ethics. Anchored in the ideas of Aristotle (1953) and Confucius (Reid, 1999), virtue is seen in embracing a 'golden mean.' Here, righteous action is sought by people with practical wisdom by finding a 'temperate' point between extremes. Such temperance is found in the 'right place' between excess and deficiency, between overdoing and underdoing. Emphasis is placed on rational and pragmatic solutions through a 'right' and 'fair' compromise sensitive to competing interests. By identifying opposing options or extremes that are possible in handling a situation or resolving a dilemma, and then finding a tempered 'golden mean' that is both right and fair, virtue ethicists seek the wisdom of good character.

Care

Central to Judeo-Christian ideals, care ethics embrace the Golden Rule by using the notion of reversibility in seeking to treat others as you would want to be treated in similar circumstances. More than a Judeo-Christian concept, the goal of 'other respecting care' is seen across world religions with the ethics of care a key feature of feminist ethics stressing cooperation, compassion, and human dignity in conflict resolution and ethical action (Gilligan, 1982; Noddings, 1984). The normative ethic of 'loving thy neighbor' is seen in the Christian concept of *agape*, or unselfish 'other directed love' that embraces loyalty to others in loving them as they are. The care-based lens is most useful in assessing breaches of dignity and justice.

Justice

Approaching justice from a perspective of fairness, rather than reversibility, justice-based ethical theory is anchored in social contract theory (Morris, 2000) and egalitarianism. Foundational to law in democratic societies, the social contract

seeks equal treatment and to eliminate arbitrary distinctions in guiding judgments. Combatting the actuality that some having more resources and power
than others can skew the social contract, Rawls (1971) advanced justice-based
ethical theory with his 'veil of ignorance' tactic, which calls for all involved or
affected by a decision over an ethical dilemma to step back from who they actually are to an 'original position' where you are stripped of your identity. Here,
you are asked to make a decision that is just regardless of who you emerge as
when the veil is lifted. This process seeks to eliminate bias and insure basic liberties, and further, remedy historic unjust treatment.

Ethical Theory and Moral Reasoning

Beyond familiarity with these and other approaches to ethical theory, scholars
new to ethical inquiry need to find a path to sort out ethical assessments in communicative situations. Here, using a basic model of moral reasoning often helps
clarify the dynamics of a situation and assess what ought to be, has, or should
have been done. Common approaches in communication ethics include the
Potter Box model (see Christians et al., 2015), Day's (2006) SAD (situation,
analysis, decision) model, and Plaisance's (2014) MERIT (Multidimensional
Ethical Reasoning and Inquiry Task Sheet) model. Moral reasoning models
such as these share bringing order and rigor to moral reasoning. They demand
dispassionate definition of the situation, an assessment of the values, principles,
loyalties, and duties at play, and facilitate a decision about what ought to be, has,
or should have been done informed by the weight and directional guidance of
applicable ethical theories.

Ethical Inquiry and Criticism

There are broad possibilities for engaging ethics in the study of communication
and sport. Empirically oriented scholars may wish to begin by measuring offsets
in moral and ethical values and priorities amongst those participating in a communicative transaction. Indeed, there are many moral/ethical scales available, such
as Aquino and Reed's (2002) Self-Importance of Moral Identity Scale, Forsyth's
(1980) Ethics Position Questionnaire, to guide inquiry. While little study of this
sort has been done, assessing gaps in moral sensibilities, such as those between
sport reporters and fans, or fans rooting for opposing teams, or between coaches
and athletes, may be integral to understanding communication in sporting contexts. Certainly moral values can clash between those prioritizing utilitarian
consequence-oriented 'win at all costs' values and those prioritizing the duty to
play fair and minimize harm to opponents.

More explored and more relevant to critical communication scholars engaging rhetorical and cultural studies in their work is ethical criticism. Focused on

how ethics are revealed in narratives that are the backbone of both literature and communication, advocates see ethical criticism as "inescapable" (Gregory, 1998, p. 196) and its applicability universal. Burke (1967) has called narratives "equipment for living" (p. 294) as they inherently make claims and exhibit "implied judgments about how to live and what to believe about how to live" (Booth, 1998, p. 353). As they characterize situations, narratives press us to "define and create our own moral agency" (Gregory, 1998, p. 213). In this, Booth (1968, p. 11) sees the central tendencies of ethical criticism:

> If "virtue" covers every kind of genuine strength or power, and if a person's ethos is the total range of his or her virtues [to behave badly or well], then ethical criticism will be any effort to show how the virtues of narratives relate to the virtues of selves and societies, or how the ethos of any story affects or is affected by the ethos—the collection of virtues—of any given reader.

Whether applied to literature, art, or communication, the goal of that 'effort' is to reveal and clarify moral standpoint. The ethical critic explores "the pathways we are invited to follow" with an eye "on the probity of the moral experience" that a given communication "shapes or prescribes as a condition for correctly assimilating it" (Carroll, 1998, p. 370).

As advocates of ethical criticism (Clausen, 1986; Gregory, 1998) see the practice as complementary to, rather than replacing or displacing, other critical approaches, and argue that much conservative, radical, feminist, poststructural, and postmodern criticism merely masks what is an inherent ethical stance in taking political positions about right or wrong, diverse critical scholars may find this lens appealing in studying the probity of communicative action in sporting contexts. While overt ethical criticism in this context has thus far been limited, some key formations are considered in the next section.

Programmatic Research on Sport and the Communication of Ethics

Two notable developing lines of inquiry feature an overt 'ethical impulse' and hold promise for communication and sport research. Featuring universal tendencies, these research agendas, focusing on (1) the workings of communicative "dirt" (Wenner, 2007) as contagion, particularly in the commodity environment of promotional communication, and (2) how moral lines are drawn and reshaped as sport heroes publicly fall from grace in scandal and attempt to recover, portend long-term viability. The next sections consider strategies and development in these areas.

Dirt and Contagion

Growing from the seminal notion of Douglas (1966, p. 35) that "(d)irt is matter out of place" (p. 35) and evolving over nearly 20 studies dating back to the 1990s (Wenner, 2013b), a "dirt theory of narrative ethics" (Wenner, 2007, 2009) was developed with an eye to deconstructing sport narratives and their reading in the commodity context, and further, to interrogating the ethics of that transaction. As developed in communication and media theory (Enzenberger, 1972; Hartley, 1984; Leach, 1976), cultural dirt, such as meanings emanating from sport, is significant because of its abilities to transcend boundaries, moving from one place to "hail" you (Althusser, 1971/2001) in another where it may be improper. This process of "cultural borrowing" (Wenner, 1991, p. 392), necessary to the transfer of meaning in all communication, becomes problematic when galvanizing familiar understandings to pollute meaning. Such ethical breaches garner power by applying old logics to new stories to shape meanings, something recognized when we speak of sports' appeal in selling other products.

Applying dirt theory to sport communication requires a three-layer process. In approaching narratives, one first 'follows the dirt,' asking about its character, origins, importation, and trajectory. Inquiry examines how imported communicative dirt and logics about it are used in constructing new narratives and what fallacies or distortions are facilitated as a result. Second, dirt theory engages the reading process, using tactics from reader–oriented criticism and reception theory (Machor & Goldstein, 2001; Tompkins, 1980) in recognition that readers necessarily soil new texts with old dirt. Central to interrogating dirt are concerns with (1) the contextualization of implied readers, (2) drawing of readers in and by the text, and (3) the nature of the reading act (Iser, 1978). Focus is given to assertions about sporting "interpretive communities" (Fish, 1980) in the 'dirtied' narrative, the painting of textual surrogates, strategies used to encourage preferred reading, and how redundancies and gaps in texts may stimulate readerly disposition. Crystallized in this process are improprieties taken in characterizing readers, in imagining their community (Anderson, 1983), and narrative sense-making. Thus, dirt theory's third step focuses on the ethical assessment of the transition between dirt and its reading. Attention centers on ethical tension in texts and reading by raising questions about greater good, minimizing harm, other respecting care, veracity, fairness, and other issues. In its focus on 'dirty transactions' and moral flaws in sport communication, ethical criticism illuminates breaches in cultural assertions.

Research exploring the workings of communicative dirt relative to sport has centered on how idealized (or imagined) understandings about sport are used strategically in promotional communication and marketing. Studies have examined the ethos of infusing sport logics in the selling of beer, creating deceptive synergies through cross-promoting products in Olympics broadcasts, using hegemonic masculinity to naturalize public space in the sports bar, creating a culture of nonaccountability in the Janet Jackson Super Bowl exposure fiasco, contributing to a knee-jerk moral cooling in Super Bowl advertising in response to the Jackson public relations disaster, creating disingenuous idealized portraits of fans in television advertising, naturalizing oppositional stereotypes of gender and gender relations in advertising narratives, celebrating hypermasculinity and homophobia in male bonding over beer in sporting contexts, mocking men and institutionalizing misandry in television commercials, stereotyping and undercutting the legitimacy of the female fan in both television advertising and user-generated web videos, and examining the deceptive ways that advertisers use sporting events to define their products (see Wenner, 2013b). This research program has coalesced in the resultant articulation of the "mediasport interpellation" (Wenner, 2013b, 2014, 2015) as a theoretical corollary to dirt theory. This corollary poses that ethically problematic logics about sport 'hail' and contain us in our understandings about gender, fanship, and consumer roles relative to sport.

Scandal and Apologia

Rather than being anchored in how sport-entailed communication may be ethically problematic or 'dirty,' a second developed research agenda examines how moral failings in sport are communicated, understood, and responded to. This line of inquiry builds on recognition that a felt paucity of heroes in contemporary times has been remediated, in often problematic ways, by the rise of a mediated celebrityhood within which the sport hero plays an outsized role along with other 'stars' and celebrities of popular culture (Allison & Goethals, 2011). With the regularized rise of this new type of hero, known not only for abilities to act, sing, entertain, and play sport but for increasingly living one's life in public, has come the regular occurrence of falling from grace in scandal (Rowe, 1997). And seemingly no class of hero in the age of celebrity culture has fallen more regularly than the sport star (Whannel, 2002).

Two major works have centered on this phenomenon. The first, Wenner's (2013a) *Fallen Sport Heroes, Media, and Celebrity Culture*, brings together a diverse group of international critical scholars from media and sport studies, anchored in a cultural studies lens. The volume builds on diverse research on the communication of scandal (Lull & Hinerman, 1997) showing how media characterizations of public sphere improprieties illuminate where moral lines are drawn in culture, as well as foundational work by Rowe (1994, 1997) interrogating the particularized workings of the fallen sport hero in cases such as NBA star 'tragic Magic' Johnson's AIDS scandal and NFL football legend O.J. Simpson's murder scandal. Reaching beyond analysis of narratives about moral fissures that drive sport scandals, studies in Wenner's (2013a) collection reveal broader understanding by examining media complicity in the creation of a rise–fall–redemption communicative arc in assessing morally tarnished heroes.

This larger context showcases how moral judgment (or lack thereof) is inherent in sport journalism fueled by the need to create virtuous sport heroes, a journalism that tends to blame athletes for individual moral failings rather than examining the structural forces, including sport and media systems, that help create elite athlete cultures.

Many studies in Wenner's volume consider the communicative dimensions of 'predictable' moral pratfalls of athletes, over such things as sexual transgressions in the cases of golfer Tiger Woods (Billings, 2013), UK soccer star John Terry (Grantham, 2013), and Australian rules football 'King' Wayne Carey (McKay & Brooks, 2013), wanton gunplay in the cases of the NFL's Plaxico Burress and the NBA's Gilbert Arenas (Lavelle, 2013), and drug use, for enhancing performance as was the case with track star Marion Jones (Meân, 2013) or for recreation in the case of professional skateboarding's Christian Hosoi (Beal, 2013). Other studies provide insight into the communication of more 'surprising' offenses such as the criminal dogfighting of NFL star quarterback Michael Vick (Giardina & Magnusen, 2013), or more complex moral dilemmas, such as how sport institutions should pass judgment over gender verification in the case of South African runner Caster Semenya (Cooky & Dworkin, 2013). Finally, the volume is significant in looking beyond moral fissures by athletes, to narratives, such as those about coaches and sport broadcasters, who provide moral leadership in and judgment about sport. Here, studies such as Hardin and Lavoi's (2013) analysis contrasting the 'lesbian problem' stories about two women coaches, one homophobic and one predatory, and Hundley's (2013) comparative analysis of sportscasters who have taken moral tumbles for racist, sexist, and homophobic comments, show how diverse ethical breaches can be in the sporting context.

The second key work, Blaney, Lippert, and Smith's (2013) *Repairing the Athlete's Image: Studies in Sports Image Restoration*, building on a set of theoretical approaches to the rhetorical analysis of "apologia" (Ware & Linkugel, 1973) and "purification" (Burke, 1968), is reliant on the "gold standard for analyzing image repair discourse" (Blaney, 2013, p. 2), Benoit's (1995, 1997) image restoration theory, which has ready application for public relations crisis management. Studies in the Blaney et al. (2013) volume feature U.S. cases and scholars seated in communication in a more limited and focused manner, with much analysis of discourse structured by Benoit's (1995) five stages typifying image recovery: (1) denial, (2) evasion of responsibility, (3) reducing offensiveness, (4) assuring corrective action, and (5) mortification.

For communication scholars, studies in the collection are important in using discipline-specific tactics that have been used to study apologia and recovery strategies more broadly as well as building on a line of rhetorical analysis emerging in the sport context. Good examples of earlier applications include Benoit and Hanczor's (1994) analysis of skater Tonya Harding's mishandling of her assault on a fellow Olympic team member and McDorman's (2003, p. 1) assessment of the "rhetorical resurgence" and "second chance apologia" of disgraced baseball star Pete Rose. The collection is useful in other ways. Its organizational strategy, with sections on drugs, marital infidelity and sexual misconduct, social deviance and integrity, on-field actions, and organizational misconduct, portends a stable classification scheme for ethical breaches and moral offenses that fuel image repair discourse. Further, many individual studies offer useful contrasting analyses of the cases of Tiger Woods (Benoit, 2013), Marion Jones (Kramer, 2013), John Terry (Huxford, 2013), Michael Vick (Smith, 2013), Gilbert Arenas (Sheckels, 2013), and Plaxico Burress (Glantz, 2013) seen in the Wenner (2013a) collection. Finally, a set of studies in the Blaney et al. (2013) collection, focusing on responses by sport organizations such as Major League Baseball (Meyer & Cutbirth, 2013), the NCAA (Milford, 2013), and the National Hockey League (DiSanza, Legge, Allen, & Wilde, 2013) to ethical problems, provides good case examples showcasing opportunities for organizational communication and public relations scholars.

Key Areas for Future Research on Sport and the Communication of Ethics

While programmatic research on sport and the communication of ethics has been limited, there are some encouraging signs seen in studies displaying a clear 'ethical impulse' and diverse opportunities in areas calling for development. Select consideration of these follows.

Encouraging Signs

Sport Journalism

Sport journalism is often characterized as a 'toy department' (Rowe, 2007) where the professionalism and ethos desired of 'serious' journalism may be less engaged. Indeed, the unique culture and practice of sport journalism provokes compromises to gain access, tensions between truth-telling and privacy, and an overarching press to serve as cheerleaders rather than muckrakers of sport (Boyle, 2006; Lowes, 1999). Yet, while the study of journalism ethics has been the preeminent concern of media ethicists, the ethics of sport journalism, perhaps because its 'toy department' may not be seen to have worldly import, has received little systematic scholarly attention. Scholars such as Oates and Pauly (2007) are increasingly recognizing the need to "refigure sports reporting as a legitimate object of ethical reflection" (p. 333) as sport journalism inherently offers "moral and ethical discourse" (p. 332) in telling stories about sport and its actors.

With much evidence that sport journalism's 'toy department' is a gendered space so dominated by male journalists that it might be called a 'boy department,' there is a need for ethical interrogation of sport journalism on justice and egalitarianism grounds. Studies across cultures (Boyle, 2006; Bruce, 2000;

Hardin & Shain, 2006; Strong, 2007) provide vivid evidence of double standards and the hostile environment that female sport reporters face. Indeed, studies of the discourse ethics of sport journalism (Holt, 2000) suggest an ethical climate reliant on the language ripe with metaphors of violence, the military and war, and machines, all features of male-dominated environments.

Climatic Assessments

Studies of the ethics of sport journalism and the moral compasses relied upon within its practice have led the way in addressing a broader need to take stock of the ethical climates at play across the creation and consumption of sport communication. Certainly, the research environment is ripe for 'ethical audits' of subcultures, using standardized scales and questionnaires mentioned earlier, and studies of how different ethical values affect communication in and about sport. In the case of sport journalism, research to date suggests that ethical concerns, such as taking 'freebies' or exhibiting home team boosterism, are not a high priority, especially amongst younger sport journalists on less prestigious local beats (Hardin, 2005; Hardin & Zhong, 2010). Other research finds the ethical climate for sport journalism offset from other parts of the newsroom on issues such as the appropriateness of sport gambling, recognizing conflicts of interests stemming from relationships with those they cover, and related 'cozy' relationships with and boosterism for their subjects (Hardin, Zhong, & Whiteside, 2009).

Moving beyond the climate for sport journalism, Raney's (2011) study uses disposition theory, a cornerstone approach to studying the enjoyment of viewing sports, to examine how morality influences the way we watch sports. In considering the dynamic of viewer morality, the study puts forward the need to confirm whether sport fans view their favorite teams as morally superior and whether 'moral amnesty' is granted by fans in a way that permits moral disengagement from select rule-breaking by their favorite teams.

Needs and Opportunities

Digital and Social Media

It is clear that much attention in recent scholarly research has been focused on the increasing importance of digital and social 'new' media, citizen journalism, and user-generated content. Here, too, there has been little formal concern over ethics. While studies have explicitly explored the ethical breaches seen in online coverage of high school athlete recruitment for intercollegiate sports (Yanity & Edmonson, 2011) and raised questions about the ethical propriety of product placement in sport video games (Kim & McClung, 2010), the ethical dynamics of the digital communication environment are rarely explored. With topics emerging such as the use of performance-enhancing drugs in competitive fantasy sports and a 'wild west' absent of a climate of professional ethical standards in user-generated content, blogging, memes, and the Twitterization of everything, finding coherent paths for ethical analysis of new communication content will be both essential and challenging.

Leadership and Organizations

We know that coaches can be abusive in motivation and the quest for winning. At the same time, we know that coaches can be highly valued for their ethical leadership and fairness (Denison & Avner, 2011; Kassing & Pappas, 2007). On other fronts, most sport fans know that team owners, professional leagues and their executives, and leaders in NGOs (non-governmental organizations) in sport, such as the IOC and FIFA, have played hardball, breaching ethics and sometimes breaking laws, to gain advantage and profit. Thus, the study of the ethical dimensions of leadership and the ethical climate of sport organizations is particularly ripe for communication inquiry. Here scholars, most particularly those seated in organizational communication, who study the improper wielding of power by management and leaders can help advance understanding in sporting contexts.

Interpersonal and Group Communication

One need only attend a Little League baseball game to realize the often intense pressures put on young athletes by parents. Indeed, it's hard not to recognize how 'out of control' some parents get with vitriolic language aimed not only at their children, but also at opponents, their coaches, and game officials. We know as well that within teams communication often transacts on less than egalitarian grounds between those with higher or lower status and often with little tact or care and can facilitate moral disengagement (Hodge & Gucciardi, 2015). While little examined using lenses from communication studies, understanding the ethical climate of communication, both among its participants, and between its participants and others, remains a basic need. Given the sport fervor seen in some parents, the ethical climate of family communication concerning sport, and most particularly between parents and children, calls out for attention in the scholarly community.

Contextualizing Sport and the Communication of Ethics

Sport provides constant and influential public staging grounds for ethics. Here, we see noble and heroic behavior that may fulfill our hopes that sport can indeed build good character. Yet, we know at the same time that there is much in the climate of sport, in its ever present drive to win, and in the everyday on- and off-the-field actions of its participants, that shows evidence of an ethical compass that frequently loses its bearings. For communication and media studies scholars, studying the communication of ethics in this powerful and public sphere offers many opportunities. In important ways those opportunities extend well beyond sport because as we examine ethical action in the sport world we also come to understand communication about where broader ethical lines in contemporary culture stand and should be drawn. We also get to consider what kind of ethical mirror we want sport to be of our society, a funhouse mirror that is distorted, or a reflection of the good and the best that we can be. For these reasons, for communication of sport scholars, studying sport and the communication of ethics seems a winning combination.

References

Aristotle. (1953). *Nichomachean ethics*. New York: Modern Library.

Allison, S.T., & Goethals, G.R. (2011). *Heroes: What they do and why we need them*. New York: Oxford University Press.

Althusser, L. (1971/2001). *Lenin and philosophy and other essays* (Ben Brewster, Trans.). New York: Monthly Review Press.

Anderson, B. (1983). *Imagined communities*. London: Verso.

Aquino, K., & Reed, A.I.I. (2002) The self-importance of moral identity. *Journal of Personality and Social Psychology, 83*, 1423–1440.

Baggini, J., & Fosi, P.S. (2007). *The ethics toolkit: A compendium of ethical concepts and methods*. Malden, MA: Wiley-Blackwell.

Beal, B. (2013). Ups and downs of skating vertical: Christian Hosoi, crystal meth, and Christianity. In L.A. Wenner (Ed.), *Fallen sports heroes, media, and celebrity culture* (pp. 92–106). New York: Peter Lang.

Benoit, W.L. (1995). *Accounts, excuses, and apologies: A theory of image restoration discourse*. Albany, NY: State University of New York Press.

Benoit, W.L. (1997). Image restoration discourse and crisis communications. *Public Relations Review, 23*, 177–186.

Benoit, W.L. (2013). Tiger Woods's image repair: Could he hit one out of the rough? In J.R. Blaney, L.R. Lippert, & J.S. Smith (Eds.), *Repairing the athlete's image: Studies in sports image restoration* (pp. 89–96). Lanham, MD: Lexington Books.

Benoit, W.L., & Hanczor, R. (1994). The Tonya Harding controversy: An analysis of image repair strategies. *Communication Quarterly, 42*, 416–433.

Bentham, J. (1948). *An introduction to the principles of morals and legislation*. New York: Hafner.

Billings, A.C. (2013). Tiger Woods lands in the "rough": Golf, apologia, and heroic limits of privacy. In L.A. Wenner (Ed.), *Fallen sports heroes, media, and celebrity culture* (pp. 51–63). New York: Peter Lang.

Bird, F.B. (2002). *The muted conscience: Moral silence and the practice of business ethics* (Rev. ed.). Westport, CT: Quorum Books.

Bivins, T. (2009). *Mixed media: Moral distinctions in advertising, public relations, and journalism* (2nd ed.). New York: Routledge.

Blaney, J.R. (2013). Introduction: Why sports image restoration and how shall we proceed? In J.R. Blaney, L.R. Lippert, & J.S. Smith (Eds.), *Repairing the athlete's image: Studies in sports image restoration* (pp. 1–5). Lanham, MD: Lexington Books.

Blaney, J.R., Lippert, L.R., & Smith, J.S. (Eds.). (2013). *Repairing the athlete's image: Studies in sports image restoration*. Lanham, MD: Lexington Books.

Booth, W.C. (1988). *The company we keep: An ethics of fiction*. Berkeley, CA: University of California Press.

Booth, W.C. (1998). Why ethical criticism can never be simple. *Style, 32*, 351–364.

Boyle, R. (2006) *Sports journalism: Context and issues*. London: Sage.

Bruce, T. (2000). Never let the bastards see you cry. *Sociology of Sport Journal, 17*, 69–74.

Burke, K. (1967). *The philosophy of literary form: Studies in symbolic action* (2nd ed.). Baton Rouge, LA: University of Louisiana Press.

Burke, K. (1968). *A rhetoric of motives*. Berkeley, CA: University of California Press.

Carroll, N. (1998). *A philosophy of mass art*. Oxford: Clarendon Press.

Cheney, G., May, S., & Munshi, D. (Eds.). (2011). *Handbook of communication ethics*. New York: Routledge.

Christians, C.G., Fackler, M., Richardson, K.B., Kreshel, P.J., & Woods, R.H. (2015). *Media ethics: Cases and moral reasoning* (9th ed.). New York: Routledge.

Clausen, C. (1986). *The moral imagination: Essays on literature and ethics*. Iowa City, IA: University of Iowa Press.

Cooky, C., & Dworkin, S.L. (2013). Running down what comes naturally: Gender verification and South Africa's Caster Semenya. In L.A. Wenner (Ed.), *Fallen sports heroes, media, and celebrity culture* (pp. 148–162). New York: Peter Lang.

Day, L.A. (2006). *Ethics in media communications: Cases and controversies* (5th ed.). Belmont, CA: Thomson Wadsworth.

Denison, J., & Avner, Z. (2011). Positive coaching: Ethical practices for athlete development. *Quest, 63*, 209–227.

DiSanza, J.R., Legge, N.J., Allen, H.R., & Wilde, J.T. (2013). The puck stops here: The NHL's image repair strategies during the 2004–2005 lockout. In J.R. Blaney, L.R. Lippert, & J.S. Smith (Eds.), *Repairing the athlete's image: Studies in sports image restoration* (pp. 319–391). Lanham, MD: Lexington Books.

Douglas, M. (1966). *Purity and danger: An analysis of the concepts of pollution and taboo*. London: Routledge and Kegan Paul.

Drumwright, M.E., & Murphy, P.E. (2004). How advertising practitioners view ethics. *Journal of Advertising, 33*(2), 7–24.

Enzenberger, H.M. (1972). Constituents of a theory of the media. In D. McQuail (Ed.), *Sociology of mass communication* (pp. 99–112). Harmondsworth, UK: Penguin.

Fish, S. (1980). *Is there a text in this class? The authority of interpretive communities*. Cambridge, MA: Harvard University Press.

Forsyth, D.R. (1980). A taxonomy of ethical ideologies. *Journal of Personality and Social Psychology, 39*, 175–184.

Giardina, M.D., & Magnusen, M. (2013). Dog bites man? The criminalization and rehabilitation of Michael Vick. In L.A. Wenner (Ed.), *Fallen sports heroes, media, and celebrity culture* (pp. 165–178). New York: Peter Lang.

Gilligan, C. (1982). *In a different voice: Psychological theory and women's development*. Cambridge, MA: Harvard University Press.

Glantz, M. (2013). Plaxico Burress takes his best shot. In J.R. Blaney, L.R. Lippert, & J.S. Smith (Eds.), *Repairing the athlete's image: Studies in sports image restoration* (pp. 187–202). Lanham, MD: Lexington Books.

Grantham, B. (2013). No gagging matter: John Terry plays centre back from dad of the year to (alleged) debauchery. In L.A. Wenner (Ed.), *Fallen sports heroes, media, and celebrity culture* (pp. 222–235). New York: Peter Lang.

Gregory, M. (1998). Ethical criticism: What it is and why it matters. *Style, 32,* 194–220.

Hardin, M. (2005). Survey finds boosterism, freebies remain problem for newspaper sports departments. *Newspaper Research Journal, 26*(1), 66–72.

Hardin, M., & Lavoi N.M. (2013). The "bully" and the "girl who did what she did": Neo-homophobia in coverage of two women's college basketball coaches. In L.A. Wenner (Ed.), *Fallen sports heroes, media, and celebrity culture* (pp. 267–283). New York: Peter Lang.

Hardin, M., & Shain, S. (2006). "Feeling much smaller than you know you are": The fragmented professional identity of female sports journalists. *Critical Studies in Media Communication, 23,* 322–338.

Hardin, M., & Zhong, B. (2010). Sports reporters' attitudes about ethics vary based on beat. *Newspaper Research Journal, 31*(2), 6–19.

Hardin, M., Zhong, B., & Whiteside, E. (2009). Sports coverage: "Toy department" or public-service journalism? The relationship between reporters' ethics and attitudes towards the profession. *International Journal of Sport Communication, 2,* 319–339.

Hartley, J. (1984). Encouraging signs: TV and the power of dirt, speech, and scandalous categories. In W. Rowland & B. Watkins (Eds.), *Interpreting television: Current research perspectives* (pp. 119–141). Beverly Hills, CA: Sage.

Hodge, K., & Gucciardi, D.F. (2015). Antisocial and prosocial behavior in sport: The role of motivational climate, basic psychological needs, and moral disengagement. *Journal of Sport & Exercise Psychology, 37,* 257–273.

Holt, R. (2000). The discourse ethics of sports print journalism. *Culture, Sport, Society, 3,* 88–103.

Hundley, H. (2013). Who's sorry now? Sportcasters falling from grace, saving face. In L.A. Wenner (Ed.), *Fallen sports heroes, media, and celebrity culture* (pp. 313–329). New York: Peter Lang.

Hurka, T. (2007). Games and the good. In W.J. Morgan (Ed.), *Ethics in sport* (2nd ed.) (pp. 21–33). Champaign, IL: Human Kinetics.

Huxford, J. (2013). Strategies of silence: The John Terry affair and the British press. In J.R. Blaney, L.R. Lippert, & J.S. Smith (Eds.), *Repairing the athlete's image: Studies in sports image restoration* (pp. 123–148). Lanham, MD: Lexington Books.

Iser, W. (1978). *The act of reading: A theory of aesthetic response.* Baltimore, MD: Johns Hopkins University Press.

Jensen, J.V. (1997). *Ethical issues in the communication process.* Mahwah, NJ: Erlbaum.

Johannesen, R.L., Valde, K.S., & Whedbe, K.E. (2007). *Ethics in human communication* (6th ed.). Prospect Heights, IL: Waveland Press.

Josephson, M. (2002). *Making ethical decisions* (2nd ed.). Marina del Rey, CA: Josephson Institute of Ethics.

Kant, I. (1959). *Foundations of metaphysics of morals* (L.W. Beck, Trans.). Indianapolis, IN: Bobbs-Merrill. (Original work published 1785.)

Kassing, J.W., & Pappas, M.E. (2007). "Champions are built in the off season": An exploration of high school coaches' memorable passages. *Human Communication, 10*(4), 537–546.

Kim, M.S., & McClung, S.R. (2010). Acceptability and ethics of product placement in sport video games. *Journal of Promotion Management, 16,* 411–427.

Kramer, M.J. (2013). Image repair media interview as apologia and antapologia: Marion Jones on the *Oprah Winfrey Show.* In J.R. Blaney, L.R. Lippert, & J.S. Smith (Eds.), *Repairing the athlete's image: Studies in sports image restoration* (pp. 59–70). Lanham, MD: Lexington Books.

Lavelle, K.L. (2013). "Guns are no joke": Framing Plaxico Burress, Gilbert Arenas, and gunplay in professional sports. In L.A. Wenner (Ed.), *Fallen sports heroes, media, and celebrity culture* (pp. 179–192). New York: Peter Lang.

Leach, E. (1976). *Culture and communication.* Cambridge: Cambridge University Press.

Lowes, M.D. (1999). *Inside the sports pages: Work routines, professional ideologies, and the manufacture of sports news.* Toronto, ON: University of Toronto Press.

Lull, J., & Hinerman, S. (Eds.). (1997). *Media scandals: Morality and desire in the popular culture marketplace.* New York: Columbia University Press.

Machor, J.L., & Goldstein, P. (Eds.). (2001). *Reception study: From literary theory to cultural studies.* London: Routledge.

Mather, V. (2013, June 17). The biggest cheats in team sports. *New York Times.* Retrieved July 23, 2015, from http://www.nytimes.com/interactive/2015/06/17/sports/cardinals-astros-cheat-teams.html?_r=0.

McDorman, T. (2003). The rhetorical resurgence of Pete Rose: A second chance apologia. In R.S. Brown & D.J. O'Rourke (Eds.), *Case studies in sport communication* (pp. 1–25). Westport, CT: Praeger.

McKay, J., & Brooks, K. (2013). "Wayne's World": Media narratives of downfall and redemption about Australian football "King" Wayne Carey. In L.A. Wenner (Ed.), *Fallen sports heroes, media, and celebrity culture* (pp. 236–250). New York: Peter Lang.

McNamee, M. (2010). *The ethics of sport: A reader.* London: Routledge.

McNamee, M.J., & Parry, S.J. (1998). *Ethics and sport.* London: E & FN Spon.

Meân, L.J. (2013). On track, off track, on *Oprah*: The framing of Marion Jones as golden girl and American fraud. In L.A. Wenner (Ed.), *Fallen sports heroes, media, and celebrity culture* (pp. 77–91). New York: Peter Lang.

Merrill, J. (1999). Overview: Foundations for media ethics. In A.D. Gordon & J.M. Kitross (Eds.), *Controversies in media ethics* (2nd ed., pp. 1–25). New York: Longman.

Meyer, K.R., & Cutbirth, C.W. (2013). No pepper: Apologia and image repair in the 2002 labor negotiations between Major League Baseball and the players association. In J.R. Blaney, L.R. Lippert, & J.S. Smith (Eds.), *Repairing the athlete's image: Studies in sports image restoration* (pp. 267–282). Lanham, MD: Lexington Books.

Milford, M. (2013). Giving them the ol' misdirection: The NCAA and the student-athlete. In J.R. Blaney, L.R. Lippert, & J.S. Smith (Eds.), *Repairing the athlete's image: Studies in sports image restoration* (pp. 283–296). Lanham, MD: Lexington Books.

Mill, J.S. (1861). *Utilitarianism.* London: Dent.

Morgan, W.J. (Ed.). (2007). *Ethics in sport* (2nd ed.). Champaign, IL: Human Kinetics.

Morris, C.W. (2000). *The social contract theorists: Critical essays on Hobbes, Locke, and Rousseau.* Lanham, MD: Rowman & Littlefield.

Neher, W.W., & Sandin, P.J. (2007). *Communicating ethically: Character, duties, consequences, and relationships.* Boston, MA: Pearson.

Noddings, N. (1984). *Caring: A feminine approach to ethical and moral education.* Berkeley, CA: University of California Press.

Oates, T.P., & Pauly, J. (2007). Sports journalism as moral and ethical discourse. *Journal of Mass Media Ethics, 22,* 332–347.

Parsons, P.J. (2008). *Ethics in public relations* (2nd ed.). London: Kogan Page.

Patterson, P., & Wilkins, L. (2013). *Media ethics: Issues and cases* (8th ed.). New York: McGraw-Hill.

Plaisance, P.L. (2014). *Media ethics: Key principles for responsible practice* (2nd ed.). Thousand Oaks, CA: Sage.

Raney, A.A. (2011). Fair ball? Exploring the relationship between media sports and viewer morality. In A.C. Billings (Ed.), *Sports media: Transformation, integration, consumption* (pp. 77–93). New York: Routledge.

Rawls, J. (1971). *A theory of justice*. Cambridge, MA: Harvard University Press.

Reid, T.R. (1999). *Confucius lives next door: What living in the East teaches us about living in the West*. Berkeley, CA: University of California Press.

Rowe, D. (1994). Accommodating bodies: Celebrity, sexuality, and "tragic Magic." *Journal of Sport and Social Issues, 18*(1), 6–26.

Rowe, D. (1997). Apollo undone: The sports scandal. In J. Lull & S. Hinerman (Eds.), *Media scandals: Morality and desire in the popular culture marketplace* (pp. 203–221). New York: Columbia University Press.

Rowe, D. (2007). Sports journalism: Still the "toy department" of the news media. *Journalism, 8*, 385–405.

Sheckels, T.F. (2013). Failed comedy of the NBA's Gilbert Arenas: Image restoration in context. In J.R. Blaney, L.R. Lippert, & J.S. Smith (Eds.), *Repairing the athlete's image: Studies in sports image restoration* (pp. 169–186). Lanham, MD: Lexington Books.

Shogan, D. (2007). *Sport ethics in context*. Toronto: Canadian Scholar's Press.

Simon, R.L. (2010). *Fair play: The ethics of sport* (3rd ed.). Boulder, CO: Westview Press.

Smith, J.S. (2013). Bad newz kennels: Michael Vick and dogfighting. In J.R. Blaney, L.R. Lippert, & J.S. Smith (Eds.), *Repairing the athlete's image: Studies in sports image restoration* (pp. 151–168). Lanham, MD: Lexington Books.

Spence, E.H., Alexandra, A., Quinn, A., & Dunn, A. (2011). *Media, markets, and morals*. Malden, MA: Wiley-Blackwell.

Spence, E. & Van Heerkeren, B. (2004). *Advertising ethics*. New York: Pearson.

Strong, C. (2007). Female journalists shun sports reporting: Lack of opportunity or lack of attractiveness? *Communication Journal of New Zealand, 8*(2), 7–18.

Tompkins, J.P. (Ed.). (1980). *Reader-response criticism: From formalism to post-structuralism*. Baltimore: MD: Johns Hopkins University Press.

Ware, B.L., & Linkugel, W.A. (1973). They spoke in defense of themselves: On the generic criticism of apologia. *Quarterly Journal of Speech, 59*, 273–283.

Wenner, L.A. (1991). One part alcohol, one part sport, one part dirt, stir gently: Beer commercials and television sport. In L.R. Vande Berg & L.A. Wenner (Eds.), *Television criticism: Approaches and applications* (pp. 388–407). New York: Longman.

Wenner, L.A. (2007). Towards a dirty theory of narrative ethics: Prolegomenon on media, sport and commodity value. *International Journal of Media and Cultural Politics, 3*, 11–129.

Wenner, L.A. (2009). The unbearable dirtiness of being: On the commodification of mediasport and the need for ethical criticism. *Journal of Sports Media, 4*(1), 85–94.

Wenner, L.A. (Ed.). (2013a). *Fallen sports heroes, media, and celebrity culture*. New York: Peter Lang.

Wenner, L.A. (2013b). The mediasport interpellation: Gender, fanship, and consumer culture. *Sociology of Sport Journal, 30*, 83–103.

Wenner, L.A. (2014). On the limits of the new and the lasting power of the mediasport interpellation. *Television and New Media, 15*, 732–740.

Wenner, L.A. (2015). Assessing the sociology of sport: On the mediasport interpellation and commodity narratives. *International Review for the Sociology of Sport, 50*, 628–633.

Whannel, G. (2002). *Media sport stars: Masculinities and moralities*. London: Routledge.

Wilkins, L., & Christians, C.G. (Eds.). (2009). *Handbook of mass media ethics*. New York: Routledge.

Yanity, M., & Edmondson, A.C. (2011). The ethics of online coverage of recruiting high school athletes. *International Journal of Sport Communication, 4*, 403–421.

4

SPORT AND ETHNOGRAPHY

An Embodied Practice Meets an Embodied Method

Robert L. Krizek

SAINT LOUIS UNIVERSITY

By selecting the title, *Defining Sport Communication*, the editor of this volume charged contributors with what might appear to be a fairly specific, even mundane task. In retrospect, however, the editor's charge has proven more taxing than I had anticipated. First, I was forced to make explicit what I had taken for granted about sport, about communication, and about the intersection of the two. Surfacing taken-for-granted assumptions is always a challenge. In addition, I have discovered that perhaps the only task as challenging as defining 'sport communication' is positing a rationale for how to conduct meaningful research for much of what resides at that intersection. Those of us who have played sport or studied sport realize that how fans, commentators, critics, writers, and myriad support personnel talk about sport, and how participants communicatively engage in sport is not always easily measured or readily observable.

In this chapter, I offer ethnography as a viable, yet unfortunately underutilized, research method for examining those not-so-easily-measured or observed aspects of the sport and communication intersection. I begin by defining key terms to create an argument for the existence of an 'embodied' connection that binds sport and ethnography. Second, I briefly review three of the principal theoretical underpinnings of ethnography and in doing so demonstrate how ethnography enables the understanding of significant facets of sport communication. Third, after responding to two questions regarding the dearth of 'real' ethnographies in sport communication, I discuss examples of ethnographic scholarship found within sport communication. Fourth, and finally, I present some possibilities for future ethnographic research within our subdiscipline. I offer these possibilities to encourage current and future sport communication scholars to engage ethnography in all of its incarnations, including auto-ethnography and personal narrative, to better understand the realm of communication and sport.

Defining Communication, Sport, and Ethnography

In this section, I provide definitions of communication, sport, sport communication, and ethnography. I also detail a key definitional connection between sport and ethnography, thereby creating the basis for this chapter's primary argument. That argument asserts that sport and ethnography are inextricably linked as embodied practices. In addition, because of that link, I propose that ethnography is a method well suited for understanding those aspects of sport not always easily measured or readily observed. For example, ethnography is particularly adept at surfacing the cultural practices of individuals who inhabit the community of sport and the systems of *meanings* that motivate and result from those practices (Vidali & Peterson, 2012).

Page considerations do not allow for an expanded review of the many and diverse definitions of communication. Regardless of their specifics, however, these definitions primarily emerge from models of communication grounded in either a humanistic or scientific approach to the examination of human communication (see Miller, 1975, for a discussion of humanistic and scientific approaches). The latter approach has led to definitions favored by functionalist and post-positivist scholars, while the former has given rise to definitions preferred by interpretive and critical scholars. As an interpretivist (the label with which I primarily identify), my definition of communication aligns with a humanistic approach. It is reasonably contrite yet massively complex. *Human communication is the creation and sharing of meaning through the use of symbolic codes.*

While there are numerous, varied, and often competing scholarly definitions of communication, by contrast few scholars and almost no one in our discipline have offered a clear, or even an explicit, definition of sport. One notable recent exception is Billings, Butterworth, and Turman (2015), who invoke Guttman's (1978) definition of sport. Guttman states that sports are "'playful' physical contests, that is, as non-utilitarian contests which include an important measure of physical as well as intellectual skill" (p. 7). Billings et al. (2015) embrace Guttman's definition and proceed to differentiate between their use of 'sports' and 'sport.' "Sports," they say, are "specific contests such as basketball or golf" while they "refer to the institutional arrangement of leagues, teams, officials, players, fans, and media" (p. 11) as "sport." Most other sport communication publications, however, simply invoke the terms 'sports' and 'sport' without making even a cursory attempt to define them. The authors of these publications, including me at times, either act as if the meanings of these terms are completely self-evident or as if they implicitly trust the reader to be the best adjudicator of *the* meaning of each. Perhaps the Australian Sport Commission's position on the definition of sport suffices. Something is a sport if it "is competitive and generally is accepted as being a sport" (Australian Sport Commission, n.d., ASC Recognition section 3).

Although the Guttman to Billings et al. definition of sport works on several levels, when applied to a specific activity such as 'Frisbee' golf,[1] drag racing, or rock climbing, declaring that something is or is not a sport (as compared with a physical activity, play, a game, a competition, or an athletic contest) remains problematic. In order to move closer to enabling such a determination, over the past several years teaching a course entitled *Sport Communication* I have asked students to create a definition of sport that would allow us to reasonably decide if, for example, Frisbee golf is or isn't a sport. Although their definitions did not entirely eliminate the 'is or is not' debate, students across classes more or less agreed on some variation of the following definition of sport. A sport:

> requires both physical and mental exertion and execution. As such it is an embodied activity, neither strictly mental nor strictly physical. Individuals engaged in a sport use and improve through practice specialized neuro-muscular skills, tactics, and strategies, with a substantial degree of difficulty, risk, and/or effort. In sports, competition determines a clear winner and that competition normally occurs within a structured environment with an explicit or implicit code of conduct and fosters the development of officials, certified coaches and miscellaneous training personnel.

Is Frisbee golf a sport? My students consistently said "no." The important take-away from this definition of sport for the present discussion isn't, however, that it facilitates a decision regarding the status of Frisbee golf as a sport. What is important for my current purpose is that sport is an embodied practice. Sport requires the training, use, and improved application of both physical and mental capacities in concert.

Given the definitions of communication and sport put forth in this chapter, what is sport communication? The easiest answer would be to combine the two definitions; however, while the result certainly would enhance clarity and reduce ambiguity, it would at best be cumbersome and perhaps even hyperbolic. A 'combination' definition also would focus our attention exclusively on the creation and sharing of meaning by *only* the individuals participating in sport. Instead, I propose that we adopt a broader definition that encompasses, as Bruce (2013) puts it, "communicating about, through, and in sport" (p. 126). As such I offer the following definition:

> Sport communication is the process of creating and sharing meanings by individuals participating in the embodied (combining physical and men-tal exertion and execution) activity of sport. Sport communication also includes the meaning-making of individuals observing that activity as well as governing, directing, or commenting on that activity. As a discipline 'sport communication' examines the influence of the communicative practices associated with sport on individuals and on society.

And although the 'who' and 'what' elements included in the second sentence of this definition can and should be open for conjecture, the embodied nature of sport underscored in the first sentence for me is beyond dispute.

Likewise, just as sport is an embodied practice, ethnography is as well. There are, however, many nuances to the term 'ethnography' to explore before accepting this claim. Tracy (2013), focusing on the etymology of the term, states that ethnography "combines two ancient Greek words: *ethnos*, which meant 'tribe, nation, people,' and *graphien*, 'to write'" (p. 29). Moving away from purely etymological definitions, some scholars define it as a process while others frame ethnography as a product of that process. As an example of the former, Fetterman (2010) describes ethnography as the art and science of understanding a culture. On the other hand, and as an example of the latter, Van Maanen (1988) defines ethnography as a written representation of culture. I view ethnography as both process and product, both a "doing" and "writing" (Krizek, 2003). The 'doing' demands that ethnographers "live intimately beside and among" (Tracy, 2013) cultural members, while the 'writing' involves making choices about how to record and share "the understanding that emerges" from and that is based upon "firsthand experience and exploration" of fieldwork in a culture (Atkinson, Coffey, Delamont, Lofland, & Lofland, 2001, p. 4). Conquergood (1991) moves us closer to the claim that ethnography is an embodied experience by reminding us that qualitative researchers, including ethnographers, are always bodies in the field. Similarly, Stoller (1989) asserts that ethnographers should embrace a full-bodied approach to the cultural constructions of meaning. Lindlof and Taylor (2011) clearly frame ethnography as an embodied practice when describing the researcher-as-ethnographer experience and exploration as "embodiment" (p. 137).

In sum, just as participants in sport are fully engaged mentally, physically, and emotionally, so are ethnographers. Ethnographers are the embodied 'conductors' of research. An ethnographer accomplishes his or her embodied engagement through "(F)irsthand participation in some initially unfamiliar social world" followed by producing "written accounts of that world by drawing upon that participation" (Emerson, Fretz, & Shaw, 1995, p. 1). These embodied 'conductors' live inside and experience a culture first-hand with all aspects of their bodies (senses) and minds (emotionally, rationally, and even spiritually). They record those experiences using field notes, audio and video files, personal journals, expanded field notes, and research stories. They then analyze and interpret those 'records' in order to share their experiences. Sharing until recently meant writing; however, ethnographers now may share their understandings through the written word, through video or audio productions, or through performances (Goodall, 2000). Ethnography, therefore, is a method well suited for describing and understanding the cultural practices that constitute sport. It is also well suited for excavating and sharing those not so easily observed or measured meanings associated with those practices of the individuals who communicate in, through, and about sport.

Principal Theoretical Underpinnings of Ethnography

Although describing and understanding cultural practices and the meanings that cultural members associate with those practices are its goals, ethnography, unlike some other research methods, does not generally promote or encourage the generation of formal theory (Hammersley & Atkinson, 2007). While there are exceptions to this 'rule,' ethnographers are mostly interested in generating local knowledge that has potential for transferability[2] (Lincoln & Guba, 1985) as opposed to creating theories that allow for generalizability about phenomena across time and space.[3] Despite its focus on local knowledge, ethnography is not devoid of theory. To the contrary, ethnography is grounded in various theoretical traditions. In addition, ethnographers draw upon theoretical knowledge to help them understand and describe the cultural practices and meanings for those practices, and ethnographers generate local theories that they often frame as understandings as opposed to theory. In the remainder of this section I discuss three of the principal theoretical traditions contributing to ethnography and a key concept from each of these traditions that is especially salient for ethnographers from the communication discipline studying sport.

While ethnography draws upon multiple theoretical traditions, for the purposes of a discussion centering on aspects of sport communication, three have particular relevance—hermeneutics, phenomenology, and symbolic interactionism. Common to all three is the desire to discern the meanings associated with some aspect of the human experience; however, among the three there are also other important similarities germane to ethnography. For example, hermeneutics and phenomenology share a mutual emphasis on the philosophical notion of 'verstehen,' or attempting to empathetically understand another's experience (Lindlof & Taylor, 2011). Phenomenology also shares a significant element with symbolic interactionism in that both consider issues of intentionality. Phenomenologists (see Husserl, 1931) believe that we perceive objects according to the practical intentions we have when we encounter them, while symbolic interactionists such as Mead (1934) claim that during interactions participants use significant symbols to determine each other's intentions.

In addition to their similarities, these three traditions make significant individual contributions to ethnography as currently practiced by communication scholars as well. For the purpose of brevity, I discuss one contribution from each tradition starting with the oldest of the three. Hermeneutics focuses our attention on the holistic study of meanings in context, although the examination of the human experience was not its initial focus. Hermeneutics was originally concerned with interpreting ancient scripture. It evolved from its scriptural focus as a result of the work of German philosophers such as Wilhelm Dilthey (1907/1954, 1910/2010) and Hans Gadamer (1976a, 1976b) to include other socio-historical texts. Ricoeur (1977), in unpacking the hermeneutical practices advanced by Dilthey and Gadamer and their philosophical offspring, tells us that the method of hermeneutics seeks to interpret meaning by moving back and forth between the features of a text and its context to generate holistic knowledge through empathetic understanding/verstehen. Tracy (2013) states that, "Max Weber brought the concept [verstehen] to the study of social sciences, where it refers to an interpretive study of groups on their own terms and from their own viewpoint" (p. 41). In ethnography the researcher, in an effort to achieve verstehen, considers context, actions, both stated and perceived intentions, as well as his or her subjectivities.

Employing the philosophical underpinnings of hermeneutics and the concept of verstehen as starting points, phenomenologists such as Husserl (1931) and Schutz (1967) move us to the concept of intersubjectivity, or how we come to share meanings as a group or culture. Lindlof and Taylor (2011) tell us that Schutz resolved issues associated with intersubjectivity "by claiming that individuals unquestioningly accept that a mundane world exists and that others share our understandings of its essential features" (p. 37). Ethnographers seek to understand the intersubjective meanings that inhabit collective realities. Symbolic interactionists examine intersubjective meaning-making as well; however, they focus on the symbols individuals use to create and manage those shared meanings. Many of the concepts of symbolic interactionism, including emergent realities, significant symbols, and role-taking, originated in the philosophy of pragmatism (see Dewey, 1927/1954; Mead, 1934). Pragmatism proposes that meaning is invoked in practical/concrete circumstances and that participants' reactions to those circumstances are mediated through symbols (words, language) and signs (gestures, nonverbals). Ethnographers trained in the communication discipline are well situated to interpret intersubjective meanings by virtue of their theoretical knowledge of the use of signs and symbols.

Ethnography is an embodied research method. Ethnographers, as the embodied 'conductors' of research, use all of their senses to examine the practices of a culture, group, or collective and the meanings that the members of that collective share regarding those practices. In the 'doing' of ethnography these researchers rely on principles stemming from various theoretical traditions, including hermeneutics, phenomenology, and symbolic interactionism. These traditions focus the ethnographer's attention, among other things, on contextualized empathetic understanding (also known as 'verstehen'), on intersubjective/collective meanings, and on the symbols that cultural members use to create and share these meanings. In achieving their understandings, however, ethnographers also employ additional theoretical knowledge as they sort through and interpret their data. Ethnographers in the communication discipline turn to theories from a variety of communication's subdisciplines, including interpersonal, family, group and organizational communication. They also draw upon theories from media studies and the critical rhetorical traditions as well as theories from psychology, sociology, and other related social and humanistic sciences. In the next section I address two questions associated with ethnographies conducted (or not) at the intersection of communication and sport. In doing so, I introduce the idea of 'real' ethnography, which simply means that the 'doing' and 'writing' follows the principles and practices of traditional ethnographic work. The next section also discusses specific ethnographic studies of sport communication and how each incorporates theoretical knowledge.

Ethnographic Studies at the Intersection of Sport and Communication

While the theories upon which ethnographers trained in communication and who examine sport might draw are virtually limitless, the number of 'real' ethnographies conducted in sport communication unfortunately is not. I begin this section, therefore, by addressing two questions associated with the scarcity of 'real' ethnographies conducted at the intersection of sport and communication. The first question inquires about the legitimacy of the use of the label ethnography by scholars across all disciplines, including communication, while the second pursues explanations. Following my responses to these two questions, I then review seminal and current ethnographic work published by sport communication scholars. In these discussions I consider both the theories that the authors of these articles employ in forming and framing their understandings as well as the local theories that emerge from their ethnographies.

First, are all researchers who invoke the label of ethnography actually engaged in the doing and writing of ethnography? It appears that some scholars invoke the label 'ethnography' to describe their research when, in fact, it may not be. Tracy (2013) hints at the tensions underlying this issue in the following statement.

> Ethnographers focus on a wide range of cultural aspects, including language use, rituals, ceremonies, relationships, and artifacts. Some researchers frame their work slightly differently, by adopting the label ethnographic methods or approaches to specific contextual needs. Researchers who use ethnographic methods tend to engage in participant observation and interviewing.
>
> *(p. 29)*

In other words, researchers have a choice between two labels, 'ethnography' and 'ethnographic methods,' to designate their project. In an ideal world, researchers who observe naturalistic behavior and/or conduct interviews *without* an immersive embodied research experience that allows them to empathetically understand a wide range of cultural aspects should be using the label 'ethnographic methods' to describe their approach. Likewise, researchers who have an immersive embodied research experience *without* fulfilling the ethnographic charge of writing culture also should be using the label 'ethnographic methods' to describe their approach. Many researchers from both categories, nevertheless, elect the label of 'ethnography.' One explanation for their choice could be that the term 'ethnography' currently has high cultural currency. It is important to note, however, that the products emerging from the second category are much more closely aligned with 'real' ethnography than the products of the first. Before reviewing the ethnographic work in sport communication, therefore, one should consider what research is 'real' ethnography and what research simply invokes the label 'ethnography.' Even with the inclusion of some of the research in the second category, however, there are still only a small number of manuscripts to discuss. The next question then is 'why?'

In response to the explanation question, "What reasons might explain why so few ethnographies focusing on sport communication have been published?" I offer four possibilities, although most assuredly there are others. The answer more than likely lies somewhere in a combination of many factors. First, media scholars to a large extent and rhetorical, interpersonal, and organizational scholars to a lesser extent have championed sport communication. And because these media, interpersonal, and organizational scholars historically tend to adhere to a scientific approach to examining human communication, they are not trained in and, therefore, do not engage ethnography. In addition, because of the research questions they ask as well as their methodological roots and training, rhetoricians normally do not employ ethnography as a method either. Methodological training and research questions posed have conspired to act against the use of ethnography at the intersection of sport and communication. Beyond this unintentional conspiracy, it also is important to acknowledge that sport communication is a relatively young area of scholarship and ethnographic research programs require a considerable amount of time and effort to be developed. As a second explanation for why there are so few sport communication ethnographies, there may be research agendas that embrace the ethnographic tradition that are being developed by communication scholars and in time the products of these agendas will reach publication.

In addition to the explanations of an unintended conspiracy and time, as a third potential reason, many influential 'mainstream' scholars for different reasons have viewed sport communication and ethnography, independent of each other, with some skepticism. For example, scholars from across the social sciences, including communication, have not always seen sport as a worthwhile or serious area of scholarship (see Trujillo, 2003). Likewise, scholars trained in the dominant narrative of the scientific method historically have viewed ethnography with skepticism because it did not generate objective, generalizable knowledge. This form of skepticism relegated much ethnographic work to the margins of edited volumes and lesser-known or lightly regarded journals. Taken together, sport was not a serious area of scholarship and ethnography did not produce generalizable knowledge. With the creation of journals such as *Communication and Sport* and divisions in our associations dedicated to sport (ICA and NCA) and ethnography (NCA), however, both sport communication and ethnography have begun to be accorded a somewhat enhanced degree of legitimization. Perhaps along with this legitimization may come more ethnographic research at the intersection of communication and sport. Finally, as a fourth explanation, the prolonged access to research sites necessary to conduct quality ethnographic research is often near impossible to obtain. While the challenge of access confronts all ethnographers, sport appears to present an even more imposing obstacle. Sport teams, franchises, and organizations have somewhat impermeable boundaries. The gatekeepers of these collectives do not trust outsiders to have the best interests of the athletes or their athletes' public identities in mind. These gatekeepers, therefore, rarely allow outsiders such as ethnographers the long-term backstage access required to conduct their research.

Despite all of the above issues and challenges, there are examples of ethnography in the area of sport communication that are models to consider and follow. The classic example of 'doing' and 'writing' ethnography is Trujillo's (1992) study of baseball/ballpark culture following his two-and-a-half year association with the Texas Rangers. This article teaches us much about the practice of 'doing' ethnography. In his last published article before his death (see Trujillo, 2013), Trujillo discussed four lessons he learned during that 1988/1989 ethnography "that might be helpful to other scholars who study sport and communication" (p. 73). While readers should look carefully at all four lessons, one and two have particular salience for all scholars interested in studying the intersection of sport and communication ethnographically. These lessons specifically address access issues raised above. The first instructs us to use the off-season to develop relationships with those teams, groups, and organizations we seek to study, while the second advises us to gain access to these settings through the less visible (nonathlete) members of sport collectives such as public relations personnel.

In addition to introducing a template for gaining access, Trujillo (1992) provides us with a glimpse of how a skilled ethnographer collects data and draws upon theory to help generate understandings. In regard to data collection and management, in addition to engaging a prolonged and embodied field experience, Trujillo described a number of his other techniques:

> During these interview and observation sessions at the ballpark, I took extensive fieldnotes that reconstructed the verbatim communicative actions of workers. I adopted certain practices to capture more details and to reinforce the representativeness of my fieldnotes. First, I asked frequent questions of the ballpark subjects as I observed them that helped me to write and understand idiomatic expressions. Second, I elaborated my fieldnotes during 'lulls' in ballpark action and soon after my observational periods; I also dictated additional notes into a tape recorder as I drove home after the game and then elaborated those notes in writing when I arrived home, sometimes while watching the rebroadcast of the game

(my 'video fieldnotes'). Finally, I took notes openly while I was observing. As an invited observer, my note-taking behavior was expected, just like reporters' note-taking behaviors are expected; in fact, in the pre-game dugout and locker room, I 'passed' as one of many reporters who also were taking notes.

(pp. 354–355)

Turning to his use of theory, in his ballpark ethnography Trujillo cited, among others, theories associated with ideology, community, impression management, organizational culture, and critical theories of commodification. Trujillo introduced and discussed these various theories and theorists at relevant points as he unpacked his understandings and interpretations of ballpark culture. Then, in his final remarks, when offering a summary of his understandings, Trujillo theorized (presented his understandings) that ballparks are social dramas of commodification and community.

During the period of his ballpark ethnography, beyond generating context-specific empathetic understandings, Trujillo's embodied research experience also produced an important byproduct. Researchers contemplating ethnography as a method for answering their research questions often overlook the potential benefit of this byproduct. The copious amount of rich data that Trujillo collected during his 'doing' of ethnography triggered the writing of multiple manuscripts, some of which did not fulfill the charge of writing ethnography. For example, he published an article (Trujillo, 1991) and a book (Trujillo, 1994) focusing on media representations of hegemonic masculinity associated with Nolan Ryan and an article that demonstrated elements of power and privilege that inhabit the business of baseball (Trujillo, 2000). The embodied practice of ethnography, therefore, has the potential to yield data that can be interpreted, critiqued, and discussed through the application of a variety of theoretical lenses. For example, his book and article examining media portrayals of Nolan Ryan incorporated various theoretical treatments of hegemonic masculinity, gender ideology, and mass media's (re)production of patriarchal values. In the end Trujillo (1991) described five distinguishing features of hegemonic masculinity and theorized about how the media reproduces those features in its portrayal of Nolan Ryan as an American hero.

At approximately the same time that Trujillo was publishing manuscripts based upon his ballpark ethnography, Krizek (1992a, 1992b) also was conducting an ethnographic study that centered on a ballpark. For that project, which I presented at the 1991 Cooperstown Symposium on Baseball and the American Culture, and discussed in my dissertation (Krizek, 1995), I built upon Gergen's (1991) argument that in the postmodern moment "small and enduring communities, with a limited cast of significant others, are being replaced by a vast and ever-expanding array of relationships" (p. ix). I claimed that traditional ethnography is a modernist endeavor examining communities, collectives or cultures "as if single communities, a neighborhood, a factory, a school, exist is some sociocultural vacuum" (Krizek, 1995, p. 33). In other words, in an effort to focus on the norms and practices of a single community or culture, ethnographers more or less disregard or at least ignore all other potential overlapping and conflicting memberships in other cultures or communities. To complement and not replace traditional ethnography, I offered an ethnographic form compatible with postmodernity. This form of ethnography maintained the 'doing' and 'writing' of traditional ethnography while examining nonroutine public events, such as the closing of the Chicago White Sox's Old Comiskey Park, that inhabit the postmodern moment. I claimed that the intersubjective meanings for these nonroutine public events exist at the intersection of personal identities and not as the properties of distinct communities or cultures. Although I engaged these events with the same embodied practices and immersive data collection techniques of Trujillo, the vehicle for my ethnographic understandings was confined primarily to the stories I 'excavated' from those fans in attendance at a single event. The theoretical lenses guiding my project's understandings were narrative theory (Fisher, 1987; Langellier, 1989; Polkinghorne, 1998), ritual (Goffman, 1967; Turner, 1974), theories of identity (Burke, 1945/1969; Gergen, 1991; Mischler, 1992), and theories of place (Meyrowitz, 1985; Oldenburg, 1989). In regard to the closing of Old Comiskey Park, I theorized that "as we destroy in the name of progress, sanitation, and comforter connections with the past, as a society we alter the identities of those who have infused those connections with very private, real, and emotionally anchored meanings" (Krizek, 1992a, p. 49).

Completing the category of seminal sport communication ethnographies is yet another ballpark project. Trujillo and Krizek (1994) collaborated on this undertaking. Our data collection methods followed Krizek's (1992a, 1992b) techniques for excavating stories in order to empathetically understand the meanings of those in attendance at the final game played at Arlington Stadium, home of the Texas Ranges. Individually and together, Nick and I walked and talked with event-goers recording our observations using photographs, fieldnotes, and audio-recordings. After collecting data at this nonroutine public event, we then combined that data with the data I had collected at the closing of Old Comiskey. Our goal was to understand how event-goers enacted their emotions and expressed their identities at these two ballpark closings. In order to help create and frame our understandings we tapped into, for example, theories of sport as religion (Prebish, 1983; Sage, 1981), sport as therapy (Wenner, 1990), sport and symbolism (Duncan, 1983), and sport as a search for community (Anderson & Stone, 1981). We described fans and ballpark employees as expressing "genuine affection for baseball and for how baseball affects their lives" (p. 321) and in doing so theorized that these baseball fans possess "powerful senses of identity, community, continuity, narrativity, therapy, spirituality, and self-discovery" (p. 321). In addition, in this article we each provided a "confessional tale" (Van Maanen, 1988) in which we offered our autobiographical accounts of the meaning baseball and ballparks had held for each of us. In doing so, we ventured into the realm of autoethnography and personal narrative as forms for the 'writing' of ethnography.

Trujillo and Krizek's seminal pieces are not, however, the only 'real' ethnographies that have been conducted at the intersection of sport and communication. In particular, the work of Lindemann (2008, 2010) quickly comes to mind. Lindemann not only conducted a 'real' ethnographic project, he also followed Trujillo's lead by using the data from his ethnography focusing on wheelchair athletes to write and publish multiple pieces from a single data set. In addition, Lindemann also employs rigorous data collection and analysis techniques indicative of solid ethnographic work. In regard to methods, Lindemann (2008, 2010) and Lindemann and Cherney (2008) to some degree each discuss the specific techniques employed to collect the substantial amount of data necessary to support the writing of multiple articles. For example, in reference to Lindemann's embodied research methods, Lindemann and Cherney (2008) state:

> The first author conducted 3 years of participant observations of two United States Quad Rugby Association (USQRA) national tournaments, and practices and games of two teams. . . . The first author transcribed scratch notes from these 124 hours of participant observations approximately 48 hours after each observation. This approach yielded 496 pages of typed, single-spaced field notes. The author also conducted a total of 25 ethnographic and semistructured interviews. Interview respondents included 19 players, 16 male and 3 female, two referees, and four friends and family members, all of whom were given the option to choose a pseudonym or have one assigned to them by the researcher. The transcriptions of these interviews amounted to 133 typed, single-spaced pages.
>
> *(p. 111)*

In reference to his data analysis techniques, Lindemann (2010) shares that, "(C)lose readings of field notes and the 19 interviews with athletes allowed 'fuzzy' categories regarding sexuality to emerge. I pared these down to more specific thematic groupings of (a) breaking with the past, (b) emulating" (p. 439).

In conjunction with addressing how the data collection and analysis methods were both embodied and rigorous, Lindemann (2008, 2010) and Lindemann and Cherney (2008) also integrated a number of theories and theorists throughout these articles. While the overall research emphasis of these three articles was the communicative practices surrounding wheelchair or 'quad' rugby, Lindemann and Cherney (2008) split their theoretical focus between the performance of masculinity and disability by the wheelchair athletes. By contrast, Lindemann (2008) concentrated more on the communicative performance of disability, while Lindemann (2010) took up more of the issues involving the communicative performance of masculinity and sexuality by the disabled athletes. Across the three articles Lindemann invoked, among others, theories of disability, stigma, heteronormativity, sexuality, sport and disability, masculinity, heroic masculinity, and gender. He also mixed in some theoretical discussions of narrative, performance, organizational culture, and socialization. In sum, these three articles are well grounded in theory that supports the understandings that emerge in each article.

Although there are numerous important understandings in and across these articles, each provides a principal local theory that stems directly from the ethnographic data. In Lindemann (2008) the dominant understanding/local theory that emerges posits that the wheelchair rugby athletes "play with their impairment and use the visibility of their 'stigma,' or bodily differences, to 'tweak' the dominant script of disability. Thus, this study creates new inroads towards understanding the power of play in helping disabled persons claim agency over their 'stigmatized' self" (p. 113). Lindemann and Cherney (2008) summarize their major understanding as "quad rugby participation as communication and player communication about their participation illustrates that sport's highly influential status as a pervasive cultural institution works as a double-edged sword in the rehabilitation process. Physically disabled quad rugby players may find participation empowering while their participation simultaneously fosters potentially harmful and exclusionary attitudes about ability and gender" (p. 122). Finally, Lindemann (2010) uses personal narrative involving his recollections of coming of age with a disabled father to put forward a very interesting local theory/understanding of the communicative performance of sexuality by these disabled athletes:

> As I write this, I realize that maybe that's what many of the players in this study were doing. It's easier to remember the simple, stereotypical portrayals of women that inhabit a hegemonic masculinity than the complexities of a more nuanced understanding of masculinity and sexuality. By striving to understand the partial and multifaceted narrative constructions of disabled sexualities, however, we can begin to write a different story.
>
> *(p. 448)*

Beyond the work of Lindemann, Trujillo, and Krizek, there have been few, if any, 'real' ethnographies conducted at the intersection of sport and communication. As exceptions, however, it is important to recognize Hartman's (2014) personal narrative, a specific type of autoethnographic account, and the digital ethnography of Armstrong, Delia, and Giardina (2014). Both of these articles display many significant aspects of the 'doing' or 'writing' associated with traditional ethnographic work and yet both also introduce nontraditional ethnographic forms to sport communication. While Trujillo and Krizek (1994) included autobiographical components that could now be labeled autoethnography or personal narrative, Hartman (2014) is probably the first communication scholar to invoke either personal narrative or autoethnography as labels for his or her published work in the area of sport communication. Likewise, Armstrong et al. (2014) appear to be the first scholars to publish a digital ethnography that focuses on an area of sport communication in a communication journal.

In her work Hartman (2014) draws upon her experience as a Division I basketball player who had her one-year scholarship revoked before her senior year. Her narrative representation of that experience follows Lindemann's (2009) description of an autoethnographic form known as personal narrative. Lindemann (2009) claims that personal narrative as a type of reflective scholarship is different than standard autoethographic work in that it provides a linear story uninterrupted in its telling. In following this model, Hartman provides a complete story in its entirety that prompts the reader to reflect upon his or her own experiences, emotions, and understandings. Her personal narrative does not adhere to Ellis's (2004) charge that autoethnography should "connect the autobiographical and personal to the cultural, social, and political" (p. xix). Hartman (2014) writes a compelling uninterrupted story, but opts to make no theoretical connections between her experiences and broader cultural concerns, such as organizational culture, gender, or power.

By contrast, Armstrong et al.'s (2014) digital ethnography does integrate theory throughout their article. Digital ethnography is a research method that affords researchers the opportunity to unobtrusively observe the interactions of individuals in a virtual space (Kozinets, 2002; Murthy, 2011). Moreover, digital ethnography allows a "sustained longitudinal involvement" through which the researcher may both "watch and participate in the unfolding of norms, patterns, rhythms, relationships, and folktales" (Ruhleder, 2000, p. 5). The authors' sustained involvement with a digital community focused on "[T]he innovative social media marketing practices of the Los Angeles Kings hockey organization, most especially through its twitter account @LAKings" (Armstrong et al., 2014, p. 1). These authors call upon theories of media convergence, message spreadability, brand community, and brand animation before extending their local theory of the outcomes of the LA Kings' social media marketing practices. Armstrong et al. (2014) summarize their understandings that emerged during their digital ethnography by stating, "[B]y embracing social media and more precisely, the social in social media, the Los Angeles Kings have charted new waters in illustrating how optimizing the interaction potential of a brand with social media users can encourage relationship and community development between an organization and its consumers" (p. 17). What is absent in their digital ethnography is the total embodied experience that comes only with the physical immersion associated with traditional ethnographic projects. As more and more of our interactions are taking place in a virtual digital world, however, the notion of an embodied experience might be evolving, making physical immersion in a setting a moot point.

Directions for Future Ethnographic Research and Sport Communication

I began this chapter claiming that research at the intersection of sport and communication is challenging because, in part, how participants communicatively engage in sport is not always easily measured or readily observable. In response to this challenge I offered the research method of ethnography as a viable alternative for understanding those not-so-easily-measured or observed aspects. Ethnography, like sport, is an embodied experience. In both sport and ethnography participants are fully engaged mentally, physically, emotionally, and perhaps even spiritually for some. The goal of an ethnographer is to empathetically understand the experiences of a collective from the inside, from those individuals who comprise the collective's culture. And while ethnographic research may help us understand many and varied aspects of sport, in particular it is a valuable method for understanding the meanings, cultural practices, values, norms, and beliefs that communicatively constitute sport.

I leave it to the readers to determine if ethnography is the preferred method for answering their research questions; however, I also offer some suggestions for those still grappling with a research focus. These suggestions are not an exhaustive list; instead I present them only as possibilities and a stimulus for thought. To begin, ethnography can help us surface and understand the taken-for-granted values, beliefs, and norms associated with cultural practices. For example, ethnographers might ask questions about what norms and communication practices exist that at least partially determine who will or won't emerge as a team leader. Also, although momentum plays a significant role in the outcome of individual games and teams' seasons, we know little about how athletes and organizations actually experience momentum. How does momentum get constructed through the interaction between and among teammates, coaches, fans, and management? In regard to an athlete's use of social media, digital ethnographers could ask, how does an athlete use social media to interact with fans in co-constructing identities? Moreover, what norms guide social media interaction between athletes and fans? Now that many athletes and fans are digital natives, questions such as these are becoming more and more important to ask and answer. Potential research questions and foci are limitless.

Ethnography, however, also is a method well suited for excavating and sharing the not-so-easily-observed or measured meanings and emotions associated with those practices of the individuals who communicate in, through, and about sport. In plying his or her method of knowing, the ethnographer will come to understand those meanings through observation and personal experience. What meanings do athletes associate with competition? And more specifically related to creating and sharing meanings, what sorts of messages do athletes find motivating or inspiring? What messages do athletes and team leaders use to motivate or inspire themselves and/or teammates, both during and in preparation for competition? Also, when scouts and coaches mention the intangibles or the 'x factors' that are desirable for recruits or draftees to possess, what do they mean? How do they communicatively construct and rationalize something as ephemeral as the 'x factor' when discussing an athlete? In regard to the role of emotion in sport, communication scholars might pursue research agendas that center on the communicative performance of emotion by fans that attend games or contests in person and fans that attend virtually. Alternatively, researchers could inquire about what meanings fans assign to their superstitions that either promote winning or losing by their favored athlete, team, or rival. In the realm of fan experience, possibilities for ethnographically oriented research questions again are unlimited.

Thus far, the possible research foci I have offered imply that sport is a socially uncomplicated or unbiased institution. It is neither. There are practices tainting the community of sport. In regard to these practices, ethnographers could, for example, consider bullying and hazing in sport. How do the alleged offenders communicatively construct their practices and, conversely, how do the victims construct theirs? How do victims communicatively resist bullying behaviors? The issues of bullying and hazing along with the experiences of whistleblowers in amateur and professional sports would be particularly ripe for autoethnographic and personal narrative examinations. In addition, questions about the use of performance enhancement drugs by amateur athletes and accepted forms of cheating such as sign stealing in baseball and football would be interesting and enlightening ethnographic projects in that the understandings emerging from these studies would invite numerous opportunities for transferability. Ethnographers also could examine the racial and ethnic stereotypes and discriminatory practices that exist in the institutions, leagues, governing bodies, and front offices that inhabit and inhibit the community of sport. And although these research agendas would be difficult to undertake, the understandings and local theories that emerge might help sports to avoid further pitfalls predicted by Lipsyte (1977) in his classic book, *Sportsworld: An American Dreamland*. Again, possibilities are endless for ethnographers to examine the socially and morally undesirable aspects of sport; however, ethnographers seeking to examine these and other tainted practices that exist at the intersection of communication and sport should proceed with caution.

Trujillo (2013) ends his contribution to the first issue of the journal *Communication and Sport* by referencing an introduction (Trujillo, 2003) he wrote a decade prior. About that introduction, Trujillo (2013) stated that "the future of research about communication and sport is even brighter than when I wrote the paragraph" (p. 74) that opened his 2003 essay. In 2003 Trujillo predicted that there would be no journal in communication solely dedicated to sport and communication. I also imagine that back in 2003 he would not have anticipated volumes such as this one that has invited dozens of communication scholars to discuss the intersection of communication and sport from a variety of interesting and very different areas of expertise. But the 2013 Trujillo also was right. The future of research about sport and communication is brighter and ethnography certainly can help with the illumination. If sport communication is *the process of creating and sharing meanings by individuals participating in the embodied (combining physical and mental exertion and execution) activity of sport*, ethnography as an embodied practice can and should play an important role in understanding those processes and meanings. And if sport communication also includes *the meaning-making of individuals observing that activity as well as governing, directing, or commenting on that activity*, ethnography moves from a position of importance to a position of preeminence in understanding those meanings. Sport as an embodied practice meets ethnography, an embodied research method.

Notes

1 Frisbee golf, also known as Frisbee disc or disc golf, is a game in which individual players throw a flying disc at various targets or 'holes.' The object of the game is for a player to make his or her way around a course from beginning to end in the fewest number of throws of the disc. The targets are normally elevated metal baskets. As players make their way around the course, just as in regular golf, they must make each consecutive throw from the spot where the previous shot, or in this case 'throw,' had landed. The trees, bushes, and any terrain changes located in and around the course provide challenging obstacles for the player.

2 Transferability empowers the reader and not the researcher. The reader decides whether or not the author's interpretation of the cultural setting, actions, and meanings have value in helping him or her gain insight into some aspect of human experience.

3 The ethnography of communication (EOC) is one exception found in the communication discipline. In EOC the researcher seeks to discover 'codes' or sets of rules or patterns that "inform cultural members how to use and interpret particular categories of signs" such as linguistic practices (Lindlof & Taylor, 2011, p. 46). See Carbaugh, 2005, for an extensive review of EOC.

References

Anderson, G.F., & Stone, G.P. (1981). A search for community. In S.L. Greendorfer and A. Yiannakis (Eds.), *Sociology of sport: Diverse perspectives* (pp. 160–175). West Point, NY: Leisure.

Atkinson, P., Coffey, A., Delamont, S., Lofland, J., & Lofland, L. (Eds.). (2001). *Handbook of ethnography*. London: Sage. doi: http://dx.doi.org/10.4135/9781848608337.

Armstrong, C.G., Delia, E.B., & Giardina, M.D. (2014). Embracing the social in social media: An analysis of the social media marketing strategies of the Los Angeles Kings. *Communication and Sport, 2*(2), 1–21. doi: 10.1177/2167479514532914.

Australian Sports Commission AIS (n.d.). Retrieved December 22, 2015, from http://www.ausport.gov.au/supporting/nso/asc_recognition.

Billings, A.C., Butterworth, M.L., & Turman, P.D. (2015). *Communication and sport* (2nd ed.). Thousand Oaks, CA: Sage.

Bruce, T. (2013). Reflections on communication and sport: On women and femininities. *Communication and Sport, 1*(1/2), 125–137. doi: 10.1177/2167479512472883.

Burke, K. (1969). *A grammar of motives.* Berkeley, CA: University of California Press. (Original work published 1945.)

Carbaugh, D. (2005). *Cultures in conversation.* Mahwah, NJ: Lawrence Erlbaum Associates.

Conquergood, D. (1991). Rethinking ethnography: Towards a critical cultural politics. *Communication Monographs, 58,* 179–194.

Dewey, J. (1954). *The public and its problems.* New York: Henry Holt. (Original work published 1927.)

Dilthey, W. (1954). *The essence of philosophy.* Chapel Hill, NC: University of North Carolina Press. (Original work published 1907.)

Dilthey, W. (2010). *Selected works, vol. III: The formation of the historical world in the human sciences.* Princeton, NJ: Princeton University Press. (Original work published 1910.)

Duncan, M.C. (1983). The symbolic dimensions of spectator sport. *Quest, 35,* 29–36.

Ellis, C. (2004). *The ethnographic I: A methodological novel about autoethnography.* Lanham, MD: Rowman & Littlefield.

Emerson, R.M., Fretz, R.I., & Shaw, L.L. (1995). *Writing ethnographic fieldnotes.* Chicago, IL: University of Chicago Press.

Fetterman, D.M. (2010). *Ethnography: Step by step (applied social research methods)* (3rd ed.). Thousand Oak, CA: Sage.

Fisher, W.R. (1987). *Human communication as narration: Toward a philosophy of reason, value, and action.* Columbia, SC: University of South Carolina Press.

Gadamer, H. (1976a). *Hegel's dialectic: Five hermeneutical studies.* (P. Christopher Smith, Trans.). New Haven, CT: Yale University Press.

Gadamer, H. (1976b). *Philosophical hermeneutics.* (D. Linge, Trans.). Berkeley, CA: University of California Press.

Gergen, K.J. (1991). *The saturated self: Dilemmas of identity in contemporary life.* New York: Basic Books.

Goffman, E. (1967). *Interaction ritual: Essays on face-to-face behavior.* New York: Anchor.

Goodall, H.L., Jr. (2000). *Writing the new ethnography.* Walnut Creek, CA: AltaMira Press.

Guttman, A. (1978). *From ritual to record: The nature of modern sports.* New York: Columbia University Press.

Hammersley, M., & Atkinson, P. (2007). *Ethnography: Principles and practice.* London: Routledge.

Hartman, K.L. (2014). "The most evil thing about college sports": The 1-year scholarship and a NCAA athlete's personal narrative. *International Journal of Sport Communication, 7,* 425–440. http://dx.doi.org/10.1123/IJSC.2014-0049.

Husserl, E. (1931). *Ideas: General introduction to pure phenomenology* (W.R.B. Gibson, Trans.). New York: Macmillan.

Kozinets, R.V. (2002). The field behind the screen: Using netnography for marketing research in online communities. *Journal of Marketing Research, 39,* 61–72.

Krizek, R.L. (1992a). Goodbye old friend: A son's farewell to Comiskey Park. *OMEGA: Journal of Death and Dying, 25,* 87–93. doi: 10.2190/P5RF-G50T-MEYY-P8KU.

Krizek, R.L. (1992b). Remembrances and expectations: The investment of identity in the changing of Comiskey. *Elysian Fields Quarterly, 11*(2), 30–50.

Krizek, R.L. (1995). *The ethnography of events: A narrative analysis of non-routine public events.* Retrieved from WorldCat Digital Dissertation. (OCLC Number: 39049944).

Krizek, B. (2003). Ethnography as the excavation of personal narrative. In R.P. Clair (Ed.), *Expressions of ethnography: Novel approaches to qualitative methods* (pp. 141–152). Albany, NY: State University New York Press.

Langellier, K.M. (1989). Personal narratives: Perspectives on theory and research. *Text and Performance Quarterly, 9*, 243–276.

Lincoln, Y.S., & Guba, E.G. (1985). *Naturalistic inquiry*. Beverly Hills, CA: Sage.

Lindemann, K. (2008). "I can't be standing up out there": Communicative performances of (dis)ability in wheelchair rugby. *Text and Performance Quarterly, 28*, 98–115. doi: 10.1080/10462930701754366.

Lindemann, K. (2009). Self-reflection and our sporting lives: Communication research in the community of sport. *Electronic Journal of Communication, 14*(21 A). Retrieved July 15, 2016, from http://www.cios.org/EJCPUBLIC/019/2/019344.html.

Lindemann, K. (2010). Masculinity, disability, and access-ability: Ethnography as alternative practice in the study of disabled sexualities. *Southern Journal of Communication, 75*, 433–451. doi: 10.1080/1041794x.2010.504454.

Lindemann, K., & Cherney, J.L. (2008). Communicating in and through "Murderball": Masculinity and disability in wheelchair rugby. *Western Journal of Communication, 72*, 107–125. doi: 10.1080/10570310802038382.

Lindlof, T.R., & Taylor, B.C. (2011). *Qualitative communication research methods* (3rd ed.). Thousand Oaks, CA: Sage.

Lipsyte, R. (1977). *Sportsworld: An American dreamland*. New York: Quadrangle.

Mead, G.H. (1934). *Mind, self, and society*. Chicago, IL: University of Chicago Press.

Meyrowitz, J. (1985). *No sense of place: The impact of electronic media on social behavior*. New York: Oxford University Press.

Miller, G.R. (1975). Humanistic and scientific approaches to speech communication inquiry: Rivalry, redundancy, or rapprochement. *Western Journal of Communication, 39*, 230–239. doi:10.1080/10570317509373872.

Mischler, E.G. (1992). Work, identity, and narrative: An artist-craftsman's story. In G.C. Rosenwald & R.L. Ochberg (Eds.), *Storied lives* (pp. 21–40). New Haven, CT: Yale University Press.

Murthy, D. (2011). Twitter: Microphone for the masses? *Media, Culture &Society, 33*, 779–789.

Oldenburg, R. (1989). *The great good place*. New York: Paragon House.

Polkinghorne, D.E. (1988). *Narrative knowing and the human sciences*. Albany, NY: State University of New York Press.

Prebish, C.S. (1983). "Heavenly father, divine goalie": Sport and religion. In D.S. Eitzen (Eds.), *Sport in contemporary society: An anthology* (3rd ed., pp. 283–293). New York: St. Martin's.

Ricoeur, P. (1977). The model of the text: Meaningful action considered as text. In F.R. Dallmayr & T.A. McCarthy (Eds.), *Understanding and social inquiry* (pp. 316–334). Notre Dame, IN: University of Notre Dame Press.

Ruhleder, K. (2000). The virtual ethnographer: Fieldwork in distributed electronic environments. *Field Methods, 12*, 3–17.

Sage, G.S. (1981). Sport and religion. In G.R.F. Luschen and G.S. Sage (Eds.), *Handbook of social science of sport* (pp. 135–156). Champaign, IL: Sipes.

Schutz, A. (1967). *The phenomenology of the social world*. Evanston, IL: Northwestern University Press.

Stoller, P. (1989). *The taste of ethnographic things: The senses in anthropology*. Philadelphia, PA: University of Pennsylvania Press

Tracy, S.J. (2013). *Qualitative research methods: Collecting evidence, crafting analysis, communicating impact.* Oxford: Wiley-Blackwell.

Trujillo, N. (1991). Hegemonic masculinity on the mound: Media representations of Nolan Ryan and American sports culture. *Critical Studies in Mass Communication, 8,* 290–308.

Trujillo, N. (1992). Interpreting (the work and talk of) baseball: Perspectives on ballpark culture. *Western Journal of Communication, 56,* 350–371.

Trujillo, N. (1994). *The meaning of Nolan Ryan.* College Station, TX: Texas A&M University Press.

Trujillo, N. (2000). Baseball, business, politics, and privilege: An interview with George W. Bush, *Management Communication Quarterly, 14,* 307–316. doi: 10.1177/0893318900142004.

Trujillo, N. (2003). Introduction. In R.S. Brown & D.J. O'Rourke, III. (Eds.), *Case studies in sport communication* (pp. 11–15). Westport, CT: Praeger.

Trujillo, N. (2013). Reflections on communication and sport: On ethnography and organizations. *Communication and Sport, 1*(1/2), 68–75.

Trujillo, N., & Krizek, B. (1994). Emotionality in the stands and in the field: Expressing self through baseball. *Journal of Sport and Social Issues, 18,* 303–325. doi: 10.1177/019372394018004002.

Turner, V. (1974). *Dramas, fields, and metaphors: Symbolic actions in human society.* Ithaca, NY: Cornell University Press.

Van Maanen, J. (1988). *Tales of the field: On writing ethnography.* Chicago, IL: University of Chicago Press.

Vidali, D.S., & Peterson, M. (2012). Ethnography as theory and method in the study of political communication. In H.A. Semetko & M. Scammell (Eds.), *The SAGE handbook of political communication* (pp. 264–275). London: Sage.

Wenner, L.A. (1990). Therapeutic engagement in mediated sports. In G. Gumpert & S.L. Fish (Eds.), *Talking to strangers* (pp. 223–244). Norwood, NJ: Ablex.

5

SPORT AND POLITICAL COMMUNICATION/POLITICAL COMMUNICATION AND SPORT

Taking the Flame

Davis W. Houck

FLORIDA STATE UNIVERSITY

After sailing more than 400 miles from Potidaea, the decorated 40-year-old son-of-a-brick-mason did a curious thing: he headed with dispatch to a house of wrestling. Not a WWE smackdown extravaganza, mind you, but a local gym—technically a *palaestra*—to get back in touch with old friends, familiar places, and catch up on a lot of hometown gossip. The heroic warrior had been away nearly two years from his beloved Athens, so what better meeting place than a local *gymnos*, where young, naked, and olive-oiled bodies on display mingled easily with thoughts of the civic and philosophic?[1]

As luck, the gods, or a really good dramatist would have it, Socrates had picked just the right time and place for his return in 429 BCE: his friend Critias' cousin, the sublimely endowed and beguiling Charmides, was just then entering the *Palaestra* for a bit of grappling with his aristocratic bros. All of 16 or 17 years old, Socrates had been aware of Charmides' charms even before sailing north to perform his hoplite duties.

Nowhere in the Platonic corpus is the prose quite so breathless and down-right ribald; fawns Socrates, "But at that moment, when I saw him, I confess that I was quite astonished at his beauty and stature. . . . Amazement and confusion reigned when he entered." Socrates admits to Critias that the lad indeed possesses a beautiful face. But "you would think nothing of his face, [Critias] replies, if you could see his naked form; he is absolutely perfect." Laying a trap to get the dazzling youth to join their company—Socrates feigning a medicine man to cure Charmides' thinly cloaked, so to speak, "morning headaches"—a seating scrum ensues. Charmides eventually finds his way seated next to the smitten mason/warrior: "And all the people in the palaestra crowded about us, and at that moment, my good friend, I caught a sight of the inwards of his garment, and took the flame. Then I could no longer contain myself" (Jowett, 1989, pp. 101–102). Before Michael Douglas, Sharon Stone, and *Basic Instinct*, there was a differently gendered erotic leg (un)crossing.

Took the flame indeed. But even with his passions aroused—"overcome by a sort of wild-beast appetite"—Socrates eventually finds his dialectical footing with his otherworldly interlocutor (Jowett, 1989, p. 102). Slowly regaining his confidence, question by question, Socrates reassures us that "my natural heat returned to me" (Jowett, 1989, p. 103). And thus can the cool pursuit of wisdom proceed.

★★★★★★

Two thousand three hundred and eighty-nine years later (give or take), a youthful aristocratic veteran won over audiences with his beguiling charms and good looks. Narrowly defeating the shadowy Richard Nixon, a bronzed John F. Kennedy performed a curious rhetorical duty as president-elect in December 1960: the heroic warrior of PT-109 fame penned an article for *Sports Illustrated* magazine. In it, the lithe golfer and sailor began with the ancient Greeks and the quadrennial festival known as the Olympic Games: "the Greeks prized physical excellence and athletic skills among man's greatest goals and among the prime foundations of a vigorous state," wrote the new president. "Thus the same civilizations which produced some of our highest achievements of philosophy and drama, government and art, also gave us a belief in the importance of physical soundness which has become a part of Western tradition" (Kennedy, 1960, para. 1 and 2).

That tradition was imperiled, claimed Kennedy, as evidenced by several studies in which the fitness of young Americans paled in comparison with European youth.[2] Moreover, American 'soft bodies' threatened the future of the nation's military might: "in a very real and immediate sense, our growing softness, our increasing lack of physical fitness, is a menace to our security." That menace loomed materially to the east: "We face in the Soviet Union a powerful and implacable adversary determined to show the world that only the Communist system possesses the vigor and determination necessary to satisfy awakening aspirations for progress and the elimination of poverty and want. To meet the challenge of this enemy will require determination and will and effort on the part of all Americans. Only if our citizens are physically fit will they be fully capable of such an effort" (Kennedy, 1960, para. 11, 13). Kennedy's rather direful soft-body warning, apotheothized on film years later in the characters of Rocky Balboa and Ivan Drago, uncannily mirrors Plato's celebration of the hard-body glories of Athenian military might on the eve of the Peloponnesian War—Athens' not-so-cold war with its Evil Empire, Sparta.

Stated differently, a country's bodies, particularly its youthful bodies, serve as a telling barometer of its fitness—whether measured empirically in the form of a physical education test or rendered philosophically in dialogue form at a local gym. What both president-elect Kennedy and the Platonic Socrates under-stood was that a physically active and accomplished country or city-state was also a healthy (and powerful) country: 'body and mind' in the secular argot of American presidential politics, and 'body and soul' in Socratic philosophy.

These two highly decorated military and aristocratic veterans, while sepa-rated by thousands of years and thousands of miles, understood from their own deeply embodied experiences that bodily health and fitness were the *sine qua non* of civic health and military prowess. Kennedy makes the point explicitly several times in *Sports Illustrated*, while Plato's symbolic setting of the *palaestra* is criti-cal to the dialogic search for *sophrosyne*.[3] The glories of Olympic victory served rhetorically as only the most obvious sporting sign of athletic excellence and as a civic sign of Socratic 'arête' and Kennedy 'vigor/vig-ah.' They still do—perhaps even more so. Yes, Al Michaels, we believe.

This brings us to our subject: political communication and sport. As suggested by my opening, I take an admittedly narrow approach to the rather querulous phrase, 'political communication.' In choosing to limit the term to a civic con-text in which politicians, elected and otherwise, leverage sport for rhetorical ends, perhaps even partisan ones, I am not unaware of the critical/cultural turn in studies of sport.[4] That turn, enormously influential and productive, has trans-formed a generic category—political discourse—and instead seeks to unearth the power/knowledge relations in discourses of all 'types.' In fact, a typology of discourse is itself an effect of a 'will to truth' that the post-structural turn eagerly interrogates. But I cede to my fellow colleagues in this volume the task of delin-eating the broader critical and cultural ground.

In addition, I am less interested in the local than I am the more national and global. Borrowing from a tradition in rhetorical studies, 'political' typically denotes politicians and political institutions working at a national or interna-tional level, usually the president and the executive branch. That choice has been influenced by a number of considerations, such as archived documents and access to texts. But the most important factor is degree of potential influence: the president and his (still) executive team can not only influence millions both at home and abroad, but we can also chart with increasing sophistication reac-tion to those attempts at influence (Kiewe & Houck, 2015). A similar argument can be made for other politicians, present and past, who occupy a national stage, as well as those running for national political office: scope of audience matters. That said, there certainly are important projects awaiting scholars interested in political communication and sport at very local levels. The county commission honoring Champion Team A and not Champion Team B might make for a fascinating case study, but in sketching a broad area of inquiry, I opt here for the paint roller rather than fine-nibbed pen, the five-gallon bucket rather than the ink well.

One final caveat: If we change the valence from 'political communication and sport' to 'sport and political communication,' what are the consequences?

To my mind, and as I hope to document below, when we privilege sport (e.g., teams, star athletes, not-so-star athletes, mega-spectacles) and trace its impact on political communication, we see that the early 21st century is an auspicious moment for what Khan (2012) deems the 'activist athlete.' Unlike the very public, bold, and embodied performances of a Jackie Robinson, a Muhammad Ali, a John Carlos and Tommie Smith, a Billie Jean King, or an Annika Sorenstam, contemporary athletes are but a tweet away, and an Instagram photo from, the fraught world of policy and politics.

In what follows, I attempt to rather briefly document possibilities for future scholarship by highlighting broad areas of inquiry. Rather than leave those areas untethered to specifics, I offer historic and contemporary examples, less as sustained case studies, and far more as suggestive tokens. I will begin with the valence on the political, switch that valence to sport, and conclude with a brief comment on pedagogy and audiences.

In mapping the terrain of the political and sporting, it seems logical to start with the presidential body. Long gone are the days of a corpulent Commander-in-Chief like William Howard Taft or a leader with the invalid-ic legs of a Franklin D. Roosevelt (Houck & Kiewe, 2003).[5] Given the metonymic importance of the 'world's only superpower,' it is imperative that the president embody something of the hard-bodied nationalism of the world's 'strongest' nation. Not only do we expect our presidents to be fit and athletic, but our nation's visual appetite demands something of a practiced, if not expert, body. Who can forget the halcyon images of Bobby and John tossing the football at Hyannis Port? George W. Bush was frequently photographed or filmed on his mountain bike while vacationing at his Crawford, Texas, ranch. How can we erase from memory images of Bill Clinton as he sashayed around the capitol in impossibly small shorts? While Barack Obama drew jeers for throwing a gutter ball on the campaign trail, his love of full-court basketball has helped define his presidential personality (Maraniss, 2012). And Gerald Ford and Ronald Reagan both played college football; the latter so identified with Notre Dame running back George Gipp that 'winning one for the Gipper' took on resonances far beyond the exigencies of a tight football game.

And yet, even as we demand fit and active presidential bodies, ambivalence enters. In August 2010, for example, President Obama brought the first family for a vacation to the panhandle of Florida; it was not innocent of political motives as, following the Exxon Deepwater Horizon oil spill in the Gulf of Mexico, the president sought to bring back tourism and commerce to the area. The official White House photographer took many pictures, and yet only one photograph of a swimming president was ever published; it depicted a smiling Obama with his youngest daughter Sasha neck deep in the presumably clean, oil-free Gulf waters. Note the omission: We did not see a shirtless president in his swim trunks. God forbid a nearly naked picture of the Commander-in-Chief expose any corporeal, and thus national, vulnerabilities.[6] Lest we forget, official

Washington went Mel Gibson-berserk over the President's choice of a light tan suit at an official DC press conference in August 2014 (Murray, 2014). In a word, the King must have clothes—and those clothes better be the right cut and color.

A different sort of vulnerability hurt Senator John Kerry's presidential ambitions in 2004. Instead of being filmed at play performing one of the more traditional American sports, the northeastern and aristocratic Kerry was shown windsurfing. Attacked by many as an 'elitist' sport, the Bush campaign went so far as to make an attack ad out of the athletic senator's exploits. So not every sport is equal in the eyes of the American electorate. Suffice it to say that presidential aspirants will avoid windsurfing, polo, and other monied games for the foreseeable future. Even the uber-presidential game of golf might be on the campaign chopping block as the '1 percent' economic class continues to take a beating in American public discourse.

Speaking of golf and national leaders, America is not the only country to celebrate sporting prowess among its executive elite. In the early 1990s, word trickled out of Salinger-ian North Korea that dictator Kim Jong-il played golf for the first time. His score? According to the North Korean news agency, who had no fewer than 17 security guards on the course, Dear Leader shot a whopping 38 under par score of 34—with no fewer than 11 hole-in-ones (Posnanski, 2012). Take that Seoul, Tokyo, and Washington! Pyongyang has nukes *and* otherworldly sporting acumen.

Back in the United States, even the First Lady is venturing out into the public and athletic world of fit bodies. Michelle Obama, for example, has helped transform the President's Council on Fitness and Sports into the President's Council on Fitness, Sports and Nutrition. Leading by example, the First Lady is often seen exercising under the aegis of her 'Let's Move' campaign to eradicate childhood obesity. Perhaps not surprisingly, her official visibility in our often overheated public sphere has engendered all manner of racist and sexist taunts about her body shape; physical movement, it seems, provides the requisite cover for many to criticize what had once been largely off limits, or smuggled in under the auspices of 'first lady fashion.'

This leads to a logical and perhaps pressing question: What, then, of a woman seeking the presidency? What sort of sporting activity validates a Hillary Clinton or a Carly Fiorina in the eyes of a 'strong' nation? Is it enough for a female candidate to merely participate somewhat vicariously in the sporting life? Will a carefully orchestrated first pitch safely close to the catcher suffice? Will a photo-op with the women's World Cup team do? Does she need to fill out an NCAA bracket to buck up her sporting bona fides? Could a NASCAR lap or two provide a suitable frame to validate our sporting appetite? Or, does a serious presidential contender, who happens to be a woman, have 'to play like one of the boys'?

Must she talk like one, too? As Butterworth (forthcoming), among many others, has noted, presidential politics is rife with the argot of sport. Not surprisingly, much of that sporting vernacular is rooted deeply in the violent masculinity of football and boxing. We frequently hear talk on the campaign trail and elsewhere of 'knockout punches,' 'jabs,' 'head butting,' 'low blows,' 'pulling punches,' 'dancing around an issue,' being 'on the ropes,' and 'heavyweights.' In certain contexts such as presidential debates, the terminology hardly registers as metaphorical, such is the antagonistic context of national politics. Similarly, football terminology such as 'blitzing,' 'fumbling,' being 'out of bounds,' or 'blind-sided,' 'quarterbacking,' and 'punting' appear frequently in our political discourse. Beyond football and boxing, though, we hear talk of 'slam dunks,' 'home runs,' 'getting thrown a curve ball,' and always the 'horse race' with the latest poll about who's up, who's down, who's trending and who's not. Of course the language of sport is not unique to political aspirants; it is also the lingua franca of media analysts who are forever speculating on the latest 'game changer,' or lamenting someone 'kicking the can down the road.' And so the question remains: Are women at a competitive disadvantage in a rhetorical universe so dominated by the physical, the violent, and the hyper-competitive? Or, are we in the midst of a backlash in which epithets such as 'throwing like a girl' get reconfigured for gendered electoral ends?

Since President Jimmy Carter instituted the practice back in 1977, and when they are not playing sports, presidents habitually cultivate cultural capital by inviting championship-winning teams or teams representing the nation to the White House. These photo-ops, rich in jock/sports bra-sniffing bonhomie, cast a winning glow on the occupants at 1600 Pennsylvania Avenue. Of course it is not uncommon for a member of the team to strategically miss the event, and thus by omission cast a proxy vote on the president's policies. Only because the hosting practice has become so institutionalized does the press eagerly pounce on such absences.

Perhaps the imbrication of sports, fitness, the presidency, and politics more generally also can help us make sense of a relatively new phenomenon: the athlete-turned-candidate. In an age of the commodification of celebrity, is it any surprise that politics serve as a fitting career for ex-athletes who long for celebrity and glory well after their playing days? Football players such as Steve Largent, J.C. Watts, Jack Kemp, and Heath Shuler have translated athletic accomplishment and celebrity into national politics. Bodybuilder extraordinaire Arnold Schwarzenegger took his 'walnuts-in-a-condom' body straight to Sacramento, as did 'wrestler,' Jesse 'The Body' Ventura in Minnesota. Former National Basketball Association (NBA) stars Bill Bradley, Kevin Johnson, and Dave Bing have also traded successful careers on the hardwood for executive positions in the U.S. Senate, and mayor positions in Sacramento and Detroit. National figure skating champion and Olympic silver medalist Michelle Kwan now works for the State Department. Even former successful coaches have gotten in on the action: former Nebraska Cornhuskers football coach Tom Osborne traded his headset in for the governorship of the state. Annually, it seems, does

NBA Hall of Famer and sports analyst Charles Barkley threaten to run for the governorship of his home state of Alabama. Internationally, boxing sensation Manny Pacquiao transformed his fame and wealth into an elected position in the Philippine Congress. One suspects, given the ever-increasing confluence of politics and sport, to say nothing of money, celebrity, and receptive audiences, that this trend will only multiply in the coming years.

And speaking of international politics, more than 40 years after the sport of ping pong helped facilitate amicable diplomatic relations between the United States and China, the State Department dipped deeply into the wellsprings of sport in trying to bring North Korea into the community of nations. Specifically, Secretary of State Madeline Albright and the Clinton administration attempted something of a 'Hail Mary' in October 2000. Nearing the end of its term in office, State Department officials knew that the reclusive Kim Jong-il was a fanatical devotee of the NBA: Kim was rumored "to have regulation courts at most of his palaces plus a video library of practically every game Michael Jordan ever played for the Bulls" (Zeigler, 2006). As such, diplomats did the logical thing when it came time to present Kim with a token of the United States' appreciation for the visit: it gave him an official NBA basketball personally auto-graphed by Chicago Bulls mega-star, Michael Jordan. Said chief CIA analyst for North Korea, Bob Carlin: "He may have been initially surprised by it, but you could tell he was pleased. I don't think he expected it. It was a very personal gesture, in a sense" (Zeigler, 2006). The auspices were so favorable following the Air Jordan diplomacy that the State Department reached out to the basket-ball star about the possibilities of a goodwill tour. North Korean officials even authorized Jordan to visit with Kim—a venture that would be underwritten by Seoul-based Samsung. The infamously apolitical Jordan declined the request: Democrats, Republicans *and* East Asians buy sneakers, too!

Albright's gift and Kim Jong-il's Basketball Jones help us make sense of what took place nearly 13 years later: NBA Hall of Famer and former Chicago Bull Dennis Rodman, along with the Harlem Globetrotters, traveled to North Korea to meet his new fan-boy, Kim Jong-un. While Rodman has been roundly exco-riated for his diplomatic boners with the 5 foot 1 inch new Dear Leader—none of his six trips have taken place under the State Department's imprimatur—he remains convinced that basketball can function as a diplomatic bridge between Kim, his hoops-obsessed nation, and the United States (Silberman, 2014). Even as Kim continues to execute family members and top military leaders, it will be interesting to see to what degree, if any, basketball and its celebrities might play in diplomacy with the most isolated nation on earth.

Sport and media scholars have explored the long tentacles of U.S. sporting empire, but in an age when at least one country in the George W. Bush-defined 'axis of evil'—Iran—seeks to enter into dialogue with the West, one wonders what, if any, role sport might play in that evolving relationship. Surely, and back in the Americas, baseball will play an important role in the ongoing thaw between Cuba and the United States. As the Castro brothers get further into their Depends years, and as trade treaties get signed and Cuba is removed from the state sponsors of terrorism list, baseball (and yes, cigars) will serve as a bridge between neighbors. Certainly, in the short term, that bridge will likely be one-way as long as American dollars are involved, but the auspices are favorable for no more Yasiel Puig-level intrigue, either.[7]

Talk of Michael Jordan, Dennis Rodman, and the Harlem Globetrotters leads logically to the activist athlete and reversing the valence to sport and political communication. Perhaps no other area in communication and sport is as intriguing and auspicious as this one. In our present age of digital activism, athletes can take to Twitter, Facebook, Instagram and other social media outlets to instantly register their opinion on current political events. Minus the filter of traditional media, not only is this activism relatively instantaneous, but it can take countless forms. Athletes no longer need to register their political opinions with the well-crafted journalism of Minnesota Vikings ex-punter, Chris Kluwe, who very memorably supported gay marriage on the website Deadspin by claiming such support "won't magically turn you in to a lustful cockmonster" (Kluwe, 2012). No, these days the activist athlete can choreograph a team picture with each member wearing a hoodie to honor the memory of a Trayvon Martin; s/he can wear a warm-up shirt emblazoned with "I Can't Breathe" to protest the death of an Eric Garner; and s/he can post a picture of a same-sexed smooch on draft night. Furthermore, a 'like' or a 're-tweet' or a hashtag can function rhetorically to register support for a candidate, a cause, a policy, an event, or a fallen victim. In brief, social media has completely redefined the activist athlete (Pierce, 2015).

BMX star Colton Satterfield did not need to rely exclusively on social media for his activism at the X Games Big Air event held in Austin, Texas, in June 2015. Eschewing a sponsor's uniform or jersey, Satterfield wore a long-sleeve t-shirt featuring an iconic image of Dr. Martin Luther King, Jr., from when he was booked into the Montgomery, Alabama, jail in 1956. Instead of a prison ID, the tag King holds reads simply "love." As Satterfield nailed the impossibly hard 'double flair' jump to win the gold, televised nationally on ESPN, the audience couldn't miss King's visage. After the miraculous jump, social media quickly noted Satterfield's shirt and registered its approbation.[8] Just two weeks later on his Twitter feed, Satterfield ventured into presidential electoral politics, imploring his nearly 7,500 followers to watch a Rand Paul video on the flat tax and to send money to his campaign. While some might note the rather incongruous pairing of King and Paul, the point is that activist athletes have multiple forums to engage the political; to focus on Satterfield's ideological (in)consistency is to miss the larger message.

For some scholars the quadrennial Olympics is the cynosure of the sport and political communication paradigm: a nation represented by a team on an international stage materializes its identity (Hogan, 2003; Barney & Heine, 2015).

Of course that identity remains bound up with medal counts, world records, and dominance in key 'nationalistic' sports: just as sprinting 'belongs' to the Jamaicans and distance running to the Kenyans, basketball 'belongs' to the United States and soccer to the Brazilians and Germans. Moreover, we do not need to reprise Jesse Owens' heroics in the 1936 Berlin Games or the 1980 American ice hockey team to make the argument that sporting excellence on an international stage functions as political rebuttal argument. The Olympics still matter.

Similarly, team sports like the Ryder Cup, the Solheim Cup, and the Walker Cup in Golf, the Davis Cup and Fed Cup in tennis, and the America's Cup in sailing, function as arbiters of sporting worth and, thus, national ideals. And yet, when half or more of the European Ryder Cup team calls Jupiter Island and Lake Nona, Florida, home, the feigned jingoism of the competition—promoted breathlessly by flag-waving television outlets in particular—is increasingly anachronistic. But well beyond a toney zip code, social media traverses national lines in an instant; flags mean less when the brand in question is an athlete or a team, not a country; and international sport of all types is so much easier to watch, follow, and share in our hyper-connected digital age. American 'friends' on my Facebook feed are constantly updating me on the arcana of the English Premier League, among other distant competitions. 'Friendlies/Friendly's' no longer refer exclusively to my favorite ice cream shop.

The news, of course, is mixed: On the one hand, perhaps with less invest-ment in flags and borders, the activist athlete can reach enormous audiences in an instant with very few filters. On the other hand, in an age ruled by the six seconds of Vine, the abracadabra of Snapchat, and the 140 charac-ters of Twitter, our collective ability to engage each other with argument, evidence, and, God forbid, nuance, spirals into quaint oblivion. The digital lynch mob that quickly formed and called for Penn State football coach Joe Paterno's head—corporeally and ceramicly—and got it, is just one of countless episodes in which a 'trending' topic ought to give us pause rather than speed us up (Brown, Billings, & Brown, 2015). On the other side of the ideological coin, with the murder of nine black members of Emanuel AME Church in Charleston, South Carolina, and the accompanying photos of accused shooter Dylann Roof posing with the Confederate flag, the 'Stars and Bars' have come down in public places with astonishing speed. Even NASCAR, long associated with the flag among its southern venues and fans, is seeking to dissociate the organization from it. All in the span of less than two weeks. Curiously, what well-reasoned public argument could not do for more than 50 years got done in an instant thanks to the vertiginous multiplier effects inherent in our digital networks. Speed kills, yes.

There are, of course, many more venues for scholarship on political com-munication and sport and sport and political communication. The annual Army All-American high school football showcases, endless military apprecia-tion nights, the omnipresent Flyover as Defense Department encomium, the

President as sportsman/commentator-in-chief, sporting bodies and the politics and economics of Chronic Traumatic Encephalopathy, golf and environmental degradation, and current event x, social media response y. Yes, the national anthem. Always the Olympics. And perennially, Caitlyn Jenner, Michael Sam, Serena, and Caster Semenya.

Coda: Pedagogy, Effect, and the Politics of Pessimism

In trying to teach my students in rhetorical studies about critical approaches to the study of contemporary sport, the feedback is often unenthusiastic—sometimes hostile—usually nonplussed. No doubt part of that is bound up with the resistance of thinking hard about the popular and taken for granted, typified by that perennial plaint, thinly disguised as a question: "Aren't you reading a bit too much into this?" The late Janice Hocker Rushing had the best response to the question: If ever there was an object lesson in hegemony, power, and culture, it lurks in the insinuation that there is nothing here to critique; it's just sport, after all. Power indeed masks when it doesn't totally efface or erase (Bochner, 2006).

Too, some of my students' lack of enthusiasm and/or hostility is also on me: Part of my job as a teacher of rhetorical criticism is to coax students into believing that significance often lies in the mundane text, the (seemingly) transparent text, and the texts we interact with every day. Arguably, that coaxing is the most important part of my/our job.

I would also offer, however tentatively, a third possibility for my students' reaction: The collective conclusions of our critical work on sport are often damning indictments of sport and sport media content that students eagerly, and enthusiastically, consume. Not unlike the Bill Lumbergh character from *Office Space*, we critics of sport tend to be eager with the bad news. My students do not like to be called out, however implicitly, for their missionary position heteronormativity, their not-so-latent red state homophobia, a systemic commitment to anti-black racism, a jingoism that far exceeds their red, white, and blue J-Crew outfit, and a pervasive and entrenched sexism that tsk-tsks their hard-bodied cult of exercise showcased at the most recent fraternity/sorority mixer. So where is the good news about sport, more than one has asked? If sport is so awful, why are so many of us consumed by it? The defensiveness grows louder: I am not a queer-baiting racist who hates my jock kid sister, makes Greg Louganis jokes, and who sings the National Anthem before going to bed every night. At this point in my classes, things get a bit loud and steamy; thermostats need some adjusting.

Whether they know it or not, and my guess is that they do not, students have identified two of the most important issues confronting critical scholars of all stripes: audience and effect. Claims of ideology, of interpolation, of consumptive practices, of marginalization—all are claims, at some level, of effect. On an audience. Real, not hypothetical. But claims about the harmful functioning of power, discursive and otherwise, are rather quaint without a corresponding audience upon whom that power is exercised. Thus have we arrived at the twin scholarly personages of Debbie Downer and Gary Gloom that so riled my students.

But my students are not alone. In media studies, more than 30 years ago, Fred Fejes (1984) posed the question of whether all the hidden meanings unearthed by his colleagues actually had any material effects. In rhetorical studies, Carole Blair (2015) raises the same objection: The meanings identified by a rhetorical critic are not the same thing as effects on an audience. And in the inaugural volume of *Communication & Sport*, no fewer than three luminaries call for more work on how mediated messages are being consumed by actual audiences (Bruce, 2013; Gantz, 2013; Wenner, 2013). We might profitably heed these warnings—and the complaints of my/our students: To continue the prose trumpet blast of bad news about sport without a corresponding analysis of how audiences receive that news privileges the (pessimistic) voice of the critic at the expense of those about whom we supposedly care so much.

The irony of the critical/cultural studies turn is that a stated commitment to the low, the marginalized, the lived experience of the working-class functions all too often as a valorization of the lonely voice of the well-meaning and middle-classed Gary and Debbie, crying out in the sporting wilderness. Might we not want, instead, to celebrate audiences, inquire eagerly with them, and celebrate their virtues? Perhaps even sit snuggly with them in our own modern *palaestras*, catching and taking their flame.

Notes

My thanks to Michael Butterworth, Doug Fowler, Abraham Iqbal Khan, and David Levenson for reading an earlier draft of this chapter.

1 For a detailed explanation of the social status and civic significance of nudity and Greek athletics, see Donald G. Kyle (2007, pp. 83–90). Summarizing Bonfante, Kyle argues that "The costume of civic nudity communicated one's social status and made a claim to political participation" (p. 87).

2 These studies provided the impetus for the Eisenhower administration to create in 1956 the President's Council on Youth Fitness. The name was altered in 1963 by John F. Kennedy to the President's Council on Physical Fitness to reflect a more global concern with Americans' bodily fitness. Five years later the Johnson administration again changed the name, this time to the President's Council on Physical Fitness and Sports. Most recently, in 2010, the Obama administration changed the name to the President's Council on Physical Fitness, Sports and Nutrition.

3 In Jowett's (1989, p. 99) brief introduction to his translation of *Charmides*, he describes *sophrosyne* as "an ideal second to none in importance" for the Greeks; it meant "accepting the bounds which excellence lays down for human nature, restraining impulses to unrestricted freedom, to all excess, obeying the inner laws of harmony and proportion."

4 For a recent anthology highlighting some of this scholarship, see Andrews and Carrington (2013).

5 New Jersey Governor Chris Christie's weight, long a punch-line of late-night comedy, likely will be a topic in the 2016 presidential primary season. Should he secure the Republican Party's nomination, that topic will likely blossom into an 'issue.' Interestingly, one prominent candidate, former Florida Governor Jeb Bush, has lost significant weight ahead of the brutal campaign season, perhaps best detailed in Richard Ben Cramer's magnificent opus, *What It Takes* (1992).

6 The prudishness with which we treat American presidential bodies is comically juxtaposed with Russian President Vladimir Putin's beefcake blitz. Whether doing martial arts, hunting big game, fishing, riding bareback, swimming, or pretty much being anywhere beyond the boundaries of the Kremlin, Putin's shirtless and hairless torso is as omnipresent as any Kardashian.

7 For the impossibly bizarre story of Puig's escape from Cuba to multimillionaire outfielder for the Los Angeles Dodgers, see Katz (2014).

8 Satterfield's jump (and shirt) can be seen at: http://xgames.espn.go.com/xgames/video/13027186/colton-satterfield-wins-gold-bmx-big-air.

References

Andrews, D.L., & Carrington, B. (Eds.). (2013). *A companion to sport*. Malden, MA: Wiley Blackwell.

Barney, R.K., & Heine, M.H. (2015). "The emblem of one united body . . . one great sporting Maple leaf": The Olympic games and Canada's quest for self-identity. *Sport in Society, 18*, 816–834.

Blair, C. (2015). "We are all just prisoners here of our own device": Rhetoric in speech communication after Wingspread. In A. Kiewe and D.W. Houck (Eds.), *The effects of rhetoric and the rhetoric of effects: Past, present, future* (pp. 31–58). Columbia, SC: University of South Carolina Press.

Bochner, A.P. (2006). Janice's voice. *Southern Communication Journal, 71*, 183–193.

Brown, N., Billings, A.C., & Brown, K. (2015). "May no act of ours bring shame": Fan enacted crisis communication surrounding the Penn State sex abuse scandal. *Communication & Sport, 3*, 288–311.

Bruce, T. (2013). Reflections on communication and sport: On women and femininities. *Communication & Sport, 1*, 125–137.

Butterworth, M. (forthcoming). Sport and politics in the United States. In J. Kelley, A. Bairner, & J.W. Lee (Eds.), *The Routledge handbook of sport and politics*. New York: Routledge.

Cramer, R.B. (1992). *What it takes: The way to the White House*. New York: Vintage.

Fejes, F. (1984). Critical mass communications research and media effects: The problem of the disappearing audience. *Media, Culture and Society, 6*, 219–232.

Gantz, W. (2013). Reflections on communication and sport: On fanship and social relationships. *Communication & Sport, 1*, 176–187.

Hogan, J. (2003). Staging the nation: Gendered and ethnicized discourses of national identity in Olympic opening ceremonies. *Journal of Sport & Social Issues, 27*, 100–123.

Houck, D.W., & Kiewe, A. (2003). *FDR's body politics: The rhetoric of disability*. College Station, TX: Texas A&M University Press.

Jowett, B. (1989). Charmides. In E. Hamilton and H. Cairns (Eds.), *The collected dialogues of Plato* (pp. 99–122). Princeton, NJ: Princeton University Press.

Katz, J. (2014, April 14). Escape from Cuba: Yasiel Puig's untold journey to the Dodgers. *Los Angeles Magazine*. Retrieved July 6, 2016, from http://www.lamag.com/long form/escape-from-cuba-yasiel-puigs-untold-journey-to-the-dodgers/.

Kennedy, J.F. (December 26, 1960). The vigor we need. *Sports Illustrated.* Retrieved June 14, 2016, from http://www.presidency.ucsb.edu/ws/?pid=8771.

Khan, A. (2012). *Curt Flood in the media: Baseball, race, and the demise of the activist-athlete.* Jackson, MS: University Press of Mississippi.

Kiewe, A., & Houck, D.W. (2015). Introduction. In A. Kiewe & D.W. Houck (Eds.), *The effects of rhetoric and the rhetoric of effects: Past, present, future* (pp. 1–28). Columbia, SC: University of South Carolina Press.

Kluwe, K. (2012). Letter to Emmett C. Burns Jr. *Deadspin.* Retrieved June 14, 2016, from http://deadspin.com/5941348/they-wont-magically-turn-you-into-a-lustful-cock monster-chris-kluwe-explains-gay-marriage-to-the-politician-who-is-offended-by-an-nfl-player-supporting-it.

Kyle, D.G. (2007). *Sport and spectacle in the ancient world.* Malden, MA: Blackwell.

Maraniss, D. (June 9, 2012). President Obama's basketball love affair has roots in Hawaii high school team. *Washington Post.* Retrieved June 14, 2016, from https://www.washingtonpost.com/sports/president-obamas-basketball-love-affair-has-roots-in-hawaii-high-school-team/2012/06/09/gJQApU2mQV_story.html.

Murray, R. (August 28, 2014). Social media explodes over President Obama's tan suit. Retrieved June 14, 2016, from http://abcnews.go.com/US/social-media-explodes-president-obamas-tan-suit/story?id=25166551.

Pierce, C.P. (June 29, 2015). NASCAR's Confederate flag ban and the explosion of the activist athlete. *Grantland.* Retrieved June 14, 2016, from https://grantland.com/the-triangle/nascar-confederate-flag-ban-sonoma-lebron-james-racing/.

Posnanski, J. (February 14, 2012). Kim Jong-il's record setting round may not have been all it was cracked up to be. *Golf Magazine.* Retrieved June 14, 2016, from http://www.golf.com/tour-and-news/kim-jong-ils-record-setting-round-may-not-have-been-all-it-was-cracked-be.

Silberman, L. (May 4, 2014). Rodman's revelations. *Dujour.* Retrieved June 14, 2016, from http://dujour.com/culture/dennis-rodman-north-korea-kim-jong-un-interview/.

Wenner, L.A. (2013). Reflections on communication and sport: On reading sport and narrative ethics. *Communication & Sport, 1,* 188–199.

Zeigler, M. (October 29, 2006). While the rest of the world watches Kim Jong il, fearful of North Korea's nuclear threat, the dictator often can't take his eyes off . . . the NBA. *San Diego Union-Tribune.* Retrieved June 14, 2016, from http://legacy.utsand iego.com/news/world/20061029-9999-1n29kim.html.

6

SPORT AS GENDER/FEMINIST STUDIES

Lindsey J. Meân

ARIZONA STATE UNIVERSITY

The significance of sport as a key site for the study of gender and gendered practices is widely acknowledged (e.g., Creedon, 2014; Griffin, 2011). Sport is a highly ideological site that remains strongly connected to men and particular forms of masculinity in historical and contemporary U.S. culture, making gender an important component of sport's ideological focus and impact. Sport is also pervasive; the proliferation of sport as media (i.e., sport-media) over the last 30 years has only increased the centrality and significance of sport as a powerful site for the construction of mainstreamed, hegemonic gender, gendered understandings, values, and identities that impact wider culture. A powerful communicator of gender and gendered values and understandings, sport-media is also particularly acknowledged to be a pivotal site of communicative action (e.g., Creedon, 2014; Wenner, 2014) with newer digital forms contributing to sport as "a global media microcosm communicating gender values" (Creedon, 2014, p. 714). Whannel (2000, p. 293) notes the ideological impact of sport-media as the naturalization of "competitive individualism, local regional and national identities and male superiority." Nonetheless, while sport-media comprises a substantive site for the study of sport and gender, sport is more widely explored as a multi-level site that has long been associated with men, male identities, masculinity, hypermasculinity, and heroic (male) formations (e.g., Dworkin & Messner, 1999).

To provide some context, this chapter starts with a brief summary of the key issues that have been at the center of feminist and gender studies of sport, all of which remain relevant in contemporary culture. The theoretical underpinnings and some of the research interrogating gender(ed) sport and sport-media then follow. However, it is important to note that sport is so central and pervasive that the range of sites and levels of interest for feminist and/or gender scholars is too widespread and diffuse to be fully represented in this chapter. A large proportion of the feminist and gender sport research does focus on sport-media, reflecting both the prominence of sport as media and the power of the sport-media complex (Jhally, 1989). But while sport-media impacts wider sport identities and practices, we also experience sport in a multitude of ways as children and continue to encounter it throughout our lives in family, school, leisure, and professional contexts as athletes, coaches, fans (and haters), parents, children, organizers, regulators, reporters, and so forth. (See Nussbaum & Worthington, Chapter 12, this volume.) We also frequently experience sport as metaphoric, idiomatic, and intertextual forms in everyday interactions alongside marketing, branding, and merchandizing imperatives. As such, sport manifests as ordinary and special events, as education, entertainment, and competition, and in banal, everyday manifestations that are routinely encountered, communicated, and consumed as identities.

Gender Issues in Sport

Traditional feminist studies initially emphasized women's exclusion from and invisibility in sport, focusing on equal access, opportunity, and representation. Research sought to undermine myths about sporting female femininity and sexuality (Hall, 1988), but increasingly recognized these as a response to the ideological threat women's sporting presence posed to the dominant, hegemonic gender formations given sport's centrality for constructing heterosexual masculinity. The shift to critical perspectives emphasizing power relations increasingly focused feminist and gender scholars on the management, negotiation, organization, and representation of females and female athleticism in sport and sport-media, and, in turn, attention to the narrow and restrictive versions of heterosexual sporting (hyper)masculinity idealized in sport. As such, gender and sexuality remain problematically intersected and conflated in sport ideology and discourses, making it difficult to extricate sexuality from the discussion of gender in sport. For many, sport research continues to focus on the persistent cyclical production and reproduction (i.e., re/production) of hegemonic binary gender formations and their intersection with sexuality, resistance to alternative male and female forms, sexualities and other gender formations, and the evidence of resistance and change within sport.

While gender and sex are not the same,[1] they are frequently conflated in and through sport. Organized sport remains primarily sex-segregated based on notions of fair competition and biological differences in ways that intersect with gender (although biological sex is also problematized as a false, constructed binary). Routine sex-testing is often referred to as gender verification and was a mandatory part of organized sport for female athletes in the second half of the 20th century. No longer mandatory in the Olympics since 1999, female athletes recently subjected to this testing reveal the continued power of these categories and their connection to gender as a culturally disciplined, embodied performance. Sex and/or gender questioning (disciplining) of female athletes reveals concerns about nonorthodox or nontraditionally feminized bodies and continued anxieties surrounding women, muscle, and (hetero)femininity. This is also evident in the continued sport-media practice of including female athletes who conform to traditional feminine beauty discourses and manage their muscles, gender, and (hetero)sexuality (e.g., Christopherson, Janning, & McConnell, 2002), rendering invisible female athletes whose performances and/or body types do not fit this standard. The recent sport and sport-media treatment of Caster Semenya informs us about contemporary gender(ed) understandings and hegemonic formations (Amy-Chinn, 2011; Sloop, 2012) and evidences the way that race, culture, and power are integral to the gender/sex questioning and disciplining of athletes whose bodies and gender performance do not fit within White, Western discourses of femininity and sexuality (Young, 2015). Race intersects in many ways with gender in sport and sport-media, particularly for constructions of Black masculinity (e.g., Angelini, Billings, MacArthur, Bissell, & Smith, 2014; Leonard, 2010). Thus, while race is directly addressed elsewhere in this book (see Khan, Chapter 7), it is often made relevant in sport constructions of gender given that Black sporting femininities and masculinities are frequently racialized compared with the unraced, unmarked White male sporting heroic (Butterworth, 2007).

Theoretical Perspectives

Many contemporary scholars studying sport and gender have a feminist and/or critical orientation rather than explicitly adopting traditional feminist theories. Ideology and power are central to the study of gender and sport, and pivotal to the communicative action and practices through which gender categories, associations, and the status quo are socially constructed, maintained, resisted, and undermined (Foucault, 1972). Discourses are significant, as ideological action-oriented systems of meaning that construct and define categories, identities, understandings, and, therefore, power and power relations because we are subject to discourses and associated identities. But we are particularly emotionally connected and subject to the powerful discourses from which our strongest identities arise, and both gender and sport are key cultural identities which also potently intersect since sport is so highly gendered (e.g., Messner, 1988). The impetus (or motivation) to re/produce, collaborate with, resist, and/or respond to their threat is then evident within the discursive and rhetorical practices of everyday communicative and social action (Potter, 1996), revealing their power (Foucault, 1972). As such, sport fans are highly susceptible to collaborate with the meanings and action of sport texts (e.g., Scherer, 2007; Wenner, 1991).

People re/produce or enact the identities, discourses, and so forth, to which we are subject as/within communicative action and re/presentational practices (talk, text, social action, etc.). Re/producing these forms is often described as collaborating with them and challenging or undermining them as resisting, but they are often simultaneously re/produced and resisted (Krane, 2001; Meân & Kassing, 2008). The most dominant or accepted cultural forms are often referred to as hegemonic forms because they are re/produced as naturalized truths, making them particularly powerful and resilient to contestation and resistance. But, for some, the concept of hegemony and its structural origins make it problematic despite many scholars using an unfixed process-oriented reformulation (Connell & Messerschmidt, 2005). Regardless, the significance of these discourses and identities means we are subject to them in many ways and collaboration is widely used to account for gender(ed), sporting action directed at ourselves, others, events, and so forth—for example, female athletes' collaboration or adherence (self-disciplining) to the traditional Western feminine beauty standards that distinguish them as heterosexual and position them as acceptable for inclusion in media coverage (Caudwell, 1999; Christopherson et al., 2002). These practices and actions simultaneously re/produce familiar discourses about sexuality and athleticism, framing and defining female athletes as lesbian unless they perform heterosexuality, which in sport also often means avoiding feminist framings (Dworkin & Messner, 1999; Meân & Kassing, 2008). These examples allude to the powerful intersectionality and intertextual connections between gender, sport, and sexuality in the familiar, hegemonic narratives and discourses—alongside the marketing, promotional, and commercial imperatives of the sport-media complex.

Consequently, beyond the focus on individuals as athletes, coaches, and so forth, sport-media and organizations are usefully conceived as connected to the individual people producing and enacting them rather than abstracted structures that have their own action. Equally, the concept of framing typically applied to media texts is also relevant for the analysis of talk and other everyday communicative action given framing is a rhetorical act that impacts *how* something is understood—positioned and interconnected within a discursive realm—rather than merely raising a topic of interest (although mere inclusion also frames content/people as 'newsworthy' and relevant). This is especially significant given that the power of sport identities renders audiences (interpretive communities) highly susceptible to collaborate with the meanings and action of sport texts (e.g., Scherer, 2007; Wenner, 1991) and organizations (Fielding-Lloyd & Meân, 2008). But it also needs to be recognized that some texts/people are more authoritative and persuasive than others, and that the global, multiplatform presence of some sport-media and organizations enhances their power and authority over gender(ed) meaning-making in/through sport (Meân, 2010, 2011; Oates, 2009).

Cultural disciplining of gender and sexuality is evident in sport-media and organizational responses to and framings of athletes and events through a number of discursive strategies: exclusion, invisibility (symbolic annihilation), re/presentational framing, and content (positive and negative). While women's exclusion, peripheralization, and invisibility in sport, sport organizations, and sport-media alongside efforts to change this (e.g., Title IX) continue to be evidenced (e.g., Billings, Angelini, MacArthur, Bissell, Smith, & Brown, 2014; Fielding-Lloyd & Meân, 2008; Hardin, 2005), analysis continues to explore what female inclusion comprises and the extent and ways in which change is arising. This extends to gender(ed) formations beyond the traditional male–female binary, but it needs to be acknowledged that evidence suggests that sport and sport-media remain predominantly male (e.g., Hardin, 2005) with the inclusion of women who fit traditional heterosexual, feminine formations. However, cultural disciplining and peripheralization should be understood as a wide-ranging process that is not only done by heterosexual males or directed only at other people. Disciplining and self-disciplining arises from the consistent negotiation of sport as an exclusive heterosexual male space (Wellard, 2002) that is ideologically contested gender terrain (Messner, 1988) across all the levels and actions of sport, sport-media, and sport organization(s).

Sport comprises a powerful site for the re/production of a *naturalized* male superiority at which sex, gender, sexuality, and race are conflated and intersected. The celebrated, competitive male sport heroic relevant to local, regional, and national identities is evident in the narratives, traditions, and other mythic and invented formations of sport and their resistance. While this masculinist orientation is apparent throughout sport, it is especially evident when women participate in 'men's sport' (i.e., male sex-typed sport), team sport, directly combative sports, and as fans of men's sport despite little evidence of gender differences in sporting identities, interests, abilities, and so forth. Ironically, efforts to gain women's equal inclusion have in many ways further reified the gender binary and the push to shift definitions of gender comprise a dilemma for those sport scholars and advocates who have worked so hard to develop the arena of women's sport (Griffin, 2011). As such, sport continues to comprise a challenging and culturally relevant multi-level site for studying rhetorical, discursive, and disciplinary gender(ed) action.

Research

The gender differences naturalized in sport are extensively re/produced and resisted, yet there is little evidence to substantiate the existence of gender differences and increasing evidence of continued disruption and resistance (notably at grassroots and peripheral sport sites). Sullivan's (2004) study of communication amongst athletes reported no significant differences between male and female athletes on a variety of quantitative measures, including team sport settings. Studies of injury management and athletes' talk suggest no gender differences in injury rates, reporting, management, or pain (Young & White, 1995) and that male and female athletes both re/produce injury risk as acceptable and normative (Theberge, 2008). Nonetheless, ideas that women and girls are more easily or seriously injured are widely circulated manifesting in efforts to protect women from sport injuries (based on notions of biological frailty) and a failure to protect male athletes (Theberge, 2012). Speer (2002, p. 352) identified three rhetorical resources men used to exclude women from male sex-typed sport: First, it's worse for women to get injured; second, injury is unfeminine; and, given the risks, third, it's irrational for women to want to participate. These ideas are often evident in the statements and decision-making of sport regulating organizations around the exclusion of women from sport or rule adaptations for the women's game (i.e. ice hockey, lacrosse) and echoed in other historically masculine fields where resistance to female participation protects traditional gendered identities and beliefs. For example, despite policy changes, deployment of females into elite American military units and active operational roles (e.g., combat roles) remains controversial and problematic (e.g., Archer, 2013) and men's interest, injuries, and sacrifices rarely questioned (e.g., Benatar, 2012).

Hypermasculinity and Negotiating Gender(ed) Identities

The hypermasculine formation of sport is a key component of such practices. Media-sport studies reveal how production values and commentary devices construct the top American men's sport as violent, exciting, and spectacular—especially compared with women's sport—re/producing these gender(ed) understandings (Greer, Hardin, & Homan, 2009; Oates, 2012). Similarly, the narratives of a hard-working, aggressive male heroic of which playing through pain remains a significant component continues to be prominent and valued in sport and sport-media (Messner, 1990; Pappas, McKenry, & Catlett, 2004). These narratives construct a narrow and potentially damaging version of heterosexual sporting masculinity and simultaneously exclude women from sport. Yet this remains widely re/produced as *the* idealized model of the male heterosexual heroic in sport and wider culture to the extent that the ideal of the hard-working athlete managing pain and injury has become the ideal for virtually all athletes, irrespective of gender and sexuality (e.g., Malcom, 2006; Meân & Kassing, 2008). Athletes have to constantly negotiate this form of masculinity (Wellard, 2002), which is especially complex for those who do not 'fit' this male, heterosexual formation.

Many studies focus on the negotiation and management of hegemonic masculinist discourses in communicative practices of identity work or consumption (performance) given these male forms are privileged as the *real* thing—as fans, athletes, coaches, reporters (e.g., Krane, 2001; Meân & Kassing, 2008; Messner, 1988; Mewett & Toffoletti, 2011). This is more problematic and contentious for those who do not clearly fit heterosexual male normativity, for whom non-collaboration is riskier. For women this includes simultaneous positioning outside traditional femininity with the potential to be *othered* as lesbian and/or feminist (e.g., Krane, 2001; Meân & Kassing, 2008). But it is complicated, of course, as identities are not singular or consistent but contradictory, intertwined, and fragmented with shifting fluidity. Women in a number of sporting contexts have been observed to distance themselves from 'ordinary' women and traditional feminine formations as nonsporting while simultaneously performing traditional heterosexual femininity (Fielding-Lloyd & Meân, 2008; Meân & Kassing, 2008; Mewett & Toffoletti, 2011) and overtly contravening and resisting (Plymire & Forman, 2000; Thompson & Üstüner, 2015). Similarly, Miller (2010) observed the fluidity and shifting gender identities of girls participating in combat sports as they managed their nonconformativity, while Bridel and Rail (2007) observed the discursive constructions of bodies by gay male marathon runners. Thorpe explored masculinities (2010) and femininities (2008) in snowboarding and their relation to media discourses, while my own research observed how male referees manage identities via collaboratively working *with* male athletes and noncollaboratively responding/reacting *to* female athletes, despite all athletes deploying the same discursive strategies and devices (Meân, 2001).

Fans and Fandom

For fans of sport, gender divisions demarcate men's sport as territory for male fans, and women's sports for females and children. Historically sport fandom has surrounded male sport and is 'passed down' by significant male figures (fathers, grandfathers, uncles, etc.) to younger males. Consequently, female fans of men's sport tend to learn and privilege male formations of fandom and distance themselves from women's sport and forms of fandom associated with women (e.g., Mewett & Toffoletti, 2011). But, increasingly, evidence also reveals some of the disruption of these practices (Hardin & Whiteside, 2012; Toffoletti & Mewett, 2012) and the carving out of alternative fan communities in digital spaces (Plymire & Forman, 2000). Mainstream sport websites designated for female interest and constructed for the female audiences of sport still evidence 'feminized' content and the re/production of hegemonic gender(ed) understandings of women's sport and its fans (e.g., espnW.com; Wolter, 2014; WNBA. com; Meân, 2011). Such practices potentially alienate established fans and fail to build new audiences, providing questionable content to guide young consumers into sport fandom, although there remains promise given that Wolter (2015, p. 168) also reports "unprecedented" numbers of professional and competitive representations of women athletes on espnW.com. The way that gender and sport fandom manifest and intersect in digital spaces, especially the 'prosumer' (consumers as producers) spaces like Twitter, warrant much more attention.

Coaches and Coaching

Gender and feminist studies of coaching report evidence of related unsubstantiated gendered beliefs about coaching that perpetuate the higher value placed on male coaches (Knoppers, 1989, 1992; Knoppers & Anthonissen, 2008). Research also shows coaches (male and female) and other sport professionals continue to re/produce naturalized gender distinctions about athletes using self-fulfilling evidence from their own experience (Fielding-Lloyd & Meân, 2008), which is relevant given evidence that gender-based coaching and expectations contribute to the performance gap between men and women athletes and the evaluation and training of coaches (Fielding-Lloyd & Meân, 2008, 2011, in press; Knoppers & Anthonissen, 2008). Indeed, coaching is so associated with men that it permeates men's parental roles—even those who are not 'athletic'—with women far less likely to coach their children's recreational sport despite being 'expert' compared to fathers with little to no experience (Coakley, 2006; Harrington, 2006). Similarly, professional American female athletes with no experience of female coaches reported men as better suited as coaches for emotional reasons, despite their own aspirations to be a coach (Meân & Kassing, 2008), while comparative elite athletes in Europe with experience of male and female coaches reported a preference for women coaches (Fasting & Pfister, 2000).

The continued interrogation of coaching as a gender(ed) site remains important given the impact and role of coaching and coaches in sport and wider culture. This is especially notable for the young and vulnerable populations of youth sport given the importance of positive role models, early experiences, and the influence and impact of coach communication content and style. Youth sport remains highly traditionally gendered, with far more boys than girls participating and much higher rates of dropout amongst girls in early adolescence. The cultural privileging of men's and boys' sporting knowledge and interest over women's and girls' is also evident in family communication and contexts around sport and youth sport participation. Patterns of parental focus and attention tend to privilege fathers' sporting attention over mothers', and boys' sporting interest over girls'—which, in turn, impacts family dynamics and youth sport participation or dropout. As noted above, these gender(ed) patterns permeate family life even when mothers have sporting expertise and fathers do not.

Sport-Media

Research in sport-media finds a continued and compelling set of differences in the reporting of men and women's sport. At the most basic level, research consistently reports substantively less coverage of women's sport compared with men's sport in all media types. Cooky, Messner, and Hextrum (2013) report a drop in women's coverage in U.S. television sport news to 1.9% in 2009, the lowest in two decades. Further, men's sport not only dominates televised news and sport highlight shows, but is presented in more exciting ways than women's sport (Cooky, Messner, & Musto, 2015). Similarly, a series of studies of NBC's Summer and Winter Olympic coverage from Billings, Angelini, and colleagues continues to evidence little substantive change in the higher coverage and promotion of men's sport over women's despite the Summer Olympics generally having more equitable amounts of coverage of women's sport (Angelini, MacArthur, & Billings, 2012; Billings et al., 2010). The privileging of male sports in terms of space, placement, and promotion has also been noted in newspapers (e.g., Godoy-Pressland, 2014; Kim, Walkosz, & Iverson, 2006) and online media (e.g., Jones, 2013). However, while the comparative invisibility of women in sport-media frames them as less newsworthy and relevant to sport audiences, the ways that female athletes and women's sports are represented further compounds the dominant heterosexual and gender hegemonies of sport.

As noted earlier, sport-media coverage typically focuses on sports that re/produce established gender differences as sex-typed (e.g., football for men, gymnastics for women) or gender-neutral sports such as tennis and track (Greer et al., 2009). Similarly, there is greater coverage of men and women who fit the dominant gender norms of masculinity and femininity alongside effort to manage the contravention of gender norms (Angelini et al., 2012; Angelini, MacArthur, & Billings, 2014; Billings et al., 2010; Christopherson et al., 2002). Indeed, a range of studies provide a well-documented series of representational practices and techniques serving to subtly and implicitly re/produce the traditional, hegemonic gendered formations as naturalized differences (e.g., Greer et al., 2009). Research on multiple sports and events reported in a variety of sport-media contexts evidence a similar pervasive and systemic pattern of practices that include production techniques and/or photographs (camera angles, edits, special effects), commentary, interviews, and written content (descriptions, language choices, topics) that function to frame men's sport as 'naturally' more spectacular and women's as less exciting, construct male athletes as strong, aggressive, and competitive while depicting female athletes as emotional and weak, and differentially account for male and female athletes' success, failure, skills, and achievements (e.g., Billings et al., 2010; Christopherson et al., 2002; Greer et al., 2009; Jones, 2013), often attributing female success as arising from male coaches, fathers, or partners.

While evidence of increased female presence is available, studies generally show that these are still disproportionately small and include a predominance of female athletes who fit the Western, heterosexual feminine ideal and who are further framed within these discourses across sport-media types and contexts (e.g., Christopherson et al., 2002; Meân, 2010, 2015). Equally, language and practices that could be considered as empowering are frequently accompanied by content (language choices, details and descriptions, visual images) that undermine the empowering content in ways that continue to trivialize and minimize women's athletic achievement (e.g., Christopherson et al., 2002). Caudwell (1999) argued that, in many ways, women's growing participation in sport has increased—rather than decreased—pressure for many female athletes to conform to the traditional beauty regimes to manage cultural anxiety about strong women as a threat to masculinity, and evidence from sport-media continues to show the need for women athletes to 'manage their muscle'. Indeed, the recent sport-media and sport organizational disciplining of Caster Semenya remains a powerful example of the impact of responses to female sporting bodies that transgress hegemonic forms of femininity in mainstream sports such as track and field (Amy-Chinn, 2011; Sloop, 2012; Young, 2015). Similarly, the disciplining of women who transgress the boundaries of male sport, such as driving race cars, have been usefully documented (Sloop, 2005). In contrast, the spectacular and aggressive heterosexual hypermasculinity of male athletes and men's sport remains consistently framed in sport-media, contraventions of these hegemonic forms raising discomfort given that sport requires the close scrutiny of apparently heterosexual male bodies by heterosexual/ized male audiences (e.g., Oates, 2007).

The significance of traditional masculinity and masculinist discourses for sport in combination with the predominance of men in sport-media as owners, editors, reporters, and so forth, in part account for the perpetuation of these practices and beliefs (Hardin, 2005). Indeed, Hardin, Simpson, Whiteside, and Garris (2007) reported the gender of the reporter as one factor impacting the framing of newspaper reports about Title IX and a failure in sport journalist education to encourage challenges to the hegemonic male norms (Hardin, Dodd, & Lauffer, 2009). Employment in sport-media remains challenging for women across multiple levels of production, reporting, and commentary, with increasing complexities becoming evident (e.g., Genovese, 2015). The optimism that digital spaces would ultimately offer opportunities to disrupt and provide alternative sport-media and mediated sport communities has been born out in some ways (e.g., Plymire & Forman, 2000), but there is substantive evidence that these remain peripheral while digital space has largely been colonized by mainstream sport-media organizations and sport fans re/producing traditionally gendered sport discourses and formations (Oates, 2009). Thus while change and resistance can be found in sport-media, Wenner (2014) argues the power and ideological significance of sport-media for gendered identities means these are likely to remain deeply entrenched in new media forms.

Concluding Remarks

In this chapter, some of the key ways sport is studied from gender and feminist orientations were discussed, but this required the simplification of a complex set of issues occurring across a wide range of sporting and sport-media action. Studies of gender and gender(ed) practices in sport have taken a critical and/ or feminist focus on masculinity, femininity, and the ways in which these are constructed and disciplined in and through the multiple levels of sport as communicative action and/or practices: that is, as people talk, write, perform, and engage in the individual, social, cultural, organizational action of sport or sport-media (as athletes, parents, fans, coaches, umpires, reporters, pundits, organizers, regulators, and so forth). While traditional feminist theories inform the field, a critical and/or feminist orientation to gender in sport is prominent and emphasis remains on the ideological significance of sport for gender: notably hegemonic hypermasculinity and its intersection and interpellation with heterosexuality as central to the interrogation of sport as a gendered site.

Sport continues to provide a significant site for exploring gender, masculinity, and femininity given its prominence, pervasiveness, and ideological significance. This makes sport impactful on wider gender(ed) cultural formations and power relations and primed for use within a plethora of promotional imperatives. Sport prominently remains a (heterosexual) male domain and the ways in which certain forms of masculinity and femininity are re/produced, excluded, resisted, and framed continues to warrant scrutiny and interrogation. However, the narrow, dichotomous, binary definition of the gender formation remains problematic and of concern to contemporary critical feminist and gender studies and the future requires increased attention to the multiplicity of genders and, imminently, concerns for the inclusion and reproduction of nontraditional gender-identifying and transgender athletes. Indeed, the International Olympic Committee has publicly stated that transgender athletes will be included.

Consequently, sport will be providing a significant site through which to continue to interrogate gender and the potential shifting to greater inclusivity and wider definitions of gender forms, especially given cultural anxieties about muscle and injuries. But Griffin (2011) notes this also raises a dilemma for critical gender sport scholars who support this shift but have also fought for the increased opportunities for (traditionally gendered) women athletes. Indeed, despite its widely claimed success in targeting gender inequity in colleges, Title IX has arguably served to perpetuate, naturalize, and institutionalize the simple gender binary of male–female. The challenge then lies in how to progress with competitive equity in sport while simultaneously expanding or eradicating gender as an oppressive construction.

Note

1 Commonly *sex* is (problematically) viewed as a more 'fixed' biological construct, while *gender* is more widely understood as a social and cultural construct manifesting as masculinity and femininity. Their historical and ideological interconnection means they are frequently used interchangeably and causally connected.

References

Amy-Chinn, D. (2011). Doing epistemic (in)justice to Semenya. *International Journal of Media & Cultural Politics, 6,* 311–326.

Angelini, J.R., Billings, A.C., MacArthur, P.J., Bissell, K., & Smith, L.R. (2014). Competing separately, medaling equally: Racial depictions of athletes in NBC's Primetime broadcast of the 2012 London Olympic Games. *The Howard Journal of Communications, 25,* 115–133.

Angelini, J.R., MacArthur, P.J., & Billings, A.C. (2012). What's the gendered story? Vancouver's primetime Olympic glory on NBC. *Journal of Broadcasting & Electronic Media, 56*, 261–279.

Angelini, J.R., MacArthur, P.J., & Billings, A.C. (2014). Spiraling into or out of stereotypes? NBC's primetime coverage of male figure skaters at the 2010 Olympic Games. *Journal of Language & Social Psychology, 33*, 226–235.

Archer, E.M. (2013). The power of gendered stereotypes in the US Marine Corps. *Armed Forces & Society, 39*, 359–391.

Benatar, D. (2012). *The second sexism: Discrimination against men and boys.* Chichester, UK: Wiley-Blackwell.

Billings, A.C., Angelini, J.R., & Duke, A.H. (2010). Gendered profiles of Olympic history: Sportscaster dialogue in the 2008 Beijing Olympics. *Journal of Broadcasting & Electronic Media, 54*, 9–23.

Billings, A.C., Angelini, J.R., MacArthur, P.J., Bissell, K., Smith, L.R., & Brown, N.A. (2014). Where the gender differences really reside: The "big five" sports featured in NBC's 2012 London primetime Olympic broadcast. *Communication Research Reports, 31*(2), 141–153.

Bridel, W., & Rail, G. (2007). Sport, sexuality, and the production of (resistant) bodies: De-/Re-constructing the meanings of gay male marathon corporeality. *Sociology of Sport Journal, 24*, 127–144.

Butterworth, M.L. (2007). Race in "The Race": Mark McGwire, Sammy Sosa, and heroic constructions of whiteness. *Critical Studies in Media Communication, 24*, 228–244.

Caudwell, J. (1999). Women's football in the United Kingdom. *Journal of Sport and Social Issues, 23*, 390–402.

Christopherson, N., Janning, M., & McConnell, E.D. (2002). Two kicks forward, one kick back: A content analysis of media discourses on the 1999 Women's World Cup soccer championship. *Sociology of Sport Journal, 19*, 170–188.

Connell, R.W., & Messerschmidt, J.W. (2005). Hegemonic masculinity: Rethinking the concept. *Gender & Society, 19*, 829–859.

Coakley, J. (2006). The good father: Parental expectations and youth sports. *Leisure Studies, 25*, 153–263.

Cooky, C., Messner, M.A., & Hextrum, R.H. (2013). Women play sport, but not on TV: A longitudinal study of televised news media. *Communication & Sport, 1*, 203–230.

Cooky, C., Messner, M.A., & Musto, M. (2015). "It's dude time!": A quarter century of excluding women's sports in televised news and highlight shows. *Communication & Sport, 3*, 261–287.

Creedon, P. (2014). Women, social media, and sport: Global digital communication weaves a web. *Television & New Media, 15*, 711–716.

Dworkin, S.L., & Messner, M.A. (1999). Just do . . . what? Sport, bodies, gender. In M. Ferree, J. Lorber, & B. Hess (Eds.), *Revisioning gender.* Thousand Oaks, CA: Sage.

Fasting, K., & Pfister, G. (2000). Female and male coaches in the eyes of female elite soccer players. *European Physical Education Review, 6*, 91–110.

Fielding-Lloyd, B., & Meân, L.J. (2008). Standards and separatism: The discursive construction of gender in English football coach education. *Sex Roles, 58*, 24–39.

Fielding-Lloyd, B., & Meân, L.J. (2011). "I don't think I can catch it": Women, confidence and responsibility in football coach education. *Soccer and Society, 12*, 345–364.

Fielding-Lloyd, B., & Meân, L.J. (in press). Women training to coach a male sport: Managing gendered identities and masculinity discourses. *Journal of Sport & Communication.*

Foucault, M. (1972). *The archeology of knowledge.* London: Tavistock.

Genovese, J. (2015). Sports television reporters and the negotiation of fragmented professional identities. *Communication, Culture & Critique, 8*, 55–72.

Godoy-Pressland, A. (2014). "Nothing to report": A semi-longitudinal investigation of the print media coverage of sportswomen in British Sunday newspapers. *Media, Culture & Society, 36*, 595–609.

Greer, J.D., Hardin, M., & Homan, C. (2009). "Naturally" less exciting? Visual production of men's and women's track and field coverage during the 2004 Olympics. *Journal of Broadcasting & Electronic Media, 53*, 173–189.

Griffin, P. (2011). The paradox of being a sport feminist. A response to Cahn's "Testing sex, attributing gender: What Caster Semenya means to women's sports." *Journal of Intercollegiate Sport, 4*, 49–53.

Hall, M.A. (1988). The discourse of gender and sport: From femininity to feminism. *Sociology of Sport Journal, 5*, 330–340.

Hardin, M. (2005). Stopped at the gate: Women's sports, "reader interest," and decision making by editors. *Journalism & Mass Communication Quarterly, 82*, 62–77.

Hardin, M., Dodd, J.E., & Lauffer, K. (2009). Passing it on: The reinforcement of male hegemony in sports journalism textbooks. *Mass Communication & Society, 9*, 429–446.

Hardin, M., Simpson, S., Whiteside, E., & Garris, K. (2007). The gender war in U.S. sport: Winners and losers in news coverage of Title IX. *Mass Communication & Society, 10*, 211–233.

Hardin, M., & Whiteside, E. (2012). How do women talk sports? Women sports fans in a blog community. In K. Toffoletti & P. Mewett (Eds.), *Sport and its female fans* (pp. 152–168). New York: Routledge.

Harrington, M. (2006). Sport and leisure as contexts for fathering in Australian families. *Leisure Studies, 25*, 165–183.

Jhally, S. (1989). Cultural Studies and the sport/media complex. In L.A. Wenner (Ed.), *Sport, media and society* (pp. 70–93). Newbury Park, CA: Sage.

Jones, D. (2013). Online coverage of the 2008 Olympic Games on the ABC, BBC, CBC, and TVNZ. *Pacific Journalism Review, 19*, 244–263.

Kim, E., Walkosz, B.J., & Iverson, J. (2006). USA Today's coverage of the top women golfers, 1998–2001. *Howard Journal of Communications, 17*, 307–321.

Krane, V. (2001). We can be athletic and feminine, but do we want to? Challenging hegemonic femininity in women's sport. *Quest, 53*, 115–133.

Knoppers, A. (1989). Coaching: An equal opportunity occupation? *Journal of Physical Education, Recreation and Dance, 60*, 38–43.

Knoppers, A. (1992). Explaining male dominance and sex segregation in coaching: Three approaches. *Quest, 44*, 210–227.

Knoppers, A., & Anthonissen. A. (2008). Gendered managerial discourses in sport organizations: Multiplicity and complexity. *Sex Roles, 58*, 93–103.

Leonard, D.J. (2010). Jumping the gun: Sporting cultures and the criminalization of Black masculinity. *Journal of Sport and Social Issues, 34*, 252–262.

Malcom, N.L. (2006). "Shaking it off" and "toughing it out" socialization to pain and injury in girls' softball. *Journal of Contemporary Ethnography, 35*, 495–525.

Meân, L.J. (2001). Identity and discursive practice: Doing gender on the football pitch. *Discourse & Society, 12*(6), 789–815.

Meân, L.J. (2010). Making masculinity and framing femininity: FIFA, soccer and World Cup websites. In H. Hundley & A. Billings (Eds.), *Examining identity in sports media* (pp. 65–86). Thousand Oaks, CA: Sage Publications.

Meân, L.J. (2011). Sport, identities, and consumption: The construction of sport at ESPN.com. In A.C. Billings (Ed.), *Sports media: Transformation, integration, consumption* (pp. 162–180). London/New York: Routledge.

Meân, L.J. (2015). The 99ers: Celebrating the mythological. *Journal of Sports Media, 10,* 31–43.

Meân, L.J., & Kassing, J. (2008) "I would just like to be known as an athlete": Managing hegemony, femininity, and heterosexuality in female sport. *Western Journal of Communication, 72,* 126–144.

Messner, M.A. (1988). Sports and male domination: The female athlete as contested ideological terrain. *Sociology of Sport Journal, 5,* 197–211.

Messner, M.A. (1990). When bodies are weapons: Masculinity and violence in sport. *International Review for the Sociology of Sport, 25,* 203–220.

Mewett, P., & Toffoletti, K. (2011). Finding footy: Female fan socialization and Australian rules football. *Sport in Society, 14,* 553–568.

Miller, S.A. (2010). Making the boys cry: The performative dimensions of fluid gender. *Text & Performance Quarterly, 30,* 163–182.

Oates, T.P. (2007). The erotic gaze in the NFL Draft. *Communication & Critical/Cultural Studies, 4,* 74–90.

Oates, T.P. (2009). New media and the repackaging of NFL fandom. *Sociology of Sport Journal, 26,* 31–49.

Oates, T.P. (2012). Representing the audience: The gendered politics of sport media. *Feminist Media Studies, 12*(4), 603–607.

Pappas, N.T., McKenry, P.C., & Catlett, B.S. (2004). Athlete aggression on the rink and off the ice. *Men & Masculinities, 6,* 291–313.

Plymire, D., & Forman, P. (2000). Breaking the silence: Lesbian fans, the internet, and the sexual politics of women's sport. *International Journal of Sexuality & Gender, 5,* 141–153.

Potter, J. (1996). *Representing reality: Discourse, rhetoric and social construction.* London: Sage.

Scherer, J. (2007). Globalization, promotional culture and the production/consumption of online games: Emerging Adidas's "Beat Rugby" campaign. *New Media & Society, 9,* 475–496.

Sloop, J.M. (2005). Riding in cars between men. *Communication & Critical/Cultural Studies, 2,* 191–213.

Sloop, J.M. (2012). "This is not natural": Caster Semenya's gender threats. *Critical Studies in Media Communication, 29,* 81–96.

Speer, S.A. (2002). Sexist talk: Gender categories, participants' orientations and irony. *Journal of Sociolinguistics, 6,* 347–377.

Sullivan, P. (2004). Communication differences between male and female team sport athletes. *Communication Reports, 17,* 121–128.

Theberge, N. (2008). Just a normal bad part of what I do: Elite athletes' accounts of the relationship between sport participation and health. *Sociology of Sport Journal, 25,* 206–222.

Theberge, N. (2012). Studying gender and injuries: A comparative analysis of the literatures on women's injuries in sport and work. *Ergonomics, 55,* 183–193.

Thompson, C.J., & Üstüner, T. (2015). Women skating on the edge: Marketplace performances as ideological edgework. *Journal of Consumer Research, 42,* 235–265.

Thorpe, H. (2008). Foucault, technologies of self, and the media discourses of femininity in snowboarding culture. *Journal of Sport and Social Issues, 32,* 199–229.

Thorpe, H. (2010). Bourdieu, gender reflexivity, and physical culture: A case of masculinities in the snowboarding field. *Journal of Sport and Social Issues, 34*, 176–214.

Toffoletti, K., & Mewett, P. (2012). "Oh yes, he is hot": Female football fans and the sexual objectification of sportsmen's bodies. In K. Toffoletti & P. Mewett (Eds.), *Sport and its female fans* (pp. 99–114). New York: Routledge.

Wellard, I. (2002). Men, sport, body performance and the maintenance of "exclusive masculinity". *Leisure Studies, 21*, 235–247.

Wenner, L.A. (1991). One part alcohol, one part sport, one part dirt, stir gently: Beer commercial and television sports. In L.R. Vande Berg & L.A. Wenner (Eds.), *Television criticism: Approaches and applications.* New York: Longman.

Wenner, L.A. (2014). On the limits of the new and the lasting power of the mediasport interpellation. *Television & New Media, 15*, 732–740.

Whannel, G. (2000). Sport and the media. In J. Coakley & E. Dunning (Eds.), *Handbook of Sport Studies* (pp. 291–308). London/Thousand Oaks, CA: Sage.

Wolter, S. (2014). "It just makes good business sense": A media political economy analysis of espnW. *Journal of Sports Media, 9*, 73–96.

Wolter, S. (2015). A quantitative analysis of photographs and articles on espnW: Positive progress for female athletes. *Communication & Sport, 3*, 168–195.

Young, K., & White, P. (1995). Sport, physical danger, and injury: The experiences of elite women athletes. *Journal of Sport & Social Issues, 19*, 45–61.

Young, S.L. (2015). Running like a man, sitting like a girl: Visual enthymeme and the case of Caster Semenya. *Women's Studies in Communication, 38*, 331–350.

7

SPORT AND RACE

A Disciplinary History and Exhortation

Abraham I. Khan

PENNSYLVANIA STATE UNIVERSITY

For sociologists, the study of sport left the 'toy department' in 1973. Such bold periodization is risky historiography, but 1973 marked the publication of what now amounts to a founding document. For sport's close observers, Harry Edwards might be best known for his role in the Olympic Project for Human Rights (OPHR), the organization that took shape in 1967 and helped to institutionalize the 1968 protests in Mexico City. Edwards wrote *Revolt of the Black Athlete* in 1969, an account of those events so dense with poetic insight that it reads today like a manifesto. Four years later, Edwards would write *Sociology of Sport* (1973), "the first monograph to seriously analyse the role of sport in America, and sports' interconnection and influence on other societal institutions" (Wiggins, 2014, p. 764). The *American Journal of Sociology* reviewed Edwards's text in 1974, affirming that "sport touches all institutions and strata in American Society and, because of its pervasiveness, is appropriate for sociological investigation" (Snyder, 1974, p. 280). In a comprehensive study of the OPHR, Douglas Hartmann (2003) calls *Sociology of Sport* "widely used and frequently cited in academia" owing to its critique of "the prevailing ideology that sport was a separate and sacred social space and moral force in the United States" (p. 204).

I begin with Harry Edwards for two reasons. First, I hope to remind communication scholars that the academic study of sport boasts a history now in its sixth decade. The most acute anxieties about sport's legitimacy as an object of inquiry may have abated, but as communication studies wrestles with sport's arrival, we often miss that we are, in fact, the progeny of cognate fields within which we patiently gestated. Second, I want to draw attention to the depth of sport scholarship's racialized genealogy. Edwards's signature insight was that sport, in contrast to its image as an apolitical haven for American meri-tocracy, reflects and reproduces the social contexts in which it is situated. For Edwards, this was an insight derived not simply from scholarly reflection, but also from his experiences as a black athlete in the 1960s, as an activist, as the philosopher-in-residence of a social movement presenting itself, quite delib-erately, as radicalized. "America's response to what the black athlete is saying and doing," Edwards proclaimed in 1969, "will affect all racial and social relations between blacks and whites in this country" (p. xvii). He may have overreached, but perhaps no better motivation could be found to authorize the study of sport in the subsequent decades. It is worth remembering that our field, sport communication, owes its existence (at least in part) to this legacy of black radicalism; an abiding concern for the entailments of racial difference is in sport communication's academic DNA. Edwards came to understand the interface of sport and society through his racial identity, and while those among us today may study different dimensions of that interface, Edwards's accent is audible in our concern for power, ideology, representation, and the other axes of identity, such as gender and sexuality, with which sport is bound up. Both delivering rewards and imposing obligations, Edwards's accent has helped to position communication at the forefront of the schol-arly study of sport. In its popularity, its mass mediation, and its generative relation to national cultures and imagined communities some 40 years after Edwards's seminal text, sport is much more than a microcosm of society; it is an expressive force, shaping the contours of social and public life in complex communicative processes.

The History

In the 21st century, the field of scholarship marked by the specific relation of race to sport has become thoroughly interdisciplinary. Everyone who arrives here takes a slightly different path, but my formative experiences included Susan Birrell and Mary McDonald's *Reading Sport* (2000), which, in addition to Nick Trujillo's widely beloved essay on Nolan Ryan (1991), contains Leola Johnson and David Roediger's piece on O.J. Simpson's shifting racial identity and David Andrews's impressively detailed work on the erasure of Michael Jordan's blackness. In those essays alone, the study of race in sport drew on intellectual resources from fields as diverse as American studies and kinesiology, in addition to communication, in offering "points of access to the constitutive meanings and power relations of the larger world we inhabit" (Birrell & McDonald, 2000, p. 3). Around the same time, I encountered Todd Boyd and Kenneth Shropshire's (2000) *Basketball Jones*, an anthology at the forefront of attempts to make sense of the NBA's vexing articulation of sport and race to global capitalism. I was pleased as a graduate student to find Davis Houck's "Attacking the Rim: The Cultural Politics of Dunking" in its table of contents because it meant that rhetorical scholars could talk about sport without embarrassment, but the volume was an interdisciplinary marvel, drawing on scholarship in law, education, sociology, economics, and English literature. A few years later came David Wiggins and Patrick Miller's *Sport and the Color Line* (2004). And a few years after that came Michael Lomax's *Sports and the Racial Divide* (2008), which examines African-American experiences alongside those of Latinos in an attempt to "explore the intersections among race, ethnicity, and sport" (p. xv). I mention these works not only to highlight the interdisciplinary nature of inquiry into race and sport, but also to illuminate the concordant rationales through which race and ethnicity have become touchstones for sport communication scholars in the US.

Cultural studies and the critical epistemologies with which it is often associated have played an important role in these developments. Andrews's (2000) essay on Jordan, for example, marshals the cultural studies all-star team (Paul Gilroy, Kobena Mercer, Stuart Hall, among others) to the task of providing a "contextual interpretation of the dominant racial discourses that have fashioned the mediated icon, Michael Jordan, in accordance with the shifting imperatives of the reactionary post-Reaganite cultural agenda" (p. 167). In the late 1990s and early 2000s, Walter LaFeber's (1999) *Michael Jordan and the New Global Capitalism* served as an excellent companion piece to Andrews's essay. LaFeber places Jordan within the historical context of imperialism, "including the rise of what has come to be known as cultural imperialism" (p. 13), so that we might come to see how race and sport are deployed as instruments of geopolitical influence. Recent scholarship, especially that which studies sport in a post-colonial global context, has made consequential use of the cultural studies tradition. In particular, the work of Kevin Hylton (2009) and Ben Carrington (2009, 2010) applies critical race theory, postcolonialism, and British cultural studies to account for the emergence of "the black athlete," a figure whose invention "was (and remains) an attempt to reduce blackness itself and black people in general into a semi-humanized category of radical otherness" (Carrington, 2010, p. 2). I am inclined to say that this globalized reckoning of race and sport sets the edge (to borrow a football metaphor) for contemporary scholarship, and that communication studies would be wise to follow its blockers around the corner. Be that as it may, I bracket the turn to the global here because the interrelationship of race and sport assumes sociopolitical forms in the U.S. context that we have yet to fully unpack. As Michael Ezra (2010) puts it, "sports provide a unique canvas for people to paint their version of an ideal America" (p. 185), and there is still much to be learned about what those canvases, like paintings covering a stain on the wallpaper, tend to hide.

Edwards's revolution, for example, never fully materialized. As if to confirm the main thesis of *Sociology of Sport*, the 1970s in sport were defined by the same kind of fraught racial negotiations characteristic of Nixon's America. Hartmann (2003) argues that challenges represented by the OPHR were met with "racial practices and policies to absorb or incorporate the more moderate and publicly legitimate aspects of African American athletic activism" (p. 207). However, by the 1980s, the ideology of racism that had simply murmured beneath the surface of economic accommodation and institutional reform would return with crass vengeance in public discourse. In 1975, Frank Robinson had become Major League Baseball's first black manager, but on April 6, 1986, *Nightline* wondered why greater progress since then had not been made. Los Angeles Dodger General Manager Al Campanis guessed that it was because black ballplayers "may not have some of the necessities to be a field manager." Pressed by Ted Koppel, Campanis resorted to rhetorical questions, "how many quarterbacks to you have? How many pitchers do you have that are black?" as if cognitive inferiority was simply self-evident in blackness (Weinbaum, 2012). Less than a year later, Jimmy "the Greek" Snyder appeared on a televised news broadcast expressing a dubious theory about black athletic superiority. "The black is a better athlete," Snyder explained, owing to "big thighs that goes up into his back," and "the slave owner" who "would breed his big black to his big woman so that he could have a big black kid" (Sharbutt, 1988). In case any mystery remained about how this white racial anxiety linked to Campanis's astonishing racism, Snyder made matters explicit: if blacks "take over coaching jobs, like everybody wants them to, there's not going to be anything left for white people." Both Campanis and Snyder were fired from their respective jobs within days of their comments, but taken together they disclosed the new character of white backlash.

Mike Marqusee (1999) writes that in place of old myths about white athletic superiority (perhaps undermined finally by Jesse Owens in 1936), the 20th century gave way to "the equally insidious myth of black physical superiority—with its unspoken concomitant, black intellectual ineptitude" (p. 295). Provoked in part by Richard Herrnstein and Charles Murray's (1994) notorious *The Bell Curve*, which purported to discover scientific proof that intelligence is a genetic trait, scholarship in race and sport would take up the problems associated with racial mythology. In this regard, John Hoberman's (1997) *Darwin's Athletes* stands as a landmark work from which many communication scholars would adopt stances. "Ideas about the 'natural' physical talents of dark-skinned peoples, and the media generated images that sustain them," Hoberman lamented, "probably do more than anything else in our public life to encourage the idea that blacks and white are biologically different in any meaningful way" (p. xxvii). Drawing on a staggering array of social and scientific histories from colonialism to genetics, Hoberman attempted to undo America's "racial folklore" and undermine the assumptions that underwrite sport's illusory promise of black socioeconomic mobility. Of course, a rejoinder would come in the form of journalist John Entine's (2000) *Taboo: Why Black Athletes Dominate Sports and Why We're Afraid to Talk About It*, but after *Darwin's Athletes*, the racialized "mind-body dualism that has dominated popular racial discourse related to males of African descent" (Andrews, 2000, p. 169) faced a powerful resource with which it might be critiqued.

The enduring importance of Hoberman's work consists in historicizing race and in situating it within shifting sociopolitical terrain. The error made by Entine (and others who rely on the human sciences to prove racial difference) is to rely on categories whose apparent stability creates the impression of neutrality and disinterest. But the way science both conditions and authorizes patterns in social life is neither neutral nor disinterested. Entine (2000) claims that "respecting human differences enhances the possibility that we can constructively, but critically confront the breathtaking changes genetics is spurring" (p. xiv). Fair enough, but the crucial worry is that sport repeats in 21st-century form the recommendations of 19th-century polygenist Louis Agassiz, who in 1850 declared:

> human affairs with reference to the colored races would be far more judiciously conducted if [. . .] guided by a full consciousness of the real difference existing between us and them, and a desire to foster those dispositions that are eminently marked in them, rather than by treating them on terms of equality.
>
> *(quoted in Gould, 1996, p. 145)*

Or, as Gould insightfully paraphrases: "train blacks in hand work, whites in mind work" (p. 145). Both 'human difference' and the kind of 'respect' it is owed are subject to the whims of the social form and its prevailing discourses. In the 19th century, scientific respect for human difference buttressed the institution of slavery. Today, perhaps, the same assumptions buttress the institution of sport.

To situate race historically is to render it contingent, a goal commonly expressed in the axiom that "race is a social construction." Some version of this axiom now works as a backdrop against which nearly all communication research on race operates. Recognizing race's synthetic character is not, however, the same as saying that race and racism aren't 'real.' As Angela Davis (2012) reminds us, "it would be erroneous to assume that we can willfully extricate ourselves from histories of race and racism. Whether we acknowledge it or not, we continue to inhabit these histories, which help to constitute our social and psychic worlds" (p. 169). Race, in short, continues to *mean* something, to figure into our present, and it must continually be *made* to mean something. Though not a media scholar, Hoberman remained keen to the power of mediated imagery. Sport, he argued, "has become an image factory that disseminates and even intensifies our racial preoccupations" (1997, p. xxviii). And this is where, in both empiricist and critical modes, communication scholarship on sport and race does its most prolific work. Mass mediation, put simply, shapes the meaning of racial identity in ways that often reinforce commonly held stereotypes, particularly those that resonate with the echoes of the racialized mind/body dualism. The phenomenon known as 'stacking,' which "relates to the placement of people in roles that closely fit societal expectations of identity groups," works as an important example of this kind of communication scholarship (Billings, Butterworth, & Turman, 2015, p. 150). When black athletes disproportionately play certain positions in football (such as running back), or Latino athletes disproportionately play certain positions in baseball (such as shortstop), or even when white commentators are disproportionately assigned to cover certain sports (such as golf or tennis), sport's mass mediation pushes familiar stereotypes along. Communication scholars have become adept at mapping the social construction of race in American culture, establishing what Lawrence Wenner (2015) calls the "glue" that holds "the Media, Sports, and Society disposition" together (p. 251).

Exactly to what origin we might trace this line of inquiry is unclear, but among a handful of key citations is Eastman and Billings's (2001) analysis of college basketball coverage. Armed with framing theory and the diligence necessary for careful content analysis, they examined college basketball telecasts on five national networks during "peak basketball season" (p. 189). Their findings revealed "embedded stereotypes," which "consistently reinforced the formulaic notion that Blacks are naturally athletic, while Whites are less so and thus need to work especially hard to keep up," reinforcing "the unfortunate notion that Whites have more mental ability and leadership qualities, while Blacks lack those characteristics" (p. 198). That studies like these (and findings like these) constitute the core of communication scholarship in sport is clear in both the variety of sports to which such inquiry is applied and in its traversal of the transmission model of communication. That is to say, communication researchers have studied mediated racial stereotypes in the Olympics (Daddario & Wigley, 2007), in baseball (Ferucci, Tandoc, Painter, & Leshner, 2013), in college football (Billings, 2004), in professional football (Mercurio & Filak, 2010), in relation to football coaches (Cunningham & Bopp, 2010), and from the perspective of both the announcers who might express racial stereotypes (Cranmer, Bowman, Chory, & Weber, 2014) and the audiences positioned to receive them (Kobach & Potter, 2013). In the context of this media studies tradition, the racialized mind/body dualism has acquired the terminological shorthand "brawn vs. brains" (Rada & Wulfemeyer, 2005, p. 67), which continues to have considerable explanatory force.

Because of its unique relationship (real or perceived) to the 'brains' side of the binary, the quarterback has been the subject of frequent scholarly scrutiny along these lines. In the last decade or so, there is reason to believe that routine stereotypes associated with black and white quarterbacks have abated. Billings (2004) surmises that "the fact that White and Black quarterbacks were not found to be described in markedly different ways in the large majority of categories should indicate progress." And wondering if stereotypical coverage of black athletes is "dead as disco," Byrd and Ustler (2007) examine print media, specifically *Sports Illustrated*, finding reason to think that "media have become more sensitive to racialized portrayals of athletes," and that media portrayals of quarterbacks have "nothing to do with pigmentation and everything to do with performance" (pp. 21, 23). These empiricist projects notwithstanding, worry about the brains vs. brawn binary remains, especially considering the dearth of black quarterbacks relative to other positions in professional football. Luke

Winslow (2014) combines critical sociology drawn from Carrington (2010) with insights derived from social psychology to evince a "widely held explanation for why black men tend to dominate sports that require speed, coordination, jumping ability, quick instincts, and reaction time" (p. 35). Winslow is not interested in moderating culture's debate with science, but prefers to concede that "the validity of the myth matters less than its presence" (p. 32). It is difficult to discern from all this precisely what we know about racial stereotypes in sport, other than that they are there and that they are worrisome. Scholarship in communication and sport would be wise to consider this problem further, especially as it elucidates the manner in which race continues to circumscribe access to reason, embodiment, and even humanity itself.

Perhaps the limit of the brawn vs. brains debate, whether measured empirically or theorized critically, consists in overlooking the subject position that surreptitiously moves racialized identities to the margins of society and politics. Since its emergence through critical race theory in the work of scholars such as David Roediger (1991), Ruth Frankenburg (1993), Richard Dyer (1997), and George Lipsitz (1995), whiteness studies has acquired considerable disciplinary traction in communication, particularly in critical rhetoric (Nakayama & Krizek, 1995; Crenshaw, 1997; Shome, 2000). Any attempt to reduce whiteness studies to a single line of inquiry is bound to fail, but from a broad perspective, it works to reveal "the structural and discursive machinations responsible for the implicit, yet unspoken, location of whiteness as the normative racial center of American culture and society" (Andrews, 2012, p. 158). It refigures 'bias' and 'stereotypes' as the entrenchment of white supremacy, attuning scholarship to the strategies by which whiteness both goes unmarked and retains the privilege to mark the 'otherness' of racialized subjects. Andrews (2012) points out that sport studies scholars have "vanguarded the recognition of, and engagement with, whiteness as a subjectivity at the epicenter of power relations within modern society" (p. 158). It is surprising that sport communication scholars have not marshaled whiteness studies to greater effect in understanding the exclusionary discourses at work in coaching, quarterbacking, and other contexts (like playing point guard) in which whiteness seems to inscribe the locus of sporting intellection. Having said that, Andrews is right to identify sport communication as a vanguard of whiteness studies, particularly in relation to mass mediation. Michael Butterworth (2007) identifies the operation of whiteness in the way media framed baseball's home run race in 1996, a number of scholars (Vavrus, 2007; Newman & Beissel, 2009) see whiteness as crucial to understanding NASCAR's production of southern masculinity, and Davie, King, and Leonard (2010) find whiteness lurking within media characterizations of Tiger Woods's infidelity scandal in 2009.

Even if it does nothing else, whiteness studies alerts us to a variety of ways in which sport fits into and helps organize a racial order constituted by identities that are often unintelligible within prevailing racial frames. Woods is instructive in this regard. Houck (2006) writes that since his arrival in the American consciousness, "Tiger Woods has been a carefully packaged, a meticulously choreographed mediated representation" (p. 508). Woods, we are reminded, once described himself as 'Cablinasian,' a neologism derived from Caucasian, black, Indian, and Asian. Whereas this confounding multiraciality once offered the promise of political transcendence, Woods's career (at least until the scandal) followed the arc established by Michael Jordan, where transcendence entailed acclimation to the race-effacing demands of corporate sponsorship. From a much different angle, but with a dovetailing conclusion, Billings (2003) conducts a content analysis of Woods's media portrayals in an attempt to come to grips with "differences in characterizations between Tiger Woods and other White golfers as well as determine how depictions of Tiger Woods reinforce or redefine characterizations of Black athletes" (p. 30). Billings attends to the fact that Woods is often perceived as a black athlete in a white sport, and finds that Woods's "partial" blackness cuts both ways; when Woods won, racial stereotypes were largely absent from coverage, but when he played poorly, "Woods was often portrayed as being entirely Black" (p. 36). Despite the transgressive appeal incipient in Woods's multiracial identity, corporate discourses and media frames find ways to delimit his meaning within the familiar confines of black and white.

The black/white binary for making sense of American sport is perhaps nowhere more pronounced than in basketball. From the Magic Johnson-Larry Bird rivalry of the 1980s to the vilification of Allen Iverson in the 2000s, basketball has long served as a stage for American racial theater. Entire books can be written on this topic—in fact, entire books *have* been written (Boyd, 2003)—so I cannot summarize it here. Instead, I want to point to the racialized context in which Jeremy Lin found himself, and which he complicated, upon his fleeting rise to superstardom with the New York Knicks in 2012. Lin's story is piquant for communication scholars concerned with the relationship between race and sport. Not only does 'Linsanity' complicate basketball's black/white frame, but it also raises questions regarding sport's regard for Asian identity, urges a consideration of race's intersection with other dimensions of subjectivity, and incites a turn to the global for making proper sense of racialization as an ongoing (post)colonial project. Noticing the dearth of sport scholarship on the range of American racial identities, Andrews (2012) reports "anticipation for the hopefully forthcoming deluge of racial/ethnic deconstructions of Jeremy Lin" (p. 158). Though 'deluge' might overstate present conditions, sport communication scholars have certainly caught on. With a story about whiteness lingering in the background, Kathleen McElroy (2014) uses media frame analysis, Gramscian theories of hegemony, and 'racial triangulation' in an analysis of commentary across multiple media. McElroy found "four frames—Lin as an oddity and underdog, a reminder of racism, an agent of change, and as an antidote to Blackness—that pitted Asian Americans against Blacks fighting for position under mainstream America's rim" (p. 446). Where McElroy finds the intersection of Asianness and blackness in media coverage, Michael Park (2014) finds the intersection of Asianness and masculinity. Lin, says Park, contravened cultural expectations regarding the athletic abilities of Asian men, and as an exception, mobilized representations that work to strip them of the masculinity still required to find an unmarked place in American sport.

Clearly, intersectionality scholarship (beginning primarily with Collins, 1990) ought to have something to say about Linsanity and other situations that not only resist comprehension in black and white, but also articulate sport's commitments to prevailing orders of gender, sexuality, and class. How else to come to terms with gendered anxieties regarding Serena Williams's body, or racialized anxieties regarding the presence of Michael Sam in an NFL locker room, or the gendered triumphalism embedded in nationalist narratives about Chinese tennis player Li Na, or the persistence of 'hoop dreams' that remain a mainstay for celebrating the anomalous financial achievements of African-American athletes? Obviously, there are productive ways to address these questions without reference to intersectionality, but apart from a handful of projects (i.e., Anderson & McCormack, 2010), occurring outside of our field, intersectionality remains undertheorized and underutilized in sport communication. We have become adept at tracking the evolution and movement of racial stereotypes, and even better at celebrating (or urging the celebration of) racial difference, but we have some yards to go before we even reach mid-field on the ways in which race figures into the vast array of standpoints, locations, and criss-crossing power relations in American society.

The Exhortation

I am tempted to leave things as they are, noting that the study of race and sport in communication is swimming along nicely, particularly as it is done in media studies, even if there are clearly new things to be learned. However, I am nagged to redress an omission—one that I take a bit personally. To wit, a quick story: Before my book, *Curt Flood in the Media*, was published in 2012, I had some thoughtful negotiations with the publisher over the title. New to this sort of thing, I had wanted to call it "Baseball in the Black Public Sphere," the title I gave proudly to the doctoral dissertation from which its main ideas were derived. University presses, it turns out, actually *are* worried about book sales, and gently insisted that the word 'media' would help its marketing. I wasn't exactly seeing dollar signs, but the rationale was convincing. Still, I worried that the word 'media' in the title would lead (potential) readers to locate my work in a media studies tradition of which I never considered myself a part. I am a *rhetorical critic*, I said to myself, not a media scholar. Last I checked, the book has yet to crack the *New York Times* bestseller list, but as I reflect at this short distance, I am grateful to be associated with the media tradition in sport and race, even as I still see myself as a rhetorical critic, and even as I remain hopeful that more rhetorical scholars will endeavor to study sport. Yes, work on race and sport in communication lends itself to the facts of its mass mediation, and, like I did, rhetorical critics must rely on mediated texts to find things to critique. Be that as it may, rhetorical scholarship defines its object domain in ways from which the study of race and sport would benefit, and the historical development of the interface of society and sport contains texts, images, and events that rhetorical critics are bound to find provocative.

By way of example, at the same time rhetorical studies was complicating its own understanding of racialized speech—most notably in the late 1960s and early 1970s when Robert L. Scott and Donald K. Smith were theorizing confrontational rhetoric (1969) and black power—Harry Edwards had declared in *Revolt* (1969) that "the black athlete has left the facade of locker room equality and justice to take his long vacant place as a primary participant in the black revolution" (p. xvi). Scott and Brockriede (1969) had, in fact, theorized black power as "a revolutionary force in American life" (p. 1), yet among their analyses of Martin Luther King and Stokely Carmichael, nary a reference to Edwards or the OPHR can be found. I do not mean to fault Scott and Brockriede for their choices; Carmichael, after all, is the rhetorical inventor of 'black power.' Moreover, as scholars like Hartmann (2003) and Amy Bass (2002) are quick to remind us, the OPHR explicitly distanced itself from black power's most extreme connotations. Yet, in a context producing one of the most memorable images in American history, the public address accompanying John Carlos and Tommie Smith's black-gloved fists occupies little but a void in rhetorical scholarship. Michael Ezra (2010) contends that understanding race and sport in relation to the 'symbolic' is a "sucker bet that fails at giving us insightful conclusions" (p. 190). Ezra sees the 'the symbolic' as inaptly connected to a banal progress narrative "in a post-civil-rights era that can no longer identify integrative firsts as the measure" (p. 190). Since Scott and Brockriede in the late 1960s, to social movement rhetoric in the 1970s to critical rhetoric in the 1980s, and even including the materialist turns taken in the 2000s, challenging the limits of grand progress narratives has been a central preoccupation for scholars in rhetoric and public address.

My gesture toward 'public address' is intentional, since situating rhetorical discourse within theories of the public sphere has also been a preoccupation, especially for scholars whose work is guided by Habermasian debates (see the citational webs spun by Calhoun, 1992, for example). Robert Asen and Daniel Brouwer (2001) along with Michael Warner (2002) and Catherine Squires (2002), have moved these debates along, helping us to theorize publics and counterpublics, recognize how public discourse circulates, notice the exclusions contained in the idea of the public, and reconsider our understanding of democratic deliberation. Scholars pursuing these lines of inquiry would be wise to pay attention to what Charles Korr, baseball's definitive labor historian, is up to these days. A few years ago, Korr (Korr & Close, 2008) found himself on Robben

Island, South Africa's infamous political prison during apartheid. By a stroke of amazing happenstance, he stumbled into a room containing the archival papers of the Makana Football Association, a soccer league formed in the 1960s by many of the very people who would come to occupy South Africa's first democratic government in 1994. For example, Dikgang Moseneke, who was until recently the Chief Justice of South Africa, was appointed the first Makana FA chairman. There are three surprises here: First, that the prisoners managed to form such a league at all, given their brutally repressive circumstances. Second, that the papers Korr discovered were truly voluminous. Korr described it as reminiscent of the final scene from *Raiders of the Lost Ark*, where boxes appear in endless rows. Third, that the league kept such meticulous records of league rules, game scores, league standings, and even the arbitration of grievances, in an explicit, self-conscious attempt to *practice the democracy they believed they would one day inherit*. Korr rightly frames this as a testament to sport's ability to manufacture hope from despair, but consider the possibilities for rhetorical scholarship and public sphere theory: from within the cauldron of modern racism's most violent expression of colonialist repression emerged a theory of public deliberation enacted in the texts produced by the very individuals who would come to govern South Africa and abolish apartheid.

So, yes, I exhort rhetorical scholars to take a closer look at sport. Funding for travel to South Africa does not come easy, but Korr's remarkable story is surely not the only one worth our finding. One wonders about the rhetorical circumstances of Jackie Robinson's testimony to the House Un-American Activities Committee in 1949, or what was at stake for Jesse Owens in the tortured color-blind wish that is his 1970 book *Blackthink*. If history fails to deliver its own rewards, rhetorical scholars might consider how the symbolic action of athletes like LeBron James and Derrick Rose lend public presence to the increasing urgency to insist that #blacklivesmatter. For my own part, I am thinking about how to track the movement of slavery as trope from Curt Flood to college athletes, who as we all know work without wages. A promising book by a kinesiologist, Billy Hawkins's *The New Plantation* (2010), just arrived in the mail.

References

Anderson, E., & McCormack, M. (2010). Intersectionality, critical race theory, and American sporting oppression: Examining black and gay male athletes. *Journal of Homosexuality, 57*(8), 949–967.

Andrews, D. (2000). Excavating Michael Jordan's blackness. In S. Birrell & M. McDonald (Eds.), *Reading sport: Critical essays on power and representation* (pp. 166–205). Boston, MA: Northeastern University Press.

Andrews, D. (2012). Reflections on communication and sport: On celebrity and race. *Communication & Sport, 1*(1/2), 151–163.

Asen, R., & Brouwer, D. (2001). *Counterpublics and the state.* Albany, NY: SUNY Press.

Bass, A. (2002). *Not the triumph but the struggle: The 1968 Olympics and the making of the black athlete*. Minneapolis, MN: University of Minnesota Press.

Billings, A.C. (2003). Portraying Tiger Woods: Characterizations of a "black" athlete in a "white" sport. *Howard Journal of Communications, 14*(1), 29–37.

Billings, A.C. (2004). Depicting the quarterback in black and white: A content analysis of college and professional football broadcast commentary. *Howard Journal of Communications, 15*, 201–210.

Billings, A.C., Butterworth, M.L., & Turman, P.D. (2015). *Communication and sport: Surveying the field* (2nd ed.). Los Angeles, CA: Sage.

Birrell, S., & McDonald, M. (Eds.). (2000). *Reading sport: Critical essays on power and representation*. Boston, MA: Northeastern University Press.

Boyd, T. (2003). *Young, black, rich, and famous*. New York: Doubleday.

Boyd, T., & Shropshire, K. (2000). *Basketball Jones: America above the rim*. New York: NYU Press.

Butterworth, M. (2007). Race in "the race": Mark McGwire, Sammy Sosa, and heroic constructions of whiteness. *Critical Studies in Media Communication, 24*(3), 228–244.

Byrd, J., & Ustler, M. (2007). Is stereotypical coverage of African-American athletes "dead as disco"?: An analysis of NFL quarterbacks in the pages of *Sports Illustrated*. *Journal of Sports Media, 2*, 1–28.

Calhoun, C. (Ed.). (1992). *Habermas and the public sphere*. Cambridge, MA: MIT Press.

Carrington, B. (2010). *Race, sport, and politics: The sporting black diaspora*. London: Sage.

Carrington, B., & McDonald, I. (Eds.). (2009). *Marxism, cultural studies, and sport*. New York: Routledge.

Collins, P.H. (1990). *Black feminist thought*. New York: Routledge.

Cranmer, G.A., Bowman, N.D., Chory, R.M., & Weber, K.D. (2014). Race as an antecedent condition in the framing of Heisman finalists. *Howard Journal of Communications, 25*(2), 171–191.

Crenshaw, C. (1997). Resisting whiteness' rhetorical silence. *Western Journal of Communication, 61*(3), 253–278.

Cunningham, G.B., & Bopp, T. (2010). Race ideology perpetuated: Media representations of newly hired football coaches. *Journal of Sports Media, 5*(1), 1–19.

Daddario, G., & Wigley, B.J. (2007). Gender marking and racial stereotyping at the 2004 Athens Games. *Journal of Sports Media, 2*, 29–51.

Davie, W.R., King, C.R., & Leonard, D.J. (2010). A media look at Tiger Woods: Two views. *Journal of Sports Media, 5*(2), 107–116.

Davis, A.Y. (2012). *The meaning of freedom*. San Francisco, CA: City Lights.

Dyer, R. (1997). *White*. London: Routledge.

Eastman, S.T., & Billings, A.C. (2001). Biased voices of sports: Racial and gender stereotyping in college basketball announcing. *Howard Journal of Communications, 12*(4), 183–201.

Edwards, H. (1969). *Revolt of the black athlete*. New York: Free Press.

Edwards, H. (1973). *Sociology of sport*. Homewood, IL: Dorsey Press.

Entine, J. (2000). *Taboo*. New York: PublicAffairs.

Ezra, M. (2010). Progress narratives, racism, and level playing fields: Recent academic literature on sports. *American Studies, 51*(3/4), 185–192.

Ferruci, P., Tandoc, E.C., Jr., Painter, C.E., & Leshner, G. (2013). A black and white game: Racial stereotypes in baseball. *Howard Journal of Communications, 24*(3), 309–325.

Frankenburg, R. (1993). *White women, race matters: The social construction of whiteness.* Minneapolis, MN: University of Minnesota Press.

Gould, S.J. (1996). *The Mismeasure of Man.* New York: Norton.

Hartmann, D. (2003). *Race, culture, and the revolt of the black athlete.* Chicago, IL: University of Chicago Press.

Hawkins, B. (2010). *The new plantation: Black athletes, college sports, and predominantly white NCAA institutions.* New York: Palgrave Macmillan.

Herrnstein, R., & Murray, C. (1994). *The bell curve: Intelligence and class structure in American life.* New York: Free Press.

Hoberman, J. (1997). *Darwin's athletes.* Boston, MA: Houghton Mifflin

Houck, D. (2000). Attacking the rim: The cultural politics of dunking. In T. Boyd & K. Shropshire (Eds.), *Basketball Jones: America above the rim.* New York: NYU Press.

Houck, D. (2006). Crouching Tiger, hidden blackness: Tiger Woods and the disappearance of race. In A. Raney & J. Bryant (Eds.), *Handbook of sports and media.* London: Taylor & Francis.

Hylton, K. (2009). *"Race" and sport: Critical race theory.* London: Routledge.

Khan, A.I. (2012). *Curt Flood in the media: Baseball, race, and the demise of the activist athlete.* Oxford, MS: University Press of Mississippi.

Kobach, M., & Potter, R.F. (2013). The role of mediated sports programming on implicit racial stereotypes. *Sport in Society, 16*(10), 1414–1428.

Korr, C.P., & Close, M. (2008). *More than just a game: Soccer vs. Apartheid.* New York: St. Martin's Press.

LaFeber, W. (1999). *Michael Jordan and the new global capitalism.* New York: Norton.

Lipsitz, G. (1995). The possessive investment in whiteness: Racialized social democracy and the "white" problem in American studies. *American Quarterly, 47*(3), 369–387.

Lomax, M. (Ed.). (2008). *Sports and the racial divide.* Jackson, MS: University Press of Mississippi.

Marqusee, M. (1999). *Redemption Song: Muhammad Ali and the spirit of the sixties.* London: Verso.

McElroy, K. (2014). Basket case: Framing the intersection of "Linsanity" and blackness. *Howard Journal of Communications, 25*(4), 431–451.

Mercurio, E., & Filak, V.F. (2010). Roughing the passer: The framing of black and white quarterbacks prior to the NFL draft. *Howard Journal of Communications, 21*(1), 56–71.

Nakayama, T.K., & Krizek, R.L. (1995). Whiteness: A strategic rhetoric. *Quarterly Journal of Speech, 81*(3), 291–309.

Newman, J., & Beissel, A.S. (2009). The limits to "NASCAR Nation": Sport and the "Recovery Movement" in disjunctural times. *Sociology of Sport Journal, 26*, 517–539.

Owens, J. (1970). *Blackthink: My life as a black man and white man.* New York: HarperCollins.

Park, M.K. (2014). Race, hegemonic masculinity, and the "Linpossible!": An analysis of media representations of Jeremy Lin. *Communication and Sport, 3*, 1–23.

Rada, J.A., & Wulfemeyer, K.T. (2005). Color coded: Racial descriptors in television coverage of intercollegiate sports. *Journal of Broadcasting & Electronic Media, 49*, 65–85.

Roediger, D. (1991). *The wages of whiteness.* New York: Verso.

Scott, R.L., & Brockriede, W. (1969). *The rhetoric of black power.* New York: Harper & Row.

Scott, R.L., & Smith, D.K. (1969). The rhetoric of confrontation. *Quarterly Journal of Speech, 55*(1), 1–8.

Sharbutt, J. (January 17, 1988). Jimmy 'the Greek' is fired by CBS. *Los Angeles Times*. Retrieved June 17, 2016, from http://articles.latimes.com/1988-01-17/sports/sp-36803_1_jimmy-snyder.

Shome, R. (2000). Outing whiteness. *Critical Studies in Media Communication, 17*(3), 366–371.

Snyder, E. (1974). [Review of the book *Sociology of Sport,* by Edwards, H.]. *American Journal of Sociology, 80*(1), 280–282.

Squires, C. (2002). Rethinking the Black public sphere: An alternative vocabulary for multiple public spheres. *Communication Theory, 12*(4), 446–468.

Trujillo, N. (1991). Hegemonic masculinity on the mound: Media representations of Nolan Ryan and American sports culture. *Critical Studies in Mass Communication, 8*(3), 290–308.

Vavrus, M.D. (2007). The politics of NASCAR dads: Branded media paternity. *Critical Studies in Media Communication, 24*(3), 245–261.

Warner, M. (2002). *Publics and counterpublics.* New York: Zone Press.

Weinbaum, W. (April 1, 2012). The legacy of Al Campanis. ESPN. Retrieved June 17, 2016, from http://espn.go.com/espn/otl/story/_/id/7751398/how-al-campanis-controversial-racial-remarks-cost-career-highlighted-mlb-hiring-practices.

Wenner, L. (2015). Communication and sport, where art thou? Epistemological reflections on the moment and field(s) of play. *Communication & Sport, 3*(3), 247–260.

Wiggins, D. (2014). "The struggle that must be": Harry Edwards, sport and the fight for racial equality. *International Journal of the History of Sport, 31*(7), 760–777.

Wiggins, D., & Miller, P. (Eds.). (2004). *Sport and the color line: Black athletes and race relations in 20th century America.* New York: Routledge.

Winslow, L. (2014). Brawn, brains, and the dearth of black NFL quarterbacks. In B. Brummet & A. Ishak (Eds.), *Sports and identity.* New York: Routledge.

8

SPORT AND LGBTQ ISSUES

Edward (Ted) M. Kian

OKLAHOMA STATE UNIVERSITY

The gay rights movement in the United States celebrated its landmark achievement in June 2015 when a U.S. Supreme Court ruling made same-sex marriage a legal right nationwide.

"No longer may this liberty be denied," Justice Anthony M. Kennedy wrote for the majority in the decision. "No union is more profound than marriage, for it embodies the highest ideals of love, fidelity, devotion, sacrifice and family. In forming a marital union, two people become something greater than once they were" (Liptak, 2015).

This judicial decision followed a decade of legal, legislative, and societal victories for sexual minorities in the US. Among those achievements were (a) the 2010 repeal of the U.S. military's "Don't Ask, Don't Tell" policy prohibiting gays and lesbians from openly serving in the armed services; (b) a majority of Americans supporting the right to same-sex marriage in every credible, national poll since 2012; (c) Barack Obama becoming the first sitting U.S. president to express support for same-sex marriage equality—which he did before easily winning re-election to a second term in 2012—and (d) 63% of Americans saying gay and lesbian relationships were morally acceptable by 2015 (McCarthy, 2014; Newport, 2015).

It is amazing that all of these changes occurred in roughly a decade. Former U.S. President George W. Bush's successful 2004 re-election campaign hinged largely upon his opposition of gay rights and calling for a constitutional amendment to permanently ban gay marriage, a then-prudent strategy based on a 2004 Gallup poll showing U.S. adults opposed gay marriage, 61%–32% (MSNBC.com, 2004).

Pop culture (e.g., television, movies, music) undoubtedly played a major part in the rapid acceptance of gays and lesbians in the United States. Gay characters in television sitcoms like *Will and Grace*, *Queer Eye for the Straight Guy*, and *Modern Family* helped communicate to viewers that gays and lesbians are normal people. Vice-President Joe Biden specifically stated that *Will and Grace* "had done more to educate the public" on gay issues than anything else (Collins & Blake, 2015).

However, the most popular professional and major-college men's team sports have provided few openly gay role models, and none who were household names, even among sport fans. In fact, it was not until 2014 that Jason Collins—previously a journeyman player only known to the most ardent NBA basketball fans—became the first openly gay athlete to compete in one of the United States' 'Big 4' professional men's team-sport leagues: Major League Baseball (MLB), National Basketball Association (NBA), National Football League, National Hockey League (NHL). Collins' self-outing in the spring of 2013 came while he was technically a member of the NBA's Washington Wizards. However, he had finished the 2012–13 season on the injured-reserve list and the Wizards' season was already over when he came out through a self-authored essay published initially on *SI.com* during the then-ongoing NBA playoffs and then later appearing as a cover story for the parent magazine, *Sports Illustrated*.

Nevertheless, an openly gay athlete in major professional American men's team sports was so overdue that Collins' public revelation drew public comments and praise from the likes of Obama, former U.S. President Bill Clinton, and numerous cultural icons from sport (e.g., past and present basketball superstars Kobe Bryant, Magic Johnson, and LeBron James, pro football Hall of Famer Barry Sanders), pop culture (e.g., talk-show host Oprah Winfrey, actor Charlie Sheen), and many other high-profile professions (Kian, Anderson, & Shipka, 2015).

The seven-foot Collins had spent the previous 12 seasons continuously on NBA rosters for multiple teams and expressed a desire to play again during the 2013–14 season following his coming-out. However, no franchise offered him a tryout until the Brooklyn Nets signed Collins to an initial 10-day contract in March 2014—nearly a full year after his announcement. Despite much optimism expressed following his announcement and that he did indeed play in the NBA again, Collins' experiences ultimately may encourage other closeted athletes to not come out during their playing careers.

Accordingly, despite many individual athletes expressing their support for gay rights and all major professional sport leagues in the United States enacting policies to prohibit discrimination against gays and lesbians because of their sexual orientation during the 21st century, the most popular men's team sports remain one part of pop culture that has not contributed much to the assimilation of gays and lesbians into mainstream American society over the past decade. Professional women's sports, in comparison, receive little media coverage, and thus open lesbians in those sports—who are still rare—do not raise as much attention as openly gay male athletes. More than likely, the culture of sport—particularly men's team sports—has instead helped to teach and reinforce masculine norms for boys and men throughout American society, among which are that heterosexuality is the standard and being gay is effeminate, deviant, or abnormal (Messner, 2002). Those norms, however, are increasingly being challenged more often—altered as society becomes more accepting of sexual minorities and their lifestyles (Anderson, 2009). But before discussing gay and lesbians in sport or the coverage of sexual minorities in sport media content, it is beneficial to first explain some key terms in this realm that are commonly used, but still often misunderstood.

Understanding LGBTQ

Surveys historically revealed that 1.5–8% of Americans self-identified as gay or lesbian (e.g., Indiana University Center for Sexual Health Promotion, 2010; Laumann, Gagnon, Michael, & Michaels, 1994), a much smaller number than the general public in the United States estimated in 2015, as they believed 23% of Americans are gay or lesbian (Newport, 2015). In addition to many gays and lesbians likely not openly admitting their orientation on anonymous surveys, another reason for the variance of these results is that a person's sexual orientation is never absolute. Gender identity and sexual desires are fluid over time, place, and with experiences—a prime tenet of Queer Theory (Diamond, 2015; Halberstam, 2005).

Most people identify as heterosexuals, including the majority of those who acknowledge having homosexual experiences with others (Laumann et al., 1994). Another reason why so many who have gay experiences or desires still identify as heterosexuals is the prevalence of *homophobia* (the fear and intolerance of gays and lesbians) and *biphobia* (an aversion toward bisexuality) that have historically existed throughout society, but especially in organized team sport (Griffin, 2012; Kian & Vincent, 2014).

Most people—including many academics—still incorrectly use the terms *sex* and *gender* synonymously. Gender, however, implies an identity that can be self-altered at any time, whereas one's sex is determined at birth and is usually only altered through medical procedures (Halberstam, 2005). The acronym LGBT (lesbian, gay, bisexual, and transgender) is commonly used to lump together all sexual minorities. In recent years, gay advocates have employed the acronym LGBTQ more often, adding the 'Q' for *queer* to include those who are *questioning* their sexual identity (Payne & Smith, 2012).

However, even more than bisexuals, the trans community (i.e., *transgender* and *transsexuals*) is more likely to be discriminated against and not accepted in society or sport by both heterosexuals and gays (Lucas-Carr & Krane, 2012). Transgender means that an individual's gender identity does not match their biological sex (Halberstam, 2005). Theoretically, one could change their transgender identity multiple times each day (e.g., dressing to work and exhibiting what are socially construed as masculine traits during the day, while crossdressing as a woman at night).

Transsexuals, in contrast, consistently identify with a gender opposite of their biological sex, with most undergoing medical procedures in efforts to alter their physical appearances, such as men having breast augmentation (Kuper, Nussbaum, & Mastanski, 2012). Whereas bisexuals, transgendered individuals, and transsexuals will be discussed, most of this chapter focuses on gays and lesbians in sport and sport media, in part because more past and present athletes have come out as gay or lesbian, and gays and lesbians have received more media attention (in both sport and society) than bisexuals or the trans community.

The major exception was former 1976 Olympic decathlon gold medalist Bruce Jenner publicly coming out as transgender woman Caitlyn Jenner in 2015, a revelation that received a plethora of international media coverage, culminated by Caitlyn Jenner accepting the Arthur Ashe Courage Award at the 2015 ESPYs. Many of the most popular American athletes attended those ESPYs, where Jenner received standing ovations from the crowd, while a worldwide, record audience watched through ESPN television and discussed/debated the merits of this award through social media (Battaglio, 2015). Based on conference submissions, there will likely be several upcoming research articles published on media coverage and social media responses to Jenner's coming out as a transgender woman.

LGBTQ in Sport

This section will show that openly gay female and male athletes are both now far more accepted and prevalent than ever before in Western societies, but yet remain obscure minorities who face many challenges within their sports if they come out publicly through media. The support for—and subsequent rise of—organized youth sport for boys in the 19th century was largely because of fears that men would become soft and weak as the United States transitioned from predominantly an agriculture-based society to the Industrial Revolution (Rader, 2008). Thus, a masculine 'warrior' narrative was regularly taught through organized sport, where young boys learned that to exhibit weakness was effeminate, or worse, gay (Anderson & Kian, 2012). The use of sport to train young boys to be masculine men continued in similar fashion for more than a century, with little change and few challenges to this line of thinking. Messner (1992) concluded, "The extent of homophobia in the sport world is staggering. Boys (in sport) learn early that to be gay, to be suspected of being gay, or even to be unable to prove one's heterosexual status is not acceptable" (p. 34).

Because young boys were usually mocked in sport for exhibiting any traits or characteristics perceived as effeminate, it is not surprising that few openly gay athletes have acknowledged their sexual identity publicly through media, particularly from the most popular professional men's team sports. Those men who did acknowledge their homosexuality, generally did so after their playing careers were over. Only eight athletes who participated in at least one regular-season game in any of the 'Big 4' American men's professional team sports have publicly acknowledged they were gay, with Jason Collins (NBA) the only one who did so while active in his sport. The others were MLB's Billy Bean and Glen Burke, the NBA's John Amaechi, and the NFL's Kwame Harris, Dave Kopay, Roy Simmons, and Esera Tuaolo. Through 2015, no past or present athlete from the NHL had revealed his homosexuality or even bisexuality.

Additionally, football player Michael Sam, the co-defensive player of the year in the powerful Southeastern Conference in 2013 while a college student at the University of Missouri, came out in advance of the 2014 NFL Draft through a primetime interview telecast on ESPN. The St. Louis Rams selected Sam in the 7th round, making him the first openly gay athlete drafted in one of the 'Big 4' American men's team sports. Sam, however, never made an NFL regular-season roster or played in a regular-season game, although he did compete in preseason games for the Rams and was a member of the Dallas Cowboys' practice squad for part of the 2014 season. Sam eventually signed with the Canadian Football League's (CFL) Montreal Alouettes in May 2015, but left the team for personal reasons shortly after signing. He returned and played in one CFL regular-season game, but then left the Alouettes a second time, citing depression, mental health concerns, and pressure from the immense attention he had received since coming out as a gay football player (Zeigler, 2015a).

U.S. professional soccer player Robbie Rogers came out publicly and played in a regular-season match before Jason Collins followed suit. However, while professional and international soccer are becoming immensely popular with the American public—evident by recent record-setting men's and women's World Cup television ratings—Major League Soccer (MLS) is not yet considered one of the 'Big 4' U.S. professional team sport leagues. In August 2015, David Denson became the first active professional baseball player affiliated with a MLB franchise to reveal his homosexuality. Denson, however, spent the 2015 season assigned to the lowest level of the Milwaukee Brewers' minor league affiliates in Helena, Montana, so the likelihood of the former 15th-round selection ever making the Major Leagues is statistically low (Boren, 2015).

More successful male gay athletes came out in individual sports, although their numbers are still minimal compared with the likely proportion of actual gay athletes participating. Further, the few famous and highly successful openly gay U.S. male athletes (e.g., figure skaters Rudy Galindo and Johnny Weir, diver Greg Louganis, etc.) competed in sports (e.g., diving, figure skating, gymnastics, etc.) that media have historically construed as more appropriate for women (Angelini, MacArthur, & Billings, 2014; Kian, 2014; Vincent, Imwold, Johnson, & Massey, 2003).

A few more prominent U.S. female athletes in team sports have come out, most notably 2015 U.S. Women's World Cup soccer gold medalists Abby Wambach and Megan Rapinoe, and basketball superstars Sheryl Swoopes and Brittney Griner. When she came out as a lesbian, Swoopes was pregnant with a child that she said was conceived through sex with a man, thus showing the fluidity of sexual preferences and identities (Chawansky & Francombe, 2011; King, 2009). Whereas Swoopes' coming-out was mostly framed positively by sport media (Chawansky & Francombe, 2011), gay female athletes or even those suspected of being gay have historically been subjected to criticism, ridicule, and negative stereotypes by some coaches, fans, and media (Griffin, 2012; Hardin & Whiteside, 2010; Lenskyj, 2013; Walker & Melton, 2015). Accordingly, the most prominent homosexual American athletes were women competing in individual sports, highlighted by tennis icons Billie Jean King and Martina Navratilova, both of whom came out during their careers. Of course, King and Navratilova both endured much animosity from sport fans and media after they revealed their lesbianism (Nelson, 1984).

However, their treatment by fans and especially fellow players was nowhere near as harsh as what Renee Richards had to endure. Richards was initially prohibited from continuing a professional tennis career after changing her name from Richard Raskind and undergoing sexual reassignment surgery (Birrell & Cole, 1990). The New York Supreme Court eventually overturned Richards' denial by the United States Tennis Association, enabling her to resume a professional career in women's events.

Hegemonic Masculinity vs. Inclusive Masculinity in Sport and Sport Media

Over the past 30 years, hundreds of published academic studies found hegemonic masculinity prevalent in sport media content regardless of the level of sport examined, country hosting the sporting event, or the type of media producing the content (e.g., Kane, LaVoi, & Fink, 2013; Pedersen, Whisenant, & Schneider, 2003; Smith & Bissell, 2014). Utilizing *hegemony* by Gramsci (1971) in his writings on power, Connell (1987; 2005) coined the phrase *hegemonic masculinity* to describe gendered practices that strengthen the dominance of men throughout society who conform to and exhibit the most desirable characteristics of masculinity as construed, taught, and reinforced by the ruling classes of society.

Hegemonic masculinity has been used to guide or interpret results for many sport media scholarly studies, the vast majority of which compared media content of men's and women's sports. Among the major and consistent findings of those studies that led scholars to conclude hegemonic masculinity was dominant in sport media were (a) that male athletes—especially those in sports construed as the most masculine in societies—collectively receive far more media coverage than female athletes in most sports; (b) that the overwhelmingly male sport media personnel use descriptors in the content they produce that trivialize or delegitimize female athletic accomplishments; and (c) that female athletes are highly sexualized by sport media, who are far more likely to delve into their personal lives than when covering male athletes (e.g., Billings, Angelini, & Duke, 2010; Cooky, Messner, & Hextrum, 2013).

In hegemonic masculine social structures, however, openly gay males fall below most heterosexual women who exhibit ideal traits of femininity in hegemonic masculine social structures (Anderson, 2002; Connell, 2005). Whereas hegemonic masculinity is always being challenged, constantly in flux, and never absolute, openly gay men, by their mere presence, challenge hegemonic masculinity (Anderson, 2009; Connell, 2005; Kian, Clavio, Vincent, & Shaw, 2011), especially in environments where rugged, stereotypical traits of masculinity (e.g., toughness, physical strength, ability to withstand pain, etc.) are most valued, such as organized team sports (Anderson & Kian, 2012; Connell, 1992).

Collins was overwhelming accepted as an openly gay athlete in the Nets' locker room, by past and present players from all teams throughout the NBA, and via the sport media. This is indicative of a society that is perpetually evolving and becoming more inclusive toward sexual minorities, even within the most masculine male team sports (Billings, Moscowitz, Rae, & Brown-Devlin, 2015; Kian et al., 2015). In other words, hegemonic masculinity is challenged in society and sport by *inclusive masculinity*, a phrase Anderson (2009) developed in arguing that hegemonic masculinity and homophobia are no longer dominant in many cultures because of various types of masculinities becoming acceptable for men, along with mainstream cultural acceptance of gay and lesbian lifestyles throughout Western societies. Both hegemonic and inclusive masculinity can be used to examine major findings from research on the framing of LGBTQ in sport media coverage, as well in discussing the future of LGBTQ in sport and sport media coverage.

Academic Research on Sport Media and LGBTQ

Mass media historically provided little attention to gays and lesbians in sport, likely because so few athletes of any prominence publicly revealed their homosexuality, and most did so long after their playing careers were over (Bernstein & Kian, 2013; Plymire & Forman, 2000). Moreover, even when focusing on gay athletes in sport or even just LGBTQ issues in sport, media still framed heterosexual relationships as the standard even when the same media members publicly expressed support for gay and lesbian lifestyles and called for acceptance (Butterworth, 2006; Nylund, 2004). With little media attention published on issues related to LGBTQ in sport and nearly all gay and lesbian athletes in the closet to the greater public until recent years, communication and sport scholars largely ignored LGBTQ in sport media content, because there was not much to research.

Accordingly, much of the early scholarly research on LGBTQ in sport media was on covert innuendo used by sport media to discuss gay athletes or insinuate that some sports featured many gay participants and coaches. Some of these studies noted that media suspected athletes were lesbians within sports construed as gender-appropriate for women (by those athletes' or coaches' appearances) or just through mere female participation in sports often construed as gender-inappropriate for women, where most athletes and coaches are perceived to be lesbian (Crosset, 1995; Griffin, 2012; Staurowsky, 2012).

The most seminal of these works, however, focused on media framing of HIV-infected male athletes in the early 1990s, when HIV and AIDS were still largely correlated with gay males by most of society (Dworkin & Wachs, 1998). A textual analysis of national newspaper coverage on basketball superstar Magic Johnson, Olympic gold medalist diver Greg Louganis, and boxer Tommy Morrison found that most of the articles on Johnson and Morrison expressed shock that both athletes had contracted the HIV virus, while also noting multiple times that each athlete had proclaimed they were heterosexual (Dworkin & Wachs, 1998). However, no article in any of the examined newspapers on the openly gay Louganis noted how he had contracted a virus that at that time was associated predominantly with gay men (Dworkin & Wachs, 1998).

The trend of more athletes coming out in recent years has provided scholarly opportunities on media framing of LGBTQ athletes. A trio of studies examined John Amaechi becoming the first former NBA player to come out publicly in 2007. Sport journalists expressed support for Amaechi (Kian & Anderson, 2009), or at least did not exhibit overt homophobia (Hardin, Kuehn, Jones, Genovese, & Balaji, 2009), but also were skeptical that pro sports were ready for openly gay males (Hardin et al., 2009; Kian & Anderson, 2009). Cassidy (2012) found that journalists rarely interviewed those close to Amaechi or gay-rights advocates, instead choosing to primarily use sport figures as sources in their articles and columns.

There will likely be several research articles published on Collins, because his coming-out in 2013 received more media attention than that of any previous openly gay athletes in the United States, and it came during a time of both great societal change and majority acceptance of gay lifestyles rights throughout most of the Western world. At least three had already been published in prominent journals at the time this chapter was submitted. In examining newspaper and online sport articles, and tweets, Billings et al. (2015) and Kian et al. (2015) both found that sport journalists overwhelmingly framed Collins' coming-out as a positive and placed it as a historic moment in sport and American society. In a second part of their study, Kian et al. (2015) also found no reports of any problems with teammates, other players, or fan backlash after Collins later signed with the Nets and played in actual games, thus alleviating past fears that openly gay athletes would not be accepted in locker rooms, and would instead serve as lightning rods for negative media attention and hatred from opposing fans (Butterworth, 2006). Kian (2015) looked at social media posts on the coming-outs of Collins and Sam published on a political website, finding that homosexuality in sport remains a highly contested political and social issue falling largely on ideological divides between social conservatives (largely unaccepting) and social liberals (very accepting).

Reporter-espoused homophobia is now nearly non-existent in mainstream U.S. sport media content as sport journalists are more willing to focus attention on openly gay athletes or gay issues in sport (Kian et al., 2015). However, only two published studies actually examined sport media members' attitudes toward gays and lesbians, with Hardin and Whiteside (2009) finding that most surveyed sport journalists thought homophobia was a problem within sport and said they were not comfortable writing about gay athletes' sexual orientation. Of course, societal and seemingly sport journalist attitudes toward LGBTQ have changed greatly since that survey was administered in 2007. Sport journalists interviewed by Kian, Anderson, Vincent, and Murray (2013) expressed strong support for sexual minorities while also acknowledging that openly gay sport members were rare and nonexistent (to their knowledge) in the departments where they had worked. Moreover, these journalists said that they did not like delving into gay sexual orientation unless athletes self-publicized their homosexuality.

No data exists on statistical representation of sexual minorities in U.S. sport media, although few have publicly come out even to their colleagues (Kian et al., 2013). Former *Los Angeles Times* sport writer Mike Penner received national attention for publicizing in a 2007 column that he was a transsexual and changing his byline to Christine Daniels. Fifteen months later and without ever providing a reason, his byline switched back to Mike Penner, roughly a year before he died of an apparent suicide (Pieper, 2015). ESPN columnist/reporter and commentator Israel Gutierrez became the most famous openly gay male sport media member in 2015 after coming out publicly through an emotional blog post, in which he announced his upcoming marriage to his long-time partner (Zeigler, 2015b).

Future of LGBTQ in Sport and Sport Media

More opportunities to research sexual minorities in sport media content will be available as additional past and present athletes eventually come out. There still has not been one prominent past or present athlete from the major American men's professional team sport leagues publicly reveal his homosexuality. However, the United States appears ready for this athlete to come out. A survey from the Public Religion Research Institute and Religion News Service released in 2015 showed 73% of Americans support the signings of openly gay and lesbian athletes by sport franchises, compared with only 19% who were opposed (Waldron, 2015).

The trend toward increasing acceptance for gays and lesbians in U.S. sport has also been shown through recent scholarship on athletes (Cohen, Melton, & Peachey, 2014; Fink, Burton, Farrell, & Parker, 2012), coaches and administrators (Cunningham, 2010), and sport marketers and advertisers (Parker & Fink, 2012). Once more prominent athletes do publicly come out, researchers can examine responses from not only media, but also reactions and interactions directly from sport fans and consumers through social media research. It will be particularly interesting to see audience reactions—through social media posts and anonymous message-board comments—from both hometown fans and fans of rival teams when the first superstar male professional team sport athlete in the United States comes out.

In general, though, research on LGBTQ in sport and sport media is needed in nearly all areas by communication scholars, because so little scholarship currently exists. Will long-standing misogynist attitudes among sport fans toward open lesbian athletes who do not exhibit stereotypical feminine qualities and appearances change as rapidly as they have toward acceptance of gays in pop culture? This seemed unlikely to occur just a few years ago, but not now. For example, despite losing her starting job, open lesbian Abby Wambach, who is a towering five-foot-11 and 179 pounds in a sport dominated by smaller athletes, was the media's most popular woman to interview and a fan favorite on the World Cup-winning 2016 U.S. women's World Cup soccer team, which captivated American society and shattered television ratings records (Deitsch, 2015).

LGBTQ in sport and sport media scholarship also needs to be conducted by researchers housed in different areas. It has historically been largely conducted by sport sociologists and sport studies academics, who often focus on qualitative or textual analyses through feminist lenses. But communications, and sport management and marketing scholars are now recognizing the value and need of this research, evident by many more studies in recent years in areas such as athletic administration, advertising, branding, and marketing of LGBTQ athletes through sport media (e.g., Bass, Hardin, & Taylor, 2015; Cunningham & Melton, 2014; Fink, 2014).

References

Anderson, E. (2002). Openly gay athletes: Contesting hegemonic masculinity in a homophobic environment. *Gender and Society, 16*(6), 860–877.

Anderson, E. (2009). *Inclusive masculinity: The changing nature of masculinities.* London: Routledge.

Anderson, E., & Kian, E.M. (2012). Examining media contestation of masculinity and head trauma in the National Football League. *Men and Masculinities, 15*(2), 152–173.

Angelini, J.R., MacArthur, P.J., & Billings, A.C. (2014). Spiraling into or out of stereotypes? NBC's primetime coverage of male figure skaters at the 2010 Olympic Games. *Journal of Language and Social Psychology, 33*(2), 226–235.

Bass, J., Hardin, R., & Taylor, E.A. (2015). The glass closet: Perceptions of homosexuality in intercollegiate sport. *Journal of Applied Sport Management, 7*(4), 32–36.

Battaglio, S. (2015, July 16). Caitlyn Jenner boosts ESPY awards ratings to record high. *Los Angeles Times* online. Retrieved June 20, 2016, from http://www.latimes.com/entertainment/envelope/cotown/la-et-ct-caitlyn-jenner-espy-award-ratings-20150716-story.html.

Bernstein, A., & Kian E.M. (2013). Gender and sexualities in sport media. In P.M. Pedersen (Ed.), *Handbook of sport communication* (pp. 319–327). London: Routledge.

Billings, A.C., Angelini, J.R., & Duke, A.H. (2010). Gendered profiles of Olympic history: Sportscaster dialogue in the 2008 Beijing Olympics. *Journal of Broadcasting & Electronic Media, 54*(1), 9–23.

Billings, A.C., Moscowitz, L.M., Rae, C., & Brown-Devlin, N. (2015). The art of coming out: Traditional and social media frames surrounding the NBA's Jason Collins. *Journalism & Mass Communication Quarterly, 92*(1), 142–160.

Birrell, S., & Cole, C.L. (1990). Double fault: Renee Richards and the naturalization of difference. *Sociology of Sport Journal, 7*(1), 1–21.

Boren, C. (August 16, 2015). A Milwaukee Brewers minor-leaguer makes history by coming out as gay. *The Washington Post* online. Retrieved June 20, 2016, from https://www.washingtonpost.com/news/early-lead/wp/2015/08/16/a-milwaukee-brewers-minor-leaguer-makes-baseball-history-by-coming-out-as-gay/.

Butterworth, M.L. (2006). Pitchers and catchers: Mike Piazza and the discourse of gay identity in the national pastime. *Journal of Sport & Social Issues, 30*(2), 138–157.

Cassidy, W.P. (2012). Beyond the game or business as usual? Daily newspaper and wire-service coverage of John Amaechi's coming out. *Journal of Sports Media, 7*(2), 23–39.

Chawansky, M., & Francombe, J.M. (2011). Cruising for Olivia: Lesbian celebrity and the cultural politics of coming out in sport. *Sociology of Sport Journal, 28*(4), 461–477.

Cohen, A., Melton, N.E., & Peachey, J.W. (2014). Investigating a coed sport's ability to encourage inclusion and equality. *Journal of Sport Management, 28*(2), 220–235.

Collins, S., & Blake, M. (2015, June 27). Years before court ruling, pop culture shaped same-sex marriage debate. *Los Angeles Times* online. Retrieved June 20, 2016, from http://www.latimes.com/entertainment/la-et-st-0628-media-gay-marriage-20150628-story.html.

Connell, R.W. (1987). *Gender and power*. Stanford, CA: Stanford University Press.

Connell, R.W. (1992). A very straight gay: Masculinity, homosexual experience, and the dynamics of gender. *American Sociological Review, 57*(6), 735–751.

Connell, R.W. (2005). *Masculinities* (2nd ed.). Berkeley, CA: University of California.

Cooky, C., Messner, M.A., & Hextrum, R.H. (2013). Women play sport, but not on TV: A longitudinal study of televised news media. *Communication & Sport, 1*(3), 203–230.

Crosset, T. (1995). *Outsiders in the clubhouse: The world of professional women's golf*. Albany, NY: State University of New York Press.

Cunningham, G.B. (2010). Predictors of sexual orientation diversity in intercollegiate athletics departments. *Journal of Intercollegiate Sport, 3*(2), 256–269.

Cunningham, G.B., & Melton, E.N. (2014). Signals and cues; LGBT inclusive advertising and consumer attraction. *Sport Marketing Quarterly, 23*(1), 37–46.

Deitsch, R. (July 6, 2015). USA-Japan Women's World Cup final shatters American TV ratings record. *SI.com*. Retrieved June 20, 2016, from http://www.si.com/planet-futbol/2015/07/06/usa-japan-womens-world-cup-tv-ratings-record.

Diamond, L.M. (2015). Sexual fluidity. *The International Encyclopedia of Human Sexuality*, 1115–1354. DOI: 10.1002/9781118896877.wbiehs452.

Dworkin, S.L., & Wachs, F.L. (1998). "Disciplining the body": HIV-positive male athletes, media surveillance, and the policing of sexuality. *Sociology of Sport Journal, 15*(1), 1–20.

Fink, J.S. (2014). Female athletes, women's sport, and the sport media complex: Have we really "come a long way, baby"? *Sport Management Review, 18*(3), 331–342.

Fink, J.S., Burton, L.J., Farrell, A.O., & Parker, H.M. (2012). Playing it out: Female intercollegiate athletes' experiences in revealing their sexual identities. *Journal for the Study of Sports and Athletes in Education, 6*(1), 83–106.

Gramsci, A. (1971). *Selections from the prison notebooks.* New York: International Publishers.

Griffin, P. (2012). LGBT equality in sports: Celebrating our successes and facing our challenges. In G.B. Cunningham (Ed.), *Sexual orientation and gender identity in sport: Essays from activists, coaches, and scholars* (pp. 1–12). College Station, TX: Center for Sport Management Research and Education.

Halberstam, J. (2005). *In a queer time and place: Transgender bodies, subcultural lives.* New York: NYU Press.

Hardin, M., Kuehn, K.M., Jones, H., Genovese, J., & Balaji, M. (2009). "Have you got game?" Hegemonic masculinity and neo-homophobia in U.S. newspaper sports columns. *Communication, Culture, & Critique, 2*(2), 182–200.

Hardin, M., & Whiteside, E. (2009). Sports reporters divided over concerns about Title IX. *Newspaper Research Journal, 30*(1), 58–80.

Hardin, M., & Whiteside, E. (2010). The Rene Portland case: New homophobia and heterosexism in women's sports coverage. In H.L. Hundley & A.C. Billings (Eds.), *Examining identity in sports media* (pp. 17–36). Thousand Oaks, CA: Sage.

Indiana University Center for Sexual Health Promotion. (2010). *National survey of sexual health and behavior.* Retrieved June 20, 2016, from http://www.nationalsexstudy.indiana.edu/.

Kane, M.J., Lavoi, N.M., & Fink, J.S. (2013). Exploring elite female athletes' interpretations of sport media images: A window into the construction of social identity and "selling sex" in women's sports. *Communication & Sport, 1*(3), 269–298.

Kian, E.M. (2014). Sexuality in the mediation of sport. In J. Hargreaves & E. Anderson (Eds.), *Handbook of sport, gender, and sexuality* (pp. 461–469). London: Routledge.

Kian, E.M. (2015). A case study on message board and media framing of gay males athletes on a politically liberal website. *International Journal of Sport Communication, 8*(4), 500–518.

Kian, E.M., & Anderson, E. (2009). John Amaechi: Changing the way reporters examine gay athletes. *Journal of Homosexuality, 56*(7), 799–818.

Kian, E.M., Anderson, E., & Shipka, D. (2015). "I am happy to start the conversation": Examining sport media framing of Jason Collins' coming out. *Sexualities, 18*(5–6), 618–640.

Kian, E.M., Anderson, E., Vincent, J., & Murray, R. (2015). Sport journalists' views on gay men in sport, society and within sport media. *International Review for the Sociology of Sport, 50*(8), 895–911. Epub ahead of print. doi: 10.1177/10126902213504101.

Kian, E.M., Clavio, G., Vincent, J., & Shaw, S.D. (2011). Homophobic and sexist yet uncontested: Examining football fan postings on Internet message boards. *Journal of Homosexuality, 58*(5), 680–699.

Kian, E.M., & Vincent, J. (2014). Examining gays and lesbians in sport via traditional and new media. In A.C. Billings & M. Hardin (Eds.), *The Routledge handbook of sport and new media* (pp. 342–352). London: Routledge.

King, S. (2009). Homonormativity and the politics of race: Reading Sheryl Swoopes. *Journal of Lesbian Studies, 13*(3), 272–290.

Kuper, L.E., Nussbaum, R., & Mustanski, B. (2012). Exploring the diversity of gender and sexual orientation identities in an online sample of transgender individuals. *Journal of Sex Research, 49*(2–3), 244–254.

Laumann, E., Gagnon, J.H., Michael, R.T., & Michaels, S. (1994). *The social organization of sexuality: Sexual practices in the United States.* Chicago, IL: University of Chicago Press.

Lenskyj, H.J. (2013). Reflections on communication and sport: On heteronormativity and gender identities. *Communication & Sport, 1*(1/2), 138–150.

Liptak, A. (June 26, 2015). Supreme Court ruling makes same-sex marriage a right nationwide. *New York Times.* Retrieved July 15, 2016 from http://www.nytimes.com/2015/06/27/us/supreme-court-same-sex-marriage.html?_r=0.

Lucas-Carr, C.B., & Krane, V. (2012). Troubling sport or trouble by sport: Experiences of transgender athletes. *Journal of the Study of Sports and Athletes in Education, 6*(1), 21–44.

McCarthy, J. (May 21, 2014). Same-sex marriage support reaches new high at 55%. *Gallup Politics* online. Retrieved June 20, 2016, from http://www.gallup.com/poll/169640/sex-marriage-support-reaches-new-high.aspx.

Messner, M.A. (1992). *Power at play: Sports and the problem of masculinity.* Boston, MA: Beacon Press.

Messner, M.A. (2002). *Taking the field: Women, men, and sports.* Minneapolis, MN: University of Minnesota Press.

MSNBC.com. (2004). Civil unions for gays favored, polls show: Same-sex marriage debate increases support for such recognition. Retrieved June 20, 2016, from http://www.msnbc.msn.com/id/4496265/ns/us_news-same-sex_marriage/.

Nelson, J. (1984). The defense of Billie Jean King. *Western Journal of Speech Communication, 48*(1), 92–102.

Newport, F. (May 21, 2015). Americans greatly overestimate percent gay, lesbian in U.S. *Gallup.* Retrieved June 20, 2016, from http://www.gallup.com/poll/183383/americans-greatly-overestimate-percent-gay-lesbian.aspx.

Nylund, D. (2004). When in Rome: Heterosexism, homophobia, and sports talk radio. *Journal of Sport & Social Issues, 28*(2), 136–168.

Parker, H.M., & Fink, J.S. (2012). Arrest record or openly gay: The impact of athletes' personal lives on endorser effectiveness. *Sport Marketing Quarterly, 21*(2), 70–79.

Payne, E.C., & Smith, M.J. (2012). Safety, celebration, and risk: Educator responses to LGBTQ professional development. *Teaching Education, 23*(3), 265–285.

Pedersen, P.M., Whisenant, W.A., & Schneider, R.G. (2003). Using a content analysis to examine the gendering of sports newspaper personnel and their coverage. *Journal of Sport Management, 17*(4), 376–393.

Pieper, L.P. (2015). Mike Penner "or" Christine Daniels: The US media and the fractured representation of a transgender sportswriter. *Sport in Society: Cultures, Commerce, Media, Politics, 18*(2), 186–201.

Plymire, D.C., & Forman, P.J. (2000). Breaking the silence: Lesbian fans, the Internet, and the sexual politics of women's sport. *International Journal of Sexuality and Gender Studies, 5*(2), 141–153.

Rader B.G. (2008). *American sports: From the age of folk games to the age of televised sports* (6th ed.). Upper Saddle River, NJ: Prentice Hall.

Smith, L.R., & Bissell, K. (2014). Nice dig! An analysis of men's and women's beach volleyball during the 2008 Olympic Games. *Communication & Sport, 2*(1), 48–64.

Staurowsky, E.J. (2012). Sexual prejudice and sport media coverage: Exploring an ethical framework for college sports journalists. *Journal of the Study of Sports and Athletes in Education, 6*(2), 121–140.

Vincent, J., Imwold, C., Johnson, J.T., & Massey, D. (2003). Newspaper coverage of female athletes competing in selected sports in the 1996 centennial Olympic Games: The more things change the more they stay the same. *Women in Sport & Physical Activity Journal, 12*(1), 1–22.

Waldron, T. (January 29, 2015). Only 19 percent of Americans oppose gay athletes in pro sports. *ThinkProgress.org*. Retrieved June 20, 2016, from http://thinkprogress.org/sports/2015/01/29/3616510/three-fourths-americans-support-openly-gay-athletes-pro-sports/.

Walker, N.A., & Melton, E.N. (2015). The tipping point: The intersection of race, gender, and sexual orientation in intercollegiate sports. *Journal of Sport Management, 29*(3), 257–271.

Zeigler, C. (August 14, 2015a). Michael Sam has left the Montreal Alouettes, his football future in doubt. *OutSports.com*. Retrieved June 20, 2016, from http://www.outsports.com/2015/8/14/9157639/michael-sam-left-montreal-alouettes.

Zeigler, C. (September 4, 2015b). ESPN commentator Israel Gutierrez announces marriage in heartfelt coming-out message. *OutSports.com*. Retrieved June 20, 2016, from http://www.outsports.com/2015/9/4/9262367/israel-gutierrez-gay-espn-nba.

PART II

Organizational/Relational Approaches to Sport

9

SPORT AND ORGANIZATIONAL COMMUNICATION

Jeffrey W. Kassing and Robyn Matthews

ARIZONA STATE UNIVERSITY

In a previous review, Kassing et al. (2004) recognized that organizing sport entailed both internal and external communication from sport organizations. These authors placed particular emphasis on how sport organizations exchanged internal and external messages to 'organize' sport. Accordingly, organizing externally entails communication emanating from sport organizations, whereas organizing internally refers to communication between and among stakeholders within an organization. The former includes marketing, advertising (see Chapter 21), and public relations (see Chapter 22). The latter, with a focus on messages exchanged within organizations, is the focus of this chapter.

Historically, organizational communication concerns communication taking place in settings marked by interdependent relationships, common and shared goals, and some degree of formalized relationships. That is, organizations are places where people's actions and interactions are linked, where they have been charged with a clear and apparent objective to achieve both in the short and long term, and where members experience direction and restriction regarding about what and with whom to communicate. Modern organizations can no longer be thought of as traditional workplaces bound by physical offices but rather should be recognized as shape-shifting entities that span time and space (Leonardi, Treem, & Jackson, 2010). Employees now connect via communication technologies far and wide. Thus, the notion of shared physical space and location has dissipated, but not the aforementioned attributes as organizational members remain interdependent, goal-directed, and formally arranged into prescribed relationships.

Given these attributes, the study of communication in organizations can include traditional business and corporate settings, for profit and nonprofit organizations, and formal structured hierarchical and more democratic arrangements.

As a point of focus, then, organizational communication casts a wide net, examining what we routinely take to mean organizations (i.e., formal, hierarchical corporations) but also nontraditional organizations such as running clubs, worker co-operatives, and community theatre groups (Harter & Krone, 2001; Kramer, 2005, 2006). The same breadth applied to the sport context allows for studying the 'organized' groups affiliated with sport. Those range from the formal sport organization or sport franchise to the fan club, from the governing body of a given sport to the organizing committees of mega-sporting events like the Olympics and the World Cup that come together temporarily, and also includes sport teams from the professional to the amateur and youth levels.

This chapter review begins by considering traditional and contemporary approaches to the study of organizations, providing examples of work in sport that exemplifies each perspective. Subsequently, it considers specific lines of research that demonstrate clear connections between sport and organizational communication. Finally, it closes by identifying opportunities for future research at the intersection of organizational communication and sport.

Organizational Communication Perspectives and Sport Applications

Tracing the historical perspectives promoting differing approaches to explaining the connection between organizations and communication is a particularly effective way to map the possibilities for how sport and organizational communication might connect. Several approaches to the study of organizational communication have been advanced. These include a set of early, classical approaches and a more recent set of contemporary approaches. In the sections that follow, each of the perspectives is described and an example sport study is discussed to illustrate how the perspectives surface in particular research efforts.

Classical Approaches

The *classical management* perspective (Taylor, 1911) evolved when the Industrial Revolution promoted a move away from the craft guild model emphasizing matriculation based on skill mastery and task-continuous work—whereby a single craftsman was responsible for the entire production of a given product. With the onset of the Industrial Revolution, work changed from something continuous and craft-like to the mass production of goods. As a result, workers adjusted to division of labor (discreet duties assigned to specific people), the specialization of tasks and duties (performing a single repetitive task), and the introduction of hierarchy (as supervision needed to be formalized). Communication became primarily top-down from management and supervisors to employees, task-centered, and formal.

Sanderson's (2011) study of the social media policies of NCAA Division I athletic departments illustrates how a classical management perspective can manifest in sport organizations. In this work, Sanderson consulted 159 student-athlete handbooks and social media policies to determine the nature of what athletic departments were communicating to college athletes about their use of social media. His analysis revealed that policies relied heavily on content restriction and external monitoring. This tack aligns with the top-down, task-centered, and formal kinds of communication that follow when classical management is apparent. This is not to say that athletic departments rely exclusively on this approach and fail to adopt and use others, but rather to illustrate that, with regard to this specific issue (athletes' social media use), most university athletic departments have adopted an approach informed by classical management. This makes sense as athletes' use of social media is something that athletic departments recognize is risk-laden and therefore have structured communication around it to be formal and direct.

While many organizations still operate with division of labor, specialization of tasks, and hierarchy firmly in place, they have shifted to more worker-centered approaches. These include the human relations and human resources perspectives discussed next. The *human relations* perspective (Herzberg, 1976; McGregor, 1960) recognized the importance of employees to the process of production, seeking to correct shortcomings of the classical management perspective. This was achieved by redirecting the focus to motivating and managing employees. Accordingly, emphasis rests upon fostering commitment, shared responsibility, creativity, and problem-solving. The underlying assumption was that employees found gratification in work beyond simply receiving a paycheck. Communication shifts from being almost exclusively top-down and formal to being multidirectional and even occasionally informal. Yet, despite focusing on employee needs and motivation, control (in the form of supervision) remains clear and apparent.

Athletes in a team setting are analogous to members in an organization—with the implicit understanding that the team, like an organization, will function better when members are committed and motivated. While there are ample studies considering athlete motivation, a recent entry helps bring into focus an approach underpinned by the human relations perspective. Mazer, Barnes, Grevious, and Boger (2013) examined student-athletes' perceptions of coaches and the effect those perceptions had on their self-reported motivation, finding that athletes were more motivated to play for coaches who possessed an affirming communication style compared with athletes who reported about coaches who possessed a verbally aggressive communication style. Implied in this approach and the relevant findings is the idea that coaches can be more autocratic and dictatorial or, conversely, more affirming and engaged with athletes. That is, they can approach the management of athletes quite differently, particularly with regard to what will produce more motivated team members. The human relations perspective suggests that athletes are motivated by communication that is two-way and, at times, informal. These results support this reasoning, demonstrating that athletes reported being motivated when coaches appeared to be supportive and concerned.

The *human resources* perspective (Blake & Mouton, 1964) expanded upon its predecessor by leveraging the intellect and not just the motivation of employees. Employees were understood to be capable of sharing ideas and acting in the best interest of the corporation. This approach demanded a rethinking of the structural arrangements of organizations so that they afforded workers the opportunity to be more engaged in determining organizational functions and structure. The perspective was a step forward, but turned out to be riddled with potential paradoxes (Stohl & Cheney, 2001). For example, management builds participation systems to empower employees, yet employees have little or no say in how these systems get constructed. Similarly, emphasis on group productivity often ironically limits individual autonomy—and the time it takes to make decisions more democratically counteracts management's expectations for those decisions to be made quickly. From this perspective, communication is both social and task-oriented, traversing organizations between coworkers as well as up and down the chain of command.

The new owner of Aston Villa Football Club in the Barclays Premier League, Randy Lerner, seemed to operate from a human resources perspective. Arriving at a time when another foreign club owner—particularly an American one—easily could have produced a public backlash, Lerner was considerate in his approach to managing the club and steering it through an organizational leadership change. According to a case study conducted by Coombs and Osborne (2012), employees identified Lerner's leadership transition as one that empowered democratic participation because he actively engaged employees for suggestions on how to initiate change and fostered an entrepreneurial environment. As part of the leadership change Lerner infused a 'team spirit' throughout the staff. This case indicates that Lerner understood the need not just to manage employees but also to take their opinions into account when determining the next phase of the club's evolution—something he apparently did with aplomb.

Yet Lerner's early success became a cautionary tale as he sold the club in 2015–16 after the team suffered relegation from the Premier League for the first time in its history. This followed several years of poor club management, a carousel of managers, and the loss of many key players. Lerner shared in a public statement posted on the club's website that "I knew that personal and professional matters made it impossible for me to contribute the time I did in my first five years with the Club" ("Farewell Message from Randy Lerner," 2016). His statement and the misfortune of the organization in the latter years of his tenure suggest that the paradoxes of operating democratically, particularly the time required to do so, eroded the earlier success achieved under his leadership.

Contemporary Approaches

The *systems* perspective (Katz & Kahn, 1966) contends that organizations can be thought of as intricate patterns of regularly occurring interaction. As such, these patterns should be both observable and routine. People, departments, and divisions are connected through structural arrangements (e.g., as team members), hierarchical relationships (i.e., a reporting chain of command), and despite geographic or spatial limitations (i.e., via communication technology). From a systems perspective an organization functions akin to an organism, subject to both internal and external influences. Thus, communication in one part of the system likely affects interaction and feedback in another part. Routinized patterned interactions are considered networks. Networks, in turn, can be formal or informal, well-established or emergent, and densely composed with a greater number of connections or more loosely coupled ones.

Barnes, Cousens, and MacLean (2007) deployed a systems perspective to gauge how coordinated efforts were in the network of sport providers in the national sport system of Canada. They were particularly interested in the regional sport policy and found there were low levels of integration in the network of sport providers because of weak ties between actors in the system as well as administrative structure. Consistent with a systems perspective, the analysis revealed that the sport system would benefit not only from better cooperation and collaboration among actors but also from identifying and addressing barriers preventing better integration within the system. In this example, the entire sport system (an organized entity) is the object of study and the systems perspective the analytic tool, illustrating how organizational communication from a systems perspective can be used to study large sport entities.

The next approach, the *cultural-interpretive* perspective (Pacanowsky & O'Donnell-Trujillo, 1983), marked a significant departure from previous positions. From this perspective, communication was not seen as a separate entity to be identified and studied within an organizational context, but rather as the very fabric of what constitutes organizations. Said another way, the cultural-interpretive perspective contends that organizations are constituted and reconstituted continuously through communication between members. This can be seen in how rules, belief systems, and values take shape as the result of rituals, ceremonies, and narratives. In essence, communication is how employees perform the culture of their respective organizations, with performance referring to both the act of performing and the gauging of accomplishment. Thus, communication continuously builds organizational culture.

Trujillo (1992) used the critical-cultural perspective to unpack ballpark culture in baseball. In particular, he examined how people structured their experiences at the ballpark. His ethnographic approach revealed that three distinct interpretations of ballpark culture as an organized site emerged. The first emerged from employees who understood the ballpark as a place of business and their interaction with it as a source of labor. For these employees, the ballpark was not much different than working in other organizational settings; formal training procedures and orientation of staff was conducted through formal communication. Employees were taught to greet customers, dress appropriately, and perform tasks according to set guidelines (ranging from controlling traffic to pouring beer). The sense that the ballpark was, in many ways, commodified also contributed to this perspective. This could be seen in interactions framing goods and services as money (e.g., food spoilage and reserve tickets) along with employee conversations about being underpaid and expendable.

A second interpretation was that of the ballpark as community as realized through informal activities before and after games and outside of work (e.g., softball tournaments, barbeques, and drinks at a local bar). The seasonal nature of the work also allowed for reconnecting with coworkers through an annual renewal of sorts, framed by many employees as a family reunion.

The final interpretation of the ballpark was as theatre. Employees understood that games were an event and that they needed to put on a show each time one occurred. This was true for the front-stage employees such as roving vendors who interacted humorously with fans in the stands as well as the cleaning crew who returned the facility to a fresh state. Fans also understood their role in the drama. Trujillo concluded that players, workers, and fans created a shared sense of reality through ritual and tradition, thereby enacting and (re)creating a social drama.

The *critical* perspective (Deetz & Mumby, 1990) recognizes the constitutive role of communication in organizations but, as the name suggests, directs attention to the entities that are served by particular communication practices—with a specific interest in uncovering dominant power interests in organizations and how those interests are maintained subtly through everyday interactions. Communication and power link when certain views of reality are given preference while others remain obscured or excluded. Power, then, is not understood to be fixed but rather continuously reconstituted through particular uncontested interactions while protecting dominant interests. Power resides with those who can control communication so as to fix meaning in ways that benefit them.

This perspective is evident in the work of Fielding-Lloyd and Meân (2008), who examined the discourse of people involved in a training program run by a regional section of the Football Association or 'FA'—soccer's governing body in England. After interviewing staff members, coach educators, and participants in coaching courses, they concluded that the identification and separation of women-specific courses served to support discourse that undermined the viability of female coaches. The fact that separate courses were warranted marked them as inferior and only available out of the necessity to promote inclusion. Additionally, they found that people framed accommodations made to support and develop women's football not as "equal opportunities, but unfair opportunities" (p. 32). Perceived favoritism for female coaches and discrimination against male coaches characterized this discourse. Together these themes typified talk positioning female coach training and contributing to the marginalization of women in football—all of which serve to reinforce and protect football and sport as a highly masculinized site. This work illustrates how a critical orientation to organizational communication can reveal how certain interests persist while others are rebuffed.

Like the cultural-interpretive and the critical perspectives, the *discursive* perspective (Fairhurst & Putnam, 2004) stands upon the fundamental premise that language and social action build organizational life. However, the focus here shifts to the study of language in use (or discourse), with a broader focus than how such talk serves particular dominant interests well. Discourse refers to everyday talk and discourses that background all interaction. It is through everyday talk that widely held discourses are perpetuated or contested. This perspective recognizes how discourse can define reality in powerful ways—one of which is through intertextuality or referencing one of the larger omnipresent discourses in routine talk (e.g., the statement 'you play like a girl' mobilizes a much larger discourse about gender and sport). Doing so demonstrates the ongoing interplay between our everyday interactions and the larger societal and organizational discourses that shape how we orient to the world.

Working from the perspective that mere presence is not necessarily akin to acceptance, inclusion, and equity, Fielding-Lloyd and Meân (2011) continued their examination of coach training practices at a regional division of the FA by focusing on the discursive practices related to gender inequity. Arguing that an organization is "a process constructed and enacted by its individual members" (p. 346), they sought to determine how everyday gendered discursive practice surfaced in coach training—and how it served to undermine women's membership in coaching. In particular, they found that discourse about women lacking confidence contributed to arguments for their absence in the coaching ranks. So, too, did discourse about women needing to take responsibility (not the organization) for changes related to gender equity in the coach training courses and the coaching ranks. These apparent discursive practices drew upon larger discourses about gender and gender inequity, combining powerfully to problematize the inclusion of women in coaching and coach training. Such work shows how organizations take shape and function through discursive practices and how a discursive approach can identify and expose particular discourses and the tendencies they provoke.

Studies Connecting Sport and Organizational Communication

In addition to the aforementioned sport-related studies that demonstrate the various approaches to the study of organizational communication, there are other lines of research showing the connection between sport and organizational communication. This section reviews some of the more pronounced lines of research surfacing at the intersection of sport and organizational communication.

One of these lines of research features the coach–athlete relationship, with a collection of researchers showing how it resembles and functions similarly to the superior–subordinate relationship in organizations. For example, Cranmer and Myers (2014) examined the influence perceived relationship status had on the coach–athlete relationship, finding that former high school athletes who perceived that they have comparatively higher-quality relationships with their coaches also reported higher levels of satisfaction with their coaches and perceived greater levels of reciprocal communication within the coach–athlete relationship. Additionally, athletes with higher-quality coach–athlete relationships also perceived greater levels of team cohesion and cooperative communication between teammates. In a follow-up study, Cranmer (in press) discovered that athletes' perception of coach-initiated social support was the major contributor to the development of high-quality coach–athlete relationships.

Coaches, like supervisors, exercise power within organizational structures. Teams represent one such organizational structure. Ruggiero and Lattin (2008) considered this phenomenon when they explored how female intercollegiate coaches used verbal aggression towards African-American female athletes. Interview data from athletes revealed that coaches often used threats (e.g., threatening to take away scholarships or to add extra practice time) and instilled a sense of indebtedness among players (i.e., the feeling that athletes owed coaches for providing scholarships), leading to feelings of fear and intimidation. Coaches also used aggressive communication to undermine the self-confidence and self-concept of players. This manifested, for example, in athletes being told they did not belong on the team or that they were not good enough to play. Through these practices, coaches could exert and maintain power over players.

One of the ways in which employees counter power imbalances in the workplace is by sharing dissent (i.e., the expression of disagreement or contradictory opinions about organizational practices and policies). Kassing and Anderson (2014) reasoned that athletes—like subordinates—might feel the need to express dissent to coaches. They discovered that athletes were more likely to share dissent when they were in the starting lineup and when they perceived that their coaches were open to hearing athlete feedback. These findings aligned closely with dissent expression patterns within organizational settings, with higher employee rank and supervisor openness predicting employee dissent to supervisors. Conversely, athletes shared more dissent with teammates when they played less and when they perceived that their coaches were less receptive to athlete feedback. Here, too, were parallels to organizational dissent expression, with lower-ranking employees who see their bosses as less receptive to feedback often choosing to express dissent laterally to coworkers.

Whistleblowing or disclosing unethical practices and organizational wrongdoing to the media, industry governing bodies, or regulatory groups has been a topic of interest in organizational communication for some time. Organizational communication scholars Richardson and McGlynn have produced a line of research that considers how whistleblowing plays out in athletic contexts. In an initial study, Richardson and McGlynn (2011) examined the accounts of a sample of whistleblowers from major college athletic departments, discovering that the unique context of collegiate athletics influenced the whistleblowing experience in two notable ways. First, the hypermasculine character of collegiate sports led to sexualized/gendered retaliation. While this was predominant for female whistleblowers, it surfaced with their male counterparts on occasion as well. Female whistleblowers were slandered with all manner of sexual remarks and innuendo; similarly they were deemed naïve, unstable, and emotional. Commentary of this sort served to separate whistleblowers, particularly female ones, from the masculinized terrain of sport. Second, highly identified fans proved to be agents of retaliation, contrasting with traditional organizational sources of retaliation that include management, supervisors, and coworkers. In the context of intercollegiate sport, whistleblowers were ostracized not just at work but also in the campus and local communities they inhabited. Thus, whistleblowers, in this context, run the risk of intensified retaliation fostered by rabid fans as well as organizational personnel.

In a follow-up study, McGlynn and Richardson (2014) found that whistleblowers experienced private support but public alienation and that they sensed a general loss of social support for having blown the whistle. In addition, the presence of alumni and fans, the orientation that college sports are a business, and the heightened role of sport on campus negatively affected whistleblowers' experience of social support. Support from family and friends eroded as community members, alumni, and fans engaged in more threatening behaviors (e.g., death threats, public confrontations). Social support was also absent from the institutions involved and the governing body. Respondents particularly singled out the failure of the NCAA to conduct what they deemed to be proper or full investigations, which, in turn, significantly limited an expected source of social support.

Their earlier efforts led Richardson and McGlynn (2015) to inductively derive a five-phase model from actual whistleblower accounts. Their model aligns with previous models, but extends those in several important ways, showing, for example, how the organizational response and the whistleblower's subsequent actions mutually inform one another. It also highlights the importance of organizational context, in this case recognizing that "the gendered construction of sport and its increasing competitiveness, marked by financial concerns and highly identified fans, may impinge on all stages of the whistleblowing process" (p. 17). Furthermore, they concluded that collegiate athletics whistleblowing moves beyond reporting unethical behavior to challenging the myth and power of sport. Together, this body of work extends whistleblowing research generally and illustrates how it unfolds specifically in the collegiate athletic context.

Other scholars have taken a similar tack, examining organizational culture within the context of sport. For example, Frontiera (2010) examined how owners and general managers of professional sport franchises in the MLB, the NBA, and the NHL managed cultural change. As with whistleblowing research, this work revealed that the sport context produced a specific model of cultural change. Accordingly, managing cultural change in the professional sport context involved addressing the symptoms of a dysfunctional culture, particularly by identifying factors contributing to a negative environment (e.g., poor leadership, outdated facilities, lack of trust and integrity) and those associated with a losing habit (i.e., becoming accustomed to mediocrity and poor decision-making). Leaders then advanced a new direction characterized by explicit communication about new vision and values, developing and promoting from within, and changing personnel as necessary. Next, leaders recognized and embraced the fact that they needed to "walk the talk" (p. 78), reiterating plans on a daily basis, reframing previous barriers as challenges rather than excuses, and improving physical facilities. Embedding the signs of success related to cultural change followed with the final step occurring when members realized that cultural change had taken root and proceeded to develop and embrace new vernacular and traditions.

In a case study of an English football club, Ogbonna and Harris (2014) discovered how cultural change was thwarted. In this instance, an intended organizational cultural change was hampered by the persistence of the existing organizational culture that organizational members sought to perpetuate. Several intracultural factors hampered the intended cultural shift. The club's historical legacy, linked to tradition and also to success, was a powerful anchor for the perpetuation of the existing culture. Additionally, former players employed at the club represented symbolic connections that linked the present and the past. Similarly, traditional values such as passion and loyalty were symbolically represented in the artifacts and accompanying video/audio presentations in the club's museum. Subculture also stymied cultural change; the authors noted that the coach and players were an influential subculture in and of themselves, one that exercised a great deal of sway over the larger organizational culture. Along with these intracultural influences, fans also contributed to the retardation of cultural change. Utilizing focus groups, the authors learned that "die-hard fanatics commonly see their primary role as one of continuing the tradition of the football club and they present a powerful counter voice to any management team that wishes to undertake radical change to the culture of the football club" (p. 681). This combination of factors—particularly the role of fans and the subcultural dimension of the team—indicates that cultural change may be more challenging for organizations operating in the sport context.

Sport also provides an avenue for exploring the emergence and management of organizational culture in temporary organizations, a phenomenon Parent and MacIntosh (2013) examined in their study of the 2010 Winter Olympics Organizing Committee. They found that several organizational cultures collided within the staging of the Games, including those associated with the International Olympic Committee: the local organizing committee, the mountain (hosted in Whistler) versus city events (hosted in Vancouver), the specific venue, and functional responsibility (or the assignment one would receive). Subcultures emerged blending different expectations and values of these various influences. The continual integration of new members as the event drew close meant that orientations were important for socializing new organizational members, but so too were organizational members who had already been integrated into the existing structure—all of which contributed to a dynamic process of socializing new members to the values of the temporary organization and navigating both complementary and contrasting subcultures. Overall, there was pressure for the values to crystalize quickly given the temporary nature of the organization and the task at hand. The authors concluded that organizational structure, socialization, and cultural evolution parallel and should inform one another in temporary organizations.

This section has traced three lines of research connecting organizational communication and sport constructs: coach–athlete relationships as hierarchical arrangements, whistleblowing in the sport context, and organizational change in sport organizations. The closing section considers possible directions for future research at the intersection of organizational and sport communication.

Directions for Future Research in Sport and Organizational Communication

Several themes emerge from this chapter that guide and direct future endeavors designed to explore the intersection of sport and organizational communication further. First, organizations in the sport contexts have unique attributes that can influence the communication processes in organizations. These include established and resistant cultures, influential fans, permeable boundaries, multiple and varied subcultures (e.g., players, ballpark employees, etc.), and complex interlinked sporting systems (e.g., regional, national, and international governing bodies). Much of the work referenced here demonstrates how sport organizations function differently than other organizations. More of this type of work is necessary to continue flushing out these distinctions.

Second, the organizational attributes of sport organizations are varied and diverse. Coach–athlete relationships can be examined as hierarchical, teams can be explored as work groups, sport franchises can be viewed as akin to businesses, and associations, leagues, and larger entities essentially form entire organizational networks. Consequently, the study of sport and organizational communication remains disparate and at times unconnected, as researchers opt for any number of entry points. The current state of relative incongruence should dissipate, though, as future work increases in volume and this terrain becomes more clearly defined and more definitively mapped.

Third, there are several lines of organizational communication research that could prove fruitful when explored in the sport context. For example, how does conflict play out in sport organizations? Does the dynamic of team subcultures and fan influence affect organizational conflict? Similarly, how does the management of emotion differ in sport organizations? Sport is an emotion-laden undertaking, for both participants and fans, so it would follow that the management of emotion (i.e., emotional displays and rules governing emotional displays) might unfold differently. Organizations are rife with team and sport metaphors deployed as organizational symbols designed to build organizational culture and corporate loyalty. But what are the metaphors that take hold in sport organizations, how do they function, and how do they serve those who forward them? These are only a few of the possible connections to be made between organizational and sport communication; many more will be revealed as work in the area progresses.

References

Barnes, M., Cousens, L., & MacLean, J. (2007). From silos to synergies: A network perspective of the Canadian sport system. *International Journal of Sport Management and Marketing, 2*(5–6), 555–571.

Blake, R., & Mouton, J. (1964). *The Managerial Grid.* Houston, TX: Gulf.

Coombs, D.S., & Osborne, A. (2012). A case study of Aston Villa Football Club. *Journal of Public Relations Research, 24*(3), 201–221.

Cranmer, G.A. (in press). A continuation of sport teams from an organizational perspective: Predictors of athlete–coach leader–member exchange. *Communication & Sport.* doi: 10.1177/2167479514542151.

Cranmer, G.A., & Myers, S.A. (2014). Sports teams as organizations: A leader–member exchange perspective of player communication with coaches and teammates. *Communication & Sport, 3*(1), 100–118.

Deetz, S., & Mumby, D.K. (1990). Power, discourse, and the workplace: Reclaiming the critical tradition. In J. Anderson (Ed.), *Communication Yearbook, 13* (pp. 18–47). Beverly Hills, CA: Sage.

Fairhurst, G.T., & Putnam, L. (2004). Organizations as discursive constructions. *Communication Theory, 14,* 5–26.

Fielding-Lloyd, B., & Meân, L.J. (2008). Standards and separatism: The discursive construction of gender in English soccer coach education. *Sex Roles, 58*(1–2), 24–39.

Fielding-Lloyd, B., & Meân, L.J. (2011). "I don't think I can catch it": Women, confidence and responsibility in football coach education. *Soccer & Society, 12*(3), 345–364.

Frontiera, J. (2010). Leadership and organizational culture transformation in professional sport. *Journal of Leadership & Organizational Studies, 17*(1), 71–86.

Harter, L.M., & Krone, K.J. (2001). The boundary-spanning role of a cooperative support organization: Managing the paradox of stability and change in nontraditional organizations. *Journal of Applied Communication Research, 29,* 248–277.

Herzberg, F. (1976). *The managerial choice: To be efficient and to be human.* Homewood, IL: Dow Jones-Irwin.

Kassing, J.W., & Anderson, R. L. (2014). Contradicting coach or grumbling to teammates: Exploring dissent expression in the coach–athlete relationship. *Communication & Sport, 2*(2), 172–185.

Kassing, J.W., Billings, A.C., Brown, R.S., Halone, K.K., Harrison, K., Krizek, B., Katz, D., & Kahn, R.L. (1966). *The social psychology of organizations.* New York: Wiley.

Kramer, M.W. (2005). An ethnography of a fundraising marathon group. *Journal of Communication, 55*(2), 257–276.

Kramer, M.W. (2006). Shared leadership in a community theater group: Filling the leadership role. *Journal of Applied Communication Research, 34*(2), 141–162.

Leonardi, P.M., Treem, J.W., & Jackson, M. (2010). The connectivity paradox: Using technology to both decrease and increase perceptions of distance in distributed work arrangements. *Journal of Applied Communication Research, 38,* 85–105.

Mazer, J.P., Barnes, K., Grevious, A., & Boger, C. (2013). Coach verbal aggression: A case study examining effects of athlete motivation and perceptions of coach credibility. *International Journal of Sport Communication, 6*(2), 203–213.

McGlynn, J., & Richardson, B.K. (2014). Public support, private alienation: Whistleblowers and the paradox of social support. *Western Journal of Communication, 78*(2), 213–237.

McGregor, D. (1960). *The human side of enterprise.* New York: McGraw Hill.

Meân, L.J., & Turman, P.D. (2004). Communication in the community of sport: The process of enacting, (re)producing, consuming, and organizing sport. In P.J. Kalbfleisch (Ed.), *Communication Yearbook* (Vol. 28, pp. 373–409). Mahwah, NJ: LEA Publishers.

Ogbonna, E., & Harris, L.C. (2014). Organizational cultural perpetuation: A case study of an English Premier League football club. *British Journal of Management, 25*(4), 667–686.

Pacanowsky, M.E., & O'Donnell-Trujillo, N. (1983). Organizational communication as cultural performance. *Communication Monographs, 50,* 126–147.

Parent, M.M., & MacIntosh, E.W. (2013). Organizational culture in temporary organizations: The case of the 2010 Olympic Winter Games. *Canadian Journal of Administrative Sciences, 30*(4), 223–237.

Richardson, B.K., & McGlynn, J. (2011). Rabid fans, death threats, and dysfunctional stakeholders: The influence of organizational and industry contexts on whistle-blowing cases. *Management Communication Quarterly, 25,* 121–150.

Richardson, B.K., & McGlynn, J. (2015). Blowing the whistle off the field of play: An empirical model of whistle-blower experiences in the intercollegiate sport industry. *Communication & Sport, 3,* 57–80.

Ruggiero, T.E., & Lattin, K.S. (2008). Intercollegiate female coaches' use of verbally aggressive communication toward African American female athletes. *Howard Journal of Communications, 19*(2), 105–124.

Sanderson, J. (2011). To tweet or not to tweet: Exploring Division I athletic departments' social-media policies. *International Journal of Sport Communication, 4*(4), 492–513.

Stohl, C., & Cheney, G. (2001). Participatory processes/paradoxical practices: Communication and the dilemmas of organizational democracy. *Management Communication Quarterly, 14*(3), 349–407.

Taylor, F.W. (1911). *The principles of scientific management.* New York: Harper & Row.

Trujillo, N. (1992). Interpreting (the work and the talk of baseball: Perspectives on ballpark culture). *Western Journal of Communication, 56*(4), 350–371.

10

SPORT AS INTERGROUP COMMUNICATION

Fans, Rivalries, Communities, and Nations

Howard Giles and Michael Stohl

UNIVERSITY OF CALIFORNIA-SANTA BARBARA

> *Serious sport is war minus the shooting.*
>
> George Orwell, 2000

Our starting point is in 1945 with George Orwell's aphorism and the highly contested nature of the response to it during the past seven decades. He argues:

> I am always amazed when I hear people saying that sport creates goodwill between the nations, and that if only the common peoples of the world could meet one another at football or cricket, they would have no inclination to meet on the battlefield. Even if one didn't know from concrete examples (the 1936 Olympic Games, for instance) that international sporting contests lead to orgies of hatred, one could deduce it from general principles . . . Serious sport has nothing to do with fair play. It is bound up with hatred, jealousy, boastfulness, disregard of all rules and sadistic pleasure in witnessing violence: in other words it is war minus the shooting.
>
> *(Orwell, 2000, pp. 41–42)*

Studies have shown that war analogies (e.g., coaches addressing their 'troops') are frequently invoked when describing sport coverage (e.g., Rowe, 2004); militarism linked to nationalism can be a feature of mega-sport events (Butterworth, 2014). But, beyond the invoking of war metaphors, it is important to also note that while Orwell only focused on how sport divides on an intergroup basis, others have also noted that sport may serve both to bridge as well as reinforce intergroup divides by breaking down stereotypes, increasing understanding, and confining battles to the playing fields rather than the battlefield (Goldberg, 2000, p. 63).

Indeed, it is difficult to watch sport and read media reports without failing to note the integral intergroup dynamics attending them. Historically, this was evident with the Berlin Olympics in 1936 being embroiled with anti-Semitic tactics by the German authorities wishing to establish Aryan superiority, through to Communist regimes (e.g., East Germany) aiming to highlight the virtues of their political system, to the many national embargos of the Olympics over decades, and to the role of Black athletes in the Civil Rights Movement. In parallel, we have clashes between players of rival teams (e.g., at hockey games, Goldschmied & Espindola, 2013), the use of ethnic slurs on the pitch in European soccer (Dunning, Murphy, Waddington, & Astrinak, 2002), the frequently reported under-representations of ethnic minorities and women in coaching and managerial positions (Cunningham & Sagas, 2005), as well as the antics of Dennis Rodman in his appeal to so-called basketball diplomacy (Jackson, 2013).

A plethora of other instances exist across sport, including class elitism in private golf clubs and the 'coming out' of gay players in major American sports (e.g., soccer player Robbie Rogers and football player Michael Sam in 2013 and 2014, respectively). The Palio horse races in Siena (since 1665) are a classic example of different neighborhoods (*Contrada*) involved in intense competition, with the winning community celebrating for a week or more after. As many nations have their own distinctive foods, different cultures also have their own unique sports (e.g., Buzkashi in Afghanistan and Seprak Takraw in Indonesia). Some have had a major role in religious practices such as *Ullamalizli* stemming from the Mayans and still played in parts of Mexico; some even having their own World Cups (e.g., *Pesäpallo* from Finland) and imperial powers such as Great Britain have introduced (or imposed) their national sports (e.g., cricket) into the cultural life of conquered nations.

The emerging group identity issue is encapsulated in Norman Tebbit's famous 'cricket test,' which derived from a question in an interview in the *Los Angeles Times*: "A large proportion of Britain's Asian population fail to pass the cricket test. Which side do they cheer for? It's an interesting test. Are you still harking back to where you came from or where you are?" (Rowe, 2012, p. 24). James (1963), in the context of his majestic memoir, *Beyond a Boundary*, noted the power of sport, and particularly cricket, to challenge all boundaries, but particularly the intergroup boundaries of race and class. More recently, O'Neill's (2008) novel, *Netherland*, celebrated how cricket provided grounding and hope to multiple groups of immigrants in post-9/11 America, incorporating cricket into the American Dream. Then there is Jacques Barzun's quote (inscribed in the Baseball Hall of Fame): "Whoever wants to know the heart and mind of America had better learn baseball" (Barzun, 1954, p. 159). No sport is seemingly immune from diverse intergroup conundrums and, beyond that, the Oscars in Hollywood and American political elections have been construed in terms of races, together with the social implications such sport metaphors invite (Lipsky, 1979).

In short, we live in a globalized, sport-saturated world (see Whannel, 2013) and when nationally prized sports come into disrepute, an entire culture can come into question. Thus, the case of many Japanese Sumo wrestlers being publicly accused of cheating and, again, when jukodas (female national judo team) complained that their coach subjected them to humiliating verbal as well as physical abuse. We also note the discussions of national 'disaster' when national teams do poorly. A sense of national despair is often communicated by sport journalists after the USA's loss in basketball to the Soviet Union in 1972 or, more recently, following Brazil's thrashing at the hands of Germany in the 2014 World Cup. Victory brings the opposite emotions and celebrations as when, following the Soviet invasion of Czechoslovakia in 1968, the Czechs defeated the Soviets in the 1969 World Hockey championships (see acts of 'BIRGing' and 'CORFing' below). In the aftermath, "People were shouting, '[4]-3' everywhere. What it meant was: 'To hell with the Russians!' You had to know it. It wasn't a sports demonstration; it was a demonstration of national pride by over one hundred thousand people, and it went on for hours" (Skoug, 2012).

In communication and sport texts (e.g., Billings, Butterworth, & Turman, 2014) and journal issues (e.g., the inaugural special issue of *Communication and Sport* in 2013), different social groups such as gender and ethnicity are typically addressed in isolation. That said, there is a small array of treatises, notably Haridakis (2010, 2012), which have attempted to explore intergroup communication dynamics across various sports (see also Bryant & Cummins, 2010; and essays in Hugenberg, Haridakis, & Earnheardt, 2008). The major theoretical framework within these works has been social identity theory (SIT: e.g., Tajfel & Turner, 1979).

While there are many intergroup relationships inherent in sport, such as athletes–coaches, athletes–management, player rivalries (see Kassing & Anderson, 2014), in this chapter we invoke the influential theoretical frame of SIT to focus mostly on fan rivalry. However, it is useful to consider the differences among spectators, fans, and supporters detailed by Giulianotti (2002). Spectators are simply consumers of the sport product; fans have a much stronger identification with the club but a relationship that is unidimensional. Supporters, on the other hand, not only see themselves as 'members' of the club, but also believe they have a reciprocal relationship (or parasocial interactions) with it. While personal circumstances and characteristics play an important role, fandom is fundamentally both a group as well as an intergroup phenomenon. Hence, to understand the interaction of relevant processes through the lens of the social psychology of intergroup relations and intergroup communication, we organize our discussion under two categories: social identification and the subsequent communication of that social identity. We conclude with some intergroup communication principles relating to sport as well as some empirical propositions.

Social Identification

SIT is a social cognitive theory of group processes, intergroup relations, and collective self-conception (e.g., Hogg, 2006; Tajfel & Turner, 1979). It defines groups cognitively as collections of individuals who share a common evaluative self-definition—a shared social identity. There is an emphasis on both the cognitive process of identifying with a group and on the various corollaries of belonging to a group. Having a specific social identity (such as practicing being a team fan) not only defines the self-concept, but also locates someone relative to other relevant people and other groups in society. A key concept characterizing fandom is loyalty—being more of a so-called 'die-hard' than a 'fair weather' fan (Wann & Branscombe, 1990). When fans become strongly identified with their team, many are willing to remain members even under conditions of high personal cost (e.g., big losses and league demotions), forgoing attractive alternatives for allying with another team. Even further, when the level of identification is high, the self may be gone and group identity can dominate who they are, illustrated by Steelers' fans swaddling their babies in fan towels at birth, while others at the end of life feature coffins clothed in team colors (Van Vugt & Hart, 2004). An extreme example of how this group identity can dominate is found in Nick Hornby's (1992) memoir *Fever Pitch*. Hornby transcribes his life and memory in terms of events, transitions, and achievements in connection to games and seasons of Arsenal Football Club. That the film was then also adapted for the United States by substituting the Boston Red Sox for Arsenal and still had the same identity dynamics, tellingly and vividly illustrates the power of the sport–identity phenomenon.

Some basic demographic and geographic identities are also fostered and reinforced by sport teams. In sport, teams are generally understood to have a fan base based on geographic location, which is most frequently associated with the city in which the team is based, but in cities with multiple teams the location of the stadium may also be an important factor. In Chicago, Cubs fans live on the North Side and White Sox fans live on the South Side. In other parts of the United States, baseball identification for many years was based not only on geographic location but also on radio coverage (Walker, 2015). Before the New York Giants and Brooklyn Dodgers moved to the West Coast for the 1958 season, much of the U.S. population west of the Mississippi rooted for the St. Louis Cardinals, whose broadcasts covered the west and southwest of the United States. In the American northeast, New England is split between Red Sox and Yankees fans following an old pattern of regional radio and subsequent television links to Boston and New York (Walker, 2015).

The cognitive process of social categorization causes people to define themselves and others as members of social groups as well as to perceive themselves and others in group prototypical terms. Group prototypes tend not only to capture intragroup or within-group similarities, but also accentuate intergroup or between-group differences on relevant dimensions so as to mold their social identities distinctively (see Bernache-Assollant, Lacassagne, & Braddock, 2007). Together, these constructs and processes form the basis for one central assumption of SIT: obtaining and maintaining a favorable and well-defined social identity motivates behavior, as it does in emotionally protecting fans when their team is defeated (Lalonde, 1992) and/or their image tarnished (Hundley & Billings, 2010). The goal of both individuals and the collective (such as a sport team) is to strive for an evaluatively positive distinctiveness, oftentimes manifest in terms of linguistic and/or communication differentiation (e.g., Giles, 1978) as discussed in the next section. Relatedly, Becker, Tausch, and Wagner (2011) found that participating in collective action brought self-directed positive affect while creating out-group-directed anger and contempt. In other words, doing something on behalf of, and communicating forcibly and visibly about, one's group helps people feel better about themselves *as individuals*.

Teams may also represent and reinforce existing social identities that casual spectators perceive as independent of them. In Glasgow, two football teams are also associated with particular religions. Glasgow Celtic is aligned with Catholics, and Glasgow Rangers are aligned with the Protestant Unionists. Foer (2004) notes that in the period from 1996 to 2003, eight deaths and hundreds of assaults in Glasgow were directly linked to the matches between them. Intergroup social comparison describes how groups and their members compare themselves on group prototypical dimensions to make the in-group seem not only distinctive from—but also evaluatively superior to—a relevant out-group. Rival sport fans (as well as players) aspire to enhance or reinforce their status in comparison with other teams in an arbitrarily set system. They compete for a higher number of game attendees and seek resources such as bragging rights, number of members in a fan club, the size of waiting lists for season ticket holders, the quality and capacity of their stadium, market share, and profits.

Because people maintain multiple identities even beyond sport, the social identity that is significant is contingent upon circumstances the individual is experiencing, or how accessible that identity is in the individual's mind (Hogg, 2006). For those living in communities where teams and their fans are prevalent, involved, and socially available, the salience of sport may be especially high. From an SIT perspective, why at-risk youth become intense fans can be explained as a motivated response to two conditions: having an unfavorable identity such as lacking a shared family structure, or feeling uncertain about their identity as well as feeling anxious and marginalized (Hogg, 2014). Hence, strongly affiliating with a team can offer the sense of belongingness that family, school, and community may not always provide: a peer group of which they can be a part, a clear personal and social identity, increased autonomy from parents or guardians, a "path to manhood" if male (Messner, 2013), and the means by which to improve their social status (cf. Hogg, Siegel, & Hohman, 2011).

After all, many nations celebrate sport and its celebrities in old and new media (Billings & Hardin, 2015); hence, constructing a meaningful and validated identity by becoming a fan is deemed societally acceptable.

More specifically, turning to fandom reduces uncertainty by providing a better conception of one's social world along with a script for how one should behave and communicate (Hogg, Meehan, & Farquharson, 2010). In this way, individuals have to learn and be socialized into the norms, beliefs, values, and ways of behaving and communicating that are shared by other members of the group (Guimond, 2000). The more uncertain one is about their self-identity, the greater the probability that one will seek a group that is high in entitativity, where entitativity is that property of a group that makes it appear to have clear boundaries, internal homogeneity, tight social interaction, clear internal structure, common goals, and common fate (Campbell, 1958). Being a sport fan is a compelling example of highly entitative groups, especially fan groups with appealing organizational structures and their own media (e.g., fanzines or sport fans' magazines) that provide a distinctive and clearly defined social identity. Fanzines for British football clubs are the most well-known, but fans of the Chicago Black Hawks and St. Louis Blues hockey teams and the Boston Red Sox baseball team have also produced them (see, e.g., http:// yawkeywayreport.com/). While entitativity refers to the structure of a group rather than the group's behaviors, the process of self-categorization reducing uncertainty through group identification with high entitativity groups readily accounts for much of the group's behavior. Self-categorization depersonalizes self-conception and self-conformity; it assigns group normative attributes—including communicative behaviors—to self and, thus, causes people to behave in line with the group's norms (e.g., Hogg & Giles, 2012; Turner, Hogg, Oakes, Reicher, & Wetherell, 1987).

If the group's norms prescribe antisocial and aggressive behaviors, as is evident among certain fans and even players (e.g., hockey), this process of self-categorization-based depersonalization can cause people to behave riskily, antisocially and aggressively (Reicher, Spears, & Postmes, 1995; regarding so-called 'soccer hooligans,' see Frosdick & Marsh, 2005). Aggression can be one way to communicate team identity to other rivals and their communities, as acting violently can send the message that fans are capable of doing anything and best left alone, enhancing their reputation and status and commanding respect from in-group peers. Figuratively, Papachristos (2009) compared violence to a 'gift' demanding reciprocation if accepted, explaining that those who reciprocate violence would be able to maintain their reputation and honor. Yet as Haridakis (2010) stated, any

> focus on negative issues should not detract from the positive ways in which the vast majority of sports fans and spectators use sports to connect with each other and use intergroup communication to satisfy their basic human needs for affiliation, belongingness, and self-esteem. . . . It is in good clean fun. More importantly, it is healthy.
>
> *(pp. 259–260)*

Novelist Nick Hornby (1992) writes:

> I have learned things from the game. Much of my knowledge of locations in Britain and Europe comes not from school, but from away games or the sports pages, and hooliganism has given me both a taste for sociology and a degree of fieldwork experience. I have learned the value of investing time and emotion in things I cannot control, and of belonging to a community whose aspirations I share completely and uncritically.
>
> *(p. 62)*

Indeed, there are many, quite different, social functions for following a sport that make fandom alluring, and different typologies have been proposed for this (e.g., Bouchet, Bodet, Bernache-Assollant, & Kada, 2010).

As above, identity at the national level has also been fostered by sport. Duke and Crolley (1996, p. 4) have argued that an international football match perfectly illustrates the power of Anderson's (1991) notion of "imagined communities". Here, it is easy to confirm a national identity when eleven players are representing their country in a game against another country. They further argue that international football served to extend a sense of nationalism to the working class in the twentieth century. Czech hockey star Jaromir Jagr played on a number of National Hockey League teams yet always wore 68 as his number in honor of the 'Prague Spring' of 1968, reminding people of the invasion of Czechoslovakia by the Soviet Union (see Morreale, 2010).

Communicating Team Identity

We turn now, more specifically, to what intergroup messages are conveyed to fans, and how (across cultures and sports) they communicate their team identities to others. Clearly, one of the ways to exhibit an intergroup bias is the label for the very sport itself as indicated by the Lady Lakers or the Ladies Professional Golf Association (which functions to differentiate them from 'standard' men's teams), and also by the apparel athletes are encouraged/required to wear. In 2004, the president of the governing body of international soccer (FIFA) tried to persuade females to wear tighter shorts (Robinson & Clegg, 2015) and the Badminton World Federation decreed women must wear skirts or dresses to create a more "attractive presentation" (Longman, 2011). While these requests were reacted to with disdain, boxers from Poland and Romania donned skirts at the 2010 European Championships. In tandem, the name given to sport teams can be controversial. For example, Native Americans claim that referring to the Washington football team as the Redskins is grossly offensive. Similarly, Atlanta Braves fans performing the 'Tomahawk Chop' and cartoonish images conveyed by the Cleveland Indians can also be regarded as inflammatory; comparable controversy attends Coachella, a Californian high school's Arab mascot. Obviously, overt messages can be sent by the sight of male owners and coaches of women's teams to fans and spectators that can reinforce gender schemas.

The media also plays a major role in the proliferation of intergroup images. Stereotypes of age in the media were vividly portrayed by Atkinson and Herro's (2010) work on the tennis player, Andre Agassi, who was described as a "kid" at 24 but, four to five years later, as a member of the "geezer brigade," "ancient mariner," and "the wise ol gnome of tennis" at 29! Billings' (2008) analysis of Olympic TV coverage (1996–2006) found that male athletes receive the majority of airtime and female athletes were the target of twice as many comments about their physical appearance. Furthermore, male success was attributed to mental toughness and overcoming emotions, while a female counterpart's failure was attributed to succumbing to emotions (for notions of hypermasculinity and heteronormativity, see Bruce, 2013). Similarly, Hundley and Billings' (2010) media analysis of Tiger Woods' performances demonstrated that he was portrayed in similar ways to black athletes (e.g., lost concentration and lack of composure), but only when he was losing. Stone, Lynch, Sjomeling, and Darley (1999) demonstrated how these social stereotypes can have behavioral consequences to other situations beyond the immediacy of watching a game. They requested that black and white students attend a college basketball game and evaluate either black or white players afterwards. As predicted, white athletes were considered to have more basketball intelligence, while blacks were deemed more naturally athletic. Thereafter, these students asked to perform a completely separate golf task which was either framed as a test of 'sports intelligence' or 'natural ability'. So-called 'stereotype threat' emerged in that whites did worse under the latter condition—whereas blacks performed worse under the former.

A compelling team identity may be reinforced through: (a) the names fans adopt for themselves (e.g., 'Cheeseheads' for Green Bay Packers fans, and 'America's Team' for the Dallas Cowboys [reinforcing the intergroup divide]), (b) the clothes members wear (team tunics with players' names), (c) team colors and scarves (e.g., the Steelers' 'Terrible Towels'), (d) the in-group company at games and beyond they keep, (e) the attitudes expressed during a game (Cikara, Botvinick, & Fiske, 2011); and (f) the activities/rituals they participate in (e.g., singing and chanting team slogans), all of which tend to be exclusionary in nature (Serazio, 2013). Music provides particular ways of communicating an in-group identity (see Giles, Hadja, & Hamilton, 2009). Liverpool soccer claims the song "You'll Never Walk Alone" by Gerry and the Pacemakers while all the NFL and MLB teams have adopted different songs to celebrate the club (Chamernik, 2015a, 2015b). For example, the New York Yankees play Frank Sinatra's recording of "New York, New York" after every game while the San Francisco Giants play Tony Bennet's recording of "I Left My Heart in San Francisco" when they win. The Boston Red Sox play Neil Diamond's "Sweet Caroline" during the 8th inning of every game (Browne, 2013). To accentuate identity-related pride, fans also adorn themselves with tattoos that identify their particular team, marking their 'turf' or territory (e.g., with banners indicating, for example, "You're in Our House"). The language fans use with each other can also convey in-group solidarity. For instance, Love and Walker (2013) found that, in an English pub, sport fans sounded more American (by adopting the postvocal /r/) when talking about National Football League teams than when they were engaged about English Premier League soccer teams.

There is a growing literature examining communicative differences between, and the kinds of messages delivered by, highly, as opposed to lowly, identified fans. Cialdini et al. (1976) introduced the term 'BIRGing' (basking in reflected glory) as exemplified in highly vested college students wearing more team paraphernalia after their team had won, talking more to other fans using the 'we' referent, and seeking out media highlights of the game than less vested fans (End, Dietz-Uhler, Harrick, & Jacquemotte, 2002). Victory, thereby, can foster self-esteem for vested fans which can be construed as a personal success, activating the pleasure center in the brain (Cikara et al., 2011). Other strategies identified as characteristic of the highly vested include 'blasting' (i.e., hostile and derogating messages) out-group fans (e.g., "we may have lost, but we're way better than their fans") as well as losses being attributed to uncontrollable external factors, such as out-group cheating and bad or biased officiating (see Bernache-Assollant, Laurin, Bouchet, Bodet, & Lacassagne, 2010). Other messages that distinguish between highly and lowly identified fans (see Wann & Grieve, 2005) include the former: attending more games, expressing more pregame anxiety, having more of an emotional experience during the game, trying to destabilize the opposing team and their fans, engaging in more hostile out-group-directed acts, being more loyal to sponsors and purchasing more team-related products, and posting more internet messages after victory and accessing the team's web page more often.

Epilogue: Towards an Intergroup Communication Theory of Sport

Meân and Halone (2010) argued that "sport is essentially *unnatural*, given that it is organized, enacted, and reproduced through language and other communicative practices in ways that echo and maintain particular cultural forms and their ideological underpinnings" (p. 254). With Billings (2010), we can see that the mix of nationality, ethnicity, and politics, together with other intergroup settings, can be a potentially "dangerous communication cocktail" (p. 105).

In this regard on the opening night of the inaugural NBC TV show *Late Night Starring Jimmy Fallon* (February 17, 2014), Jimmy Fallon mentioned in his monologue that Russia had lost an Olympic hockey game to Norway. The outcome? Rapturous applause! (See the notion of *schadenfreude*, Cikara et al., 2011.) Despite significant advances in the last forty years, many hegemonic gender biases in reporting, naming, and attributing success and failure in discourse also still persist.

But sport can also foster a healthy, balanced sense of personal esteem, oft-becoming an instrument of international cooperation, social activism, civil rights, and social change, through a more enlightened positioning of nation, gender, race, age, and disability. This is illustratively manifest each April, when all major league ballplayers wear number 42 to both honor Jackie Robinson and reinforce the continuing struggle for civil rights. Sport may also signal the development of new national relationships as with the 'ping pong diplomacy' leading to the reestablishment of U.S.–PRC relationships in 1971.

We have not, of course, detailed all of the intricacies of sport from an intergroup communication lens. Indeed, we have characterized 'fans' somewhat homogeneously, acknowledging that there can be many contrasting subgroups having their own distinctive identities and communicative practices. Bernache-Assollant et al. (2010) studied the Olympique de Marseille soccer team and its eight fan groups. The oldest and elitist—the Commando Ultra—comprised largely middle-class fans who differentiated themselves from immigrants. They had a well-equipped organizational infrastructure—even a corporate culture—and would promote their jackets, caps, and so forth, to anyone. Another group—the South Winner—was created by high school students and was younger, more working class (often from immigrant families), and was more cosmopolitan. In addition, they were more anti-authority, fiercely Marseilleise (sometimes refusing a French identification) and out-group confrontational at games. Their logos depicted the city harbor and cathedral, and were only sold to their own fans. At the other extreme are transnational supraorganizations: Red Star Belgrade has two friend clubs, namely Olympiacos (Greece) and Spartak Moscow (Russia), and the three are dubbed collectively the 'Orthodox Brothers.' Intergroup theories, such as the common group identity model (Gaertner & Dovidio, 2000), could have explanatory value of communicative practices.

So whither next? Haridakis (2012) outlined features of what an intergroup communication theory of sport might resemble. Nonetheless, it would be prudent to at least consider whether we can forge an intergroup model that can adequately deal with *all* sport, although theories of sport in general do exist (Crone, 1999). After all, sports vary on many dimensions and debate even exists around whether any given sport qualifies to be called one, such as ESPN-televised poker, competitive eating, and musical chairs (which has its own World Federation, rules, World Cup, and world records). Nonetheless, we contend that there are sufficient intergroup communalities, as discussed above, that encourage us towards proposing an intergroup model of fandom, and towards that end we offer the following five (empirically testable) principles.

PRINCIPLE A: The more fans identify with their team, the more they will:

- frequently engage in, and create, historical narratives and everyday discourse on team and sport topics;
- in pre-, during, and post-games blast and craft intergroup accounts of, and attributions about, relative team performances (e.g., in-group favoritism

and out-group derogation, image protectic) that will maintain or enhance a positive identity (even in the face of losses);

- adorn prototypical dress styles and purchase team paraphernalia for the workplace and home;
- be vested in (ever-changing) team-related communication technology and social media (see Hardin, 2014);
- cumulatively foster empowerment and, hence, in-group pride and self-esteem.

PRINCIPLE B: The lower the number of *other* nonsporting (as well as other competing sport) identities fans possess and the lower the statuses of these as well as the intragroup prestige within them (e.g., work status), the more PRINCIPLE A will be endorsed (see Giles & Johnson, 1981).

PRINCIPLE C: The more fans' other nonsporting identities overlap with a sport identity (e.g., age- and ethnicity-related sports), the more PRINCIPLE A will be endorsed.

PRINCIPLE D: The more fans perceive their team's and sport's 'relative group vitality' to be low (e.g., decreasing fan base, inadequate sport facilities and media access), legitimate, and stable (Giles & Johnson, 1981), the more they will seek fandom or other social identities elsewhere (Bernache-Assollant et al., 2010).

PRINCIPLE E: The more fans perceive their team's and sport's relative group vitality to be strong (e.g., increasing numbers, media attention), the more they will be semiotically creative, contribute to fanzines, message boards, and the like, and compete via aggressive collective action with out-groups (especially those with local and/or historical rivalries).

Finally, it has been our goal to make the intergroup perspective accessible and analytically emancipating for understanding fan behavior. A next goal will be to develop the theoretical framework herein to be parsimoniously inclusive of other relevant sport entities, including parents, coaches, and administrators, and to explore other intergroup theoretical positions (see Taylor, King, & Usborne, 2010). With complex issues of globalization (Rowe, 2012) and super leagues evident, new medical and technological advances both for athletes and the sport, social media use proliferating, and sporting events including new sports increasing, and so on and so forth, we will need to continually refine and elaborate our studies and theoretical frames. How these multidimensional and numerous changes will affect the very nature of intergroup communication is an exciting prospect to witness in the future as is the issue raised by Gantz (2013) of how a team identity for a fan may be meaningfully different across the lifespan.

References

Anderson, B.R.O'G. (1991). *Imagined communities: Reflections on the origin and spread of nationalism.* London: Verso.

Atkinson, J.L., & Herro, S.K. (2010). From the chartreuse kid to the wise old gnome of tennis: Age stereotypes as frames to describe Andre Agassi at the U.S. Open. *Journal of Sport and Social Issues, 34,* 86–104.

Barzun, J. (1954). *God's country and mine.* Boston, MA: Little & Brown.

Becker, J.C., Tausch, N., & Wagner, U. (2011). Emotional consequences of collective action participation: Differentiating self-directed and outgroup-directed emotions. *Personality and Social Psychology Bulletin, 37,* 1587–1598.

Bernache-Assolant, L., Lacassagne, M-F., & Braddock, II, J.H. (2007). Basking in reflected glory and blasting: Differences in identity-management strategies between two groups of highly identified soccer fans. *Journal of Language and Social Psychology, 26,* 381–388.

Bernache-Assollant, I., Laurin, R., Bouchet, P., Bodet, G., & Lacassagne, M-F. (2010). Refining the relationship between ingroup identification and identity management strategies in the sport context: The moderating role of gender and the mediating role of negative mood. *Group Processes and Intergroup Relations, 13,* 639–652.

Billings, A.C. (2008). *Olympic media: Inside the biggest show on television.* London: Routledge.

Billings, A.C. (2010). *Communicating about sports media: Cultures collide.* Barcelona, Spain: Aresta.

Billings, A.C., Butterworth, M.L., & Turman, P.D. (2014). *Communication and sport* (2nd ed.). Thousand Oaks, CA: Sage.

Billings, A.C., & Hardin, M. (Eds.). (2015). *The Routledge handbook of sport and new media.* London: Routledge.

Bouchet, P., Bodet, G., Bernache-Assollant, I., & Kada, F. (2010). Segmenting sports spectators: Construct and preliminary validation of the sporting event experience scale. *Sport Management Review, 14,* 42–53.

Browne, I. (2013). Fenway Park's anthem started innocuously. *MLB.com.* Retrieved June 22, 2016, from http://m.mlb.com/news/article/45075964/fenway-parks-anthem-started-innocuously.

Bruce, T. (2013). On women and femininities. *Communication and Sport, 1,* 125–137.

Bryant, J., & Cummins, R.G. (2010). The effects of outcome of mediated and live sporting events: Non sports fans' self- and social identities. In H.L. Hundley & A.C. Billings (Eds.), *Examining identity in sports media* (pp. 217–238). Thousand Oaks, CA: Sage.

Butterworth, M.L. (2014). Public memorializing in the arena: Sport, the tenth anniversary of 9/11, and the illusion of democracy. *Communication and Sport, 2,* 203–224.

Campbell, D.T. (1958). Common fate, similarity, and other indices of the status of aggregates of persons as social entities. *Behavioral Science, 3,* 14–25.

Chamernik, M. (2015a). *MLB fight songs. UNIWATCH: The obsessive study of Athletics Aesthetics.* Retrieved June 22, 2016, from http://www.uni-watch.com/2015/04/06/pro-sports-fight-songs-mlb/.

Chamernik, M. (2015b). *NFL fight songs. UNIWATCH: The obsessive study of Athletics Aesthetics.* Retrieved June 22, 2016, from http://www.uni-watch.com/2015/04/13/pro-sports-fight-songs-nfl/.

Cialdini, R.B., Borden, R.J., Thorne, A., Walker, M.R., Freeman, S., & Sloan, L.R. (1976). Basking in reflected glory: Three (football) field studies. *Journal of Personality and Social Psychology, 34,* 366–375.

Cikara, M., Botvinick, M.M., & Fiske, S.T. (2011). Us versus them: Social identity shapes neural responses to intergroup competition and harm. *Psychological Science, 22*, 306–313.

Crone, J.A. (1999). Toward a theory of sport. *Journal of Sport Behavior, 22*, 321–339.

Cunningham, G., & Sagas, M. (2005). Access discrimination in intercollegiate athletics. *Journal of Sport and Social Issues, 29*, 148–163.

Dunning, E., Murphy, P., Waddington, I., & Astrinakis, A. (Eds.). (2002). *Fighting fans: Football hooliganism as a world problem*. Dublin, Ireland: University College Dublin Press.

Duke, V., & Crolley, L. (1996). *Football, nationality and the state*. London: Routledge.

End, C.M., Dietz-Uhler, B., Harrick, E.A., & Jacquemotte, L. (2002). Identifying with winners: A reexamination of sport fans' tendency to BIRG. *Journal of Applied Social Psychology, 32*, 1017–1030.

Foer, F. (2004) *How soccer explains the world*. New York: HarperCollins.

Frosdick, S., & Marsh, P. (2005). *Football hooliganism*. Cullompton, UK: Willan.

Gaertner, S.L., & Dovidio, J.F. (2000). *Reducing intergroup bias: The common ingroup identity model*. Philadelphia, PA: Psychology Press.

Gantz, W. (2013). Reflections on communication and sports: On fanship and social relationships. *Communication and Sport, 1*, 176–187.

Giles, H. (1978). Linguistic differentiation between ethnic groups. In H. Tajfel (Ed.), *Differentiation between social groups* (pp. 361–393). London: Academic Press.

Giles, H., Hajda, J.M., & Hamilton, D.L. (Eds.). (2009). Harmony and discord: The music of intergroup relations. *Group Processes and Intergroup Relations, 12*, 291–412.

Giles, H., & Johnson, P. (1981). The role of language in ethnic group relations. In J.C. Turner & H. Giles (Eds.), *Intergroup behavior* (pp. 199–243). Oxford, UK: Blackwell.

Giulianotti, R. (2002). Supporters, followers, fans and flaneurs: A taxonomy of spectator identities in football. *Journal of Sport and Social Issues, 26*, 25–46.

Goldberg, J. (2000). Sporting diplomacy: Boosting the size of the diplomatic corps. *The Washington Quarterly, 23*, 63–70.

Goldschmied, N., & Espindola, S. (2013) "I went to a fight the other night and a hockey game broke out": Is professional hockey fighting calculated or impulsive? *Sports health: A multidisciplinary approach, 5*, 458–462.

Guimond, S. (2000). Group socialization and prejudice: The social transmission of intergroup attitudes and beliefs. *European Journal of Social Psychology, 30*, 335–354.

Hardin, M. (2014). Moving description: Putting Twitter in theoretical context. *Communication and Sport, 2*, 113–116.

Haridakis, P.M. (2010). Rival sports fans and intergroup communication. In H. Giles, S.A. Reid, & J. Harwood (Eds.), *The dynamics of intergroup communication* (pp. 249–262). New York: Peter Lang.

Haridakis, P.M. (2012). Sport viewers and intergroup communication. In H. Giles (Ed.), *The handbook of intergroup communication* (pp. 344–356). New York: Routledge.

Hogg, M.A. (2006). Social identity theory. In P.J. Burke (Ed.), *Contemporary social psychological theories* (pp. 111–136). Palo Alto, CA: Stanford University Press.

Hogg, M.A. (2014). From uncertainty to extremism: Social categorization and identity processes. *Current Directions in Psychological Science, 23*, 338–342.

Hogg, M.A., & Giles, H. (2012). Norm talk and identity in intergroup communication. In H. Giles (Ed.), *The handbook of intergroup communication* (pp. 373–388). New York: Routledge.

Hogg, M.A., Meehan, C., & Farquharson, J. (2010). The solace of radicalism: Self-uncertainty and group identification in the face of threat. *Journal of Experimental Social Psychology, 46*, 1061–1066.

Hogg, M.A., Siegel, J.T., & Hohman, Z. (2011). Groups can jeopardize your health: Identifying un-healthy groups to reduce self-uncertainty. *Self and Identity, 10*, 326–335.

Hornby, N. (1992). *Fever pitch.* London: Victor Gollancz.

Hugenberg, L.W., Haridakis, P.M., & Earnheardt, A.C. (Eds.). (2008). *Sportsmania: Essays on fandom and the media in the 21st century* (pp. 63–77). Jefferson, NC: McFarland.

Hundley, H.L., & Billings, A.C. (2010). *Views from the fairway: Media explorations of identity in golf.* Cresskill, NJ: Hampton Press.

Jackson, S.J. (2013). The contested terrain of sport diplomacy in a globalizing world. *International Area Studies Review, 16*, 274–284.

James, C.L.R. (1963). *Beyond a boundary.* London: Paul Hutchinson.

Kassing, J.W., & Anderson, R.L. (2014). Contradicting coach or grumbling to teammates: Exploring dissent expression in the coach–athlete relationship. *Communication and Sport, 2*, 172–185.

Lalonde, R.N. (1992). The dynamics of group differentiation in the face of defeat. *Personality and Social Psychology Bulletin, 18*, 336–342.

Lipsky, R. (1979). The athletization of politics: The political implication of sports and symbolism. *Journal of Sport and Social Issues, 28*, 28–38.

Longman, J. (2011). Badminton's new dress code is being criticized as sexist. *New York Times.* Retrieved June 22, 2016, from http://www.nytimes.com/2011/05/27/sports/badminton-dress-code-for-women-criticized-as-sexist.html?_r=0.

Love, J., & Walker, A. (2013). Football versus football: Effect of topic on /r/ realization in American and English fans. *Language and Speech, 56*, 443–460.

Meân. L.J., & Halone, K.K. (2010). Sport, language, and culture: Issues and intersections. *Journal of Language and Social Psychology, 29*, 253–260.

Messner, M. (2013). On men and masculinities. *Communication and Sport, 1*, 113–124.

Morreale, M. (2010). Czech-Russia rivalry defines blood feud. *NHL.com.* Retrieved May 20, 2015, from http://www.nhl.com/ice/news.htm?id=517914.

O'Neill, J. (2008). *Netherland.* New York: Pantheon.

Orwell, G. (2000). *In front of your nose, 1945–1950* (pp. 40–44). New York: Harcourt, Brace, & World.

Papachristos, A. (2009). Murder by structure: Dominance relations and the social structure of gang homicide. *American Journal of Sociology, 115*, 74–128.

Reicher, S.D., Spears, R., & Postmes, T. (1995). A social identity model of deindividuation phenomena. *European Review of Social Psychology, 6*, 161–198.

Robinson, J., & Clegg, J. (2015). Why FIFA can't get out of its own way. *Wall Street Journal.* Retrieved June 22, 2016, from http://www.wsj.com/articles/why-fifa-cant-get-out-of-its-own-way-1432242986.

Rowe, D. (2004). *Sport, culture and the media.* Maidenhead, UK: Open University Press.

Rowe, D. (2012). Reflections on communication and sport: On nation and globalization. *Communication and Sport, 1*, 18–29.

Serazio, M. (2013). The elementary forms of sports fandom: A Durkheimian exploration of team myths, kinship, and totemic rituals. *Communication and Sport, 1*, 303–325.

Skoug, K. (2012). Interview. Retrieved May 21, 2015, from http://adst.org/2012/08/blood-on-ice/.

Stone, J., Lynch, C.I., Sjomeling, M., & Darley, J.M. (1999). Stereotype threat effects on black and white athletic performance. *Journal of Personality and Social Psychology, 77*, 1213–1227.

Tajfel, H., & Turner, J.C. (1979). An integrative theory of intergroup conflict. In W.G. Austin & S. Worchel (Eds.), *The social psychology of intergroup relations* (pp. 33–47). Monterey, CA: Brooks-Cole.

Taylor, D.M., King, M., & Usborne, E. (2010). Towards theoretical diversity in inter-group communication. In H. Giles, S.A. Reid, & J. Harwood (Eds.), *The dynamics of intergroup communication* (pp. 263–276). New York: Peter Lang.

Turner, J.C., Hogg, M.A., Oakes, P.J., Reicher, S.D., & Wetherell, M.S. (1987). *Rediscovering the social group: A self-categorization theory*. Oxford, UK: Blackwell.

Van Vugt, M., & Hart, C.M. (2004). Social identity as social glue: The origins of group loyalty. *Journal of Personality and Social Psychology, 86*, 585–598.

Walker, J.R. (2015). *Crack of the bat: A history of baseball on the radio*. Lincoln, NE: University of Nebraska Press.

Wann, D.L., & Branscombe, N.R. (1990). Die-hard and fair-weather fans: Effects of identification on BIRGing and CORFing tendencies. *Journal of Sport and Social Issues, 14*, 103–117.

Wann, D.L., & Grieve, F.G. (2005). Biased evaluations of ingroup and outgroup specta-tor behavior at sporting events: The importance of team identification and threats to social identity. *Journal of Social Psychology, 145*, 531–545.

Whannel, G. (2013). On mediatization and cultural analysis. *Communication and Sport, 1*, 7–17.

11

SPORT AS INTERPERSONAL COMMUNICATION

Paul D. Turman

SOUTH DAKOTA BOARD OF REGENTS

Sport represents a complex, multilayered, and pervasive institution composed of athletes, coaches, and parents/families working collectively to shape experiences for those involved. As these individuals are presented with opportunities to engage each other around sport, they are shaped by forces that not only impact performance, but also shape how they reflect upon their experience. Athletes form relationships with their teammates allowing them to compete, resolve conflict, express themselves, and build cohesive bonds. Coaches exert influence over athletes by employing a set of soft skills emphasizing interpersonal communication necessary to shape team goals, provide instruction, enhance athletic skill, and relate to players as they confront challenges. Finally, for many families, sport consumes a significant portion of leisure activities; for larger families with multiple youth athletes, it is not uncommon for sport to constitute a central role in parent–child interaction and family leisure time (discussed at greater length in the following chapter by Nussbaum exploring Sport as Family Communication). As more family time and resources are devoted toward sport, there is further opportunity for family communication driven by sport participation.

This chapter seeks to explore the role that interpersonal communication serves in mediating relationships among athletes, coaches, and families who participate in sports. To accomplish this goal, the chapter is divided into three primary sections. First, the connection between interpersonal communication theory and sport research is discussed to assess how coaches and athletes form relationships. While specific interpersonal communication research is limited across this relationship type, there are a number of useful avenues for exploring the role of compliance-gaining, coach communication styles, and the role that specific coaching messages have for fostering coaching–athlete interaction. Second, family communication theory and research are explored to embrace the role that sport has in the important socialization process for many families. Research seeking to better understand the role of parental pressure and support are assessed, along with how communication theories can serve as a useful lens for how parents discuss sport with their children, and how relationships are formed between parents and coaches. The chapter concludes with a brief discussion of the avenues for future research that would be useful in understanding the role that interpersonal communication theory can serve to improve sport participation. In particular, areas for expanding our understanding of communication theory are assessed.

Coach Communication and Sport

Coaches serve an influential role in structuring how athletes understand, perform in, and reflect upon the broader community of sport. A small group of scholars have sought to more clearly understand the communicative influences coaches have on their athletes, examining factors such as a coach's leadership styles (Turman, 2001, 2003), argumentativeness (Kassing & Infante, 1999), and aggression and hostility (Sagar & Jowett, 2012). One theme across each of these research studies has been an emphasis on the communication that occurs at the interpersonal level between coaches and athletes. Despite the fact that coaches are in a position of power, the interaction is highly interpersonal in nature. The ability for coaches at all levels to possess the interpersonal communication skills necessary to gain compliance, persuade athletes, build intimacy, and even foster regret are a small number of the interpersonal communication perspectives that have significance when applied to a sport setting involving coaches and athletes.

Compliance-Gaining

Research examining persuasive messages at the individual level has suggested that one's successful attempt to persuade others to behave in a particular way is based on the effective utilization of various compliance-gaining techniques (Marwell & Schmitt, 1967). In their initial research examining the effectiveness of compliance-gaining messages, Marwell and Schmitt (1967) identified 16 techniques that were then collapsed into five compliance-gaining dimensions. Their findings argued that when faced with situations in which compliance-gaining was necessary, individuals would select from one of five strategies including: (a) *rewarding activity*, requiring the manipulation of the environment using positive methods such as pre-giving or making promises; (b) *punishing activity*, whereby individuals used negative manipulation of the other's environment by making specific threats or aversive stimulation; (c) the use of one's own *expertise*, which could be both negative or positive, and displayed to known rewards or consequences associated with compliance; (d) the *activation of impersonal commitments*, which were messages which focused on the other's self-esteem or made moral appeals to gain compliance; and

(e) *activation of personal commitments*, whereby the individual attempts to persuade the other by focusing on issues of debt or altruism.

Since the initial development of this typology of compliance dimensions, scholars have examined the use of compliance-gaining across a variety of contexts, including doctor–patient (Parrott, Burgoon, & Ross, 1992), supervisor–subordinate (Adams, Schlueter, & Barge, 1988), and teacher–student relationships (Kearney & Plax, 1987). Coach–athlete relationships also embody many of the same orientations to power as the relationship types examined in these research studies. Regardless of the context, individuals are predisposed to fulfill a variety of social, personal, and interpersonal needs that must be met, and Schutz's (1958) fundamental interpersonal relations orientations categorized three continua of interpersonal needs for individuals. He argued that we have a greater or lesser need for inclusion, control, and affection. When these needs are met, individual affect is increased, and when this occurs it produces more fulfilling relationships and more satisfying environments for those involved. When examined in a sport setting, Turman and Schrodt (2004) assessed the connection between athlete affect and coaching behaviors, finding a positive association between prosocial behaviors and an inverse association with antisocial ones.

Coach Communication Styles

The 'positive coaching alliance' represents a movement that impresses upon coaches to encourage athletes to enjoy sport as a positive character-building experience, and advocates a coaching philosophy that is centered around the ability to use positive feedback. The goal is to draw upon affirming messages to reflect approximately 75% of statements to players. When coaches draw upon punitive actions to influence their athletes, they invite stress; yet positive feedback and reinforcement strategies have been found to have a greater impact on athletes' optimal performance, satisfaction levels, enjoyment, and self-esteem. Similar results have been found when examining the relationship between prosocial coaching behaviors and athlete satisfaction toward their sport. Weiss and Friedrichs (1986) observed that coaches who use rewarding behavior, social support, and display a democratic decision-making style had more highly satisfied athletes.

When collapsing communication styles (democratic, training and instruction, social support, and positive feedback) into one general prosocial style, studies have found that this type of behavior is positively associated with athletes' ability to positively acquire sport knowledge (Turman & Schrodt, 2004). Contrary to prosocial behaviors enacted by coaches, an autocratic style (e.g., antisocial or custodial behaviors enacted by coaches) is inversely correlated with athletes' affect toward the sport, suggesting that coaches who rely solely on autocratic behaviors may find their athletes demonstrating less appreciation for the sport, their teammates, and—perhaps most importantly—their coach. Even when accounting for success, it has been found that an autocratic communication style in the presence of moderate to high levels of positive feedback may actually increase an athlete's affect, whereas the sole use of autocratic behaviors may lead to a decline. This tends to support 'traditional,' anecdotal notions that effective coaching is inherently a form of 'tough love.' In other words, coaches can portray an autocratic style as long as athletes know that their coaches have their best interests in mind and can occasionally communicate some form of positive feedback that fosters positive interpersonal relationships.

Coaching Messages

Coach–athlete interaction can occur across a variety of contexts (i.e., informal coaching sessions, during practice, halftime, etc.), giving coaches a range of options for communicating with athletes. The type of performance feedback a coach offers serves as an important feature of any interpersonal process, whereby coaches are afforded the opportunity to provide an assessment of athletes' overall performance in a way that best suits their goals. As the positive coaching movement might attest, the messages coaches select to frame their feedback can directly influence the attributions athletes make about their athletic experience. For example, a coach's decision to place the blame on the team's star athlete after a loss is quite different from one who might choose to encourage the player who missed the final shot that marked the end of the season. The coach may also place the blame on him- or herself or even make a point to bolster esteem of struggling players by using the pregame speech to challenge them to perform beyond their means. Gallmeier (1987) followed a professional hockey team throughout the season, noting that the coach relied upon the pregame speech to 'psych up' players, especially in situations where the coach did not have access to the players throughout the day. Players exposed to these speeches were found to have higher levels of self-efficacy and larger margins of victory.

The messages coaches select can be powerful predictors for how athletes view their athletic experiences and the nature of their relationship with the coach. The messages that coaches employ during competitive situations have also been found to produce feelings of regret as athletes are called upon to reflect on what could have or should have happened. *Regret* is defined as a complex emotion causing individuals to make judgments about events they take part in, and they have the ability to feel regretful not only about their participation in past experiences but also about how decisions concerning future events are made. For instance, Turman (2005, 2007) identified six types of regret messages used by coaches during interaction with athletes. The most predominant was *accountability regret*, which represented coaches' need to assign blame or praise for an athletic event ("If we just would have gone for it on fourth down, we could have won the game"). *Individual performance regret* messages were used to help magnify the potential self-regret felt by individual athletes after a poor performance/outcome. *Collective failure regret* signified messages that demonstrated how athlete performance was potentially linked to the disappointment of their teammates or coach. *Social significance regret* was derived from the coach's efforts to construct the game as socially significant for their players. Coaches relied on *regret reduction* to reduce the potential regret felt by athletes after a loss, and as the season drew to a close, a number of coaches relied on regret messages that described the *future regret* players would experience as a result of a team loss ("Lose this game and you'll take it to the grave"). How coaches choose to frame their messages to athletes not only has a psychological effect for how they recall their athletic experience, it also shapes the nature of the relationships they have with their players. Similar opportunities for interpersonal interaction occur among family members as they negotiate the role that sport will serve in guiding family dynamics.

Family Communication and Sport

Family communication scholars have defined socialization as an interdependent learning process allowing individuals to successfully orient themselves to the system they are exposed to (Miller, 2009). Traditionally, family socialization research has operated under two fundamental approaches by either emphasizing what is learned, or how the socialization process itself occurs for family members (Ashforth, Sluss, & Harrison, 2007). When these two approaches are applied to the socialization process occurring within sport, the strongest emphasis has been on an evaluation of behaviors (i.e., support, pressure, etc.) functioning to orient one to viewing athletic activity as a rewarding experience. Although the socialization process for children and young adults occurs across a variety of contexts or social settings (school, organization, and work), the family stands out as one of the primary sites for learning. In this context, the parent serves as highly influential as a socialization agent for children.

Sport has been shown to fulfill a number of important functions in the development of children. Roberts, Treasure and Hall (1994) stated, "in play, games, and sport, children are brought into contact with social order and the values inherent in society, and are provided a context within which desirable social behaviors are developed" (p. 631). Grounded in a family socialization model (Mead, 1934), sport socialization research argues that learning should occur through an athlete's exposure to the sport (e.g., the actual enactment of sport, interacting with other athletes, following rules and procedures developed for the sport) and the reinforcement that is received from others (e.g., role models, peers, parents, coaches). Baxter-Jones and Maffulli (2003) suggested parents with an active interest in sport are more likely to expose their children to sport at an early age and allow sport to become an important part of the family's leisure time. As more family time and resources are devoted toward sport, there is an increased opportunity for parents to provide feedback to encourage participation and influence coaching decisions. Despite the perceived benefit for parents and children, sport participation can produce emotions ranging from excitement to apprehension, and direct and indirect messages about sport participation can either foster or deter child involvement (Kidman, McKenzie, & McKenzie, 1999), stress (Hirschhorn & Loughead, 2000), and drop-out rates (Bergin & Haubusta, 2004). As a result, research has sought to examine specific types of feedback provided by parents to young athletes to evaluate the impact of messages that emphasize parental support or pressure.

Parental Support

Social support is a benefit many people seek from disclosure (Derlega, Metts, Petronio, & Margulis, 1993) and these benefits include: (a) *esteem support*, represented by support given to help a person feel loved, valued, and accepted even though the person may be going through difficult times; (b) *informational support*, in which guidance, advice, or information is given to help a person cope with a problem; (c) *instrumental support*, defined by tangible support given to a person who needs assistance; and (d) *motivational support*, represented by encouragement from others. Hirschhorn and Loughead (2000) observed that supportive parents (noninterfering with a focus on effort rather than winning) utilized more open communication and encouraged children to develop at their own pace. Additionally, Hoyle and Leff (1997) observed that when feedback was presented in a positive light, parental support was associated with athlete enjoyment toward the sport as well as perceived sport importance. Athletes who reported higher levels of enjoyment also displayed higher levels of self-esteem. When assessing technique for encouraging sport participation, Roberts et al. (1994) found parents to most commonly emphasize goal-reaching, followed by pointing out the child's personal improvement or growth, importance of trying your best, and reward for hard work and overcoming difficulties. These findings also indicate that children perceive two conceptually different types of parental involvement, one that represents *parental facilitation* of the children's activity participation, and one that suggests *parental control* of the child's activity participation and imposes performance standards. For some athletes this parental control could be perceived as a moderate form of parental pressure.

Parental Pressure

Despite the potential positive benefits resulting from parent–child sport interaction, research has also demonstrated how parental influence can produce detrimental results (Roberts et al., 1994). When examining the negative repercussions of parental involvement, messages that continually focus on success and performance-based outcomes establish an expectation in children that winning is the only way to satisfy. Ego-building involves instances where parents' natural instinct is to wish for their children's success in their respective sport. Hirschhorn and Loughead (2000) found that children can develop the fear that their standing with parents is based on their on-field performance, which can produce long-term effects that influence the parent–child relationship. Often the parents will attempt to live vicariously (i.e., living through the success/failure of another's athletic performance) through their child, believing that the performance of the child is a direct reflection of them (Hirschhorn & Loughead, 2000). This biased approach causes the child stress and lowers satisfaction of the sport itself. Roberts et al. (1994) presented a typology of negative parental attitudes that are often passed on to children, including a need to: (a) outperform their opponents; (b) show others they were the best; (c) demonstrate their superiority; (d) accomplish something others could not; and (e) exhibit dominance over others. White, Kavussanu, Tank, and Wingate (2004) found a strong correlation between parent and child sport orientation (both task and social). Specifically, young athletes who had parents who held a task orientation were also more likely to view sport in a similar fashion (i.e., effort leads to success in sport). Those parents with a high ego orientation were also more likely to have young athletes with this orientation, producing negative assumptions about sport involvement (i.e., success is achieved through deception and external factors).

Research examining interpersonal exchanges that foster parental pressure or support reinforces the need for parents to provide a combination of private and public disclosures. Much of the existing research highlights the harmful nature of such parental comments. For instance, Kidman et al. (1999) observed that 35% of comments made by parents at sporting events resulted in forms of correcting child performance, scolding for inappropriate play, or contradicting coach recommendations. Turman (2007) conducted interviews with parents of young athletes to explore the factors that necessitated a talk with the child about the nature of their sport participation in the private family setting. Four prominent themes were identified, beginning with *playing time*, which included instances where parents confronted their child's frustration about playing time by interpreting the situation from the coach's perspective. *Sport politics* focused on factors outside the control of the child's athletic ability and resting on the subjective decision-making of the coach. Issues such as favoritism and overreliance on star athletes resulted in the need for parents to talk about the politics of sport with their children. *Negative coaching behaviors* included actions where parents questioned the coach's objectivity and ethical practices with their child or the team. When faced with coaches that displayed behaviors they deemed inappropriate, parents used the private family setting as a place to interpret the coach's behavior for the child. Finally, *sport competitiveness* included instances where parents perceived sport had become too competitive by placing an overemphasis on winning. These parents perceived that winning was promoted to be more important than learning to play the sport and that overbearing parents inadvertently discouraged their own desire to have their children participate.

As a result, parents indicated a need to address this topic with their children as a way to encourage continued participation by de-emphasizing such inappropriate behavior.

Parent–Coach Interaction

Not only do parents spend time providing feedback to their children, but also parents and coaches have been found to collide over the objectives for sport participation (i.e., skill development vs. fostering competitive environment), requiring that parents and coaches must negotiate boundaries for their relationships. Communication privacy management (CPM) theory (Petronio, 1994, 2002) suggests that sharing private information is not easy and is regulated by two factors: boundary structures and rule management. Communication boundary structures identify who is and who is not allowed access to private information, while rule management represents the regulation of private information that moderates boundary linkage, boundary ownership, and boundary permeability (Petronio, 2000). Petronio further described four interrelated dimensions associated with communication boundaries, including ownership, control, permeability, and levels. *Ownership* represents an individual's right to reveal or conceal private information about themselves, whereby individuals assess the amount of risk associated with revealing private information. *Control* refers to whom private information is shared with. For instance, a connection to a child's coach may make one privy to information that is restricted to other parents. Making choices about who has access to private information influences the *permeability* of one's communication constructed boundaries. Free exchange results in permeable boundary management. Finally, *levels* represent the individuals within the subsystem who have access to information (i.e., assistant coaches, players, the team, parents).

In her description of communication privacy management (CPM), Petronio (2002) argues, "The regulation process is fundamentally communicative in nature. Consequently, CPM places communication at the core of private disclosure because it focuses on the interplay of granting or denying access to information that is defined as private" (p. 3). Taking this theoretical perspective toward parent–coach sport boundaries, Turman, Zimmerman, and Dobesh (2009) explored the techniques parents used to develop relationships with their child's coach and what necessitated the need for those relationships. These parent types include: (a) *spectators* who maximized their distance from the coach, but made conscious efforts to ensure the coach recognized their presence and level of support; (b) *enthusiasts* who made a point to offer insight or encouragement to the coach, and used these opportunities to demonstrate their level of knowledge about the particular sport as a way to establish a level of status or influence over coaching decisions; and (c) *fanatics*, consisting of parents who perceived permeable boundaries between themselves and the coach, being willing to openly address issues and topics directly, either face-to-face or over the phone.

Directions for Future Research

To date, interpersonal communication research has focused primarily on the generation of theory in more traditional relationship types, and the application of interpersonal concepts to family, instructional, organizational settings. This lack of exploration is likely due to a number of issues. First, interpersonal and family research are still considered to be new areas of communication research that are growing and expanding an original theory base that has tended to focus primarily on traditional interpersonal/family constructs. Not until more recently have researchers begun to expand beyond this theoretical foundation to establish contextual differences for same-sex couples, blended families, or alternatives to face-to-face interaction. The emphasis has traditionally been on examining the nature of interpersonal and family exchanges, rather than attempting to explore contextual factors that facilitate the need for interaction, and then the impact that context stimulus may have on the nature of the relationships that are formed. Second, and related to the infancy of the subdiscipline, the application of theory into other contexts that include relationships formed around sport consumption or participation requires a theoretical foundation from which to build. Fortunately for communication and sport scholars, the formation of this theoretical foundation now provides a framework from which to begin establishing the significance that sport can serve in these intimate relationships. Even the most casual reader can accept that interpersonal communication serves an integral role in how sport is enacted and performed. This chapter sought to focus your attention on three primary relationship types (i.e., coach–athlete, athlete–parent, and coach–parent), but there are certainly many others warranting further investigation and encompassing meaningful interpersonal relationships. For example, there is a wealth of research on the factors that aid in building cohesion among players in small group sport; however, this research base has tended to focus more broadly on task and social features of that interaction from a psychological perspective. Questions worthy of exploration for teammates include how are these relationships formed, what factors impact their formation, and how do the effects of winning and losing adversely/positively impact these relationships? Also worthy of investigation is the role a coach serves in helping to encourage strong bonds among teammates, and whether it is in the best interest of a coach to promote these relationships when simultaneously seeking to instill a heightened level of competitiveness among athletes.

From a theoretical perspective, a number of interpersonal theories lend themselves to research opportunities that may aid in enhancing the tenets of major theoretical underpinnings. For instance, Berger and Calabrese's (1975) uncertainty reduction theory has been a foundational interpersonal theory that has received considerable attention over the past three decades. Relationships formed through sport present opportunities for reducing uncertainty surrounding coaching decisions, parental motives, or conflict that may emerge as participants navigate their motives for sport involvement (winning at any cost vs. basic enjoyment achieved from playing the game). For instance, the foundation of CPM is grounded in this dialectal framework (Baxter & Montgomery, 1996), arguing that individuals experience tensions that necessitate change in their relationship. One primary tension is the desire to reveal and conceal information (i.e., openness vs. closedness), whereby coaches must negotiate parental desire to uncover playing time decisions and need for a relationship with the coach (autonomy vs. connection). A coach's power over athletes and the ability to maintain boundaries with parents often rests upon their ability to withhold information and elicit uncertainty. Of primary interest is whether our understanding of basic interpersonal theories can be further enhanced by expanding the contexts in which one seeks to apply the basic tenets to contexts such as sport, forcing one to reconsider how applicable they are across contexts.

For an alternative theoretical perspective, when seeking to evaluate verbal and nonverbal behaviors impacting interpersonal communication, Mehrabian (1969) grounded immediacy behaviors in approach–avoidance theory, suggesting that they represent behaviors that diminish psychological and physiological distance. Its central premise is that individuals would be attracted to and willing to approach those they liked, while avoiding those they disliked. Andersen (1979) described nonverbal immediate behaviors as "communication behaviors engaged in when a person maintains closer physical distance," (p. 545) including behaviors such as touching others, use of gestures and eye contact, length of interaction, informal dress, and relaxed body position. Those with high verbal immediacy used behaviors signaling openness for communication, or used words that include both the sender and receiver (e.g., we, our). Conversely, placing a focus on the individual sender or receiver (e.g., I, you, they) often produced low levels of immediacy and signaled to more avoidance qualities. When applied within a classroom setting, research on teacher immediacy has contended that physical contact has an adverse impact on students because of the parameters for physical proximity. While many coaches may fulfill similar functions as teachers due to the instructional role they perform, to suggest that research in this area easily translates to the coach–athlete relationship may be misguided. Coaches routinely come into physical contact with their athletes. In certain instances, such behavior could be interpreted as mutual affirmation, while in other instances the behavior reflects acts of aggression on the part of a coach that blur the lines of appropriate behavior. Our understanding of nonverbal immediacy behaviors may be further extended if examined as a feature of coach–athlete interpersonal interaction as one seeks to better understand the distinctions across these contexts.

There are also a range of research opportunities for applying family communication constructs to the socialization processes surrounding sport. As it relates to parental pressure and support, previous research on topic avoidance has found that openness between parents is directly tied to relationship satisfaction and solidarity (Bochner, 1982; Crohan, 1992); evaluating additional factors that contribute to the intrinsic motivation for continued sport participation would seem valuable. How does parent–child interaction about these sport topics influence athlete satisfaction and relationship with the coach? Are there certain topics that parents should avoid talking about with their children? What topics would children identify and disclose with their parents about sport? These are some questions that could be answered by examining parent–child sport-talk from a communication perspective.

Along these same lines, it is difficult to estimate how athletes view the interaction they have with their parents about sport. The interaction (both implicit and explicit) that occurs between parents and children in the private setting provides a valuable look at the true nature of the sport socialization process. As sport and family continue to intersect in meaningful ways, communication scholars are presented with the opportunity to apply a communicative lens to help families address interaction problems that emerge within and about sport. Much can be learned about the role that communication (or lack thereof) plays in producing tension that sport families might experience. Additionally, the examination of the role of sport within the family unit has the potential to better inform family research. Sport as a source of conflict, tension, cohesion, bonding, topic of talk, and/or loyalty within the family may serve as an important variable that speaks to the structure of many families within today's society. Methodologically, in-depth interviews or open-ended surveys would be appropriate to ask athletes and coaches to reflect on specific topics of talk and describe how parents address these topics when they arise. It would also be interesting to assess coach perceptions of parent relationships. It seems warranted for future researchers to interview the combination of athlete, parent, and coach. Doing so would provide an opportunity to determine how a combination of perspectives best reflects these aspects of the athletic experience.

By continuing to examine how sport is enacted, we are afforded the opportunity to evaluate factors that not only influence athlete performance, but also better comprehend how communication mediates athlete experiences within the community of sport. Specifically, interpersonal communication scholars should be encouraged to extend the boundaries of the traditional relationships and across family communication context. Doing so across the life span provides one with the opportunity to better understand how sport competition transcends the playing field and extends into many of our everyday activities and events.

References

Adams, C.H., Schlueter, D.W., & Barge, J.K. (1988). Communication and motivation within the superior-subordinate dyad: Testing the conventional wisdom of volunteer management. *Journal of Applied Communication, 16*(2), 69–81.

Andersen, J.F. (1979). Teacher immediacy: A predictor of teaching effectiveness. In D. Nimmo (Ed.), *Communication Yearbook 3* (pp. 543–559). New Brunswick, NJ: Transaction.

Ashforth, B.E., Sluss, D.M., & Harrison, S.H. (2007). Socialization in organizational contexts. In G.P. Hodgkinson & J.K. Ford (Eds.), *International review of industrial and organizational psychology* (Vol. 22, pp. 1–70). Chichester: Wiley.

Baxter, L.A., & Montgomery, B.M. (1996). *Relating: Dialogue and dialectics.* New York: Guilford Press.

Baxter-Jones, A.D., & Maffulli, N. (2003). Parental influence on sport participation in elite young athletes. *Journal of Sports Medicine and Physical Fitness, 43*(2), 250–255.

Berger, C.R., & Calabrese, R.J. (1975). Some exploration in initial interaction and beyond: Toward a developmental theory of communication. *Human Communication Research, 1*(2), 99–112.

Bergin, D.A., & Haubusta, S.F. (2004). Goal orientations of young male ice hockey players and their parents. *Journal of Genetic Psychology, 165*(4), 383–399.

Bochner, A.P. (1982). On the efficacy of openness in close relationships. In M. Burgoon (Ed.), *Communication Yearbook 6* (pp. 109–123). Beverly Hills, CA: Sage.

Crohan, S.E. (1992). Marital happiness and spousal consensus on beliefs and marital conflict: A longitudinal investigation. *Journal of Social and Personal Relationships, 9*(1), 89–102.

Derlega, V.J., Metts, S., Petronio, S., & Margulis, S.T. (1993). *Self-disclosure.* Newbury Park, CA: Sage Publications.

Gallmeier, C.P. (1987). Putting on the game face: The staging of emotions in professional hockey. *Sociology of Sport Journal, 4*(4), 347–362.

Hirschhorn, K.H., & Loughead, T.O. (2000). Parental impact on youth participation in sport: The physical educator's role. *Journal of Physical Education, Recreation & Dance, 71*(9), 26–29.

Hoyle, R.H., & Leff, S.S. (1997). The role of parental involvement in youth sport participation and performance. *Adolescence, 32*(125), 233–245.

Kassing, J.W., & Infante, D.A. (1999). Aggressive communication in the coach–athlete relationship. *Communication Research Reports, 16*, 110–120.

Kearney, P., & Plax, T.G. (1987). Situational and individual determinants of teachers' reported use of behavior alteration techniques. *Human Communication Research, 14*(2), 145–166.

Kidman, L., McKenzie, A., & McKenzie, B. (1999). The nature and target of parents' comments during youth sport competition. *Journal of Sport Behavior, 22*(1), 54–68.

Marwell, G., & Schmitt, D.R. (1967). Dimensions of compliance-gaining behavior: An empirical analysis. *Sociometry, 30*, 350–364.

Mead, G.H. (1934). *Mind, self and society.* Chicago, IL: University of Chicago Press.

Mehrabian, A. (1969). Attitudes inferred from non-immediacy of verbal communication. *Journal of Verbal Learning and Verbal Behavior, 6*(2), 294–295.

Miller, K. (2009). *Organizational communication: Approaches and processes* (5th ed.). Belmont, CA: Wadsworth, Cengage Learning.

Parrott, R., Burgoon, M., & Ross, C. (1992). Parents and pediatricians talk: Compliance-gaining strategies' use during well-child exams. *Health Communication, 4*(1), 57–66.

Petronio, S. (1994). Privacy binds in family interactions: The case of parental privacy invasion. In W.R. Cupach & B.H. Spitzberg (Eds.), *The dark side of interpersonal communication* (pp. 241–257). New York: Wiley & Sons.

Petronio, S. (2000). The boundaries of privacy: Praxis of everyday life. In S. Petronio (Ed.), *Balancing the secrets of private disclosures* (pp. 37–49). Mahwah, NJ: Erlbaum.

Petronio, S. (2002). *Boundaries of privacy: Dialectics of disclosure.* New York: State University of New York Press.

Roberts, G.C., Treasure, D.C., & Hall, H.K. (1994). Parental goal orientations and beliefs about the competitive sports experience of their child. *Journal of Social Psychology, 24*, 631–645.

Sagar, S.S., & Jowett, S. (2012). Communicative acts in coach-athlete interaction: When losing competitions and when making mistakes in training. *Western Journal of Communication, 76*(2), 148–174.

Schutz, W. (1958). *FIRO: Fundamental interpersonal relations orientation.* New York: Holt, Rinehart & Winston.

Turman, P. (2001). Situational coaching styles: The impact of success and "athlete maturity" level on coach's leadership styles over time. *Small Group Research, 32*(5), 572–590.

Turman, P. (2003). Athletic coaching from an instructional communication perspective: The influence of coach experience on high school wrestlers' preferences and perceptions of coaching behaviors across a season. *Communication Education, 52*(2), 73–86.

Turman, P. (2005). Coaches' use of anticipatory and counterfactual regret messages during competition. *Journal of Applied Communication Research, 33(2)*, 116–138.

Turman, P. (2007). Parental sport involvement: Parental influence to encourage young athlete continued sport participation. *Journal of Family Communication, 7*(3), 151–175.

Turman, P., & Schrodt, P. (2004). New avenues for instructional communication research: Relationships among coaches' leadership behaviors and athletes' affective learning. *Communication Research Reports, 21*(2), 130–143.

Turman, P., Zimmerman, A., & Dobesh, B. (2009). Parent-talk and sport participation: Interaction between parents, children, and coaches regarding level of play in sports. In T. Socha & G. Stamp (Eds.), *Interfacing outside of home: Parents and children communicating with society* (pp. 171–188). Mahwah, NJ: Lawrence Erlbaum.

Weiss, M.R., & Friedrichs, W.D. (1986). The influence of leader behavior, coach attributes, and institutional variables on performance and satisfaction of collegiate basketball teams. *Journal of Sport Psychology, 8*(4), 332–346.

White, S.A., Kavussanu. M., Tank, K.M., & Wingate, J.M. (2004). Perceived parental beliefs about the causes of success in sport: Relationship to athletes' achievement goals and personal beliefs. *Scandinavian Journal of Medicine & Science in Sports, 14*(1), 57–68.

12

SPORT AS FAMILY COMMUNICATION

Jon F. Nussbaum and Amber K. Worthington

PENNSYLVANIA STATE UNIVERSITY

I (Jon) was born into a family obsessed with sport, within a city (Pittsburgh) obsessed with sport, in a country obsessed with sport. My father played college football at Johns Hopkins University in the early 1950s; my mother nurtured and supported every imaginable organized and nonorganized sport-related activity, enabling our family to engage in sport without fear of not eating, having clean uniforms, or showing up late. All of my brothers participated in multiple sports through college, continuing to do so into their fifties and sixties. One brother and his son are attorneys representing professional sport associations; my sister was a cheerleader in high school, supporting her daughter through a successful college career in field hockey; all of my children, nephews, and nieces are active sport enthusiasts.

I (Amber) was also raised in a family obsessed with sport, in another sport-obsessed city (Baltimore). My father played baseball and basketball through high school; my mother was a competitive swimmer. Both my parents supported and coached my brother and I as we participated in a variety of sports growing up, including baseball, basketball, soccer, lacrosse, swimming, golf, track and field, and cross-country. My cousins all participated in a similarly large list of competitive sports, with some who continued to do so at the collegiate level and some whose careers are based in sport management. The rest of my extended family, including my aunts, uncles, and grandmother, are also obsessed with sport—particularly the Baltimore Ravens football team. One of my uncles has never missed attending a home football game since the opening Ravens game in 1996; another, to his chagrin, has missed just one. The very core of both of our family's identities is grounded in sport.

While the scholarly literature on sport and the effects that sport has upon our daily lives—from an individual perspective to the most macrocultural perspective—has increased exponentially over the past several decades (e.g., Billings, Butterworth, & Turman, 2015), sport as family communication has not been a primary focus of scholarly interest. Communication scholars and psychologists have made the same mistake by not focusing on, for example, emotion until recently. This chapter focuses on the notion of sport as family communication.

LePoire (2006) provides a very inclusive and progressive definition of family that incorporates the rather contentious biological, legal, and sociological grounding of family that has entered into our civic discourse. For LePoire (2006), family membership is determined by *relatedness* (the involuntary nature of families in all their various forms of connectedness both biological and legal), *nurturing* (behaviors that encourage the development of the family), and *control* (influence attempts across the lifespan). Flowing from this fundamental definition of family, LePoire (2006) provides the following definition of family communication: "Messages that are typically sent with intent, that are typically perceived as intentional, and that have consensually shared meaning among individuals who are related biologically, legally, or through marriage-like commitments who nurture and control each other" (p. 16).

Family communication shapes and reinforces the roles we play within families, the intimacy we share in families, the expectations for life we construct within our families, the management of conflict we engage in within our families, and the lifelong support and obligations we feel toward our family. Choo (2014) recently found that the degree of a family's participation in sport activities positively influenced both family resilience and communication facilitation. This chapter, grounded within the definitions of family and family communication noted above, introduces three characteristics of sport as family communication. First, we discuss *sport as family identity* by exploring the important function sport plays, as well as the mutual feeling and understanding that the very nature of family is grounded with our participation within sport. Second, we review *sport as intergenerational exchange* with a special emphasis upon parent–child interactions. Third, we present *sport as generativity* by embracing a lifespan developmental perspective of support and nurturing for the continuation of sport tradition within the family.

Sport as Family Identity

Identity, as the study of self, has been an important topic of poetic and scholarly discussion throughout most of recorded history. James (1891) and Mead (1913) are known as the 'modern' scholars who began to write about exploring the notion of individual identity from a scientific perspective. The great majority of humanistic and social scientific scholarship occurring throughout the last century in the disciplines of psychology, sociology, anthropology, and economics has focused on the nature and consequences of the individual identity. Brummett and Ishak (2014) have written that "sports as a cultural practice becomes a site for the creation and management of symbolic components of identity" (p. xiv). In addition, their edited book, *Sports and Identity: New Agendas in Communication*, considers the collective identities of towns, countries, genders, and races.

Symbolic interactionism (Blumer, 1969) emphasized social interaction with others and the perceptions formed through this interaction as the key, fundamental cause of one's identity. Thus, identity is a function of our interactive world. Hecht (1993) extended this perspective by incorporating theoretical notions from the "intergroup perspective" (Tajfel & Turner, 1979; see also Giles & Stohl, Chapter 10, this volume), communication accommodation theory (Giles & Soliz, 2015), and from his own readings of Eastern philosophy to develop the communication theory of identity, which stipulates that identity cannot be separated from communication. In addition, Hecht (2015) conceptualized four layers of identity: personal, relational, enacted, and communal. These layers are experienced simultaneously and can change across time such that "our identity at any one moment would consist of many, perhaps all, of these layers" (Hecht, 2015, p. 178). Family identity exists within these multiple layers. The construction of our family identity and how our family identity functions are grounded within our interactive network both within and beyond familial definitions.

Sport can play a significant role in the construction and maintenance of family identity. A number of 'famous' sport families serve as examples of this dynamic. Football's Manning family is known and respected as a sport family. Elisha Archibald 'Archie' Manning (the father) was an All-American college and National Football League Hall of Fame professional athlete. His two sons, Peyton and Eli, were college All-Americans and professional Pro Bowl quarterbacks. Peyton's and Eli's grandmother on their mother's side was a women's basketball All State basketball player in Mississippi. Cooper, the third son of Archie Manning, was an exceptional football player during high school, suffering a career-ending injury in high school yet joining his more famous father and brothers during personal appearances or in television commercials.

Another example can be found in the Rooney family, who own the Pittsburgh Steelers National Football League franchise. Arthur 'Art' Rooney, Sr. was an exceptional high school and college athlete who qualified for the Olympic boxing team. Rooney won a large sum of money betting on horses at Saratoga in the 1930s, parlaying the winnings to found the Pittsburgh Steelers Football Club within the National Football League. He served as owner and ran the team until his sons Dan became chairman and Art II became team president in the 1970s. The Manning family and the Rooney family are sport icons.

The Irsay family does not have such a consistently positive family sport reputation. Robert Irsay purchased the Baltimore Colts National Football League franchise in 1972. My (Amber) father's family grew up in Baltimore during the Baltimore Colts' heyday and was close family friends with the Unitas family— my father even recalls playing football with Johnny Unitas in the backyard.

In 1984, Robert moved the franchise to Indianapolis in the very early hours of the morning. The majority of the Baltimore Colts football fans, including my father and his family, had no idea that the move was planned, remaining resentful to this day because of the 'theft' of the team, their history, the 'Colts' name, and all memorabilia. The Baltimore Colts were a large part of my family's sport identity, and we still hang Baltimore Colts ornaments on our Christmas tree. Robert suffered a stroke in 1995 and his son Jim, a college football player at SMU, became principle owner and CEO of the Indianapolis Colts. Unlike Art II and Dan Rooney, Jim has led a much more public—and at times personally destructive—life (e.g., Rosenthal, 2014).

The families briefly mentioned above all have achieved their fame, fortune, identity (both individual and family), and, in one case, infamy, through participation in the business of sport. We began this chapter with a description of how our families remain linked to sport. Though precise, valid data is hard to collect, it is not unreasonable to state that the great majority of families in the United States and within the technologically advanced countries throughout the world have, at some point, had a significant connection with sport. A 2015 jointly published research report by NPR, the Robert Wood Johnson Foundation, and the Harvard T.H. Chan School of Public Health found that 76% of their randomly chosen, representative adult sample (2,506 respondents aged 18 and older) place a high priority on their children playing sport (Blendon et al., 2015). Parents report that participation in sport helps their children by (a) maintaining physical and mental health, (b) giving them something to do, (c) teaching dedication and discipline, and (d) benefiting their social lives. The parents surveyed also report that their children participate in a wide variety of sports, with baseball, soccer, and basketball having the highest participation levels. In addition, parents report an overwhelmingly positive attitude toward sport as a leisure activity for both themselves and their children. It is interesting to note that household income is negatively correlated to participation in sport or any vigorous- or moderate-intensity exercise. In other words, as income decreases from a household income of $75,000 per year or more to a household income of $25,000 per year or less, self-reported participation in sport or any vigorous- or moderate-intensity workout decreases from 64% to 40%. The higher your household income, the more likely you are to embrace sport within the family structure.

Parents are responsible for registering their children to play in organized recreational leagues as well as formal teams sponsored by the school district, public or church-related leagues, sport camps, and the more expert level of AAU teams. In addition, parents provide transportation, financial assistance, administration/ coaching, food, laundry services, and numerous other support services to help their children participate. During the period of parenting through middle childhood until the postcollege years, a family can spend considerable time, energy, and finances on sport-related activities. These families cannot help but see themselves as a sport family as their sport identity significantly constructs their identity as a family. To fully understand the dynamics of the family, one must consider the significant consequences of sport participation by the individual members of the family.

The label 'soccer mom' first became popular during the 1996 Republican National Convention. The term was meant to identify a large and important voting block that should, in the minds of the Republicans, vote for Republican candidates, who felt that suburban mothers who ferry their children to and from soccer games and practices were burdened by the 'non-family-friendly' policies of the Clinton Administration. The 'soccer mom' label can be both a positive label (mothers who care and are engaged in the sport activities of their children), or a negative label (white mothers of generally high financial means with nothing better to do than to spend their day in the suburbs driving the kids around in an expensive SUV/minivan). In either case, the label signals a family identity that is an excellent example of the link between family and sport that exists within our society. The archetype of the 'soccer mom' resonates at least in part because most individuals can cognitively envision that person demographically within American society.

Sport as Intergenerational Exchange

Our parents were most likely the first individuals who introduced us to participation in sport. As mentioned above, this is truer for middle-class families than for those at the poverty level. For many of us, then, this initial participation in sport and the family conversations about our favorite sport teams continue throughout our lifespan (Nussbaum, 1981). When we were children, our parents signed us up to participate in sport, drove us to the practice field or court, often coached the teams we played on, fed us appropriate food so that we had the energy to compete, and did their very best to support us through the highs and lows of winning, losing, and injuries. Parents and their children are afforded opportunities to talk on their way to and from the sporting events and during the meal times before and after their sporting activities. This talk contextualized by sport helps to define and construct our individual sense of self and the sense of who we are/were as a family. At times, the topic of sport is the only topic of comfortable interaction or of any interaction within a family (more on this later).

In addition, media has reinforced our sense of sport as family and sport as intergenerational bonding. Wonderful depictions of the strong bond between fathers and their sons based on sport, for instance, can be found within the adult child characters portrayed by Billy Crystal in *City Slickers* (1991), Robert Redford in *The Natural* (1984), and Kevin Costner in *Field of Dreams* (1989). In each of these popular movies, the main character's strong emotional bond with his father is linked to a first trip to Yankee Stadium, to a wish that dad were still alive to see a son succeed as a Major League Baseball player, or to have one last 'catch' with dad. The intergenerational transfer of the love of sport, the role our parents and we as parents play as a supporter of child participation in sport, and the conversations occurring during this process are key factors in every family dynamic.

Our childhood participation in sport is a context within which our parents can both control and nurture the family. We suggest that for a brief time in our lives, parent–child interaction during sport participation may be the most significant context within which family communication transpires. Indeed, Billings, Butterworth, and Turman (2015) provide an excellent extended discussion of parent–child interaction during childhood within a sport context, and we turn now to highlight several of the important findings and consequences of this interaction.

A parent who coaches or is actively engaged in his or her child's sport activities is placed within a context where positive socialization and support/comfort can readily occur. Valuable lessons of teamwork and handling adversity can be modeled and taught by parents to their children. The sport context is also a wonderful context within which children and parents can create and manage friendships with teammates and their parents (Billings et al., 2015). Roberts, Treasure, and Hall (1994) point out that parents can emphasize the positive concepts of setting and achieving goals, the importance of effort as the children try to achieve those goals, the value of overcoming the difficulties they face when attempting to accomplish goals, and the rewards children gain once goals are accomplished when interacting with their children. "When feedback is provided in a positive light, the support perceived by athletes can increase their enjoyment, perceived sport importance, increased involvement in a range of sports, and general self-esteem" (Billings et al., 2015, p. 222). Entire summers are often spent traveling to games and camps and then organizing team parties to celebrate the team experiences. The children can see and learn how their family interacts with other families in an enjoyable manner. We, also, want to mention the important role grandparents can play within this sport context as our lifespans increase, and individuals can remain both physically and mentally healthy well into their eighties and beyond.

The experience of engaging in sport for the family also has a dark side. One only needs to attend to the numerous media accounts of overzealous parents who abuse their children in an attempt to control a positive sport outcome (see also Bien-Aimé, Hardin, & Whiteside, Chapter 15, this volume). Parental messages to their children can focus too much on winning as an outcome (the only acceptable outcome), which, in turn, creates impossible expectations for the child. Turman (2007) investigated themes that parents report when interacting with their children about the nature of the child's participation in sport. Four themes emerged: (a) playing time, (b) sport politics, (c) negative coaching behaviors, and (d) sport competitiveness. Within each of these themes an opportunity for positive encouragement and support exists. However, the opportunity to criticize the lack of playing time, the 'fact' that someone else's child is being favored, the coach's inappropriate behavior, and the competitiveness of the sport is removing all the fun, can turn a positive experience into a negative one. Competent parent–child interaction within the sport context can be complex and difficult when so much emotion is involved.

Our parents always attended each of our sport games throughout our childhood up until college. They were very vocal supporters and they were not alone in the stands and sidelines. Blom and Drane (2009) investigated the feedback that parents provide to their children from the stands, finding that the majority of comments (51%) were positive, 32% were negative, and 16% were neutral. These messages, however, can at times be contradictory and very hard for the child to interpret and understand. One parent may be complimenting a certain behavior of a certain player while another parent is scolding another player or the same player as the coach is signaling a play to be run or a lesson to be learned. Blom and Drane (2009) emphasize the fact that sideline 'yellings' are chaotic, confusing, and can be very distracting for the child athletes. We were not the best at being able to separate our parents' voices from many of the other parents' voices and often were left wondering what was happening as we were competing on the field. It is not hard to imagine children becoming confused and embarrassed by their parents' communicative behavior during a game.

An additional important factor within parent–child interaction within the sport context is gender differences (see also Meân, Chapter 6, this volume). "Communication research argues that children are often socialized into either masculine or feminine communication cultures through their participation in a variety of sex-segregated games and sports as they mature" (Billings et al., p. 228). Title IX is a federal law established in the early 1970s that made gender equity the law. While this law produced profound changes in the sport world, these changes have not eliminated gender bias in sport participation, the significance of a particular sport over other sports, or the role mothers and fathers play toward their daughters and sons within the sport context. There does, however, appear to be a significant change or, at the very least, a changing trend in how parents and society view and behave toward their female and male children within the sport context, diminishing some traditional gender role biases. Nevertheless, Hardy, Kelly, Chapman, King, and Farrell (2010) found that female children were still not receiving the same level of support to participate in sport as male children.

Sport as Generativity

A significant function of the parents within a family is to provide early socialization experiences for their infants and children (Vangelisti, 2013). In addition, "it is by observing and interacting with family members that most people learn to communicate and, perhaps more importantly, where they learn to think about communication" (Vangelisti, 2013, p. 1). Nussbaum, Pecchioni, Robinson, and

Thompson (2000) extended this notion of the importance of socialization and communication within the family to cover the entire lifespan. The role of family and the interactions transpiring within the family as we move through our lifespan become increasingly important as family members cope with the various challenges of aging. As we become parents and grandparents, we attempt to ensure that our children and grandchildren become positive contributors to society.

Generativity is a concept first discussed by Erikson (1950), capturing a commitment that adults develop as they age to promote the well-being of future generations and improve the world in which they live. Williams and Nussbaum (2001) place generativity within the context of family intergenerational communication, arguing that as parents move into middle adulthood, these parents and grandparents become more concerned about their role as an active 'teacher,' passing on to their children and grandchildren the wisdom necessary for a 'good life.' This generative communication often takes the form of family life narratives (McAdams, 2011). Specifically, "highly generative adults tend to construct life stories that feature redemptive sequences, in which the protagonist is delivered from suffering to an enhanced status or state" (McAdams, 2011, p. 599).

Nussbaum (1981) was interested in the role family and friends play as their older adult family members manage the aging process. Older adults aged 65–91 living in three environments (independent living at home, independent living within a retirement community, and mentally/cognitively healthy individuals living within an age-segregated nursing home) were interviewed concerning their communicative behavior and their feelings of life satisfaction. As part of this much larger investigation, data were collected as to the topics of conversation that these older adults engaged in with their family members and friends. It was not surprising to find that topics such as family activities and health were among the most mentioned topics. However, one rather surprising topic, *sport*, was also mentioned frequently by older adults living across all three environments. It should be noted that these interviews took place within the West Lafayette/Lafayette area of Central Indiana. No professional sport teams were located within Indiana at that time, though Chicago and St. Louis teams were broadcast on local radio and television. Purdue basketball, football, the local high school teams, and the sporting activities of grandchildren were often mentioned as the precise content of these sport topics.

Nussbaum and Bettini (1984) extended this investigation into the narrative content of family interactions by documenting actual storytelling between grandparents and their grandchildren during a Thanksgiving weekend. Grandparents and their grandchildren were asked to record an important family story that has 'life meaning.' Results revealed that grandfathers often utilized a sport narrative to express the meaning of life. The stories were about how overcoming obstacles, hard work, the importance of teamwork, all led to success. It should be noted that many stories had a very strong work/military component as well, given that these grandfathers overwhelmingly served during World War II.

Grandmothers most often told stories focusing on the importance of family during an individual life crisis. The message being sent focused on the notion that when all others are no longer willing or able to help, family will be there.

The gender difference found between the content of stories told by grandparents to their grandchildren reflect the time when these stories were told. Thirty years later, this gender difference is likely disappearing (see also Meân, Chapter 6, this volume). As we write this chapter, the United States women's national soccer team has just won the 2015 FIFA Women's World Cup. All reports from the media suggest that this World Cup was the most watched and followed World Cup within the United States in the history of both men's and women's World Cup competitions (e.g., Sandomir, 2015). It would not be an overstatement to suggest that one of the primary messages that is consistently repeated not only on the media but also likely in families across this nation is the story of these women overcoming hardships, gender bias, injury, and lack of national support to triumph on the world stage. We conjecture that mothers, grandmothers, and their children of both sexes are actively engaging in family storytelling grounded within the triumph of this women's national team.

Sport narratives shared within a family serve the dual purpose of socialization and generativity. These sport narratives can be told over and over throughout the years within the family to not only reinforce family identity but also to teach valuable life lessons personalized within the family context. While not all families will be as dedicated to sport as the Manning, Rooney, and Irsay families mentioned previously within this chapter, we suspect that most families who for certain periods of their lifespan share a high level of sport activity will find their family sport narratives enjoyable and enriching. I (Jon) know I enjoy when my father (88 years old) tells his story as a Johns Hopkins quarterback, and I know that I enjoy sharing my own sport stories and listening to those of my children.

Future Research Agenda for Sport as Family Communication

Family communication scholars are known for their rich and robust multi-methodological, interdisciplinary investigations (Vangelisti, 2013). Utilizing this inclusive methodological arsenal, family communication scholars and sport scholars can make a significant contribution to our understanding of how families construct and function as a family in their day-to-day lives. We propose three domains for future research into sport as communication, largely mirroring the content of this chapter. First, we suggest that communication/sport scholars investigate the significance of family identity within 'ordinary' families as constructed and influenced by family participation within sport. Second, the actual, real-time interaction transpiring within families focused on sport must be aggressively documented and investigated. Finally, scholars should investigate a lifespan perspective, describing the changing nature of sport as family communication as these families and individuals age throughout their lives, as it can provide a richer understanding of the changing dynamics of family as that family progresses through time.

The 90% of children between the ages of 5 and 17 who take part in some form of sport translates into the fact that families are spending a significant portion of their leisure life engaged in family sport activities (Jellineck & Durant, 2004; Kassing et al., 2004; Turman, 2007). Family communication researchers are well placed to investigate how these families construct and manage their family sport identity as the parents coordinate sport activities for their children. Do families who construct a stronger sport identity utilize different styles of parenting than those families who construct a weaker or nonexistent sport family identity? Are the parents within these strong sport identity families more likely to become abusive to their children? Or, are parents more likely to become positively supportive of their children, functioning as positive teachers and mentors? How do families grow into their sport identity during their child's 4th or 5th year and then some 15 to 25 years later develop away from their family sport identity?

Given the significance of sport within the great majority of families, capturing the actual, real-time communication that transpires as parents and children talk with one another before, during, and after sport should be a priority for family communication scholars. How are these talks initiated? Are these sport talks monologues, dominated by one parent, or do both parents actively listen and respect the opinions of their children? Do these sport-related conversations change throughout the day or are there predictable times and contexts for these talks? How are these sport conversations different when comparing blended families, single-parent households, gay-parent households, or families with adopted children?

A lifespan perspective of sport as family should focus upon change across time within the family. The narratives and stories families generate can serve as data marking this change. As families develop and their children age into their teenage years and beyond, changes within the content and style of the family narrative can signal the different functions and nature of the family. It is also important to mention the significant changes occurring as parents move into middle adulthood and how the parent–child relationship changes with advancing age as well. Finally, it is important to recognize the significant role that grandparents and siblings play within the communication dynamic of the family (Nussbaum et al., 2000), as these relationships need to be included across time as well. Future research questions to be investigated include: How do sport family narratives emerge within the developing family? Do sport family narratives change across time? What roles do the different members of the family (parents, children, and grandparents) play within the sport family narratives? And, what are the relationships between sport family narratives and generativity?

Conclusion

The majority of families within technologically advanced countries throughout the world spend a significant portion of their time engaging in a variety of sports as their primary recreational activity. Family communication transpiring as these families engage in sport as recreation can be a central feature within the day-to-day activities of these families. This chapter focuses on three components of sport as family communication: sport as family identity, sport as intergenerational exchange, and sport as generativity. Investigations that explore the communication within families between children, siblings, parents, and grandparents contextualized by sport can help us to better understand the complex dynamics of family life, leading to a much richer understanding of both the positive and negative aspects of family that, in the end, can improve our overall quality of life.

References

Billings, A.C., Butterworth, M.L., & Turman, P.D. (2015). *Communication and sport: Surveying the field*. Los Angeles, CA: Sage.

Blendon, R.J., Benson, J.M., Satde, J.M., Gorski, Mann, F., Miller, C., Van Roekel, B., Gudenkauf, A., & Neel, J. (2015). *Sports and health in America*. An ongoing series of surveys developed at the Harvard Opinion Research Program at the Harvard T.H. Chan School of Public Health, the Robert Wood Johnson Foundation, and National Public Radio. Retrieved June 28, 2016, from http://www.rwjf.org/content/dam/farm/reports/reports/2015/rwjf420908.

Blom, L., & Drane, D. (2009). Parents' sideline comments: Exploring the reality of a growing issue. *Online Journal of Sport Psychology, 10*(3), 12.

Blumer, H. (1969). *Symbolic interactionism: Perspective and methods*. Berkeley, CA: University of California Press.

Brummett, B., & Ishak, A.W. (2014). *Sports and identity: New agendas in communication*. New York: Routledge.

Choo, M. (2014). The influence of family's participation in recreational sports on its resilience and communication facilitation. *Journal of Exercise Rehabilitation, 10*(5), 313–318.

Erikson, E.H. (1950). *Childhood and society*. New York: Norton.

Giles, H., & Soliz, J. (2015). Communication accommodation theory: A situated framework for relational, family, and intergroup dynamics. In D.O. Braithwaite & P. Schrodt (Eds.), *Engaging theories in interpersonal communication: Multiple perspectives* (2nd ed., pp. 161–173). Los Angeles, CA: Sage.

Hardy, L.L., Kelly, B., Chapman, K., King, L., & Farrell, L. (2010). Parental perceptions of barriers to children's participation in organized sport in Australia. *Journal of Pediatrics and Child Health, 46*, 197–203.

Hecht, M.L. (1993). 2002: A research odyssey – toward the development of a communication theory of identity. *Communication Monographs, 60*, 76–82.

Hecht, M.L. (2015). Communication theory of identity: Multilayered understandings of performed identities. In D.O. Braithwaite & P. Schrodt (Eds.), *Engaging theories in interpersonal communication: Multiple perspectives* (2nd ed., pp. 175–187). Los Angeles, CA: Sage.

James, W. (1891). *The principles of psychology (vol. 1).* Cambridge, MA: Harvard University Press. (Original work published 1890.)

Jellineck, M., & Durant, S. (2004). Parents and sports: Too much of a good thing? *Contemporary Pediatrics, 21*(9), 17–20.

Kassing, J., Billings, A.C., Brown, R., Halone, K.K., Harrison, K., Krizek, B., Mean, L., & Turman, P.D. (2004). Enacting, (re)producing, consuming, and organizing sport: Communication in the community of sport. *Communication Yearbook, 28,* 373–409.

LePoire, B.A. (2006). *Family communication: Nurturing and control in a changing world.* Thousands Oaks, CA: Sage.

McAdams, D.P. (2011). Life narratives. In K.L. Fingerman, C.A. Berg, J. Smith, & T.C. Antonucci (Eds.), *Handbook of life-span development* (pp. 589–610). New York: Springer.

Mead, G.H. (1913). The social self. *Journal of Philosophy, Psychology, and Scientific Methods, 10,* 374–380.

Nussbaum, J.F. (1981). *Interactional patterns of elderly individuals: Implications for successful adaptation to aging.* An unpublished doctoral dissertation, Purdue University, West Lafayette, Indiana.

Nussbaum, J.F., & Bettini. L.M. (1984). Shared stories of the grandparent–grandchild relationship. *International Journal of Aging and Human Development, 39,* 67–80.

Nussbaum, J.F., Pecchioni, L.L., Robinson, J.D., & Thompson, T.L. (2000). *Communication and aging* (2nd ed.). Mahwah, NJ: Lawrence Erlbaum.

Roberts, G.C., Treasure, D.C., & Hall, H.K. (1994). Parental goal orientations and beliefs about competitive sports experience of their child. *Journal of Social Psychology, 24,* 631–645.

Rosenthal, G. (2014). Colts' Jim Irsay suspended six games, fined $500K. *Around the National Football League.* Retrieved June 28, 2016, from http://www.nfl.com/news/story/0ap3000000387267/article/colts-jim-irsay-suspended-six-games-fined-500k.

Sandomir, R. (2015). Women's world cup final was most watched soccer game in United States history. *New York Times.* Retrieved June 28, 2016, from http://www.nytimes.com/2015/07/07/sports/soccer/womens-world-cup-final-was-most-watched-soccer-game-in-united-states-history.html?_r=0.

Tajfel, H., & Turner, J.C. (1979). An integrative theory of intergroup conflict. In W.C. Austin & S. Worchel (Eds.), *The social psychology of intergroup conflict* (pp. 33–53). Monterey, CA: Brooks/Cole.

Turman, P.D. (2007). Parental sport involvement: Parental influence to encourage young athlete continued sport participation. *Journal of Family Communication, 7*(3), 151–175.

Vangelisti, A.L. (2013). *The Routledge handbook of family communication.* New York: Routledge.

Williams, A., & Nussbaum, J.F. (2001). *Intergenerational communication across the life span.* Mahwah, NJ: Lawrence Erlbaum.

13

SPORT AS HEALTH COMMUNICATION

Intersections, Theories, Implications

Kim Bissell

UNIVERSITY OF ALABAMA

Research in the areas of sport and health communication have become one of the most quickly growing areas in mass communication scholarship in the last two decades. While research in either discipline represents a rich and diverse area for empirical investigation, the combination of the two is often overlooked. By its very nature, sport, participation in sport, and sporting activities are directly tied to health. An individual's health can be directly affected by involvement or participation in sport and sporting activities (U.S. Department of Health and Human Services, 1996; Croll et al., 2006). While the link between the two seems obvious, research in the combined areas is not as distinct. The overarching question for consideration is how the two are interrelated and what is known from the research about the intersection of sport and health communication. This chapter explores sport in its role in health communication, examining the way health communication is directly related to sport. Through exploring statistics and research on health, health disparities, and the correlates related to improved health in children and adults, the way sport and physical activity can serve as functions of improved health can be uncovered. Certainly, as the rates of overweight and obesity rise or remain stable rather than decline (Centers for Disease Control and Prevention, 2015), a closer examination of the intersection between health and sport is warranted.

Statistics on Obesity and Obesity in Children

Obesity is a central public health issue facing the nation, particularly in regard to younger generations. Children's attitudes toward healthy eating and exercise will likely stay with them for the remainder of their life. Currently, one in three children in the United States are overweight or obese (Centers for

Disease Control and Prevention, 2015), creating growing concerns about the health risks associated with the rapidly growing rates of childhood obesity and low levels of physical activity in the United States (Fakhouri, Hughes, Brody, Kit, & Ogden, 2013; Ogden, Carroll, Kit, & Flegal, 2014). Presently, 17.7% of U.S. children aged 6 to 11 are obese (Ogden et al., 2014); moreover, urban–rural disparities in child obesity persist: rural children have higher odds of being overweight and obese than urban children, even after adjusting for sociodemographics (Liu et al., 2012).

There is no lack of evidence documenting the health disparities among different demographic groups. Racial/ethnic disparities in health have been found showing disproportionately higher rates of certain health problems such as diabetes, asthma, and cancer among racial/ethnic minorities as well as individuals in lower socioeconomic status (SES) households. The social determinants of health cannot be overlooked in the consideration of the role of sport and health because many factors such as SES are directly related to a child's involvement in physical activity (PA) or sport. Betancourt, Green, Carrillo, and Ananeh-Firempong (2003) report on the sociocultural barriers to improved health across populations, noting that demographic factors such as race/ethnicity, SES, and education function as barriers to improved health, access to activities and preventative treatment that improve health, and the recognition of factors that result in decreased health.

Physical Activity/Inactivity Statistics

While physical inactivity among children is a national health concern, it is especially high in more rural, Southern states. According to national guidelines published by the U.S. Department of Health and Human Services, children aged 6 to 17 should engage in 60 minutes or more of physical activity (PA) of moderate or vigorous intensity most days of the week. However, only 47% of children meet this guideline nationwide. Television viewing displaces chances for more stringent exercise; however, it cannot be said that children who watch large quantities of television take part in little physical activity because there may be many factors driving the sedentary behavior, including but not limited to access to safe places to be active, household behavior that does not encourage physical activity, or lack of knowledge or understanding as to the benefits of physical activity. Several studies have documented correlations between heavy television viewing and obesity in children. For example, data collected during the National Health and Nutritional Examination Survey between 1988 and 1994 showed that obesity was least prevalent among children who watched an hour or less of television a day. The highest prevalence was documented among children who watched four or more hours of television a day (Crespo et al., 2001). A longitudinal study found that participants who watched the most television during childhood showed the largest gain in body fat between preschool and early adolescence (Proctor et al., 2003). Obesity, in turn, may affect the amount of exercise a child gets. Studies have found that obese children are less likely to exercise regularly, less likely to express confidence in their ability to perform well in physical activities, and less likely to take part in organizations focused on physical activities such as team sport (Trost, Kerr, Ward, & Pate, 2000). This self-efficacy or self-esteem specific to exercise and sport participation may certainly be a driving factor in a child's involvement in PA later in life from preferences to participation in PA. A spiral of health and sport is created: lack of exercise creates obesity, with obesity making exercise harder to pursue.

Other studies determining PA preferences among lower SES children noted similar barriers to PA described by both children and adults. Hesketh, Waters, Green, Salmon, and Williams (2005) found that barriers to PA reported by children included lack of playground equipment, unsafe roads, neighbors who complained of noise from children, and lack of money to engage in organized activities (Hesketh et al., 2005). The barriers to PA reported by parents included increasing distances between schools and homes as well as distractions in the home such as televisions and computers (Hesketh et al., 2005).

Health Disparities in Specific Populations

The significant disparity between the amount of PA recommended for children and the actual PA engaged in by children, especially those who are medically underserved, is a problem researchers should address as regular PA has many health benefits. Those who participate in at least seven hours of PA a week have a 40% lower risk of premature death compared with those who are active for less than 30 minutes a week (2008 Physical Activity Guidelines for Americans, 2008; Paffenbarger et al., 1993; Paffenbarger, Hyde, Wing, & Hsieh, 1986). Also, studies have shown that PA contributes to lower rates of a number of chronic diseases and conditions, including heart disease (Morris & Crawford, 1958), type 2 diabetes (Helmrich, Ragland, Leung, & Paffenbarger, 1991; Manson et al., 1992), obesity (Ades, Savage, & Toth, 2009), hypertension (Fagard, 2001), and osteoporosis (Borer, 2005). While children do not typically develop these aforementioned chronic diseases, risk factors begin early in life; a child who is physically active will be less likely to develop these risk factors and a physically active child is more likely to become a physically active adult. Since behavioral patterns are most formable during childhood (Baranowski, Baranowski, & Cullen, 2003), efforts should focus on implementing interventions designed to increase PA behavior in children, especially in medically underserved areas of the country, where PA levels in children are particularly low (Robinson, Wadsworth, Webster, & Bassett, 2014) and chronic disease rates are high (Sewell, Andreae, Luke, & Safford, 2011).

Veitch, Bagley, Ball, and Salmon (2006) investigated reasons why lower SES children were less physically active than higher SES children. This study examined children's access to places in their neighborhood where they engaged in PA (Veitch et al., 2006). Specifically, children were given a map showing the surrounding areas from their school, and they were instructed to mark where they lived and where they have engaged in PA in the previous week. Results indicated that children living in low SES outer-urban neighborhoods had to travel greater distances to access local parks when compared with those in inner-urban, mid-, and high SES areas.

Sociocultural factors are also important in predicting health-related behavior (Pate, Heath, Dowda, & Trost, 1996). In terms of PA participation, African-American children participate less than their white counterparts (Martin et al., 2005). In contrast, they are also engaged with sedentary activities more often. According to Chuang, Sharma, Skala, and Evans (2013), African-American preschoolers averaged more than two hours of TV every day and were also more likely to use a computer and engage with video games when compared with Hispanic or white children. African-American girls at all ages were found to be less physically active than girls from any other subgroup (Trost et al., 2002). Eaton et al. (2012), for instance, reported that 21% of African-American adolescent girls do not meet the CDC's recommended level of PA, while another 26.7% do not engage in any PA.

Decline of Physical Education (PE) in Schools

Involvement (or lack thereof) in PA is a primary contributor in the prevention of youth becoming overweight or obese. Because many children and youth spend so much time doing sedentary activities, places such as schools have unique opportunities to facilitate PA and the healthy behaviors surrounding it. However, despite the increasing waistlines of children across the US, schools have gradually reduced or eliminated opportunities for children (e.g., recess, PE) to become active while in school. Johnston, Delva, and O'Malley (2007) found a significant decline in PE requirements and student participation rates between 8th and 12th grade; 87% of 8th graders were required to take PE while only 20% of the 12th graders were required to take PE as part of their course schedule. While PA can certainly occur outside of the school environment, it is one universal mechanism for ensuring that all children are involved in some PA each day. Moving forward, it would be important to better understand the rationale behind the decline in PE in terms of what is required and what is offered in public schools around the country.

Theories Relevant to Sport within the Communication Subdiscipline

Health Promotion Model and the Children's Health Belief Model

While many theories can be used to better understand the intersection between sport and health, a few theories seem most appropriate for understanding the motivations behind involvement in PA and exercise and the factors potentially influencing the lack of involvement in PA and exercise. The Health Promotion Model (HPM) was originally proposed by Pender (Pender, 1996; Pender, Murdaugh, & Parsons, 2005), aiming to provide "a guide for exploration of the complex bio-psychosocial processes that motivate individuals to engage in health behaviors directed toward the enhancement of health" (Pender, 1996, p. 51). Applying a social cognitive approach, the HPM considers health behavior within a context of the larger social environment, identifying three domains of influence on health behaviors: (a) an individual's general background and characteristics, (b) health-related factors, and (c) behavior-specific factors (Pender et al., 2005). General background factors refer to innate individual characteristics such as demographic variables and past experience. Health-related factors are related to knowledge, perceptions, and attitudes toward health, while behavior-specific variables integrate perceptions of the specific behavior, previous related behavior, and interpersonal and situational factors (Pender, 1996; Pender et al., 2005). In short, the HPM is a comprehensive model that considers health behavior as multidimensional in use. Of particular relevance to the study of sport and health is the influence of the innate characteristics of individuals as these serve as one of the driving factors behind involvement or participation in PA, exercise, and sport.

Bush and Iannotti (1990) propose a modification of the Health Belief Model in the development of the Children's Health Belief Model (CHBM). Bush and Iannotti (1990) argue that children's lack of cognitive development along with their reliance on parents to make health decisions for them necessitated the development of this model, believing children's health behavior has to be placed within personal and social contexts, and this context has to be one that includes children's "beliefs, expectations, motives, and other cognitive elements, and recognizes that these personal attributes are influenced by families, peers, and social groups" (p. 70). The modifying factors identified by the authors included cognitive and affective variables such as health locus of control, self-esteem, health risk-taking, knowledge, and autonomy. The authors further suggest that what they call 'readiness factors'—motivations, perceived illness threat, and perceived benefit of a health treatment—predict a health behavior. Knowledge of specific health topics such as nutrition are learned from external sources such as the media, but children's health behavior can be predicted using theoretical models such as the CHBM.

In studies of children, sport, and health, researchers using the HPM or the CHBM have identified individual characteristics that have been found to be influential on children's adoption of the specific health behavior promoted. For example, Garcia et al.'s (1995) survey of 399 teens and preteens detected background characteristics or factors, specifically where gender plays an important role in predicting adolescents' exercise behavior. Frenn and Shelly's (2003) quasi-experimental, pre-post design study found that the effect of their intervention program on teens' dietary intake and duration of physical activity varied with race, sex, and social economics. They noted that technological methods could be used to promote health behavior; however, adolescents' development and social environment should also be taken into account. This argument is particularly relevant when considering the role of new media technologies into the sport and health communication equation.

Social Cognitive Theory

Social cognitive theory (SCT) serves as a theoretical bridge between cultivation theory and sociocultural theory. SCT provides a perspective for understanding the way personal factors such as cognition, affect, behavior, or biological events operate together as a means of influencing one another when it comes to an individual's behavior (Bandura, 1986). The theory suggests that perceptions of self and others are influenced by factors such as media exposure, demographic variables, and observation of other influential individuals, and, in the case of children, this could be parents, siblings, teachers, or peers. Social cognitive theory helps us better understand the psychosocial mechanisms through which "symbolic communication influences human thought, affect, and action" (Bandura, 2009). Earlier theories in mass communication have suggested a more unidirectional degree of influence on behavior; for example, exposure to violent media might lead an individual to exhibit higher levels of aggression. However, social cognitive theory offers the triadic reciprocal causation (Bandura, 1986), which is an explanation for the different types of determinants—personal, behavioral, and environmental—that are all interrelated and that all function together in order to predict human behavior. Thus, the theory allows for the introduction of a variety of factors that could influence an individual's knowledge, beliefs and attitudes, and actions. As it relates to sport and health outcomes, social cognitive theory allows for close examination of factors predicting or relating to an individual's involvement in PA or sport, which would also be directly related to health outcomes. In many ways, health outcomes or health behaviors are going to be influenced by a variety of factors on the individual and social level, which means studies should be more comprehensive in understanding the motivations behind involvement in PA and sport.

Studies Offering Connections between Sport and Communication

Studies about New Media Technologies Tying Sport to Health

Over the last decade, new media technologies have been used more frequently to help children and adults track their physical activity and eating behavior, to serve as a resource for exercise and nutrition and to help engage consumers in weight-loss challenges. Marceglia, Bonacina, Zaccaria, Pagliari, and Pinciroli (2012) note the iPad could change the face of healthcare by going beyond the consumption of information by consumers and moving into a phase of information dissemination by healthcare providers. While some of the health-related apps may not necessarily be backed by empirical evidence or even be developed by healthcare professionals, Pandey, Hasan, Dubey, and Sarangi (2013) report that 56% of the apps they analyzed for cancer-related information were backed by scientific data. While this percentage represents just over half of the apps with cancer-related information, consumers are increasingly becoming more demanding of apps that are developed based on scientific evidence (Peterson, 2015). Results from these earlier studies suggest we are only at the beginning stages of new media technologies' effect on overall health and healthcare practices. Bissell, Conlin, Bie, Zhang, and McLemore (2015) found that an app enabled children to give more accurate reports of their foods when compared with a free-response recollection of their food intake. The authors also found that children in the study did not meet USDA guidelines for suggested servings of vegetables and grains and consumed too many empty calories via sugary drinks. While this study examined children's eating behavior instead of their PA, an app similar to the one used in this study could be developed and used to help children become more aware of their health behaviors. Future studies could also examine this using the knowledge gap hypothesis by looking at the adoption of the new technology as well as the successfulness of it by factors such as socioeconomic status, cognition, and other individual factors. Limited data exists on the effectiveness of new media technologies in improving children's health and/ or physical activity, although more studies are starting to emerge that look at the role of active video games (AVG) in helping children become more physically active (Marceglia et al., 2012; Carter, Burley, Nykjaer, & Cade, 2013).

Using new media technologies as a means of changing outcomes or behavior specific to health often requires interventions as neither children nor adults will necessarily sustain behavior if the benefits are not clear and/or if use of the new technology is not easy or intuitive. A web-based intervention designed to change behavior could be beneficial to any number of students, since the majority of classrooms in the United States—including those in underserved areas—now have access to the Internet (Gray, Thomas, & Lewis, 2010). Furthermore, the importance of using technology to promote health-related behavior modification has been recognized (Doshi, Patrick, Sallis, & Calfas, 2003). Over the past decade, several studies have discussed the use of computers and web-based interventions to change PA levels of both children and adults (Baranowski et al., 2003). Internet-based interventions may be one of the more successful ways to engage individuals in more PA, exercise or even sport, in a slightly moderated way. More importantly, an Internet-based intervention used in the school setting does not depend on the effectiveness of the teacher's ability to relay the pertinent health information, but rather the health information conveyed in the Internet-based intervention can be developed and overseen by a health expert. While literature in this area is relatively scant, it appears that a few studies have been conducted that involve using a web-based intervention in an attempt to improve PA behavior (Baranowski et al., 2003). While one study showed significant increases in PA behavior following the web-based intervention (Barwais, Cuddihy, & Tomson, 2013), the two other studies did not report a significant improvement (Kosma, Cardinal, & McCubbin, 2005). A common limitation evident in all three studies was the failure of the researchers to ensure participant adherence in logging onto the online programs. Therefore, more research with higher participation adherence is warranted to determine whether web-based PA interventions are beneficial.

In recent years, the active video game (AVG) has emerged as a high-tech tool in the fight against physical inactivity and associated health complications. It is hoped that if the time used to watch TV or play traditional nonactive video games could be replaced by playing AVGs, a reduction in sedentary pastimes and an increase in physical activity would result (e.g., Biddiss & Irwin, 2010). Many studies have been conducted to examine to what extent AVGs are able to engage children (e.g., Bailey & McInnis, 2011; Biddiss & Irwin, 2010; Bissell, Zhang, & Meadows, 2014) and induce physical activity (e.g., Barnett, Cerin, & Baranowski, 2011).

In the battle against physical inactivity and associated health complications, technology has long been recognized as a double-edged sword; on one hand, Internet, computer, and video games are seen as promoting a sedentary lifestyle in young people (Bailey & McInnis, 2011), yet, on the other hand, active video games seem to promise a novel way to enhance physical engagement (Biddiss & Irwin, 2010). Defined as "a video game that provides physical activity or exercise through interactive play, these games go beyond simple hand/finger movements" (Mears & Hansen, 2009, p. 26), active video games (AVGs) take advantage of technology to track a player's body movement or reactions for the game to progress. If the time used to play traditional nonactive video games could be replaced by playing AVGs, a reduction in sedentary behavior and an increase in PA could be the result. Similarly, AVGs have the advantage of not being constrained by traditional PA barriers, such as unsafe neighborhoods, lack of transportation and severe weather (Biddiss & Irwin, 2010). Therefore, AVGs are regarded as a feasible lifestyle option, as nonstructured PA serves to sustain weight loss and fitness (Biddiss & Irwin, 2010). More specifically, it can be a useful tool in helping children to meet physical activity guidelines (Simons, Vries, Jongert, & Verheijden, 2014). McLemore et al. (2015) found that elementary-aged children who engaged in AVG experienced an increase in overall heart rate when playing more active games (boxing and running), finding that children enjoyed playing the AVG even though they indicated working hard during the exercise portion of the game. Zhang et al. (2015) examined African-American children's exertion and enjoyment while playing Wii sports games and observed significant heart rate change and high levels of enjoyment in Wii game playing, indicating that players were enjoying the play while exercising fairly hard, consistent with previous studies purporting favorable attitudes toward AVGs (e.g., Barnett et al., 2011; Hansen & Sanders, 2010). This finding also highlighted the potential of AVG as a tool to motivate African-American children in participating in physical activities (Song, Peng, & Lee, 2011).

Researchers, educators, parents, and advocates of physical activity and sport have identified multiple benefits associated with participation in these types of activities in a variety of domains: physical, lifestyle, affective, social, and cognitive (Bailey, 2006). Some researchers speak to the role of physical activity and its influence on children's respect for their own bodies, while other researchers note that involvement in PA provides individuals opportunities to meet and communicate with others and to learn new social skills (Talbot, 2001). Several studies (Biddle, Akande, Vlachopoulos, & Fox, 1996; Butcher, 1989; Virnig & McLeod, 1996) have documented that involvement in sport is related to more positive body image and fewer reports of disordered eating among females. Richman and Shaffer (2000) found in their study of 220 college females that involvement in sport prior to the start of college was related to higher levels of general and body self-esteem, and that more frequent participation in sport and PA resulted in the highest levels of self-esteem. While a positive correlation has been found between involvement in sport and increased self-esteem, recent data suggests participation rates for involvement in sport is on the decline for children in the US (Gaio, 2014).

Involvement in Sport-Related Programs Designed Specifically for Children

There is certainly no shortage of sport programs around the country for children of all ages and playing abilities. While the availability of recreational and competitive programs has increased over the years, the Sports & Fitness Industry Association (SFIA) has noted that participation across sports and demographics has declined: In 2007, 35% of children between the ages of 6 and 12 were active at least three times a week in a sporting activity (organized or unstructured); by 2014, that number dropped to 27%. The biggest declines were seen in softball and baseball, but the SFIA observed there was a notable decline of 2.6 million fewer children playing sport in the past five years. Reasons for the declining numbers include a variety of factors—social, interpersonal, and financial. From parents' fear of injury to increased costs associated with involvement in an organized sport to the increased time commitment, many parents have indicated that despite the positive effects associated with participation in sport, the negative outcomes outweigh the positive (Aspen Institute Project Play, 2015).

Despite the decline in organized youth athletics nationwide, a few smaller programs, such as Girls on the Run (GOTR, 2015), have found modest success in not only getting children—girls in this case—involved, but also helping them learn the value of involvement in PA and exercise. Established in 1996, Girls on the Run was developed to provide preadolescent girls with tools, skills, and self-esteem that would help them navigate the challenging years that were ahead of them. The nonprofit organization, which serves more than 165,000 girls in the US and Canada, has found a unique way to involve girls in a sporting activity at an age when self-esteem starts to plummet and girls, for the most part, are more insecure and self-conscious than ever. Martin, Waldron, McCabe, and Choi (2009) noted in their study of 21 girls participating in a GOTR program significant differences in each participant's overall physical fitness level, running self-concept, and fear of being fat in the pre- and post-test measures of these dimensions. The overarching takeaway from this study was that general levels of self-concept and self-perception improved following participation in this organized program. Other community-based intervention programs are also being examined as a means of taking the intervention out of the schools into the community with the hope of raising PA levels across demographic groups.

Community Interventions in Sport and Health

One type of research involving community and participant input and participation when devising research strategies or interventions is called community-based participatory research (CBPR). The W.K. Kellogg Foundation Community Health Scholars Program defines CBPR as follows:

> [CBPR] is a collaborative approach to research that equitably involves all partners in the research process and recognizes the unique strengths that each brings. CBPR begins with a research topic of importance to the community with the aim of combining knowledge and action for social change to improve community health and eliminate health disparities.
>
> *(Faridi, Grunbaum, Gray, Franks, & Simoes, 2007, A70)*

While previous PA interventions with no community input have been shown to be effective in suburban areas (Pangrazi, Beighle, Vehige, & Vack, 2003), these interventions may not necessarily be appropriate for a rural, underserved population. The use of the CBPR model is one way to ensure participant and community input when developing a PA intervention for a community. By using CBPR, a PA intervention is more likely to address unique needs of the particular participants. While little has been done in the field of exercise science to engage the community in PA intervention development, using information gained from the community to direct interventions is not a new concept (de Winter, Baerveldt, & Kooistra, 1999). For example, public health studies have been using community-directed interventions, including those utilizing children's input, for over a decade (de Winter et al., 1999). Additionally, studies involving the community in intervention development have done so in an effort to promote social justice and equity in health, specifically regarding low SES populations (Potvin, Cargo, McComber, Delormier, & Macaulay, 2003). The World Health Organization (WHO) views community involvement in intervention development as an important process that "enables people and communities to take control over their health and its determinants" (Potvin et al., 2003). According to the WHO, health should not be promoted and enhanced through a top-down, expert-driven approach, but rather should be based on community participation and insight (de Winter et al., 1999). This is because interventions incorporating the views of those being studied have been shown to improve the likelihood of success and sustainability (Hesketh et al., 2005). CBPR approaches may be just one of many directions for future research when contemplating the role of sport in health.

Directions for Future Research within Sport and the Communication Subdiscipline

Research in the area of sport and health is really in its infancy and therefore offers many possible directions for future research that will lead to theoretical and applied advancements. Several studies have identified positive outcomes as it relates to the physiological and psychological effects associated with PA, which includes mediated PA in the form of a Wii, other gaming devices, or new media technologies. The research is also fairly consistent when looking at the likelihood of a child to be involved long-term with PA, exercise, or sport, and notes that enjoyment is a key motivating factor in the equation. The more children enjoy an activity, the more likely they are to continue it. Dishman et al. (2005) found that perceived enjoyment is another key component of exercise behavior; for school-aged children and adolescents, enjoyment is an important determinant influencing the amount of time they allocate to a physical activity. This offers many directions for future research in the area of sport and health: continue the examination of AVG that help children become physically active and measure perceived enjoyment, perceived exertion, and actual exertion; continue to examine the motivations behind children's involvement (or lack thereof) in sport and identify factors relating to lower retention rates as children move from preadolescence to adolescence. Of great importance here is better understanding the complex factors relating to children's health literacy and/or knowledge of how to become and remain healthy. Certainly, involvement in sport is a key element in that equation, yet without understanding the factors influencing and shaping a child's decision-making as it relates to health behaviors, it will be difficult to develop intervention programs aimed at positive health outcomes. With a variety of populations at continued risk for overweight and obesity, it seems relevant and pertinent to further examine the role of sport in a health communication context.

While lack of physical activity is often associated with overweight and obesity in individuals, the excess of physical activity can also result in harmful effects including what is commonly referred to as the female athlete triad. Researchers from the American College of Sports Medicine examined the relationship among energy expenditure, energy availability, menstrual function, and body density to determine which courses of treatment would be most successful in helping young women with the disorder (Nattiv et al., 2007). As Bissell and Porterfield (2006) and Bissell (2004) found, disordered eating symptomatology and related psychological issues are more prevalent in athletes who compete in aesthetic sports versus strength or power sports, but affective issues such as social physique anxiety or body image distortion are increasingly becoming more common in all athletes across sports. Studies examining the role of sport involvement or PA and body image issues remain a pressing concern as young female athletes are often not receiving proper nutrition, which can lead to many other physical and mental problems later in the lifespan. The intersection of sport in health communication is an important one for future research because the issues will continue to evolve as the role of sport in health communication evolves.

References

2008 Physical Activity Guidelines for Americans Vol 1. (2008). Washington, DC: health.gov.

Ades, P.A., Savage, P.D., & Toth, M.J. (2009). High-calorie-expenditure exercise: A new approach to cardiac rehabilitation for overweight coronary patients. *Circulation, 119*(20), 2671–2678.

Aspen Institute: Project Play. (2015). *Sport for all: Play for life.* Retrieved June 29, 2016, from http://youthreport.projectplay.us.

Bailey, R. (2006). Physical education and sports in schools: A review of benefits and outcomes. *Journal of School Health, 76*(8), 397–401.

Bailey, B.W., & McInnis, K. (2011). Energy cost of exergaming: A comparison of the energy cost of 6 forms of exergaming. *Archives of Pediatrics & Adolescent Medicine, 165*(7), 597–602.

Bandura, A. (1986). *Social foundations of thought and action: A social cognitive theory.* Englewood Cliffs, NJ: Prentice-Hall.

Bandura, A. (2009). Social cognitive theory of mass communication. In J. Bryant & M.B. Oliver (Eds.), *Media effects: Advances in theory and research* (pp. 94–124). New York: Routledge.

Baranowski, T., Baranowski, J.C., & Cullen, K.W. (2003). The Fun, Food, and Fitness Project (FFFP): The Baylor GEMS pilot study. *Ethnicity & Disease, 13*(1 Suppl 1), S30–39.

Barnett, A., Cerin, E., & Baranowski, T. (2011). Active video games for youth: A systematic review. *Journal of Physical Activity and Health, 8*(5), 724–737.

Barwais, F.A., Cuddihy, T.F., & Tomson, L.M. (2013). Physical activity, sedentary behavior and total wellness changes among sedentary adults: A 4-week randomized control trial. *Health and Quality of Life Outcomes, 11*(1), 183.

Betancourt, J.R., Green, A.R., Carrillo, J.E., & Ananeh-Firempong, O. (2003). Defining cultural competence: A practical framework for addressing racial/ethnic disparities in health and health care. *Public Health Reports, 118*, 293–302.

Biddiss, E., & Irwin, J. (2010). Active video games to promote physical activity in children and youth: A systematic review. *Archives of Pediatrics & Adolescent Medicine, 164*(7), 664–672.

Biddle, S., Akande, A., Vlachopoulos, S., & Fox, K. (1996). Towards the understanding of children's motivation for physical activity: Achievement goal orientations, beliefs about sport success, and sport emotion in Zimbabwean children. *Psychology and Health, 12*, 49–55.

Bissell, K. (2004). Sports model/sports mind: The relationship between entertainment and sports media exposure, sports participation and body image distortion in Division I female athletes. *Mass Communication & Society, 7*, 453–474.

Bissell, K., Conlin, L., Bie, B., Zhang, X., & McLemore, D. (2015). *Let go of my iPad: Testing the effectiveness of new media technologies to measure children's food intake and health behaviors.* Paper presented to the Mass Communication & Society Division of the Association for Education in Journalism and Mass Communication. Annual meeting, August 7.

Bissell, K., & Porterfield, K. (2006). Who's got game? Exposure to entertainment and sports media and social physique anxiety in Division I female athletes. *Journal of Sport Media, 1*(1), 19–50.

Bissell, K., Zhang, C., & Meadows III, C.W. (2014). A Wii, a mii, and a new me? Testing the effectiveness of Wii exergames on children's enjoyment, engagement, and exertion in physical activity. *International Journal of Child Health and Human Development, 7*(1).

Borer, K.T. (2005). Physical activity in the prevention and amelioration of osteoporosis in women: Interaction of mechanical, hormonal and dietary factors. *Sports Medicine, 35*(9), 779–830.

Bush, P.J., & Iannotti, R.J. (1990). A children's health belief model. *Medical Care, 28*(1), 69–86.

Butcher, J.E. (1989). Adolescent girls' sex role development: Relationship with sports participation, self-esteem, and age at menarche. *Sex Roles, 20*(9/10), 575–593.

Carter, M.C., Burley, V.J., Nykjaer, C., & Cade, J.E. (2013). Adherence to a smartphone application for weight loss compared to website and paper diary: Pilot randomized controlled trial. *Journal of Internet Research, 15*(4), 32.

Centers for Disease Control and Prevention. (June 19, 2015). Prevalence of childhood obesity in the United States, 2011–2012. Division of Nutrition, Physical Activity, and Obesity. Retrieved June 29, 2016, from http://www.cdc.gov/obesity/data/childhood.html.

Centers for Disease Control and Prevention. (June 13, 2014). Youth risk behavior surveillance: United States, 2013. *Morbidity and Mortality Weekly Reports, 63*(4), 505–520.

Chuang, R.J., Sharma, S., Skala, K., & Evans, A. (2013). Ethnic differences in the home environment and physical activity behaviors among low-income, minority preschoolers in Texas. *American Journal of Health Promotion, 27*(4), 270–278.

Crespo, C.J., Smit, E., Troiano, R.P., Bartlett, S.J., Macera, C.A., and Andersen, R.A. (2001). Television watching, energy intake, and obesity in U.S. children: Results from the third National Health and Nutritional Examination Survey, 1988–1994. *Archives of Pediatrics and Adolescent Medicine, 155,* 360–365.

Croll, J.K., Neumark-Sztainer, D., Story, M., Wall, M., Perry, C., & Harnack, L. (2006). Adolescents involved in weight-related and power team sports have better eating patterns and nutrient intakes than non-sport involved adolescents. *Journal of the American Dietetic Association, 106*(5), 709–717.

de Winter, M., Baerveldt, C., & Kooistra, J. (1999). Enabling children: Participation as a new perspective on child-health promotion. *Child: Care, Health and Development, 25*(1), 15–23; discussion 23–25.

Dishman, R.K., Motl, R.W., Sallis, J.F., Dunn, A.L., Birnbaum, A.S., Welk, G.J., et al. (2005). Self-management strategies mediate self-efficacy and physical activity. *American Journal of Preventive Medicine, 29,* 10–18.

Doshi, A., Patrick, K., Sallis, J.F., & Calfas, K. (2003). Evaluation of physical activity websites for use of behavior change theories. *Annal of Behavioral Medicine, 25*(2), 105–111.

Eaton, D.K., Kann, L., Kinchen, S., Shanklin, S., Ross, J., Hawkins, J., et al. (2012). Youth risk behavior surveillance: United States, 2007. *Morbidity and Mortality Weekly Report. Surveillance Summaries (Washington, DC: 2002), 61*(4), 1–162.

Fagard, R.H. (2001). Exercise characteristics and the blood pressure response to dynamic physical training. *Medicine & Science in Sports & Exercise, 33*(6 Suppl), S484–492; discussion S493–494.

Fakouri, T.H.I., Hughes, J.P., Brody, D.J., Kit, B.K., & Ogden, C.L. (2013). Physical activity and screen-time viewing among elementary school-aged children in the United States from 2009–2010. *Journal of American Medical Association Pediatrics, 167*(3), 223–229.

Faridi, Z., Grunbaum, J.A., Gray, B.S., Franks, A., & Simoes, E. (2007). Community-based participatory research: Necessary next steps. *Preventing Chronic Disease, 4*(3), A70.

Frenn, M., & Shelly, M. (2003). Diet and exercise in low-income culturally diverse middle school students. *Public Health Nursing, 20*(5), 361–368.

Gaio, M. (2014). Youth participation in team sports on the decline. *Athletic Business.* Retrieved June 29, 2016, from http://www.athleticbusiness.com/high-school/youth-participation-in-team-sports-on-the-decline.html.

Garcia, A.W., Broada, M.B., Frenn, M., Coviak, C., Pender, N., & Ronis, D.L. (1995). Gender and developmental differences in exercise beliefs among youth and prediction of their exercise behavior. *Journal of School Health, 65*(6), 213–219.

Girls on the Run. (2015). How Girls on the Run began. Retrieved June 29, 2016, from http://www.girlsontherun.org/Who-We-Are/Our-History.

Gray, L., Thomas, N., & Lewis, L. (2010). Teachers' use of educational technology in U.S. public schools: 2009. *National Center for Education Statistics.*

Hansen, L., & Sanders, S. (2010). Fifth grade students' experiences participating in active gaming in physical education: The persistence to game. *ICHPER-SD Journal of Research, 5*(2), 33–40.

Helmrich, S.P., Ragland, D.R., Leung, R.W., & Paffenbarger, R.S. Jr. (1991). Physical activity and reduced occurrence of non-insulin-dependent diabetes mellitus. *New England Journal of Medicine, 325*(3), 147–152.

Hesketh, K., Waters, E., Green, J., Salmon, L., & Williams J. (2005). Healthy eating, activity and obesity prevention: A qualitative study of parent and child perceptions in Australia. *Health Promotion International, 20*(1), 19–26.

Johnston, L.D., Delva, J., & O'Malley, P.M. (2007). Sports participation and physical education in American secondary schools: Current levels and racial/ethnic and socio-economic disparities. *American Journal of Preventative Medicine, 33*, 195–208.

Kosma, M., Cardinal, B.J., & McCubbin, J.A. (2005). A pilot study of a web-based physical activity motivational program for adults with physical activities. *Disability and Rehabilitation, 27*(23), 1435–1442.

Liu, J.H., Jones, S.J., Sun, H., Probst, J.C., Merchant, A.T., & Cavicchia, P. (2012). Diet, physical activity, and sedentary behaviors as risk factors for childhood obesity: An urban and rural comparison. *Childhood Obesity, 8*(5), 440–448.

Manson, J.E., Nathan, D.M., Krolewski, A.S., Stampfer, M.J., Willett, W.C., & Hennekens, C.H. (1992). A prospective study of exercise and incidence of diabetes among US male physicians. *Journal of the American Medical Association, 268*(1), 63–67.

Marceglia, S., Bonacina, S., Zaccaria, V., Pagliari, C., & Pinciroli, F. (2012). How might the iPad change healthcare? *Journal of the Royal Society of Medicine, 105*, 223–241.

Martin, J.J., Kulinna, P.H., McCaughtry, N., Cothran, D., Dake, J., & Fahoome, G.F. (2005). The theory of planned behavior: Predicting physical activity and cardiorespiratory fitness in African American children. *Journal of Sport and Exercise Psychology, 27*(4), 456–469.

Martin, J.J., Waldron, J.J., McCabe, A., & Choi, Y.S. (2009). The impact of "Girls on the Run" on self-concept and fat attitudes. *Journal of Clinical Sport Psychology, 3*, 127–138.

McLemore, D., Conlin, L., Bie, B., Zhang, M., Bissell, K., & Parrott, S. (August 2015). *The mediating role of media use in an elementary school health intervention program.* Paper presented at the meeting of the Association for Education in Journalism and Mass Communication, San Francisco, CA.

Mears, D., & Hansen, L. (2009). Technology in physical education: Article 5 in a 6-part series: Active gaming: Definitions, options and implementation. *Strategies, 23*(2), 26–29.

Morris, J.N., & Crawford, M.D. (1958). Coronary heart disease and physical activity of work: Evidence of a national necropsy survey. *British Medical Journal, 2*(5111), 1485–1496.

Nattiv, A., Loucks, A.B., Manore, M.M., Sanborn, C.F., Sundgot-Borgen, J., & Warren, M.P. (2007). American College of Sports Medicine position stand: The female athlete triad. *Medical Science and Sports Exercise, 39*(10), 1867–1882.

Paffenbarger, R.S. Jr., Hyde, R.T., Wing, A.L., Lee, I.M., Jung, D.L., & Kampert, J.B. (1993). The association of changes in physical-activity level and other lifestyle characteristics with mortality among men. *New England Journal of Medicine, 328*(8), 538–545.

Paffenbarger, R.S. Jr., Hyde, R.T., Wing, A.L., & Hsieh, C.C. (1986). Physical activity, all-cause mortality, and longevity of college alumni. *New England Journal of Medicine, 314*(10), 605–613.

Pandey, A., Hasan, S., Dubey, D., & Sarangi, S. (2013). Smartphone apps as a source of cancer information: Changing trends in health information-seeking behavior. *Journal of Cancer Education, 28*(1), 138–142.

Pangrazi, R.P., Beighle, A., Vehige, T., & Vack, C. (2003). Impact of Promoting Lifestyle Activity for Youth (PLAY) on children's physical activity. *Journal of School Health, 73*(8), 317–321.

Pate, R.R., Heath, G.W., Dowda, M., & Trost, S.G. (1996). Associations between physical activity and other health behaviors in a representative sample of US adolescents. *American Journal of Public Health, 86*(11), 1577–1581.

Pender, N.J. (1996). *Health promotion in nursing practice* (3rd ed.). Stanford, CT: Appleton and Lange.

Pender, N.J., Murdaugh, C.L., & Parsons, M.A. (2005). *Health promotion in nursing practice* (5th ed.). Upper Saddle River, NJ: Prentice Hall.

Peterson, A. (September 17, 2015). Apps are making health claims but they may not have the science to back them up. *Washington Post.* Retrieved June 29, 2016, from https://www.washingtonpost.com/news/the-switch/wp/2015/09/17/apps-are-making-health-claims-but-they-may-not-have-the-science-to-back-them-up/.

Potvin, L., Cargo, M., McComber, A.M., Delormier, T., & Macaulay, A.C. (2003). Implementing participatory intervention and research in communities: Lessons from the Kahnawake Schools Diabetes Prevention Project in Canada. *Social Science & Medicine, 56*(6), 1295–1305.

Proctor, M.H., Moore, L.L., Gao, D., Cupples, L.A., Bradlee, M.L., Hood, M.Y., & Ellison, R.C. (2003). Television viewing and change in body fat from preschool to early adolescence: The Framingham Children's Study. *International Journal of Obesity, 27*, 827–833.

Ogden, C.L., Carroll, M.D., Kit, B.K., & Flegal, K.M. (2014). Prevalence of childhood and adult obesity in the United States, 2011–2012. *Journal of the American Medical Association, 311*, 806–814.

Richman, E.L., & Shaffer, D.R. (2000). "If you let me play sports": How might sport participation influence the self-esteem of adolescent females? *Psychology of Women Quarterly, 24*, 189–199.

Robinson, L.E., Wadsworth, D.D., Webster, E.K., & Bassett, D.R. Jr. (2014). School reform: The role of physical education policy in physical activity of elementary school children in Alabama's Black Belt Region. *American Journal of Health Promotion, 28*(3 Suppl), S72–76.

Sewell, K., Andreae, S., Luke, E., & Safford, M.M. (2011). Perceptions of and barriers to use of generic medications in a rural African American population, Alabama, 2011. *Preventing Chronic Disease, 9*, E142.

Simons, M., Vries, S.I.D., Jongert, T., & Verheijden, M.W. (2014). Energy expenditure of three public and three home-based active video games in children. *Computers in Entertainment (CIE), 11*(1), 3.

Song, H., Peng, W., & Lee, K.M. (2011). Promoting exercise self-efficacy with an exergame. *Journal of Health Communication, 16*(2), 148–162.

Talbot, M. (2001). The case for physical education. In G. Doll-Tepper & D. Scoretz (Eds.), *World Summit on Physical Education.* Berlin: ICSSPE.

Trost, S.G., Kerr, L.M., Ward, D.S., & Pate, R.R. (2000). Physical activity and determinants of physical activity in obese and non-obese children. *International Journal of Obesity, 25*, 822–829.

Trost, S.G., Pate, R.R., Dowda, M., Ward, D.S., Felton, G., & Saunders, R. (2002). Psychosocial correlates of physical activity in White and African-American girls. *Journal of Adolescent Health, 31*(3), 226–233.

U.S. Department of Health and Human Services. (1996). *Physical activity and health: A report of the Surgeon General.* Atlanta, GA: U.S. Department of Health and Human

Services, Centers for Disease Control and Prevention, National Center for Chronic Disease Prevention and Health Promotion.

Veitch, J., Bagley, S., Ball, K., & Salmon, J. (2006). Where do children usually play? A qualitative study of parents' perceptions of influences on children's active free-play. *Health & Place, 12*(4), 383–393.

Virnig, A.G., & McLeod, C.R. (1996). Attitudes toward eating and exercise: A comparison of runners and triathletes. *Journal of Sport Behavior, 1,* 82–91.

Zhang, M., Bie, B., Conlin, L., McLemore, D., Bissell, K., Lowrey, P., & Parrott, S. (2015). *Active video game play in African American children: The effect of gender and BMI on exertion and enjoyment.* Paper presented to the Minorities and Communication Division at the Annual Meeting of the Association for Education in Journalism and Mass Communication, San Francisco, CA.

PART III

Mediated Approaches to Sport

14

SPORT AS INTERNATIONAL COMMUNICATION

Simon Ličen

WASHINGTON STATE UNIVERSITY

Since childhood, one of my favorite technologies in sport communication has been the 'telestrator'—the device allowing broadcasters and color commentators to draw sketches over still or moving images, such as instant replays in sport games. The first time I noticed the technology was during TV broadcasts of the National Basketball Association's (NBA) games in the late 1980s and early 1990s. Watching the wizardry of Magic Johnson was entertaining in itself; yet seeing replays with graphic highlighting of his imaginative passes allowed a fuller appreciation of Magic's vision of play and made those games even more enjoyable.

Although I grew up in Europe, the games I *saw* were the same as those seen by viewers in the United States: televised athletic events are caught on camera in full by one production company which then sells broadcasting rights to other broadcasters (sometimes worldwide). The play-by-play announcing that I *heard*, however, was different from the American. The broadcasts were aired on TV Koper-Capodistria, a television station based in Koper in Slovenia, which was then part of Yugoslavia. Despite what one might expect considering the station's geographic location, the announcers spoke Italian, rather than Slovenian (the latter being one of the three official languages of Yugoslavia). To further complicate matters, the color commentator who joined play-by-play announcer Sergio Tavčar was former coach Dan Peterson—an American.

Let me recapitulate: American basketball was shown on a Yugoslav TV network and announced in Italian by a Slovenian and an American.

This intertwinement of nations, countries, and languages (and, in the late 1980s, even social, economic, and political systems) may appear hard to comprehend to readers and sport fans in the United States; here, quintessential indicators of nationhood such as the flag and the national anthem precede athletic contests even at the middle school level, and most major professional leagues are named 'national' even though they include teams from Canada. These very leagues are indicators of the relativity of national boundaries: for instance, on opening night rosters for the 2014–15 season, NBA teams fielded 101 international players (22% of the total) from 37 countries and territories (NBA.com, 2014). This league is often cited as a model of the 'internationalization' of American professional sport—perhaps as a consequence of the global appeal of basketball. However, Major League Baseball (MLB) features even more international athletes, and American nationals in the NHL are actually a minority (242 players, only 25% of the total; Quanthockey.com, 2015) even though the United States is home to 23 of the league's 30 franchises. Although fans and consumers of American professional—and even intercollegiate—sport may not realize it, they are likely exposed to international athletes almost daily.

Relevant Theories for Sport within International Communication

The sports mentioned in the previous paragraph are most obviously consumed through mass media. Determining its effects is a complex task because of the plethora of media offerings, the diversity of consumers, their backgrounds and experiences, and their varying amount of exposure to media content. For all, the impact is seldom strong and direct; instead, it accumulates over time and media forms.

One way mass media influence those who consume them is by determining which topics and issues merit public attention. The ability of the media, especially news media, to influence the public agenda is referred to as the agenda-setting function of the media, and the theory describing this process is called agenda-setting theory. The theory originators compared media coverage of the 1968 presidential campaign with what voters identified as relevant political issues, finding a very strong correlation between the issues identified by mass media outlets and the judgment of the electorate regarding the importance of various campaign topics (McCombs & Shaw, 1972). Thus, voters tended to share the media's composite definition of what is important—even though this picture is not perfect.

Perhaps the ideal example of agenda-setting in connection with sport are the Olympic Games, which are the quintessential 'media event' staged solely to attract media coverage. They are a "pseudo-event" (Boorstin, 1961) and would not even occur if the media were not there to document them. This does not diminish their importance; rather, it highlights that the public would not care about the Olympics nearly as much had the media not made them into "the biggest show on Earth" (Billings, 2008).

The agenda-setting function does not prove a causal relationship between media contents and one's opinions: The media do not tell people what to think, but rather what to think *about* (Cohen, 1963). One may thus support or be critical of the Olympics, but very few remain indifferent. Also, agenda-setting is particularly effective with people who are undecided. Those who have already formed an opinion about an issue that is important to them tend to avoid acquiring further—and potentially diverging—information (McCombs & Shaw, 1972).

Related to but distinct from agenda-setting is agenda-building, which examines *how* issues are created and *why* some of them "come to command the attention and concern of decision makers, while others fail" (Cobb & Elder, 1971, p. 905). This theory also originates in political science as policy agenda-setting. The "sources of bias" (Cobb & Elder, 1971, p. 906) in institutional agendas include older (i.e., existing and unresolved) items, decision-makers, the media themselves, and the status of the group initiating an issue. Routine, elites, ownership, and interest groups, in addition to real-world events, thus influence the media agenda (Scheufele, 2000).

'Beats' in journalism are the epitome of 'older items' as some topics, such as men's professional sport, receive constant coverage and preempt alternatives— including international sport and women's sport (Gee & Leberman, 2011). With regard to ownership influencing agenda-building, worldwide coverage of the Olympic Games is dictated by the International Olympic Committee (IOC), which established an agency, Olympic Broadcasting Services (OBS), tasked with serving as the host broadcaster for summer, winter, and youth Olympics. OBS produces video coverage of every sport from every venue, resulting in thousands of hours of so-called 'international signal' which is then distributed to the hundreds of television stations airing the event worldwide. Similarly, many North American professional leagues (NBA TV, NFL Network, NHL Network, MLB Network), some college athletic conferences (Big Ten Network, Pac-12 Networks), and even individual teams (YES Network, Longhorn Network, Manchester United Television) own or control their television channels. These circumvent traditional news organizations, oversee news and content-generation, and control sport from production to publication.

If agenda-setting states the media are successful at telling people what to think *about*, the priming hypothesis suggests that mass media also influence people's behavior and judgment about issues and individuals by exposing them to selected stimuli and making some issues more salient than others (Iyengar & Kinder, 1987). Judgment is usually influenced by affecting what is on people's minds when they make a decision: if a news show discusses living standards or human rights violations in Russia and then switches to this country organizing the 2014 Winter Olympics or the 2018 FIFA World Cup, the viewers are primed to think Russia is not an appropriate host for the events. Frequent or longer primes have stronger effects, and their effects fade with time (Higgins, Bargh, & Lombardi, 1985).

Related to, yet distinct from, agenda-setting and priming is the concept of framing, which describes the process of selection of some elements of perceived reality, the exclusion of others, and the assembling of narratives emphasizing connections among them to promote a particular interpretation of an issue. This process unfolds through four stages: problem definition, causal analysis, moral judgment, and remedy promotion (Entman, 1993). The latter two do not necessarily employ biased wording aimed specifically at convincing the audience; instead, they may seem a natural continuation of the definition and cause analysis phases. Issues may be reported—or created—and the analysis may use neutral expressions, yet be partial and incomplete. Such selection and exclusion may evoke particular interpretations of the information presented. Sports are often said to be 'plagued' by doping, suggesting the phenomenon is grave and spreads rapidly. Depending on the causal analysis and moral judgment associated with the case at hand, doping can then be framed as a relatively isolated phenomenon, an exception—e.g., the BALCO scandal—or the norm, such as in the recent case of the allegedly state-sponsored use of performance-enhancing drugs among Russian athletes.

The idea of frames as the circumstances surrounding acts and events in everyday life derives from Erving Goffman (1974). Somewhat similar to stereotypes, which are necessary and inevitable cognitive processes that become problematic only when they are prejudicial, 'frames' are shared circumstances and schemes of interpretation that make communication possible. In everyday communication, individuals very often apply them inadvertently rather than purposely.

Mass media and news media are particularly salient producers of frames; they can change the societal status quo, yet more commonly preserve it (Goffman, 1974; Hofstetter, 1976). This perpetuating impulse is described as the 'structural bias' of mass media and is attributed to the perpetuation of existing schemes of media coverage and the pursuit of high ratings (Hofstetter, 1976).

The theories introduced thus far operate in connection with individual topics and issues. Another concept relevant to international communication and sport is broader in the scope of influence it implies, and explains the effects television has on its viewers. Television is fundamentally different from other media: it is pervasive, highly accessible, and nonselective as it does not require literacy. These characteristics are the tenets of cultivation theory (Gerbner & Gross, 1976), which suggests that television should not be studied in terms of targeted and specific events, but rather in terms of the cumulative and overarching impact on the way people see the world in which they live.

The amount of TV viewing, especially when compared with other activities that expand knowledge such as reading, learning, and studying, drove the authors of cultivation theory to describe television as the "central cultural arm of American society" (Gerbner & Gross, 1976, p. 175). They thought of it as a unique medium requiring a special study approach. Its messages form a coherent system, which produces the mainstream of American culture. Cultivation analysis thus focuses on television's cumulative contributions to the thinking and actions of the masses, which have overwhelmingly stabilizing and homogenizing consequences (Gerbner, 1990). It is a theory of learning which explains how people acquire knowledge from and through television. The more time they spend 'living' with it, the greater the effect on their opinions, values, and personal identity.

Although 'on-screen reality' is made to appear as an accurate mirror of the real world, it is not. Groups such as women, lower classes, the young, and the old are significantly underrepresented, and the disproportionate amount of crime leads viewers to think the world is much more violent than it actually is. The more viewers watch, the more they are convinced television reality is real (Gerbner & Gross, 1976). Until the penetration of some European soccer leagues on American television, international sports were not broadcasted or even mentioned in topical shows such as SportsCenter. Thus, when teams won national titles in the MLB or NBA, viewers did not challenge assertions that they became 'world' champions as most of them simply never became aware that professional baseball and basketball is played outside the United States, too.

The groups and categories mentioned in the previous paragraph—gender, nationality, age, and so forth—are often used by people to mentally organize themselves. Individuals typically develop two principal identities: a personal self and a collective self, comprising characteristics—beliefs, attitudes, behaviors—of the groups they perceive themselves as belonging to (Tajfel, 1981). These can be formal or informal and range from gender and nationality to ethnicity, religion, and even athletic or ideological affiliation. Groups and categories can be used to differentiate, as well as to compare and evaluate ourselves and others. Social identity theory assumes that individuals are motivated to evaluate themselves positively to improve their feeling of self-worth. When group membership becomes relevant to their self-definition, they are motivated to seek a positive social identity (Tajfel & Turner, 1986), hence the feeling of satisfaction and positive emotions felt after the victory of a favored or national team. When managing their social identities, individuals do not think of themselves as just being different, but also as being better or worse than others (Bryant & Cummins, 2009). This gives way to fan behavior that is rooted in group identification and can range from seemingly innocuous 'trash talk' to disruptive behavior such as brawls and even hooliganism.

Social identity is central to self-categorization theory, which suggests that people develop a sense of personal identity that incorporates the *perceived shared characteristics* of the group they belong to: The self is thus not a foundational aspect of cognition but rather a product of it (Turner, Hogg, Oakes, Riecher, & Wetherell, 1987). One way people learn about the shared characteristics of national groups (and out-groups) is through international sport: Athletes from Russia and China are often thought of as collectively perpetuating the undemocratic political systems of the countries they live in and thus expanding the divide between 'them' and 'us.' This may or may not be correct, as shown by American athletes who have very different opinions on a number of social and political issues. There is no reason to believe that athletes from other countries are less diverse in their attitudes.

Self-categorization theory examines the perception and interaction between people perceived to belong to different social categories. It is sometimes referenced as 'social identity of the group' and predicts that categories are constructed so as to ensure that differences between categories are larger than differences within them. This allows the preservation of such categorization. Individuals try to distance themselves from the norms and behaviors of out-groups. Also, out-group members are usually seen as more homogeneous than in-groups: individual differences among them disappear (Oakes, Haslam, & Turner, 1992). A bumper sticker on a Tar Heels fan's car might read, "I'll Cheer for Duke When They Play Al Qaeda"; obviously, the name of the loathed school can be easily changed, but the name of the opponent less so.

Studies Offering Connections between Sport and International Communication

Although sport is considered by some to be a unique realm of society, it can be studied using conventional approaches; the theories introduced in the previous section were developed and first used in very different contexts. To examine sport communication as international communication, scholars and fans often turn to 'mega events' (or, as previously noted, 'media events') such as the Olympic Games. In the United States, the broadcasting and electronic rights to the Olympic Games have been owned for decades by NBC Sports, a division of the National Broadcasting Company (NBC). American viewers are potentially exposed to an overwhelming amount of Olympic content: NBC provided 5,535 hours of Olympic coverage from the 2012 Summer Olympics across six television networks and a website, NBCOlympics.com (Deitsch, 2012). Despite this plentitude, viewers and researchers focus their attention on the prime-time telecasts airing on NBC's main channel. These broadcasts attract large audiences (an average 31.1 million nightly viewers for London in 2012; International Olympic Committee, 2012) and offer plenty of opportunity to discuss international sport at the elite level.

One way to explore the agenda set by sport media is to examine the topics discussed on air, or who and what is talked *about*. In 2012, *non*-American athletes received 44% of all primetime mentions (Billings, Angelini, MacArthur, Smith, & Vincent, 2014) even though they accounted for 95% of all Olympians and won 89% of all medals awarded in London. Such imbalance in Summer Olympics coverage has been observed consistently over the past two decades, for a 'grand total' 45% of primetime mentions. The dialogue is slightly less skewed during Winter editions, when 'foreign' athletes (92% of all participants and 89% of all medal winners) receive 58% of primetime mentions (see Angelini, Billings, & MacArthur, 2012; Billings, 2008). Such 'home team' overrepresentation can also be found, for instance, in American coverage of soccer's World Cup (Billings & Tambosi, 2004).

American broadcasters thus set American competitive performances as (more) important for the public agenda by dedicating a disproportionate amount of time to them. Granted, American media are not alone in this: in a seminal examination of international newspaper coverage of the 1984 Summer Olympics, Michael Real (1989) documented 'indexes of nationalism' spanning from 17% (in Mexico) to 79% (in the United States). Self-centered coverage is, thus, a widespread phenomenon among national media; they only differ in the level of disregard for international stories.

Sport coverage does not just dedicate *less* coverage to international athletes; they are also *framed differently*. Studies of the descriptors used to assess success, failure, personality, and physicality of Olympic competitors show that non-American athletes are significantly more likely to be described in terms of athletic skills and experience. In turn, dialogue concerning American athletes disproportionately engages in subjective assessments of commitment, concentration, composure, courage, intelligence, and consonance (the latter describing the influence of concepts such as 'luck' or 'stars aligning') (Angelini et al., 2012; Billings, 2008; Billings et al., 2014). Each of these differences were observed in at least three editions of the Olympic Games since 1996, indicating that such unequal representation, if not necessarily deliberate, is an integral part of the broadcasting discourse. One set of descriptors is not necessarily better or worse; rather, they are different, and American athletes receive more nuance in their depictions.

Dialogic differences likely derive from the announcers' greater familiarity with American athletes; they have the opportunity to observe them practice in the months leading up to major events such as the Olympics. Often, announcers follow athletes year-round in professional competitions and frequently become acquainted to them. Non-American athletes, in turn, remain largely unknown to NBC broadcasters, unless they happen to compete internationally (or in the United States) on a regular basis. With the exception of the Usain Bolts and Maria Sharapovas of the world, most international athletes remain brief profile notes compiled by Olympic media services or network researchers until minutes before stepping on the world's most prominent athletic stage. Those notes will list their brief athletic histories (thus providing clues about their experience) and best performances (informing commentary on their athletic prowess). An additional barrier limiting contacts between announcers and international competitors is the frequent lack of a common language; characteristics such as commitment and intelligence are difficult to assess in the absence of personal contact.

While descriptors usually relate to individuals and result in a cumulative dialogic disparity, several studies have identified instances in which announcers apply national stereotypes to individual competitors. Studies have showed how former baseball player from Japan, Hideo Nomo, and former basketball player from China, Yao Ming, were described as 'model minorities' who sacrificed personal comfort and worked hard and diligently to overcome (athletic and cultural) adversities and succeed in American teams (Lavelle, 2011; Mayeda, 1999).

While one could endorse this cultural stereotype as it involves personal qualities many people would find praiseworthy, a negative, anti-Soviet slant permeated *Sports Illustrated*'s reporting during the Cold War. The magazine disfavored the ideals of collectivism and communism, portrayed Soviet athletes as emotionless, secretive, and only focused on winning, and portrayed the Soviet Union and its athletic program as controlling and oppressive—all notions consonant with then-current negative attitudes towards the country. Interestingly, when it began crumbling in the late 1980s, *Sports Illustrated* steered towards describing Soviet athletes as *framed by* an oppressive system rather than as joyless and robotic contributors to that system (Ellingson, 2012). The discourse surrounding basketball player Jeremy Lin proves that media bias and stereotyping persist to date: although the viral wave of support that became known as 'Linsanity' contributed to changing the perception of Asian-Americans in this sport, a prerequisite for the phenomenon was the fundamentally low athletic expectations placed by the media on males belonging to this ethnic group (Park, 2014). Also, the fact that Lin graduated from Harvard University without an athletic scholarship and that he slept on his brother's couch during his first days with the New York Knicks likely perpetuates, rather than alleviates, the stereotype of Asians as 'good in math' and 'model minorities' who sacrifice to overcome adversities.

Nationalized coverage can cultivate audiences' skewed perceptions. After the 2006 Winter Olympics—a competition in which American athletes won 11% of the medals awarded—a survey asked Americans who had watched Olympic broadcasts how many medals the United States had won. Immediately following the closing ceremony, participants overestimated 'their' nation as having won 27.7% of all medals. Accuracy fell further as time progressed: four weeks later, the estimated share of medals won by the United States increased to 33.9% (Billings, 2008). The assessments of heavy viewers were actually *more accurate* than those of the casual spectator; likely a consequence of frequent exposure to the medal chart. Still, American Olympic broadcasting cultivated an appealing, yet inaccurate, image of national superiority over the rest of the world.

In general, media coverage of the Olympics does not offer a thoroughly accurate picture of the world (of sport). Recent studies have assessed the impact of televised consumption of the Olympic Games on nationalistic attitudes. In a study conducted in six nations on three continents (Billings et al., 2013), people from the United States ranked highest in measures of patriotism (pride in a common cultural heritage) and smugness (an arrogant attitude of perceived superiority over others), and lowest in terms of internationalism (understood as a sense of global citizenship). All these measures were positively correlated with media consumption of the 2012 Summer Olympics: the more viewers watched, the higher they ranked on patriotism and smugness (but also internationalism) scales.

Among the national audiences surveyed for this study, Americans seemed to be most reliant on television as a source of information and, ultimately, cultivation: It was the only audience for which increased viewing was positively correlated with an increase in all assessed nationalized attitudes (including, perhaps counterintuitively, internationalism). One might be tempted to conclude that 'Olympic viewing causes nationalism': Cultivation theory posits that watching violent programming on television leads people to believe that the world is much more dangerous than it actually is (Gerbner & Gross, 1976), so it makes sense that continued disproportionate exposure to programming showing American athletes succeed over foreign counterparts results in a perception of disproportionate athletic superiority.

Yet, correlation does not equal causation. A study of nationalistic attitudes among American viewers of the 2014 Winter Olympics (Billings, Brown, & Brown-Devlin, 2014) confirmed that the more people watched television, the higher they scored on patriotism, nationalism, smugness, and internationalism scales. A comparison across time, however, did not reveal significant differences before, surrounding, and after the Sochi Games, except in the attitude to internationalism: The more one watched, the more their sense of global citizenship *increased*. Following the Olympics does not make one a nationalist: Rather, people with more strongly expressed attitudes seem to tune in to the Olympics more. Consonant with self-categorization theory, the more they watch, the more homogeneous out-groups, or 'foreigners,' are. Also, the stronger one feels about nationalized attitudes, the more motivated a consumer of self-validating programming reaffirming in-group superiority they will be.

The media adopts nationalized narratives and themes (Maguire & Poulton, 1999), potentially resulting in biased and oversimplified coverage, especially in matters pertaining to international communication. In the United States, NBC pursues a 50/50 equilibrium between American and all other competitors (Billings, 2008). Announcer Jim Lampley describes such approach as "intelligent programming" (Billings, 2009, p. 16), and people are, indeed, significantly more likely to watch sport when their nation is playing (Kuper & Szymanski, 2009; Nüesch & Franck, 2009). Even though NBC bans announcers from using the first-person plural when referring to American athletes (Billings, 2008), the overall dialogue—as well as the biased selection of images to report about—can influence audiences. Thus, such programming is 'intelligent' only for the network, which likely witnesses increased ratings. Meanwhile, the knowledge that the audience acquires is rather skewed, partial, and incomplete—only modestly contributing to collective intelligence and media literacy.

If Olympic broadcasting pursues an even split of commentary between those who do and those who do not represent the United States, Twitter is even more skewed toward patriotism. During the 2014 FIFA World Cup matches played by the United States, foreign teams received only 22% of comments while an overwhelming 78% of tweets pointed at the American team. The attributions for success and failure did not differ between the United States and the rest of the world; still, foreign players received significantly fewer comments about appearance, emotions within their performance, and other, miscellaneous commentary (Billings, Burch, & Zimmerman, 2015). On social media, too, familiarity breeds commentary, especially with regard to personality and physicality—again subjective, immeasurable characteristics. Twitter may be a more democratic communication platform that changes the role of producer, but it is not an egalitarian forum. In Chapter 19 of this book, Jimmy Sanderson discusses in greater detail the role of social networking for fans, athletes, and reporters. For now, let us just add that George Gerbner's (1990) observation at the dawn of the Internet era that new technologies extend, rather than deflect, the reach of television's messages would turn out to be remarkably accurate.

Directions for Future Research within Sport and International Communication

The content, discourse, and effects of broadcast and social media in connection to events and organizations worldwide will continue to be major research avenues within sport and international communication in the future. The United States is a particularly prolific and influential producer of global popular culture; while scholarship examining broadcasting has been able to reach across cultures, studies in social media and sport have mostly been limited to American athletes and leagues. Other continents generate less scholarship in this field, with a particularly wide gap following the lines of the North–South divide. An exception to this is Oceania, which contributes state-of-the-art knowledge in both social media research (e.g., Hutchins & Rowe, 2012, 2013) and industry (*The Economist*, 2015). Given the current lack of transnational scholarship in an increasingly interconnected world, the impact and meaning of ever shorter messages and of new 'new media' platforms is bound to be a particularly salient research avenue in the future.

Several theories introduced in this chapter derive from political communication, with more on this aspect of sport offered by Davis Houck in Chapter 5 of this book. Given that sport influences the perception of the home and foreign nations, as well as provides clues for cultivation, one might contemplate whether sport communication branches out into the political. The following is a word-for-word excerpt from an article entitled "15 Most Memorable Stories from London" published on the website SBNation.com following the 2012 London Olympics:

> The U.S. won the final medal count in overall medals and gold medals because America KICKS THE WORLD'S ASS IN EVERYTHING. But none of it could've happened without the American women, who gave us most of the best American moments in the games and ultimately won 58 medals to the men's 45, including 29 Gold. American women, F*** YEAH.

(Sharp, 2012)

Although the acknowledgement of the (disproportionate) female contribution to American success is laudable, the assertion regarding American dominance over the rest of the world is questionable from both content and stylistic standpoints. A reader who signed his name as Todd Carton actually posted a comment describing the story as "Way too U.S. Centric," to which user TheAVA responded, "I think 7 out of 15 is a pretty good representation of other countries' accomplishments." Some perspective is in order, and 7/15 is hardly a good representation of the 89.3% of all awarded medals that were won by 84 of a total 204 participating nations. Among them, compelling stories abound: Soon after winning the gold weightlifting medal in London, Behdad Salimi was suspended from the Iranian national weightlifting team after publicly protesting the national team coach's use of offensive language in training (Zee News, 2014). While a similar story about an abusive American basketball coach generated widespread public and media reactions and literally made it onto the cover of the *New York Times* (Eder & Zernike, 2013), the weightlifter from Iran remains unknown to American audiences. Scholars and professionals must find ways to make them compelling to the American audience so that they demand more of them.

Another future research avenue will relate to cross-national announcing. American sport broadcasts inclusive of the original play-by-play announcing can now be accessed worldwide through feeds streaming to smartphones. In the United States, ratings of the English Premier League have been increasing despite—or perhaps because—they are announced by British commentators. Past research has shown that the global vs. local circulation of game feeds influence production practices (Silk, 1999). Future research will likely examine the impact such trans-national announcing has on national and international audiences and their perception of athletes, organizations, sport, and culture.

The global community is constantly evolving, and about 35 new countries emerged since 1990. Sport is one of the first avenues they use to gain legitimacy: Palestine has yet to gain full international recognition, yet its soccer and basketball national teams have already competed in Asian championships in 2014 and 2015, respectively. As years pass and these new societies—along with other developing and postcolonial nations—enter the world (athletic) stage, they face a number of communication changes and challenges. The academic community will need to welcome scholarship examining these phenomena and their impact on consolidating societies.

Finally, globalization and the increasing interconnectedness of nations in a world system are a domain in itself. Interpersonal, group, and organizational communication change as ever more non-American athletes compete at the professional, but also intercollegiate, level. The latter are likely represented on the reader's varsity teams or even college classes, and the number of athletic departments sponsored by Adidas, a German brand, is increasing. Simultaneously, institutions worldwide have started pursuing sport-themed academic collaborations with US-based universities. Not all involve 'professionalism';

rather, communication through and about sport can be used to bridge cultural differences—or erase them—and can contribute to societal development and peace—or colonization through sport. Navigating these issues will be a major challenge for scholars who will have to be wary of inadvertently spreading cultural dominance and insensitivity: The proverb says, the road to hell is paved with good intentions.

Technology has come a very long way since the days when the telestrator was a novelty. The world is becoming increasingly interconnected, and international communication is assuming an unprecedented role and magnitude. Twenty-five years ago, it involved a lone American speaking Italian on a Yugoslav channel; in 2015, I saw students in China watch ESPN Deportes' live feed of the NBA Finals. Sport offers one of the few regular peaceful opportunities to introduce people to other nations and cultures in unbiased terms. Responsible communication is vital.

References

Angelini, J.R., Billings, A.C., & MacArthur, P.J. (2012). The nationalistic revolution will be televised: The 2010 Vancouver Olympic Games on NBC. *International Journal of Sport Communication, 5*(2), 193–209.

Billings, A.C. (2008). *Olympic media: Inside the biggest show on television.* London: Routledge.

Billings, A.C. (2009). Conveying the Olympic message: NBC producer and sportscaster interviews regarding the role of identity. *Journal of Sports Media, 4*(1), 1–23.

Billings, A.C., Angelini, J.R., MacArthur, P.J., Smith, L.R., & Vincent, J. (2014). Fanfare for the American: NBC's prime-time broadcast of the 2012 London Olympiad. *Electronic News, 8*(2), 101–119.

Billings, A.C., Brown, K., & Brown-Devlin, N. (2014). Sports draped in the American flag: Impact of the 2014 Winter Olympic telecast on nationalized attitudes. *Mass Communication and Society, 18*(4), 377–398.

Billings, A.C., Brown, N.A., Brown, K.A., Guo, Q., Leeman, M.A., Ličen, S., Rowe, D. et al. (2013). From pride to smugness and the nationalism between: Olympic media consumption effects on nationalism across the globe. *Mass Communication and Society, 16*(6), 910–932.

Billings, A.C., Burch, L.M., & Zimmerman, M.H. (2015). Fragments of us, fragments of them: Social media, nationality and US perceptions of the 2014 FIFA World Cup. *Soccer & Society, 16*(5–6), 726–744.

Billings, A.C., & Tambosi, F. (2004). Portraying the United States vs portraying a champion: US network bias in the 2002 World Cup. *International Review for the Sociology of Sport, 39*(2), 157–165.

Boorstin, D.J. (1961). *The image: A guide to pseudo-events in America.* New York: Vintage.

Bryant, J.R., & Cummins, G. (2009). The effects of outcome of mediated and live sporting events of sports fans' self- and social identities. In H.L. Hundley & A.C. Billings (Eds.), *Examining identity in sports media* (pp. 217–238). Thousand Oaks, CA: Sage.

Cobb, R.W., & Elder, C. (1971). The politics of agenda-building: An alternative perspective for modern democratic theory. *Journal of Politics, 33*, 892–915.

Cohen, B.C. (1963). *The press and foreign policy.* Princeton, NJ: Princeton University Press.

Deitsch, R. (July 26, 2012). The Olympic television guide. *SI.com*. Retrieved from http://sportsillustrated.cnn.com/2012/olympics/2012/writers/richard_deitsch/07/16/olympics-NBCTV-preview/index.html.

The Economist (May 23, 2015). Kiwis as guinea pigs. *The Economist* (European edition), p. 58.

Eder, S., & Zernike, K. (April 3, 2013). Rutgers leaders are faulted on abusive coach. *New York Times* (New York edition), p. A1.

Ellingson, N. (2012). *"Sports Illustrated" and the Cold War* (Unpublished undergraduate Honors thesis). Redlands, CA: University of Redlands. Retrieved June 29, 2016, from http://inspire.redlands.edu/cas_honors/25.

Entman, R.M. (1993). Framing: Toward clarification of a fractured paradigm. *Journal of Communication, 43*(4), 51–58.

Gee, B L., & Leberman, S.I. (2011). Sports media decision making in France: How they choose what we get to see and read. *International Journal of Sport Communication, 4*(3), 321–343.

Gerbner, G. (1990). Epilogue: Advancing on the path of righteousness (maybe). In N. Signorielli & M. Morgan (Eds.), *Cultivation analysis: New directions in media effects research* (pp. 249–262). London: Sage.

Gerbner, G., & Gross, L. (1976). Living with television: The violence profile. *Journal of Communication, 26*(2), 173–199.

Goffman, E. (1974). *Frame analysis: An essay on the organization of experience*. Boston, MA: Northeastern University Press.

Higgins, E.T., Bargh, J.A., & Lombardi, W.J. (1985). Nature of priming effects on categorization. *Journal of Experimental Psychology: Learning, Memory, and Cognition, 11*(1), 59–69.

Hofstetter, C.R. (1976). *Bias in the news*. Columbus, OH: Ohio State University Press.

Hutchins, B., & Rowe, D. (2012). *Sport beyond television: The Internet, digital media and the rise of networked media sport*. London: Routledge.

Hutchins, B., & Rowe, D. (2013). *Digital media sport: Technology, power and culture in the network society*. London: Routledge.

International Olympic Committee. (2012). *Marketing Report London 2012*. Retrieved June 29, 2016, from http://www.olympic.org/Documents/IOC_Marketing/London_2012/LR_IOC_MarketingReport_medium_res1.pdf.

Iyengar, S., & Kinder, D.R. (1987). *News that matters: Television and American opinion*. Chicago, IL: University of Chicago Press.

Kuper, S., & Szymanski, S. (2009). *Soccernomics: Why England loses, why Germany and Brazil win, and why the US, Japan, Australia, Turkey—and even Iraq—are destined to become the kings of the world's most popular sport*. New York: Nation Books.

Lavelle, K.L. (2011). "One of these things is not like the others": Linguistic representations of Yao Ming in NBA game commentary. *International Journal of Sport Communication, 4*(1), 50–69.

Maguire, J., & Poulton, E.K. (1999). European identity politics in Euro 96: Invented traditions and national habitus codes. *International Review for the Sociology of Sport, 34*(1), 17–29.

Mayeda, D.T. (1999). From model minority to economic threat. *Journal of Sport and Social Issues, 23*(2), 203–217.

McCombs, M.E., & Shaw, D.L. (1972). The agenda-setting function of mass media. *Public Opinion Quarterly, 36*(2), 176–187.

NBA.com (October 2014, 2014). Record 101 international players on opening day rosters. Retrieved June 29, 2016, from http://www.nba.com/2014/news/10/28/international-players-on-opening-day-rosters-2014-15/.

Nüesch, S., & Franck, E. (2009). The role of patriotism in explaining the TV audience of national team games: Evidence from four international tournaments. *Journal of Media Economics, 22*(1), 6–19.

Oakes, P.J., Haslam, S.A., & Turner, J.C. (1994). *Stereotyping and social reality.* Oxford: Blackwell.

Park, M.K. (2014). Race, hegemonic masculinity, and the "Linpossible!": An analysis of media representations of Jeremy Lin. *Communication & Sport, 3*(4), 367–389.

Quanthockey.com (July 30, 2015). Active NHL players totals by nationality: 2014–15 stats. Retrieved June 29, 2016, from http://www.quanthockey.com/nhl/nationality-totals/active-nhl-players-2014-15-stats.html.

Real, M. (1989). *Super media: A cultural studies approach.* London: Sage.

Scheufele, D.A. (2000). Agenda-setting, priming, and framing revisited: Another look at cognitive effects of political communication. *Mass Communication and Society, 3*(2–3), 297–316.

Sharp, A. (August 13, 2012). 2012 Olympics in review: 15 most memorable stories from London. *SBNation.com.* Retrieved June 29, 2016, from http://www.sbnation.com/london-olympics-2012/2012/8/13/3233939/summer-games-best-moments-team-usa.

Silk, M. (1999). Local/global flows and altered production practices: Narrative constructions at the 1995 Canada cup of soccer. *International Review for the Sociology of Sport, 34*(2), 113–123.

Tajfel, H. (1981). *Human groups and social categories.* Cambridge: Cambridge University Press.

Tajfel, H., & Turner, J.C. (1986). The social identity theory of intergroup behaviour. In S. Worchel & W.G. Austin (Eds.), *Psychology of intergroup relations* (pp. 7–24). Chicago, IL: Nelson-Hall.

Turner, J.C., Hogg, M.A., Oakes, P.J., Riecher, S.D., & Wetherell, M.S. (1987). *Rediscovering the social group: A self-categorization theory.* Oxford: Blackwell.

Wallerstein, I. (1974). *The modern world system.* New York: Academic Press.

Zee News (2014, September 26). Asian Games: Five facts about "world's strongest man" Behdad Salimi. Retrieved June 29, 2016, from http://zeenews.india.com/sports/2014-asian-games/asian-games-five-facts-about-worlds-strongest-man-behdad-salimi_1476154.html.

15

SPORT AS JOURNALISTIC LENS

Steve Bien-Aimé

LOUISIANA STATE UNIVERSITY

Erin Whiteside

UNIVERSITY OF TENNESSEE

Marie Hardin

PENNSYLVANIA STATE UNIVERSITY

There is an expression that says silence is golden. When it comes to athletes not talking to the media, silence gets expensive. Seattle Seahawks running back Marshawn Lynch was fined $50,000 for not speaking to journalists after a November 2014 football game (Hanzus, 2014). During Media Day for the Super Bowl that same season, Lynch said, "I'm just here so I won't get fined," 29 times during a five-minute appearance with reporters (Stroud, 2015). The fine amount is somewhat understandable when considering that the Super Bowl almost always receives the highest amount of viewership in the United States: more than 112 million people watched the National Football League's championship game in 2015, and NFL games represented seven of the ten single most-watched programs of the year (Sandomir, 2015). The growth of sport leagues is largely dependent on continued robust media coverage and such content is, in part, a function of a strong relationship between journalists and the leagues, teams, and athletes themselves (Genovese, 2013; McChesney, 1989; Rowe, 1999). Thus, it is unsurprising that the NFL threatened Lynch with such strict sanctions; refusing to speak to the media destabilized that mutually beneficial relationship.

Defining the Relationship between Media, Society, and Sport

As the heralded 'fourth estate,' journalism has been described as a kind of social glue, and an institution that, when functioning properly, plays a key role in deliberative democracy (Adam & Clark, 2006). At its core, the effective practice of journalism provides citizens with a shared language and a common understanding of the critical issues in a society, thus facilitating informed and rational debate (Kovach & Rosenstiel, 2007). When a vibrant and free press is also engaged in a simultaneous practice of monitoring government and acting as an effective check against potential abuses by elected officials, democracy is in a position to flourish (e.g., Adam & Clark, 2006; Harcup, 2009; Kovach & Rosenstiel, 2007). Sport, though often thought to be occupying a less important space in the news hierarchy, is highly important to structuring societies and building community, too; as McChesney (1989) writes in his history of sport journalism, "a newspaper's coverage and promotion of sport could be considered a significant contribution to its metropolis"(p. 57). Sport and sport media also combine to foster 'conformity' among citizens while at the same time diminishing dissent in a society (Jenkins, 2013, p. 252).

The development of sport journalism and its related mission has not paralleled that of news; more specifically, sport journalism is often imagined as a decidedly *apolitical* space, where its content is considered value-neutral (Rowe, 2007). This shared definition obscures the ways in which social values and norms are produced through even the most seemingly banal sport media content (e.g., Rowe, 2007; Segrave, 2000). In evaluating the growth and changes of the field over time, scholars have noted the "symbiotic relationship" of sport and media (McChesney, 1989, p. 49). As Rowe (1999) explains, "media are both the driving economic and cultural force in sport because they provide (or attract) most of the capital that in turn creates and disseminates the images and information, which then generate more capital and more sport, in an ascending spiral" (p. 65). For example, FOX, CBS, NBC, and ESPN pay the NFL more than $1 billion each annually to broadcast its games (Ourand, 2014). That investment has yielded staggering returns; NBC charged advertisers $4.4 million for a 30-second spot during the Super Bowl, for instance (Sandomir, 2015). Ultimately, NBC and all other for-profit media companies essentially sell the sport-based audiences to advertisers, making sport content—and the vast number of individuals who follow it closely—an incredibly lucrative commodity. As Genovese (2013) notes, those financial partnerships create ethical quagmires for sport journalists, raising the question: How far can sport journalists go in critiquing sport leagues and athletes when the business ties between sport and media continue to increase?

These relationships shape even the most routine practices; sport journalists might have to constrain the scopes of their reporting in order to increase their potential for success. For instance, to attain 'scoops' and good quotes, reporters need access to practices, games, players, coaches, agents, and so forth (Boyle, 2006a, 2006b; Fatsis, 2014; Genovese, 2013; Rowe, 2007). Journalists are "bound by the limits those teams put on media access—and can get tossed from the press box for violating them" (Ellis, 2013). Thus, some reporters might feel compelled to engage in some version of self-censorship by not covering topics that are perhaps controversial to sport leagues and athletes in order to preserve precious access (Fatsis, 2014; Guthrie, 2015).

With the comingling of interests between sport and media, it would be beneficial to refer back to journalism's responsibilities in a democracy. Different scholars list various responsibilities; however, the responsibilities can be reduced to some key principles: Journalists must be independent, journalists must critique the powerful interests in society, and journalists must be loyal to news consumers (e.g., Brooks, Kennedy, Moen, & Ranly, 2014; Kovach & Rosenstiel, 2007). There are obvious tensions between sport journalism and these ideals, however. The rest of this chapter explores this thorny relationship, and how researchers can further analyze sport journalism.

"Corporate Culture" and Ethical Concerns

The sport media complex also illustrates the tension between media companies' business interests and the journalists who work for those companies (Genovese, 2013; Wolter, 2014). Genovese (2013) explains the tension as a fear that "journalists are influenced by a corporate culture to the degree that they fail to pursue certain stories or angles that might conflict with corporate interests such as a story on the falling attendance for a sport franchise owned by the parent company that owns both the franchise and the media outlet" (p. 144). He interviewed several journalists from a regional sports network that owned two sport teams in the market. One journalist explained the tension and ethical issues associated with meshing hard journalism with corporate interests:

> the (network) is a legitimate news source. But at the same time (the network) has an agenda. (The network's parent company) the company has an agenda. There are a lot of events that we'll go out and cover because of the people who are there. . . . We're putting a little bit more emphasis in it. Whereas we may not for other people. It's just the nature of the business, I mean you gotta dance with the one who brought you there or you gotta appease the people who run this place. I mean yes we're a news place but we're also there is some marketing and there is some public relations that go with working here.
>
> *(p. 151)*

Ethical concerns for sport journalism extend beyond journalists working to please corporate bosses. Hardin, Zhong, and Whiteside (2009) examined industry ethics in a survey of sport reporters. Their findings showed agreement—though slightly—from sport journalists that they need to abide by a different set of ethical rules than do other journalists. Oates and Pauly (2007) want sport journalism to push itself toward a higher ethical standard, partly because of its scope. Sport journalism is not a mere subset of news; it is a huge driver of content.

In Australia, there are more sport journalists than there are political reporters (Zion, Spaaij, & Nicholson, 2011). Sport journalists are shapers of society and should be held to high ethical standards (Rowe, 1999; Oates & Pauly, 2007).

Shifts in the Symbiotic Relationship

As the sport journalism landscape continues to change, sport journalists find themselves in a difficult position as they must compete with team- and league-produced media, many of whom enjoy built-in and ready access to key sources; creating alternative sport media content could become a more prominent strategy for journalists as they look to adapt (Ellis, 2013). One such strategy may be focusing on local content. During the 2013 Super Bowl, for instance, SB Nation reported record traffic across its blog network, crediting a focus on producing local content and unique videos, instead of Super Bowl-related items (Warzel, 2013). Among the 12 most popular sport websites, two of them are SB Nation and Deadspin, both nontraditional blog sites (Fisher, 2015). Other outlets may focus on building a niche through investigative reporting.

A growth in alternative sport media companies could begin to challenge sport's ability to be a safe space, that is, an industry that allows itself to be viewed as nonpolitical, noncontroversial, but still fun, exciting, and unifying (McChesney, 1989). Sport is not seen as divisive; rather, it unites fans into a sort of "secular religion" (Rowe, 1999, p. 69) and is often depicted as bringing a nation together to support one's country (e.g., Allison, 2000; Jenkins, 2013). Sport creates a fantasy sanctuary for many fans (Segrave, 2000). When alternative sport media bring contentious issues to light such as racism, sexism, or classism, that fantasy sanctuary is disrupted. Thus, to generate content that is both exciting, yet apparently noncontroversial in terms of real-life stakes, most sport journalists provide "their consumers with pieces building up to events, profiling the participants, and analysing performances, as well as with a steady flow of background news and features" (Andrews, 2005, p. 3) to satisfy fans' "seemingly insatiable appetite" (Bellamy, 2006, p. 63). These stories, though often assumed to be part of entertainment (Zion et al., 2011), have deeply serious implications, according to Oates and Pauly (2007). They write, "[e]ven when sports coverage does not offer citizens crucial information, it may offer them cultural narratives that frame and shape their understandings of the group identities and relations of democratic society" (p. 336). The accepted notion that sport is an apolitical space guards against critique and evaluation of its related discourse.

Investigating Sport Journalism Content and Practices: Tools and Theories

Because of its sometimes-undefined ethical standards and subject matter that some deem 'frivolous,' sport has been called the 'toy department' of the wider newsroom. Yet sport media play a fundamental role in how we make meaning around myriad sociopolitical issues through the process of framing, or what Entman (1993) describes as the outcome of information selection, interpretation, and emphasis inherent in the journalistic process. Scholars have long noted, for instance, that sport media often showcase—essentially *frame*—female athletes as feminine, through visual aesthetics or linguistic devices (e.g., Fink, 2015; Wolter, 2015). Others have described the consistent trend of sport journalists contributing to dominant racial ideologies through the practice of framing black athletes as naturally athletic and white athletes as naturally hard workers or intellectually gifted (e.g., Bigler & Jeffries, 2008; Billings, 2004). Identifying and tracking frames has been a prominent part of sport journalism scholarship and, as Carragee and Roefs (2004) suggest, can be an important step in locating the media's role in larger public ideological struggles.

Although much framing scholarship focuses on identifying frames, that is but one of four parts to building a framing research program; according to D'Angelo (2002), to fully understand the impact of frames, scholars must also investigate the conditions giving rise to those frames, exploring the ways individuals negotiate and make meaning in response to frames, and, finally, examining the ways in which this process shapes public opinion and policy outcomes. Developing a robust investigation of framing can yield a more comprehensive picture of how frames operate in the public discourse and to what effect. For instance, in his study tracking how Title IX was framed over its first thirty years, Kaiser (2011) contextualized the frames he identified by connecting them to the social milieu in which they occurred. Others have explored how individuals respond to gendered narratives and frames; Hardin and Whiteside (2009), for instance, conducted group interviews with college-aged women, noting some of the ways their participants resisted negotiating notions of gender equality in emancipatory ways. By investigating this meaning-making process, the authors offer ideas for policymakers and Title IX advocates, so they may find ways for the law to continue to resonate with younger generations.

Along with playing a role in the social meaning-making process, sport media companies are agenda-setters locally, nationally, and internationally (e.g., Denham, 2004; Frederick, Burch, & Blaszka, 2015). Agenda-setting says that events and issues of high importance to media will eventually be of utmost importance to the public (e.g., Kiousis, 2011; McCombs, 1997; McCombs & Shaw, 1972). Essentially, the more journalists prominently report on an issue, the more likely that the public will consider the issue an important one. If journalists ignore controversial issues because of powerful interests, the public good is not being served (e.g., Oates & Pauly, 2007). Thus, sport journalists have the power not just to influence the sport industry, but politics as well.

Take *Sports Illustrated*'s landmark reporting on steroid use in baseball during the 1990s and early 2000s. Major League Baseball players such as Barry Bonds, Mark McGwire, and Sammy Sosa were hitting home runs in record numbers, but journalists were not openly questioning whether players were using illegal performance-enhancing drugs (Denham, 2004). When Tom Verducci of *Sports Illustrated* wrote a 2002 exposé on steroids, the national discussion surrounding baseball changed because this story brought a previously unknown problem to light (Denham, 2004). The repetitive nature of media plays a huge role in agenda-setting in that the "redundancy in the media messages received by the public" serves to solidify the importance of the news being conveyed (McCombs, Shaw, & Weaver, 2014, p. 790). As the media continued to report on steroids in baseball, Congress held hearings on what Major League Baseball was doing to address its drug problem. One sport story in a magazine started a chain-reaction that went all the way to Capitol Hill. The process of agenda-setting in the *Sports Illustrated* situation worked as follows:

> Mainstream journalists report on a provocative cover story in a prominent magazine, citing the sources and the sources' contentions within the magazine story, and the newspaper articles, reaching a broader audience of readers, contribute to the building of a broad public agenda. Policymakers act on the agenda, based on the need to address not only the issues affecting their own sensibilities but also the issues their constituents consider important.
>
> *(Denham, 2004, p. 54)*

Prominence factors greatly into agenda-setting (e.g., Denham, 2004, 2014; Frederick, Burch, & Blaszka, 2015). Journalists often pay close attention to their competitors and report on the same stories as their competitors (e.g., Denham, 2014; Lowrey, 2012; Shoemaker & Vos, 2009). And so, publications such as *Sports Illustrated*, which at the time of its steroid story was the most popular U.S. sport magazine (Denham, 2004), and the *New York Times* (Denham, 2014; Yang, 2003) carry outsized influence in journalism because they are highly visible news sources. Denham (2014) found that print and broadcast media outlets began reporting on the scope of drug use in the horse racing industry in 2012 soon after the *New York Times* began covering that topic. Media outlets cited *The Times* and in their subsequent stories employed similar frames to *The Times*'s reporting.

Today, we see that blogs and other nontraditional forms of media can influence journalism agendas (e.g., Hutchins, 2014; McCombs et al., 2014). The "increasingly porous boundaries that structure digitally mediated social connections" (Hutchins, 2014, p. 125) were evidenced with TMZ publishing a 2014 video of then NFL star Ray Rice striking his fiancée (Brinson, 2014; Deitsch, 2014; Fatsis, 2014). The story went from not extremely visible to lead stories all over mainstream sport media (Fatsis, 2014). The growing power of nontraditional media could be a great benefit for sport media consumers. Denham (2004) notes that one of the reasons *Sports Illustrated* was able to report aggressively on steroids in Major League Baseball was because it was not financially bound to sport leagues. In fact, the reporters for the other media companies cited in this section (*New York Times* and TMZ) appear to also enjoy significant freedom to report on sport stories, and as such set the agenda through investigative reporting.

When thinking of agenda-setting, one must also consider gatekeeping. Myriad events occur daily, yet only a limited number of stories and frames actually reach the public because of economies of space and attention. Traditionally, media gatekeepers—reporters and editors—decide what news is shared with the public (Shoemaker, 1991; Shoemaker & Vos, 2009). More recently, sport media's gatekeeping power has waned a bit as teams and leagues do not need journalists in order to share information with a wide audience (Coddington & Holton, 2014). Teams and leagues can share breaking news on social media, shaping messages as they wish. In fact, athletes and fans directly communicate on social media platforms such as Twitter, "reshaping fan-athlete interaction" (Frederick, Lim, Clavio, Pedersen, & Burch, 2012; Kassing & Sanderson, 2010). Athletes are able to provide followers with insights regarding games that are not readily available, share beliefs on certain topics, or even "counter unfavorable media representations" (Kassing & Sanderson, 2010, p. 113). Through this shift in gatekeeping, athletes might be able to reframe themselves. Essentially, athletes can depict themselves on their own terms, and not the journalists' terms. The self-portrayal is contingent upon athletes' willingness to drop the gate per se and converse with fans to facilitate robust engagement; the willingness of athletes to do so is varied (Frederick et al., 2012).

Directions for Future Research within Sport and Journalism

This chapter has been written during a time when sport journalism has grown in popularity within the academy. There are 34 sport communications programs at Association for Education in Journalism and Mass Communication-accredited institutions, up from 14 in 2007 (Penn State, 2012). Therefore, it is important to understand how educators are training future media professionals. Despite what Fatsis (2014) describes as an emphasis on day-to-day transactions and hyping events, sport journalism simultaneously plays an important role in shaping the public consciousness on myriad social issues. Budding sport journalists should be aware of the role they play in this regard; an examination of courses within the growing communication and sport discipline could provide an important intervention. Without question, journalists need adequate skills training to enter the industry, but their education should also be balanced with an understanding of how their work fits in with building community and the ongoing process of negotiation over the values that knit such communities together.

Numerous scholars have critiqued the ways sport discourses uphold various social hierarchies—in both obvious and subtle ways—through textual analyses, including those grounded in the concepts of framing. Along with helping aspiring sport journalists understand their role in that process, researchers should aspire to understand the conditions by which content, including common frames, are produced. In her work examining how racial ideologies are communicated through sport media, for instance, McDonald (2005) has noted the many ways that sport media content upholds white privilege. And while such textual analyses are critical in demonstrating the communication and crystallization of social norms, she argues that researchers must turn their focus to understanding how these systems of meaning are produced. In research on sport journalism, this includes examining the workplace cultures and norms that shape the processes of content production; indeed, as Becker and Vlad (2009, p. 59) write, "news is both an individual product and an organizational product," thus making research examining organizations themselves, and the specificities of their related cultures, a vital piece in understanding the content they produce. We similarly believe more research is needed on the cultures, work routines, ethics, and other forces driving sport media production. Lowes (1999) provides a useful starting point; his ethnography illuminates the ways sport news is manufactured, and offers insights into the nuances of sport media production. More research, especially using qualitative methods that incorporate the voices of industry professionals, will provide important interpretative devices for understanding the sport media texts that are so often a point of inquiry among researchers. Sociological inquiry represents only one part of the equation, however; returning to political economic analyses will further demonstrate new ways in which the symbiotic relationship between sport and media is manifest in the contemporary sport media landscape.

Lowes' (1999) research examined the workplace of a mid-market newspaper. Such a study is unusual in that regard as Wahl-Joergensen and Hanitzsch (2009) argue that too often journalism scholars engage in a process of 'studying up,' or what they describe as the practice of prioritizing elite and large-scale media organizations in research. Doing so ignores the variability in news production and creates a "universalizing and authoritative" description of journalism (p. 12). A similar blind spot exists in research on journalism and sport; ESPN, *Sports Illustrated* and other large-scale media organizations are giants in the field, but represent only one dimension of the industry. While it is important to examine what these leaders focus on and how they cover various issues and individuals, examining a breadth of news organizations on key issues will help develop a more complex picture of sport journalism practices and norms. For instance, scholars have devoted much attention on portrayals of women in sport journalism, and it is well-established that in high-profile sport media venues women are largely invisible. There is no question that large-scale sport media outlets set a tone for the rest of the industry. Yet, there are examples of content in which female athletes do receive substantial and/or socially just coverage (e.g., Antunovic & Hardin, 2012; Billings et al., 2014; Pedersen, 2002; Wolter, 2015; Whiteside & Rightler-McDaniels, 2013). Combining analyses and critiques of the practices of elite media organizations along with a diverse array of outlets might illuminate not only where girls' and women's sport do and do not receive coverage, but the *necessary conditions* by which such coverage may embody notions of credibility and legitimacy.

Texts themselves and the production forces behind that content are incomplete by themselves, however. Schudson (2000) has suggested that a focus on these two dimensions has resulted in a process of overlooking the audience and thus denying individuals agency in how we understand sport media consumption. Audience studies is a growing research genre and sport journalism researchers have an important role to play in its development, particularly given the prominence of social media in sport journalism. In particular, that medium is changing the news media's relationship with its consumers (e.g., McCombs et al., 2014) and fans' relationships with athletes and teams (e.g., Frederick et al., 2014; Hutchins, 2014). The outcomes of such shifting relationships could impact how sport journalism is produced, including the type and breadth of content, making such a research entry point a particularly fruitful one going forward.

Overall, journalism has a key responsibility in the promotion of a vibrant democracy. Sport journalism is not immune from that duty. What sport journalists decide to cover, in addition to the manner in which they report on issues, has influence that extends beyond the sport section of a news site. Together, sport and sport media work to shape culture. Thus, researchers must continue to critique sport media content and sport journalistic practices. The use and further development of key communication theories and research methodologies can help researchers in this most-important endeavor.

References

Adam, G.S., & Clark, R.P. (2006). Introduction: Reflections on journalism and the architecture of democracy. In G.S. Adam & R.P. Clark (Eds.), *Journalism: The democratic craft* (pp. xv–xix). New York: Oxford University Press.

Allison, L. (2000). Sport and nationalism. In J. Coakley & E. Dunning (Eds.), *Handbook of sports studies* (pp. 344–355). London: Sage.

Andrews, P. (2005). *Sports journalism: A practical introduction.* London: Sage.

Antunovic, D., & Hardin, M. (2012). Activism in women's sports blogs: Fandom and feminist potential. *International Journal of Sport Communication, 5*(3), 305–322.

Bellamy Jr., R.V. (2006). Sports media: A modern institution. In A.A. Raney & J. Bryant (Eds.), *Handbook of sports and media* (pp. 63–76). Mahwah, NJ: Lawrence Erlbaum.

Becker, L.B., & Vlad, T. (2009). News organizations and routines. In K. Wahl-Jorgensen & T. Hanitzsch (Eds.), *The handbook of journalism studies* (pp. 59–72). New York: Routledge.

Bigler, M., & Jeffries, J.L. (2008). "An amazing specimen": NFL draft experts' evaluations of black quarterbacks. *Journal of African American Studies, 12*(2), 120–141.

Billings, A.C. (2004). Depicting the quarterback in Black and White: A content analysis of college and professional football broadcast commentary. *Howard Journal of Communications, 15*(4), 201–210.

Billings, A.C., Angelini, J.R., MacArthur, P.J., Bissell, K., & Smith, L.R. (2014). (Re) Calling London: The gender frame agenda within NBC's primetime broadcast of the 2012 Olympiad. *Journalism & Mass Communication Quarterly, 91*(1), 38–58.

Boyle, R. (2006a). Running away from the circus. *British Journalism Review, 17*(3), 12–17.

Boyle, R. (2006b). *Sports journalism: Context and issues.* London: Sage.

Brinson, W. (September 25, 2014). ESPN suspends Bill Simmons for calling Roger Goodell "a liar". *CBS Sports.* Retrieved June 29, 2016, from http://www.cbssports.com/nfl/eye-on-football/24724124/espn-suspends-bill-simmons-for-calling-roger-goodell-a-liar.

Brooks, B.S., Kennedy, G., Moen, D.R., & Ranly, D. (2014). The nature of news. In B.S. Brooks, G. Kennedy, D.R. Moen, & D. Ranly (Eds.), *News Reporting and Writing* (pp. 3–19). Boston, MA: Bedford/St. Martin's.

Carragee, K.M., & Roefs, W. (2004). The neglect of power in recent framing research. *Journal of Communication, 54*(2), 214–233.

Coddington, M., & Holton, A.E. (2014). When the gates swing open: Examining network gatekeeping in a social media setting. *Mass Communication and Society, 17*(2), 236–257.

D'Angelo, P. (2002). News framing as a multiparadigmatic research program: A response to Entman. *Journal of Communication, 52*(4), 870–888.

Deitsch, R. (November 7, 2014). ESPN suspends Bill Simmons for criticism of Roger Goodell. *Sports Illustrated.* Retrieved June 29, 2016, from http://www.si.com/nfl/2014/09/24/espn-bill-simmons-roger-goodell-suspension.

Denham, B.E. (2004). *Sports Illustrated*, the mainstream press and the enactment of drug policy in Major League Baseball: A study in agenda-building theory. *Journalism, 5*(1), 51–68. doi: 10.1177/1464884904039554.

Denham, B.E. (2014). Intermedia attribute agenda setting in the *New York Times*: The case of animal abuse in U.S. horse racing. *Journalism & Mass Communication, 91*(1), 17–37. doi: 10.1177/1077699013514415.

Ellis, J. (April 11, 2013). My team, my publisher: The new world of competition between leagues and media in sports. *Nieman Lab.* Retrieved June 29, 2016, from http://www.niemanlab.org/2013/04/my-team-my-publisher-the-new-world-of-competition-between-leagues-and-media-in-sports/.

Entman, R.M. (1993). Framing: Toward clarification of a fractured paradigm. *Journal of Communication, 43*, 51–58.

Fatsis, S. (September 15, 2014). Giving up on Goodell: How the NFL lost the trust of its most loyal reporters. *Slate.* Retrieved June 29, 2016, from http://www.slate.com/articles/sports/sports_nut/2014/09/roger_goodell_and_the_nfl_thought_they_had_the_press_under_control_not_any.html.

Fink, J.S. (2015). Female athletes, women's sport, and the sport media commercial complex: Have we really "come a long way, baby"? *Sport Management Review, 18*(3), 331–342.

Fisher, E. (March 13, 2015). ESPN leads ComScore rankings for 12th-straight month with 74.7 unique visitors. *Sports Business Daily/Global Journal.* Retrieved June 29, 2016, from http://www.sportsbusinessdaily.com/Daily/Issues/2015/03/13/Media/ComScore.aspx.

Frederick, E.L., Burch, L.M., & Blaszka, M. (2015). A shift in set: Examining the presence of agenda setting on Twitter during the 2012 London Olympics. *Communication & Sport, 3*(3), 312–333. doi: 10.1177/2167479513508393.

Frederick, E., Lim, C.H., Clavio, G., Pedersen, P.M., & Burch, L.M. (2014). Choosing between the one-way or two-way street: An exploration of relationship promotion by professional athletes on Twitter. *Communication & Sport, 2*(1), 80–99.

Genovese, J. (2013). "You gotta appease the people who run this place": Corporate ownership and its influence on sports television production. *Electronic News, 7*(3), 141–159.

Guthrie, M. (July 1, 2015). ESPN wants Keith Olbermann to quit doing "Commentary". *The Hollywood Reporter.* Retrieved August 11, 2015 from http://www.hollywood reporter.com/news/espn-wants-keith-olbermann-quit-806220.

Hanzus, D. (November 19, 2014). Marshawn Lynch fined $100K for avoiding media. *NFL.com.* Retrieved July 4, 2015 from http://www.nfl.com/news/story/0ap300000 0430995/article/marshawn-lynch-fined-100k-for-avoiding-media.

Harcup, T. (2009). The journalist as objective reporter. In T. Harcup (Ed.), *Journalism: Principles and practice* (2nd ed., pp. 79–94). Thousand Oaks, CA: Sage.

Hardin, M., & Whiteside, E.E. (2009). The power of "small stories": Narratives and notions of gender equality in conversations about sport. *Sociology of Sport Journal, 26*(2), 255–276.

Hardin, M., Zhong, B., & Whiteside, E. (2009). Toy department of public-service journalism? The relationship between reporters' ethics and attitudes toward the profession. *International Journal of Sport Communication, 2*(3), 319–339.

Hutchins, B. (2014). Twitter: Follow the money and look beyond sports. *Communication & Sport, 2*(2), 122–126.

Jenkins, T. (2013). The militarization of American professional sports: How the sports-war intertext influences athletic ritual and sports media. *Journal of Sport & Social Issues, 37*(3), 245–260.

Kaiser, K. (2011). Gender dynamics in producing news on equality in sports: A dual longitudinal study of Title IX reporting by journalist gender. *International Journal of Sport Communication, 4*(3), 359–374.

Kassing, J.W., & Sanderson, J. (2010). Fan-athlete interaction and Twitter: Tweeting through the Giro—A case study. *International Journal of Sport Communication, 3*(1), 113–128.

Kiousis, S. (2011). Agenda-setting and attitudes: Exploring the impact of media salience on perceived salience and public attitude strength of U.S. presidential candidates from 1984 to 2004. *Journalism Studies, 12*(3), 359–374.

Kovach, B., & Rosenstiel, T. (2007). *The elements of journalism: What newspeople should know and the public should expect.* New York: Three Rivers Press.

Lowes, M.D. (1999). *Inside the sports pages: Work routines, professional ideologies, and the manufacture of sports news.* Toronto: University of Toronto Press.

Lowrey, W. (2012). Journalism innovation and the ecology of news production: Institutional tendencies. *Journalism & Communication Monographs, 14*(4), 214–287.

McChesney, R.W. (1989). Media made sport: A history of sports coverage in the United States. In L. Wenner (Ed.), *Media, Sports, & Society* (pp. 49–69). Newbury Park, CA: Sage.

McCombs, M. (1997). Building consensus: The news media's agenda-setting roles. *Political Communication, 14*(4), 433–443.

McCombs, M.E., & Shaw, D.L. (1972). The agenda-setting function of mass media. *Public Opinion Quarterly, 36*(2), 176–187.

McCombs, M.E., Shaw, D.L., & Weaver, D.H. (2014). New directions in agenda-setting theory and research. *Mass Communication & Society, 17*(6), 781–802.

McDonald, M. (2005). Mapping Whiteness and sport: Introduction to the special issue. *Sociology of Sport Journal, 22,* 245–255.

Oates, T.P., & Pauly, J. (2007). Sports journalism as moral and ethical discourse. *Journal of Mass Media Ethics, 22*(4), 332–347.

Ourand, J. (November 3, 2014). With major media rights deals done, how will networks grow revenue? *Sports Business Daily/Global Journal.* Retrieved June 29, 2016, from http://www.sportsbusinessdaily.com/Journal/Issues/2014/11/03/In-Depth/Networks-main.aspx.

Pedersen, P.M. (2002). Investigating interscholastic equity on the sports page: A content analysis of high school athletics newspaper. *Sociology of Sport Journal, 19*(4), 419–432.

Penn State (January 23, 2012). Schools across country increase focus on sports communication. Retrieved June 29, 2016, from http://news.psu.edu/story/152329/2012/01/23/schools-across-country-increase-focus-sports-communication.

Rowe, D. (1999). *Sport, culture and the media.* Buckingham: Open Court Press.

Rowe, D. (2007). Sports journalism: Still the "toy department" of the news media? *Journalism, 8*(4), 385–405.

Sandomir, R. (2015, January 31). A mere 112 million? The Super Bowl's audience is tough to gauge. *New York Times,* p. D2.

Schudson, M. (2000). The sociology of news production revisited (again). In J. Curran & M. Gurevitch (Eds.), *Mass Media and Society* (3rd ed., pp. 175–200). London: Edward Arnold.

Segrave, J.O. (2000). Sport as escape. *Journal of Sport & Social Issues, 24*(1), 61–77.

Shoemaker, P.J. (1991). *Communication concepts 3: Gatekeeping.* Newbury Park, CA: Sage.

Shoemaker, P.J., & Vos, T.P. (2009). *Gatekeeping theory.* Routledge: New York.

Stroud, R. (January 28, 2015). Marshawn Lynch repeats his stance. A lot. *Tampa Bay Times,* p. 1C.

Wahl-Jorgensen, K., & Hanitzsch, T. (2009). Introduction: On why and how we should do journalism studies. In K. Wahl-Jorgensen & T. Hanitzsch (Eds.), *The handbook of journalism studies* (pp. 3–16). New York: Routledge.

Warzel, C. (February 8, 2013). SB Nation sets all-time daily traffic record during the Super Bowl. *Adweek.* Retrieved June 29, 2016, from http://www.adweek.com/news/technology/sb-nation-sets-all-time-daily-traffic-record-during-super-bowl-147154.

Whiteside, E., & Rightler-McDaniels, J.L. (2013). Moving toward parity? Dominant gender ideology versus community journalism in high school basketball coverage. *Mass Communication and Society, 16*(6), 808–828.

Wolter, S. (2014). "It just makes good business sense": A media political economy analysis of *ESPNW. Journal of Sports Media, 9*(2), 73–96.

Wolter, S. (2015). A quantitative analysis of photographs and articles on *ESPNW:* Positive progress for female athletes. *Communication & Sport, 3*(2), 168–195.

Yang, J. (2003). Framing the NATO air strikes on Kosovo across countries: Comparison of Chinese and U.S. newspaper coverage. *Gazette: The International Journal for Communication Studies, 65*(3), 231–249.

Zion, L., Spaaij, R., & Nicholson, M. (2011). Sport media and journalism: An introduction. *Media International Australia, 140,* 80–83.

16

SPORT AS AUDIENCE STUDIES

Walter Gantz

INDIANA UNIVERSITY

Nicky Lewis

UNIVERSITY OF MIAMI

Sport is big business. Corporations want to be associated with sport because it has become part of the mainstream fabric of contemporary American life. Media outlets want sport because its content attracts large, attractive, and hard-to-reach audiences. Rights fees to deliver sport content have increased sharply and, for major collegiate and professional sports, these fees have become quite expensive: The NFL, currently the most valuable league in the country, receives roughly $7 billion annually from media deals (Badenhausen, 2011). Media outlets as well as corporations that advertise or sponsor sport content and events rely on audience ratings (and other data) to set rights negotiations, create content, schedule programming, and design promotions that draw audiences. With so much money in play, stakeholders want to learn everything they can about the audience for sport programming, much as they do for audiences of all mediated content. This includes audience demographics, patterns of media use, attitudes about leagues, teams and their sponsors, linkages with relevant behaviors (e.g., game attendance), and purchases of sponsored products.

Sport programming is ubiquitous. Available across platforms around the clock, every day of the year, sport attracts large audiences, many of whom consume hours of sport programming each week. Scholars interested in—or concerned about—the uses and effects of mediated content have approached sport programming much as they have examined mass media (e.g., movies, newspapers, radio, television, cable, the Internet, mobile technologies) and mediated content (e.g., soap operas, news, violence in entertainment programming, popular music, advertising, children's programming, reality shows) over many decades (e.g., Billings & Angelini, 2007; Bryant, Rockwell, & Owens, 1994; Raney & DePalma, 2006). With those deeply ingrained practices in hand, scholars have examined the predictors, correlates, and consequences of exposure to sport content (Gantz & Wenner, 1991; Wenner & Gantz, 1989). In recent years, their research has included the social dimension of exposure and the ways in which sport audiences move across platforms, share reactions with others near and far, and create original content.

Sport audiences matter in ways similar to the audiences for all other content. They are bought and sold, coveted, lured and triumphantly trumpeted, cared for and cared about. Sport audiences are not a province or breed apart from the rest: those who follow sport work, play, and study; have families, colleagues, and friends; and turn to a variety of media platforms and content domains. Yet, the audience for sport stands out because the contests themselves are live and unscripted with outcomes that matter; because those who follow sport have a vested interest that reverberates through their soul—and, increasingly, through their pocketbook as well.

In all, the *audience* for sport merits study. This chapter will not focus on the demography of sport audiences. Such descriptors (i.e., that women comprise nearly half the viewers for televised NFL games or that women comprise a larger proportion of the TV audience for the NFL than they do for women's soccer) are of interest, yet those data are best mined by commercial entities (such as Nielsen) that have the resources to describe audience characteristics with a level of precision academics cannot match—but who, sadly, generally do not release their own detailed analyses to those who have not helped pick up the tab. Instead, we will focus on four areas of inquiry media scholars have used across content and platform domains: (a) the uses and gratifications approach, (b) emotion, (c) psychological theories of self, and (d) audience reception studies.

Audience Perspectives and Theories Relevant to Sport

Uses and Gratifications

The uses and gratifications perspective assumes the audience for mediated content is active. Based on needs, interests, and expected psychological and social outcomes, audience members select and attend to media and content likely to maximize the value of the exposure experience, even given the escapist nature of much content on the media (Katz & Foulkes, 1962; Katz, Blumler, & Gurevitch, 1974). At the same time, this approach recognizes that not all exposure is carefully considered: Audience members don't always control the remote and they willingly attend to content others have selected; selections driven by habit—and interest in killing time—may not be particularly thoughtful or thought through; and when audiences simply seek respite, almost any content will suffice. Rubin (1984) captured these differences when he described media orientations as instrumental (purposive, where the information in the content matters) or ritualized (driven by habit, primarily to pass time and for diversion purposes where content may not be king). Studies on radio quiz programs and soap operas (Herzog, 1940, 1944) as well as newspapers (Berelson, 1949) documented the array of reasons why audiences turn to programming or miss a medium (newspapers) when a strike makes it unavailable. By the 1970s and 1980s, lists of specific uses as well as media use typologies abounded (e.g., Greenberg, 1974; Katz et al., 1974; Rubin, 1979), generally focusing on use of television per se, the dominant medium at that time. Scholars also narrowed and stretched their focus, examining specific content genres (e.g., news, Levy, 1979; Gantz, 1978; reality programs, Papacharissi & Mendelson, 2012), comparisons across content genres (e.g., Gantz, Wang, Paul, & Potter, 2006), then-emerging technologies and media (e.g., VCRs, the Internet, Charney & Greenberg, 2002; Cohen, Levy, & Golden, 1988), and specific demographic groups (Yang, Wu, Zhu, & Southwell, 2004). Scholars (e.g., Elliott, 1974, Swanson, 1977) have long lamented the perspective's shortcomings: Its central concepts are not clearly defined; the audience is not always active; researchers typically rely on self-reports, assuming users are able to accurately identify and articulate the reasons why they turn to mediated content and the outcomes they associated from that exposure. Despite its limitations, the uses and gratifications perspective continues to be widely used. Each new mediated communication technology and genre of content that develops traction among large or demographically attractive audiences appears ripe for a uses and gratifications assessment. As we will document, this has been the case with sport.

Mass media have covered sport for well over 200 years (Bryant & Holt, 2006). We have not tried to pinpoint the exact arrival of scholarship on mediated sport. Nonetheless, interest in its study appears to have climbed dramatically in the 1970s, nearly coincidental (considering publication lags) with the uptick in coverage of sport—and the NFL—on TV, as sociologists and psychologists saw mediated sport as either a reflection of culture or as a vehicle for extending theories and principles relevant to their disciplines. Those trained in communication, itself a reasonably new and rapidly expanding field at that time, ascended into conversations using the theories, perspectives, and methods that marked their training.

Gantz (1981) appears to have been the first to examine the audience for sport employing a uses and gratifications approach. His list of uses and gratifications incorporated items others had used in their studies of entertainment television as well as those distinctly related to sport content and sport fans. That is, and like other scholars in this area, Gantz assumed that in addition to the reasons why viewers generally turned to entertainment and information programming on TV, they would turn to mediated sport for reasons and anticipated gratifications likely *unique* to sport. These included getting psyched, letting off steam, adding excitement to their day, rooting for their favorite player or team, and taking the opportunity to have an extra drink or two. Despite its limitations (e.g., a small sample of college students; no measure of fanship), Gantz's study pointed to a primarily active audience, one driven by the excitement and rush of emotions associated with live sport, where the to-be-determined out-comes mattered, in some ways perhaps as much to the fans as to those on the playing field. Gantz and Wenner followed up with three studies using larger and somewhat more broad-based samples of adults. Their first focused on motivation and gratification sets across sports, their second and third on the roles of gender and fanship, respectively, on the mediated sport expo-sure experience (Wenner & Gantz, 1989; Gantz & Wenner, 1991; Gantz & Wenner, 1995). Collectively, these studies were able to document underlying motivational set commonalities—and differences—across sport. So, for exam-ple, while viewers across the sports assessed wanted to see how their favorites performed and liked the drama associated with unknown outcomes, getting 'psyched up' was not a motivation that drove baseball enthusiasts to watch that sport. Gantz and Wenner also were able to showcase commonalities—again, and differences—between male and female sport viewers as well as between sport fans and nonfans as they approached and responded to sport on TV. Not surprisingly, gender differences emerged, although primarily as a function of fanship. Although fewer in number, women who were fans were about as passionate and emotionally involved in sport viewing as their male counterparts. On the other hand, women who were not fans stood apart as they were the least interested, least involved, and, correspondingly, the most likely to watch sport for social and diversion purposes—that is, because their friends or families were watching and they had nothing else to do.

As is the case with selected exposure to information or other entertainment content on the media, there is no single magic number of specific uses and gratifications—or underlying dimensions of either—associated with mediated sport. Instead, the number and names of the uses and gratifications vary from one study to the next, a function of researcher interests and research questions, fiscal and temporal constraints, concerns about respondent fatigue, and the tar-geted audience being studied. So, for example, while Wenner and Gantz used 14 motivation items for sport, Rubin (1983) included 27 items in his study of adult TV viewing and Greenberg (1974) used 31 studying children's use of television. Despite important differences across studies including scholarship not reliant on uses and gratification measures, Raney (2006) was able to distill three sets of core needs linked with sport consumption: emotional (entertainment, eustress, escape, and self-esteem); cognitive (learning and aesthetic appreciation); and behavioral and social (release, companionship, group affiliation, family, and economics). As Raney noted, the single most important motivation was enter-tainment: Viewers turn to sport programming to root for their favorites and to vicariously savor the emotional fruits of victory. By and large, then, the sport exposure experience is emotion-laden with cognitive and social dimensions added on top. In the decade since Raney's work, participation in fantasy sport has increased dramatically, one reason why economics may be a more salient motivation than it was some years ago.

Changes in the sport landscape (i.e., new sports and emerging media) have led to a resurgence of uses and gratifications scholarship. Several examples should suffice: Mixed martial arts (MMA) appears to be watched by its rapidly growing fan base of young males primarily for the raw competition it features (Cheever, 2009). Studies of MMA fans have documented motivations leading to exposure, linkages with attendance, and merchandise purchases—and gender-based differences in the way fans approach the sport. So it is, for example, that women are more likely to highly identify with individual fighters and with story arcs while men are more likely to identify with MMA as a sport (Brown, Devin, & Billings, 2013). Those who participate in fantasy football do so for its entertainment and escape value, the competition and arousal it offers, the surveillance it provides and the social interaction—including a heavy dose of 'trash-talking'—that goes along with participation (Dwyer & Kim, 2011; Farquhar & Meeds, 2007). Spinda and Haridakis (2008) identified two other motivations with fantasy sport not associated with exposure to contests featuring real teams: Fantasy league players, owners and managers of the teams they fielded, enjoy participation because of the control they have over their teams and, in turn, the self-esteem and sense of achievement they experience when their teams fare well. Fantasy sport enthusiasts also appear to be more highly motivated than audiences for real sport programming. Billings and Ruihley (2013) found fantasy sport players report higher levels of entertainment, enjoyment, social interaction, and surveillance than those who merely follow sport.

Sport-related blogs and Twitter feeds generate large fan bases and somewhat different sets of motivations, a function of their content. Frederick, Clavio, Burch, and Zimmerman (2012) found a host of information motivations (i.e., information gathering, evaluation) that shaped use of an MMA blog. At the same time, though, they found a competitive edginess to blog use: Bloggers enjoyed demonstrating knowledge and the opportunities for argumentation that blog offered. Twitter use, at least among those following the Canadian Football League, was marked by interest in news and game updates—but also for the interaction it offered (Gibbs, O'Reilly, & Brunette, 2014).

The handful of studies on new sports and on interactive media simultaneously reinforce the primary motivations for following mainstream sport on traditional media as well as call attention to the growing importance of the social dimension of mediated sport. Indeed, the 'active' sport viewer now consumes and engages with sport media across a variety of platforms, many of which veer away from traditional television viewing (and the foundation of most uses and gratifications research in this area). Sport consumers are now using web-based programs and apps to access a wider variety of sport information; receive game and injury updates anytime, anywhere; participate in fantasy sport leagues; and, partake in sport gambling. In this new media landscape, the outcomes of the actual games (which were largely broadcast over television or radio) can be accessed across media formats. For many in the audience, though, catching plays and following outcomes for real and fantasy teams is only part of today's participatory experience. Blogs and Twitter accounts held by players, managers, and teams provide an inside view and a para-social relationship (Bowman & Cranmer, 2014) likely to add value to fans—and increase exposure across platforms.

What is still unknown is whether the range and relative importance of motivations associated with using these new technologies, particularly among younger audiences, are inherently different than the motivations that have been outlined in over thirty years of traditional sport viewing research. There is one other interesting issue at play: Much of the uses and gratifications literature focused on either-or decisions—that is, reasons for watching TV or doing something else; motives for picking a specific show over others. With second and third screens, the decision shifts from exclusionary to inclusionary: Users may turn to second or third screens as their screen of choice to follow sport—or as means to enhance their first screen experience. Uses and gratifications researchers will need to parse out motivations for each screen, cognizant that uses of a platform to supplement the exposure experience may be quite different than the motives for using the same platform as the primary (or sole) vehicle for following a sport event. As a result, as sport expands and media platforms and audiences change, we expect uses and gratifications will continue to be fruitful in sport media studies.

Emotion

For many in the audience, exposure to sport content centers on emotion. Emotion matters for all entertainment content—and, perhaps, for information programming, too. Research about the role of emotion in the media experience, including how emotion is processed by audiences and its subsequent effects, has coincided with the general growth of media use among audiences of all ages—and has been undertaken in a variety of content types (e.g., political, educational, entertainment; Nabi & Wirth, 2008). Although scholars have not settled on a single definition of emotion, emotions are interpreted as temporary internal mental states that result from evaluative reactions to stimuli (Ortony, Clore, & Collins, 1998). Research on emotional responses to mediated stimuli has relied on three theoretical perspectives falling under the umbrella of entertainment theory (Vorderer, 2003): excitation transfer (Zillmann, 1991), mood management (Zillmann, 2000) and affective disposition (Bryant & Raney, 2000). Here, we will briefly describe each. (For a review of sport as entertainment, see Raney's chapter in this volume.)

Excitation transfer theory posits that excitation from one stimulus intensifies the response to another stimulus, no matter the valence (Bryant & Miron, 2003). Developed in the late 1960s, a series of experiments demonstrated the effects of excitation transfer across emotions (i.e., anger, pleasure) and genre types. For example, Cantor, Bryant, and Zillmann (1974) found that individuals who were exposed to highly arousing content (positive or negative in valence) rated humorous content that followed as funnier than when individuals were exposed to low arousal content. Similarly supportive results were reported after exposure to erotic content (Cantor, Zillmann, & Bryant, 1975). Because sport viewing can be a highly arousing experience, excitation transfer theory helps account for the strong and peaked emotional responses viewers experience watching sport. Suspense helps build excitement and can increase enjoyment of sport. Gan, Tuggle, Mitrook, Coussement, and Zillmann (1997) found that males' enjoyment increased as college basketball games became more suspenseful. This was not the case, though, for females. Instead, females did not find highly suspenseful games as enjoyable as games with somewhat lesser amounts of suspense. That result fits with Gantz and Wenner's (1995) finding that women who are less interested in sport also have less desire to follow suspenseful sporting events. It also meshes with the conclusion reached by Whiteside and Hardin (2011) that many women may regard watching sport as work—maintaining family relationships—rather than leisure. From that perspective, suspense may detract from spending time with the men in their lives. Beyond being influenced by the suspense associated with close games and unknown outcomes, arousal can be manipulated by production elements such as subjective camera angles and temporally related content (Cummins, Keene, & Nutting; 2012; Cummins, Wise, & Nutting, 2012).

Mood management theory assumes human beings are motivated to seek pleasure and, in that light, use media to regulate mood. Aligned with uses and gratifications and selective exposure approaches (Raney, 2006), mood management involves the process of limiting bad moods and extending good moods. It has been applied to music (Knobloch & Zillmann, 2002), film (Greenwood, 2010), and computer games (Bowman & Tamborini, 2012, 2013). Findings from these studies suggest individuals choose entertainment content at least partially based on mood: Individuals in a bad mood choose upbeat music to listen to; those in a happy mood prefer comedies or action-adventure films; and gamers choose tasks that will help them repair negative mood states. For many in the mediated sport audience, game outcomes affect moods. Fans feel good when their team wins and lousy when their team loses (Sloan, 1979). Yet, with outcomes uncertain, sport audiences can only hope the game or match they attend to will let them maintain or elevate a good mood—or turn a bad mood good. Expected outcomes come into play here, too: An entirely expected loss, for example, may not lead to a bad mood, although an upset of historic proportions might trigger unbridled joy. Similarly, an entirely expected win may bring no joy, perhaps just relief. No matter: Turning to mediated sport contests may involve considerably more risk than using other mediated content where outcomes are known and emotional involvement is lower.

Affective disposition proposes that media viewers form para-social relationships with characters and empathize with the characters they identify with (Raney, 2004). Thus, the actions and attributes of characters and the outcomes of stories influence the audience's emotional experience. The disposition theory of drama proposes that enjoyment increases when well-liked characters succeed and disliked characters fail (Raney, 2003; Weber, Tamborini, Lee, & Stipp, 2008; Zillmann & Cantor, 1976). The disposition theory of sport spectatorship was developed soon after (Zillmann, Bryant, & Sapolsky, 1989) and follows the same line of reasoning and expectations because fans have favorite teams and players (the heroes) and dislike their favorites' rivals (the villains): Enjoyment is greatest when a favored team wins or a detested team loses. Socialization and environmental factors shape fan preferences and loyalties which, in turn, drive exposure to sport entertainment. Aspects of the sport broadcast (i.e., commentary) also shape viewer dispositions about the contests they are about to see (Knobloch-Westerwick, David, Eastin, Tamborini, & Greenwood, 2009). Recent studies that examined sport media stories (not games) suggest that audiences do indeed empathize and identify with athletes (Kinally, Tuzunkan, Raney, Fitzgerald, & Smith, 2013; Lewis & Weaver, 2015). In all, mediated sport provides an environment for audiences to form dispositions toward the athletes and teams featured in such content.

Psychological Theories of Self

Media exposure allows all users to help define who they are, where they stand among others, and how to feel about themselves. Social comparison theory (Festinger, 1954) suggests individuals have an innate desire to reduce uncertainty about the self and they do so through social comparison. Social identity theory (Tajfel, 1978) proposes that group memberships help shape a large part of one's self-concept. Individuals prefer groups they belong to (in-groups) and derogate against those they are not part of (out-groups). Self-esteem can increase when individuals feel their in-groups are better than their out-groups. The role of social identity has been explored in media research: Scholars have examined how identifying with mediated characters impacts self-esteem (Knobloch-Westerwick & Hastall, 2010). We can understand the mediated sport experience through the lens of these theories. Much of the work here revolves around sport fanship. Because viewers have so much invested in the teams they root for or against and their self-identities are linked with these in-groups, self-perceptions in this context are amplified. Moreover, mediated sport consumption has increased as (perhaps coincidentally) participation in traditional social and community activities has declined. This is likely to heighten the role of mediated sport in shaping identity and self-esteem (Branscombe & Wann, 1991).

Cialdini et al. (1976) found that sport viewers express their social identity and enhance their self-esteem by basking in reflected glory (BIRG) and cutting off reflected failure (CORF). In their classic study, social identity and self-esteem was measured by participant use of possessive and non-possessive pronouns. Fans tended to refer to their school's team as 'we' after victories and 'they' after defeats, effectively identifying with the team when it was successful and distancing themselves when the team failed. The effects of BIRGing and CORFing appear to be moderated by one's level of sport fanship. Wann and Branscombe (1990) found that those higher in fan identification were more likely to BIRG and less likely to CORF. Alternatively, those lower in fan identification were less likely to BIRG and more likely to CORF. Both strategies work to maintain one's self-esteem. Hirt, Zillmann, Erickson, and Kennedy (1992) also demonstrated the impact of outcomes on fans' self-esteem. Fans considered their school team's successes and failures to be their own and predicted better outcomes (i.e., securing a date) when their team won.

Fanship itself and team identification, one of its corollaries, have been examined in light of the mediated sport experience. Both are multidimensional constructs (Gantz & Wenner, 1995; Wann, 2006). Sport audiences vary on both. Differences here influence viewing patterns as well as affective and behavioral responses to sport content (Gantz & Wenner, 1995). Personality factors and individual differences come into play, too. As a personality construct, sensation-seeking (McDonald, 2004) is tied with the intense and arousing aspects of spectator sport. Gender differences are at work as well: Males identify more strongly with being a sport fan and generally participate in more sport fan-related behavior (Dietz-Uhler, Harrick, End, & Jacquemotte, 2000).

Reception Studies

The basic premise underlying reception studies is the polysemic nature of all media texts (content, including programming): Texts can be interpreted in a variety of ways, ranging from the preferred or dominant reading, one the producers intended for the message, all the way through oppositional decoding, where audiences interpret a text in ways directly opposite to the intended reading (Hall, 1980). Using *Nationwide*, a TV news magazine, Morley (1980) was able to document distinctly different interpretations of the show's text: Audience members decoded the text in ways consistent with their place in British society. In short order, other scholars were able to document oppositional reading of texts that appeared to support the status quo, be those texts British soap operas (Hobson, 1982), popular romance novels (Radway, 1986), or *Ms.* magazine (Steiner, 1988).

Sport texts offer play-by-play coverage of activity on the field. In doing so—and in the pomp and ceremony surrounding games and matches—sport texts provide a dominant reading about social values. Real's seminal work on the Super Bowl (1975) points to the ways sporting events speak to issues of myth and ritual; gender, race, and labor; business, labor, and management; militarism and nationalism. For years, scholars have offered oppositional readings of the way games and matches are covered as well as of news coverage about those games. Duncan (2006) demonstrated and argued that sport texts shortchange women: Across media, women's sport receive scant coverage and female sportscasters, reporters, and athletes are sexually objectivized as well as demeaned as athletes and mature adults. Others have argued sport texts have maligned minorities with limited and stereotyped coverage that reinforces prejudiced views that minority athletes succeed because of natural physicality and that they have a proclivity to commit crimes and use illegal drugs. Grainger, Newman, and Andrews (2006) provide an excellent summary of those concerns.

Sport audiences have been vocal for as long as they have followed sport. Save for selected sports (i.e., tennis and golf), players and teams expect and encourage spectators—hometown fans, after all—to actively root for their teams: screaming and clapping with pleasure following great plays and wins, yelling to rattle opponents, and reigning boos (and other catcalls) at umpires who make calls against the home team. All this reflects the dominant reading, although we extended Hall's view from texts to unmediated stimuli. Call-in talk shows and, more recently, websites, blogs, and social media (i.e., Facebook and Twitter) have enabled engaged members of the mediated sport audience—sport fans—to amplify their voices during and subsequent to sporting events. Gantz, Fingerhut, and Nadorff (2012) documented the social dimension of the mediated sport exposure experience: Most in their small, online sample of fans said they called, texted, or turned to social networking sites during games to share their glee, disappointment, or anger as play progressed. Such communication reflects a truly active and engaged audience—but not one necessarily interested in or offering an oppositional reading. At times, though, fan contributions openly challenge the status quo and reflect the underlying tenets of reception studies research. In one example, Watts (2008) documented fan online activity during a turbulent period for the University of Florida's football team. Upset with how their team fared on the field, fans challenged playing-time decisions by the university's football coach, upbraided Florida's athletic director for the head coach he hired, and then pressed for his firing until that, indeed, happened. In essence, across message boards, fans challenged the dominant reading offered by University of Florida administrators—and, in this case, may have had an influence on the administration of their team's football program. A similar, anti-administration stance was taken by Penn State fans in wake of the 2011 sex abuse scandal that rocked Penn State and resulted in the firing of Joe Paterno, its iconic coach. Rather than supporting their university, many fans sided with Paterno and, instead, tweeted insults and taunts at school officials for their response to the crisis (Brown, Billings, & Brown, 2015). In all likelihood, social media such as Twitter have forever raised the visibility of oppositional readings to dominant texts about sport.

Directions for Future Research within Sport and Audience Studies

Of necessity, corporations with a vested interest in attracting audiences to sport programming routinely measure their viewers, listeners, and users.

Using quantitative surveys featuring large, representative samples, the major networks, leagues, and advertising sponsors know the demography, media use patterns, likes, dislikes, and purchasing behaviors of sport audiences. With less money in the bank and with a different set of priorities and research questions, sport communication scholars have relied on a broader array of methods and, simultaneously, a narrower swath of sport consumers. In other forums, university-based researchers need to expand their participant base beyond students enrolled at their schools. With online panels readily available (i.e., at Qualtrics and Amazon's Mechanical Turk), tapping into the American public at large has become easier to do. Rather than using this forum to harp on reaching a significantly more demographically diverse sample of sport consumers, we suggest a mix of six approaches and areas of inquiry relevant to audience studies and sport.

First, work with big numbers. Commercial firms produce plenty of quantitative, descriptive research detailing the manifest characteristics of national and regional sport audiences. Team up with those vendors to examine the ways in which team and star athlete performance coupled with long-standing, season, and short-term expectations affect viewership. Decision-making in major league sports is increasingly driven by data. We should take the same approach to assess the extent to which national, regional, and local ratings (across platforms) are influenced by expected and actual wins and losses, betting lines, press coverage, and content competing for the user's attention.

Second, work beyond the numbers. Qualitative work, characterized by in-depth interviews and fine-grained analyses of user-generated content, can flesh out the nature of the sport exposure experience. Qualitative approaches can capture how family members or friends negotiate and navigate through the mediated sport experience and document how, on a personal level, exposure to sport fits into everyday social life. Such approaches also can capture meaning-making and the ways in which audience members interpret and make sense of mediated sport messages. To keep fans engaged (and generate attention and spending), collegiate and professional leagues and teams routinely sponsor websites and blogs that encourage fan participation. Reception studies such as the one conducted by Watts (2008) can shed light on the extent to which fans decode such texts and are willing to offer oppositional readings to them.

Third, study the user experience across platforms: Content providers understand consumers want access to sport content wherever they are. With that in mind, content providers use an ever-expanding array of mobile and social platforms to reach users. In turn, sport content consumers access these platforms at work, home, school, in transit, or out on the town, turning to what ESPN calls the "best available screen" at that juncture to follow sport (Billings, 2015). These platforms vary in size, fidelity, content, and interactivity options. How does the sport audience use and integrate each platform into the overall experience they seek?

Fourth, focus on minorities in the sport-viewing audience: Women make up nearly half the audience for NFL games and a significant but minority share of the audience for other major sports. Yet, women also may use sport media within a different set of contextual constraints than men, especially if they serve as the primary caregiver for their children—or for their aging parents as well. They may not have the luxury of sitting down to watch an entire game without interruptions—or heading to a bar for a full afternoon or evening of consuming sport (and suds). Expectations may be different, too: Unlike men, where fanship is not surprising, women may need to demonstrate they are, indeed, knowledgeable and passionate consumers, turning to mediated sport for the intrinsic pleasures sport offers. How do women navigate those constraints and combat expectations?

Fifth, examine emerging sports. The sport landscape is changing and, if anything, becoming more cluttered. To attract young viewers, the International Olympic Committee has been asked to add sports such as climbing, skateboarding, and surfing to the 2020 Summer Olympics in Tokyo. Mixed martial arts has attracted a sizeable fan base with bouts aired regularly. But, there may be no better example of an emerging sport than soccer, at least in the United States. At long last, although it still has a long way to go, soccer has entered the mainstream of contemporary American culture. Attendance at Major League Soccer games is up, ratings are up for major matches, and there is more coverage of US—and European—soccer than ever before. As a sign of the times, in 2015 NBC Sports inked a multiyear, billion-dollar deal with England's Premier League, a move the network expected would help them establish a new sport weekend morning daypart (Sandomir, 2015). In all, we have a near unique opportunity to study the growing acceptance over time of a major sport and the consequences this has on other sport properties and programming. Will televised soccer matches become an appointment viewing phenomenon much as NFL football has in recent decades? In large enough numbers to make coverage profitable, will Americans embrace European leagues? Will fans find room in their hearts to passionately follow yet another team or two or will loyalties shift or passions for a single team abate? In short, how elastic is the audience's passion for sport?

Finally, focus on youth. To remain relevant, sports that are popular today need to attract young viewers. For decades, baseball was king. But, it began to lose its hold on sport fans in the 1960s when professional football rose to prominence and its audience today is growing older. Today's sports are competing with video games and, now, with e-sports whose competitions and major stars appear to attract the same sort of attention and loyalty as professional athletes. The interests of today's youth will help shape the sport programming landscape in the future. What are their interests and how are traditional and new sports conceptually arrayed in their constellation of meaningful leisure activities? After decades of research on the audience for sport, the good and bad news is there still is much to be done.

References

Badenhausen, K. (December 14, 2011). The NFL signs TV deals worth $27 billion. *Forbes*. Retrieved June 30, 2016, from http://www.forbes.com/sites/kurtbaden hausen/2011/12/14/the-nfl-signs-tv-deals-worth-26-billion/.

Berelson, B. (1949). What "missing the newspaper" means. In P.F. Lazarsfeld & F.N. Stanton (Eds.), *Communication Research 1948–1949* (pp. 111–129). New York: Harper.

Billings, A.C. (2015). Facilitating conversations through sport. In. J. McGuire, G.G, Armfield, & A. Earnheardt (Eds.), *ESPN effect: Exploring the leader in worldwide sports* (pp. 253–264). New York: Peter Lang AG.

Billings, A.C., & Angelini, J.R. (2007). Packaging the games for viewer consumption: Gender, ethnicity, and nationality in NBC's coverage of the 2004 Summer Olympics. *Communication Quarterly, 55*(1), 95–111.

Billings, A.C., & Ruihley, B.J. (2013). Why we watch, why we play: The relationship between fantasy sport and fanship motivations. *Mass Communication and Society, 16*(1), 5–25.

Bowman, N.D., & Cranmer, G.A. (2014). Socialmediasport: The fan as a (mediated) participant in spectator sports. In A.C. Billings & M. Hardin (Eds.), *Routledge handbook of sport and new media* (pp. 213–224). London: Routledge.

Bowman, N.D., & Tamborini, R. (2012). Task demand and mood repair: The intervention potential of computer games. *New Media & Society, 14*(8), 1339–1357.

Bowman, N.D., & Tamborini, R. (2013). "In the Mood to Game": Selective exposure and mood management processes in computer game play. *New Media & Society*, doi: 1461444813504274.

Branscombe, N.R., & Wann, D.L. (1991). The positive social and self-concept consequences of sports team identification. *Journal of Sport & Social Issues, 15*(2), 115–127.

Brown, N., Billings, A.C., & Brown, K. (2015). May no act of ours bring shame: Fan-enacted crisis communication surrounding the Penn State sex abuse scandal. *Communication & Sport, 3*(3), 288–311.

Brown, N., Devlin, M.B., & Billings, A.C. (2013). Fan identification gone extreme: Sports communication variables between fans and sport in the Ultimate Fighting Championship. *International Journal of Sport Communication, 6*, 19–32.

Bryant, J., & Holt, A.M. (2006). A historical overview of sports and media in the United States. In A.A. Raney & J. Bryant (Eds.), *Handbook of sports and media* (pp. 21–43). Mahwah, NJ: Lawrence Erlbaum Associates, Inc.

Bryant, J., & Miron, D. (2003). Excitation-transfer theory and three-factor theory of emotion. In J. Bryant, D. Roskos-Ewoldsen, & J. Cantor (Eds.), *Communication and emotion: Essays in honor of Dolf Zillmann* (pp. 31–59). Mahwah, NJ: Erlbaum.

Bryant, J., & Raney, A. (2000). Sports on the screen. In D. Zillmann & P. Vorderer (Eds.), *Media entertainment: The psychology of its appeal* (pp. 153–174). Mahwah, NJ: Lawrence Erlbaum Associates, Inc.

Bryant, J., Rockwell, S.C., & Owens, J.W. (1994). "Buzzer beaters" and "barn burners": The effects on enjoyment of watching the game go "down to the wire." *Journal of Sport & Social Issues, 18*(4), 326–339.

Cantor, J.R., Bryant, J., & Zillmann, D. (1974). Enhancement of humor appreciation by transferred excitation. *Journal of Personality and Social Psychology, 30*(6), 812–821.

Cantor, J.R., Zillmann, D., & Bryant, J. (1975). Enhancement of experienced sexual arousal in response to erotic stimuli through misattribution of unrelated residual excitation. *Journal of Personality and Social Psychology, 35*, 69–75.

Charney, T., & Greenberg, B.S. (2002). Uses and gratifications of the Internet. In C.A. Lin & D.J. Atkin (Eds.), *Communication technology and society: Audience adoption and uses* (pp. 379–407). New York: Hampton Press.

Cheever, N. (2009). The uses and gratifications of viewing mixed martial arts. *Journal of Sports Media, 4*(1), 25–53.

Cialdini, R.B., Borden, R.J., Thorne, A., Walker, M.R., Freeman, S., & Sloan, L.R. (1976). Basking in reflected glory: Three (football) field studies. *Journal of Personality and Social Psychology, 34*(3), 366.

Cohen, A.A., Levy, M.R., & Golden, K. (1988). Children's uses and gratifications of home VCRs: Evolution or revolution. *Communication Research, 15*(6), 772–780.

Cummins, R.G., Keene, J.R., & Nutting, B.H. (2012). The impact of subjective camera in sports on arousal and enjoyment. *Mass Communication and Society, 15*(1), 74–97.

Cummins, R.G., Wise, W.T., & Nutting, B. H. (2012). Excitation transfer effects between semantically related and temporally adjacent stimuli. *Media Psychology, 15*(4), 420–442.

Dietz-Uhler, B., Harrick, E.A., End, C., & Jacquemotte, L. (2000). Sex differences in sport fan behavior and reasons for being a sport fan. *Journal of Sport Behavior, 23*(3), 219–231.

Duncan, M.C. (2006). Gender warriors in sport: Women and the media. In A.A. Raney & J. Bryant (Eds.), *Handbook of sports and media* (pp. 231–252). Mahwah, NJ: Lawrence Erlbaum Associates, Inc.

Dwyer, B., & Kim, Y. (2011). For love or money: Developing and validating a motivational scale for fantasy football participation. *Journal of Sport Management, 25*(1), 70–83.

Elliott, P. (1974). Uses and gratifications research: A critique and a sociological alternative. In J.G. Blumler & E. Katz (Eds.), *The uses of mass communications: Current perspectives on gratifications research* (pp. 249–268). Beverly Hills, CA: Sage.

Farquhar, L.K., & Meeds, R. (2007). Types of fantasy sports users and their motivations. *Journal of Computer-Mediated Communication, 12*(4), 1208–1228.

Festinger, L. (1954). A theory of social comparison processes. *Human Relations, 7*(2), 117–140.

Frederick, E.L., Clavio, G.E., Burch, L.M., & Zimmerman, M.H. (2012). Characteristics of users of a mixed-martial-arts blog: A case study of demographics and usage trends. *International Journal of Sport Communication, 5*(1), 109–125.

Gan, S., Tuggle, C.A., Mitrook, M.A., Coussement, S.H., & Zillmann, D. (1997). The thrill of a close game: Who enjoys it and who doesn't? *Journal of Sport & Social Issues, 21*(1), 53–64.

Gantz, W. (1978). How uses and gratifications affect recall of television news. *Journalism Quarterly, 55*(4), 664–672, 681.

Gantz, W. (1981). An exploration of viewing motives and behaviors associated with television sports. *Journal of Broadcasting & Electronic Media, 25*(3), 263–275.

Gantz, W., Fingerhut, D., & Nadorff, G. (2012). The social dimension of sports fanship. In A.C. Earnheardt, P.M. Haridakis, & B.S. Hugenberg (Eds.), *Sports fans, identity, and socialization* (pp. 65–78). Lanham, MD: Lexington Books.

Gantz, W., & Wenner, L.A. (1991). Men, women, and sports: Audience experiences and effects. *Journal of Broadcasting & Electronic Media, 35*(2), 233–243.

Gantz, W., & Wenner, L.A. (1995). Fanship and television sports viewing experience. *Sociology of Sport Journal, 12*, 56–74.

Gantz, W., Wang, Z., Paul, B., & Potter, R.F. (2006). Sports versus all comers: Comparing TV sports fans with fans of other programming genres. *Journal of Broadcasting & Electronic Media, 50*(1), 95–118.

Gibbs, C., O'Reilly, N., & Brunette, M. (2014). Professional team sport and Twitter: Gratifications sought and obtained by followers. *International Journal of Sport Communication, 7*(2), 188–213.

Grainger, A., Newman, J.I., & Andrews, D.L. (2006). Sport, the media, and the construction of race. In A.A. Raney & J. Bryant (Eds.), *Handbook of sports and media* (pp. 447–468). Mahwah, NJ: Lawrence Erlbaum Associates, Inc.

Greenberg, B.S. (1974). Gratifications of television viewing and their correlates for British children. In J.G. Blumler & E. Katz (Eds.), *The uses of mass communications: Current perspectives on gratifications* (pp. 71–92). Beverly Hills, CA: Sage.

Greenwood, D. (2010). Of sad men and dark comedies: Mood and gender effects on entertainment media preferences. *Mass Communication and Society, 13*(3), 232–249.

Hall, S. (1980). Encoding/decoding. In S. Hall, D. Hobson, A. Lowe, & P. Ellis (Eds.), *Culture, media, language: Working papers in cultural studies, 1972–79* (pp. 128–138). London: Hutchison.

Herzog, H. (1940). Professor quiz: A gratification study. In P.F. Lazarsfeld & F.N. Stanton (Eds.), *Radio and the printed page* (pp. 64–93). New York: Duell, Sloan & Pearce.

Herzog, H. (1944). What do we really know about daytime serial listeners? In P.F. Lazarsfeld & F.N. Stanton (Eds.), *Radio research 1942–1943* (pp. 3–33). New York: Duell, Sloan & Pearce.

Hirt, E.R., Zillmann, D., Erickson, G.A., & Kennedy, C. (1992). Costs and benefits of allegiance: Changes in fans' self-ascribed competencies after team victory versus defeat. *Journal of Personality and Social Psychology, 63*(5), 724–738.

Hobson, D. (1982). *Crossroads: The drama of a soap opera.* London: Methuen.

Katz, E., Blumler, J., & Gurevitch, M. (1974). Utilization of mass communication by the individual. In J. Blumler & E. Katz (Eds.), *The uses of mass communication: Current perspectives on gratifications research* (pp. 19–34). Beverly Hills, CA: Sage.

Katz, E., & Foulkes, D. (1962). On the use of the mass media as "escape": Clarification of a concept. *Public Opinion Quarterly, 26*(3), 377–388.

Kinnally, W., Tuzunkan, F., Raney, A.A., Fitzgerald, M., & Smith, J.K. (2013). Using the schema-triggered affect model to examine disposition formation in the context of sports news. *Journal of Sports Media, 8*(1), 117–137.

Knobloch, S., & Zillmann, D. (2002). Mood management via the digital jukebox. *Journal of Communication, 52*(2), 351–366.

Knobloch-Westerwick, S., David, P., Eastin, M.S., Tamborini, R., & Greenwood, D. (2009). Sports spectators' suspense: Affect and uncertainty in sports entertainment. *Journal of Communication, 59*(4), 750–767.

Knobloch-Westerwick, S., & Hastall, M.R. (2010). Please your self: Social identity effects on selective exposure to news about in-and out-groups. *Journal of Communication, 60*(3), 515–535.

Levy, M.R. (1979). Watching TV news as para-social interaction. *Journal of Broadcasting & Electronic Media, 23*(1), 69–80.

Lewis, N., & Weaver, A.J. (2015). Emotional responses to social comparisons in reality television programming. *Journal of Media Psychology, 28*, 65–77.

McDonald, S.R. (2004). Sensation seeking and the consumption of televised sports. In L.J. Shrum (Ed.), *Psychology of entertainment media: Blurring the lines between entertainment and persuasion* (pp. 323–335). Mahwah, NJ: Lawrence Erlbaum Associates.

Morley, D. (1980). *The nationwide audience.* London: Film Institute.

Nabi, R.L., & Wirth, W. (2008). Exploring the role of emotion in media effects: An introduction to the special issue. *Media Psychology, 11*(1), 1–6.

Ortony, A., Clore, G.L., & Collins, A. (1988). *The cognitive structure of emotions.* Cambridge: Cambridge University Press.

Papacharissi, Z., & Mendelson, A.L. (2012). An exploratory study of reality appeal: Uses and gratifications of reality TV shows. *Journal of Broadcasting & Electronic Media, 51*(2), 355–370.

Radway, J. (1986). Identifying ideological seams: Mass culture, analytical method, and political practice. *Communication, 9*(1), 93–123.

Raney, A.A. (2003). Enjoyment of sports spectatorship. In J. Bryant, D. Roskos-Ewoldsen, & J. Cantor (Eds.), *Communication and emotion: Essays in honor of Dolf Zillmann* (pp. 397–416). Mahwah, NJ: Erlbaum.

Raney, A.A. (2004). Expanding disposition theory: Reconsidering character liking, moral evaluations, and enjoyment. *Communication Theory, 14,* 348–369.

Raney, A.A. (2006). Why we watch and enjoy mediated sports. In A.A. Raney & J. Bryant (Eds.), *Handbook of sports and media* (pp. 313–329). Mahwah, NJ: Lawrence Erlbaum Associates, Inc.

Raney, A.A., & Depalma, A.J. (2006). The effect of viewing varying levels and contexts of violent sports programming on enjoyment, mood, and perceived violence. *Mass Communication & Society, 9*(3), 321–338.

Real, M.R. (1975). Super Bowl: Mythic spectacle. *Journal of Communication, 25*(1), 31–43.

Rubin, A.M. (1979). Television use by children and adolescents. *Human Communication Research, 5*(2), 109–120.

Rubin, A.M. (1983). Television uses and gratifications: The interactions of viewing patterns and motivations. *Journal of Broadcasting & Electronic Media, 27*(1), 37–51.

Rubin, A.M. (1984). Ritualized and instrumental television viewing. *Journal of Communication, 34*(3), 6777.

Sandomir, R. (August 11, 2015). In NBC deal, English soccer proves a force in America. *New York Times,* pp. B8, B11.

Sloan, L.R. (1979). The function and impact of sports for fans: A review of theory and contemporary research. In J.H. Goldstein (Ed.), *Sports, games, and play: Social and psychological viewpoints* (pp. 219–262). New York: Erlbaum.

Spinda, J.S.W., & Haridakis, P.M. (2008). Exploring the motives of fantasy sports: A uses-and-gratifications approach. In L.W. Hugenberg, P.M. Haridakis, & A.C. Earnheardt (Eds.), *Sports mania: Essays on fandom and the media in the 21st century* (pp. 187–202). Jefferson, NC: McFarland & Company.

Steiner, L. (1988). Oppositional decoding as an act of resistance. *Critical Studies in Media Communication, 5*(1), 1–15.

Swanson, D.L. (1977). The uses and misuses of uses and gratifications. *Human Communication Research, 3*(3), 214–221.

Tajfel, H.E. (1978). *Differentiation between social groups: Studies in the social psychology of intergroup relations.* New York: Academic Press.

Vorderer, P. (2003). Entertainment theory. In J. Bryant, D.R. Roskos-Ewoldsen, & J. Cantor (Eds.), *Communication and emotion: Essays in honor of Dolf Zillmann* (pp. 131–154). Mahwah, NJ: Erlbaum.

Wann, D.L. (2006). Understanding the positive social psychological benefits of sport team identification: The team identification-social psychological health model. *Group Dynamics: Theory, Research, and Practice, 10*(4), 272–296.

Wann, D.L., & Branscombe, N.R. (1990). Die-hard and fair-weather fans: Effects of identification on BIRGing and CORFing tendencies. *Journal of Sport & Social Issues, 14*(2), 103–117.

Watts, R.B. (2008). The Florida gator nation online. In L.W. Hugenberg, P.M. Haridakis, & A.C. Earnheardt (Eds.), *Sports mania: Essays on fandom and the media in the 21st century* (pp. 243–256). Jefferson, NC: McFarland & Company.

Weber, R., Tamborini, R., Lee, H.E., & Stipp, H. (2008). Soap opera exposure and enjoyment: A longitudinal test of disposition theory. *Media Psychology, 11*(4), 462–487.

Wenner, L.A., & Gantz, W. (1989). The audience experience with sports on television. In L.A. Wenner (Ed.), *Media, sports and society* (pp. 241–268). Newbury Park, CA: Sage.

Whiteside, E., & Hardin, M. (2011). Women (not) watching women: Leisure time, television, and implications for televised coverage of women's sports. *Communication, Culture & Critique, 4,* 122–143.

Yang, C., Wu, H., Zhu, M., & Southwell, B.G. (2004). Tuning in to fit in? Acculturation and media use among Chinese students in the United States. *Asian Journal of Communication, 14*(1), 81–94.

Zillmann, D. (1991). Television viewing and physiological arousal. In J. Bryant & D. Zillmann (Eds.), *Responding to the screen: Reception and reaction processes* (pp. 103–133). Hillsdale, NJ: Erlbaum.

Zillmann, D. (2000). Mood management in the context of selective exposure theory. *Communication Yearbook, 23,* 103–122.

Zillmann, D., Bryant, J., & Sapolsky, B.S. (1989). Enjoyment from sports spectatorship. In J.H. Goldstein (Ed.), *Sports, games, and play: Social and psychological viewpoints* (2nd ed., pp. 241–278). Hillsdale, NJ: Erlbaum.

Zillmann, D., & Cantor, J.R. (1976). A disposition theory of humor and mirth. In T. Chapman & H. Foot (Eds.), *Humor and laughter: Theory, research, and applications* (pp. 93–115). London: Wiley.

17

SPORT AS ENTERTAINMENT STUDIES

Arthur A. Raney

FLORIDA STATE UNIVERSITY

To some, the title and focus of this chapter may seem odd. "Sport *is* entertainment, and thus all studies of sport are necessarily entertainment studies." On many levels that logic rings true. However, as the breadth of this volume attests, sport is much more than *just* entertainment. Nevertheless, communication scholars have for decades examined how and why we are entertained by mediated sporting events. Although such questions have been interrogated from a variety of perspectives, arguably the largest body of systematic research on the topic has been produced by media psychologists working in the subarea of entertainment theory (or, to some, entertainment psychology). In this chapter, I review and seek to explain that body of literature, offering possible directions for building upon it in the future.

Understanding Entertainment

At the outset, a brief review of some of the key goals and purposes of entertainment theory might prove helpful. In short, entertainment theory encompassed a set of psychological perspectives, concepts, and theories that seek to describe, explain, and (to some extent) predict the selection, reception, and effects of media entertainment. Generally speaking, entertainment[1] can be defined as "any activity designed to delight and, to a smaller degree, enlighten through the exhibition of the fortunes or misfortunes of others, but also through the display of special skills by others and/or self" (Zillmann & Bryant, 1994, p. 438). Using this lens, it is obvious to see how sport is universally considered an entertainment content. But the primary goal of entertainment theory is not to merely categorize content but rather to explore the experiences people have with content, or in the words of Zillmann and Bryant (1994), to explore "entertainment as media effect" (p. 437). Thus, within this research tradition, entertainment is further conceptualized as a complex reception process involving various thoughts, feelings, and behaviors. This perspective acknowledges that humans are active agents in deciding what is and is not entertaining to them. That is, we perceive and experience entertainment on an individual level. Ultimately, scholars in the area (e.g., Bosshart & Macconi, 1998; Vorderer, 2001; Zillmann & Bryant, 1994) see entertainment as being in the eye of the beholder, which, for our purposes, explains why great variance exists in the appeal of sport across the population.

Given this, one goal of entertainment psychology is to understand what motivates people to seek out particular content in the first place. Sport entertainment scholars have typically limited such examinations to the presumed social and psychological functions of entertainment, with their labors generally falling within the broader uses and gratifications (see Blumler & Katz, 1974) and selective exposure (see Zillmann & Bryant, 1985) traditions. A closer look at viewing motives is offered by Gantz and Lewis in Chapter 16 of this volume, though some of this research is discussed below. In any event, understanding why people seek out certain media content is one of the major goals of entertainment studies.

Another major goal of entertainment studies is to better understand the experiences that people have with content. As earlier noted, the entertainment reception process is multidimensional, involving various affective, cognitive, and behavioral manifestations. To date, the greatest scholarly attention has been paid to affective responses to content, specifically positive emotional responses associated with *enjoyment*. Various communication-related theories, research perspectives, and concepts explain or acknowledge the centrality of enjoyment to the entertainment experience: affective disposition theory (Zillmann & Cantor, 1976; Raney, 2004), mood management (Zillmann, 1988), arousal theory and excitation transfer (Zillmann, 1971, 1996), selective exposure (Zillmann & Bryant, 1985), uses and gratifications (Blumler & Katz, 1974), parasocial interaction (Giles, 2002; Horton & Wohl, 1956), identification (Cohen, 2001; Maccoby & Wilson, 1957), transportation (Green & Brock, 2000; Green, Brock, & Kaufman, 2004), narrative engagement (Busselle & Bilandzic, 2008), flow (Csikszentmihalyi & Csikszentmihalyi, 1988; Sherry, 2004), narrative/entertainment persuasion (Moyer-Gusé, 2008; Slater & Rouner, 2002), and catharsis (Scheele & DuBois, 2006) (to name a few); many of these approaches are relevant to the study of sports content. Within these approaches, the experience of media enjoyment is typically defined using terms associated with pleasure, perceived by viewers/users through the activation of neurotransmitters in the limbic and sympathetic nervous systems. Thus, as a key dependent variable, the *feeling* of enjoyment is generally measured as a pleasurable, emotional reaction to media content.

Of course, many forms of entertainment—particularly, sport—also involve some level of pain for the viewer: a loss by your favorite team, witnessing an injury to a player, your team 'playing down to its competition' or snatching defeat from the jaws of victory, empathizing with a devastated athlete giving a post-loss interview, suffering through a win by a hated rival. Further, other non-hedonic considerations—such as admiring extraordinary human achievement or contemplating meaningfulness—can also be associated with the consumption of entertainment. Such complexities highlight the multidimensionality of entertainment experiences, leading scholars to acknowledge that enjoyment itself is ultimately "a complex construct that includes references to physiological, affective, and cognitive dimensions" (Vorderer, Klimmt, & Ritterfeld, 2004, p. 389). However, to date these nonhedonic aspects have received relatively little attention by scholars studying sport content. Regardless, a primary goal of entertainment studies is to identify the factors through and conditions under which enjoyment arises and varies. Those factors and conditions include myriad inputs (or 'prerequisites'; see Vorderer, Klimmt, & Ritterfeld, 2004) from viewers/users themselves, their situational environment, the medium, and the content. Entertainment scholars studying sport have generally focused their attention on a particular set of inputs related to the contests, the coverage, and the viewers; much of this research is reviewed below.

Sport as a Unique Genre of Media Entertainment

Despite entertainment theory's aim to identify patterns of responses reflecting basic psychological processes in media viewers/users, the truth is that great variance in entertainment experiences exist because of the numerous inputs noted above, like unique plotlines, genre-specific storytelling devices, the delivery/reception medium, viewing situations, and the like. In the case of sport studies, scholars have historically acknowledged factors distinguishing the content from other genres of entertainment programming, factors presumed to subsequently differentiate encounters with sport from other forms of media entertainment. Bellamy (2006) summarized many of these factors when differentiating sport from other televised entertainments: (a) sporting events are typically presented live, facilitating 'real-time' suspense; (b) unlike most programming today, sport is regularly scheduled season-in, season-out, year-to-year on, generally speaking, the same days at the same times; (c) sport comes with minimal barriers of language and literacy, making international/universal sport television experiences a reality; (d) because sport is quite culturally ingrained, it engenders civic pride and celebration in ways that other forms of programming cannot; and, (e) sport seamlessly integrates advertising and other forms of promotion into the broadcasts, transforming the relationship between content and marketing.

Additionally—and perhaps most germane to discussions of enjoyment—the nature of team and athlete fanship is quite different from that for most other forms of media. While television series and movie franchises come and go, sport teams are (for the most part) eternal, with allegiances passed along as birthrights. Unlike most entertainment genre preferences, sport loyalty is often cross-generational, geographically determined, and race-/gender-/class-neutral. As a result, teams and athletes engender unparalleled partisanship among viewers. For many fans, the impact of these affiliations on motivations for seeking out events and for the enjoyment of them cannot be understated. In short, sport fanship affects the reception process in ways rarely (if ever) paralleled on the entertainment landscape. With this in mind, we now turn our attention to scientific studies exploring that process.

Exploring Mediated Sport Enjoyment

As alluded to earlier, an overarching question motivating this area has been "How is enjoyment—operationalized as a pleasurable, emotional response—derived from sport media spectatorship?" Given the question, scholars have almost exclusively investigated *in situ* viewing of live-televised sporting events, typically collecting evidence using experimental or quasi-experimental methodologies in the field or the laboratory to make claims about possible answers.

Disposition Theory of Sport Spectatorship

One theoretical perspective has driven most of this work: the disposition theory of sport spectatorship (Zillmann, Bryant, & Sapolsky, 1989; Zillmann & Paulus, 1993). According to the theory, the emotional experience of enjoyment is dependent upon the affiliations—that is, the affective dispositions—that viewers hold toward teams and athletes; these dispositions are conceptualized along a continuum of affect (or liking) from extremely positive, through indifference, to extremely negative. Ultimately, enjoyment is operationalized as a product of the intensity and valence of the affective dispositions held toward the combatants and the outcome of the contests.

More specifically, the theory states that enjoyment increases the more viewers favor the winning team and/or dislike the losing team.[2] In contrast, enjoyment decreases—that is, disappointment or negative enjoyment increases—the more the winning team is disliked and/or the more the losing team is loved by viewers. Thus, maximum enjoyment from viewing mediated sport should be experienced when an intensely liked team defeats an intensely hated one, while maximum disappointment should be experienced when a hated team defeats one that is beloved. Support for the disposition theory of sport spectatorship (and related constructs) has been found with a variety of sports: professional football (Zillmann, Bryant, & Sapolsky, 1989), college football (Raney & Kinnally, 2009), international basketball (Zillmann, Bryant, & Sapolsky, 1989), college basketball (Peterson & Raney, 2008), professional baseball (Rainey, Larsen, & Yost, 2009), Olympic gymnastics (Reichart Smith, 2012), World Cup soccer (Knoll, Schramm, & Schallhorn, 2014), Formula 1 racing (Hartmann, Stuke, & Daschmann, 2008), tennis (Tüzünkan, 2007), and professional wrestling (Lachlan & Tamborini, 2008). The vast majority of these and similar studies have paid the greatest attention to the relationship between team affiliations (along with a host of other variables) and winning, though a few studies have also examined losses and disappoinment (e.g., Hall, 2015; Kinnally, 2012; Raney & Kinnally, 2009; Rainey, Larsen, & Yost, 2009; Rainey, Yost, & Larsen, 2011).

As noted above, enjoyment is the key dependent variable in most disposition theory studies. However, scholars have explored the associated construct of mood, with fans consistently reporting more positive moods following a win by a beloved team (e.g., Knoll, Schramm, & Schallhorn, 2014), as well as increased negative moods after non-wins (e.g., Schwarz, Strack, Kommer, & Wagner, 1987).

These findings have been further supported by physiological data reflecting increased arousal in the sympathetic nervous system, which is also conceptually linked to both mood and enjoyment (see Vorderer, Klimmt, & Ritterfeld, 2004; Zillmann, 1996). For instance, the viewing of team-relevant photographs from winning and losing matches can lead to numerous markers of physiological arousal, like greater skin conductance responses and smaller startle probe-P3 reflexes (Hillmann, Cuthbert, Bradley, & Lang, 2004). Similarly, following a televised World Cup soccer match featuring bitter rivals, saliva samples from male fans contained elevated levels of testosterone (Bernhardt, Dabbs, Fielden, & Lutter, 1998). For ardent fans, such feelings may be experienced even before the game starts: Wann, Schrader, and Adamson (1998) reported that some sport fans experience increased somatic anxiety in the days leading up to an important game. Ultimately, the stress can become so great during a game that even the most loyal fans will avert their gaze from the television, cover their eyes and ears, or even turn off the set for a short period of time (Eastman & Riggs, 1994). Thus, the affective dispositions we hold not only allow us to enjoy sport but also to feel *for* and *with* the teams we love. Given this reality, it should not be surprising that empathy is considered a key explanatory mechanism for the disposition-theory formula across all forms of media enjoyment (see Zillmann, 1994).

As alluded to earlier, enjoyment of mediated sport is more complex and impacted by more situational inputs than the basic disposition-theory formula suggests. These inputs include factors and features related to the sport being played and the nature of the in-game action, the accompanying commentary and other technical issues, and the viewers themselves.

Enjoyment and the Contests

Some sports are obviously beloved more than others. Since the early 1970s, America's favorite sport to watch has been football, with basketball and baseball swapping second and third place from year to year ("Sports: Gallup Historical Trends," n.d.). A few empirical studies have examined differences across audiences in the appeal and enjoyment of various sports. Sargent,

Zillmann, and Weaver (1998) found that U.S. college students rated combative sports—football, baseball, basketball, soccer, hockey, boxing, among others—as significantly more enjoyable than both stylistic (e.g., gymnastics, diving, figure skating, swimming, tennis) and mechanized sports (e.g., golf, auto racing, fishing, archery). Perhaps mirroring the Gallup data, the researchers found that violent team sports (including football) were rated the most exciting, dangerous, violent, and enjoyable of all.

These data appear to suggest that Americans prefer their sport violent.[3] In truth, the relationship between perceptions of violence and sport enjoyment is consistent across many studies. For example, across 16 amateur hockey matches, DeNeui and Sachau (1996) found two variables that reliably and consistently predicted enjoyment: the number of penalties committed and penalty minutes assessed. Furthermore, Bryant and his colleagues (1998) found that, across all televised sport, *violence*—as opposed to features such as risk, artistry, and action—was the content characteristic rated most enjoyable. But despite these findings, relatively few studies have directly compared the enjoyment of violent and nonviolent play. In the seminal study in this area, Bryant and his colleagues (1981) found that NFL plays rated high in 'roughness' were significantly more enjoyed than those rated as less rough. Goldstein and Arms (1971), as well as Raney and Depalma (2006), also found violent sport to be rated as more enjoyable than nonviolent (although, to be fair, most recently Westerman and Tamborini [2010] did not replicate this finding). Moreover, affective dispositions can influence our perceptions of sport violence, with one study finding that games won by a favored team were judged to be more violent than those lost and with those fans perceiving higher levels of overall violence reporting greater enjoyment than those perceiving lower levels (Raney & Kinnally, 2009). In general, the trend is clear: Violence, at least in some perceived form, is highly associated with sport enjoyment.

Likewise, perceptions of suspense promote sport enjoyment. As a key component of dramatic narratives, suspense has been a concept of interest for entertainment researchers for decades (see Vorderer, Wulff, & Friedrichsen, 1996). Several sport scholars have examined the way that game features impact perceptions of suspense and enjoyment. In one of the first studies, Gan and her colleagues (1997) operationalized suspense in relation to final-point differentials between teams playing in the NCAA men's basketball tournament, with higher suspense corresponding to closer final scores. As predicted, enjoyment was highest for males viewing the closest, and thus most suspenseful, games. Peterson and Raney (2008) replicated and extended this work by testing how well a host of suspense measures—including those used in the earlier study, number of times the lead changed hands, number of times the game was tied, and the round of the tournament in which the game was played—predicted enjoyment. Ultimately, enjoyment was most strongly predicted by a measure of the *unfolding* nature of suspense: the cumulative time (in seconds) that the game scores were extremely close. Knobloch-Westerwick and her colleagues (2009) highlighted the importance of shifts in positive and negative affect as another key component of perceptions of suspense impacting enjoyment of a college football game between two long-standing rivals. Further, Hall (2015) demonstrated that suspense can even cushion the blow of a loss, reporting that suspense was more closely associated with enjoyment following the defeat of a favored team than following a win. Thus, as with violence, perceptions of suspense appear to be highly and positively correlated with sport media enjoyment.

Enjoyment and the Coverage

As previously noted, one way that media psychologists differentiate their work from others is by acknowledging that media texts/messages are constructed versions of reality. We maintain that this fact matters greatly in the entertainment reception process. Within sport media studies, no place is this more apparent than in the impact of commentary on enjoyment. This is particularly the case as commentators influence perceptions of violence and suspense.

Even a cursory view of promotional efforts reveals networks relying on, inflating, or even manufacturing hostility between teams to market sport. It should come as little surprise that such language is also found in the in-game commentary, with measurable effects on perceptions of game violence and enjoyment. For example, in one classic study, participants rated hockey clips containing the actual broadcast commentary as more intense and violent than others viewing the identical action without commentary (Comisky, Bryant, & Zillmann, 1977). Furthermore, the researchers added aggression-embellishing commentary to clips containing 'normal' play, which viewers ultimately rated as rougher than actual, rough play. Similar findings have been reported for experimentally manipulated commentary on basketball play (Sullivan, 1991) and soccer fouls (Beentjes, Van Oordt, & Van Der Voort, 2002). Further, Bryant and his colleagues demonstrated how commentary can influence perceptions of violence with even noncontact sport (Bryant, Brown, Comisky, & Zillmann, 1982). The researchers created three versions of a tennis match in which the commentators described the players as having no prior relationship, as best friends, or as bitter enemies. Viewers of the participants-as-enemies version perceived the players to be more hostile, tense, and competitive than participants viewing the other two versions; they also reported enjoying the match significantly more.

Perceptions of suspense—and thus enjoyment—can also be impacted by sport commentary. Owens and Bryant (1998) revealed how home team radio announcers can add to the level of perceived suspense experienced by listeners rooting for the home team. Further, Bryant, Rockwell, and Owens (1994) manipulated suspense in a football game through adding or omitting play-by-play announcing and through play selection. As expected, viewers of the more suspenseful version reported greater enjoyment, along with more anxiety in relation to the game outcome.

In addition to commentary, technical aspects of the medium such as screen size, image quality, vividness, and camera-angle selection can also influence enjoyment, in particular as such aspects influence perceptions of presence with and immersion into the content (Kim & Biocca, 1997). Some of these issues are discussed by Cummins in Chapter 18 of this volume, but I will mention one relevant study on the on-hold-for-now 3D sport television experience (Raney, Ellis, & Janicke, 2012). My colleagues and I compared 2D and 3D clips from various sporting events and found significantly greater attention, feelings of presence, and enjoyment in the 3D viewers. The extent to which future media technologies can improve upon our perception of 'being there' and the impacts on the entertainment reception experience will need to be further examined.

Finally, enjoying sport today increasingly involves more than just viewing or listening to the game itself. Millions of sport viewers routinely pick up their computers, tablets, smartphones, and other devices while watching sport; that is, they 'second screen' the games (with a television set generally remaining the 'first screen' or the primary means for viewing). Thus, the impact of media coverage (presumably on enjoyment) comes not only from the match itself, but also from content on the second screen. Some viewers simply use the devices to keep up with player and team statistics for the game being watched; others view different camera angles or another game altogether or fantasy statistics. However, many fans use the technologies to connect with others through social media sites such as Facebook, Snapchat, and Twitter. To date, little research has explored how all of this additional media activity is impacting enjoyment of the game being shown on the 'first screen.' One notable exception offered a sentiment analysis of Twitter messages (i.e., tweets) posted during five U.S. men's national team matches during the 2014 World Cup. Unsurprisingly, among U.S. fans, the number of tweets containing negative emotions (e.g., anger, fear) decreased when the U.S. team scored and increased when their opponents scored; as the authors correctly note, these findings are "consistent with the disposition theory of sports spectatorship" (Yu & Wang, 2015, p. 399).

Enjoyment and the Consumers

Enjoyment of mediated sport is also influenced by a variety of factors associated with the viewer/listener/user. For instance, almost by definition, self-reported sport fans *enjoy* sport more than others. Further, gender differences have been historically noted as well, with females reporting greater enjoyment of stylistic sport than men, and men reporting greater enjoyment of combative sport than women (e.g., Sargent et al., 1998; McDaniel, 2003).[4] Other studies have found that males particularly enjoy sport violence more than females, although Zillmann (1995) found that *violent* was the sport characteristic most associated with enjoyment for both males and females.

In terms of personality variables, individuals scoring high on the Sensing (S-N) dimension of the Myers-Briggs Type Indicator have shown a preference for sport programming (Nolan & Patterson, 1990), as have persons scoring higher in sensation-seeking (Krcmar & Green, 1999; McDaniel, 2003). Persons scoring high in trait hostility tend to be "particularly fond of sports violence" (Bryant, 1989, p. 287), similar to those scoring high on the surface trait Curiosity About Morbid Events (McDaniel, Lim, & Mahan, 2007). Admittedly, none of these studies examined sport enjoyment per se. But it seems reasonable to assume that some consistent relational patterns also exist between these personality variables and sport enjoyment.

Finally, as noted above, scholars examine motives for consuming entertainment, including the desire to fulfill numerous social and psychological needs. It stands to reason that the process of gratifying these needs through media can be satisfying and pleasurable and, thus, experienced as enjoyment. Therefore, variation in perceived needs across the population should (and does) impact the entertainment reception experience in general, as well as with sport content specifically. For example, some persons are motivated to consume sport for aesthetic considerations. In fact, Smith (1988) noted that "a splendid athletic performance rivals any great work of art" (p. 58). Thus, it is unsurprising that many routinely report finding enjoyment in contemplating the beauty, grace, and extraordinary displays of athleticism found in sport. Others are motivated to consume sport for social reasons: to spend time with family and friends, to experience a sense of belonging in connection to a larger group or cause, to engage in conversation with strangers at a bar, and to promote one's own self-esteem (e.g., Gantz, 1981; Gantz & Wenner, 1995; Melnick, 1993). It follows that enjoyment likely increases the extent to which these perceived needs are met while viewing a sporting event.

Avenues for Future Sport as Entertainment Studies

The entertainment landscape and the sport media world are ever-changing. So, too, the field of entertainment psychology is experiencing increased interest and growth. As a result, the future of sport as entertainment studies looks bright. In closing, I mention a few avenues of possible future exploration.

First, as I alluded to above, we must better understand how emerging media technologies and content platforms are altering the entertainment experience. In many ways, these new communication contexts call into question our basic understanding of enjoyment. For instance, when fans continually post to social media while watching a game, how do we conceptualize enjoyment? Is it the sum of enjoyment from the first and second screen? Is it the difference of the two, in that one may detract from attending to the other? Is it the product of the two? How can we determine the relative weight of each? Further, how might enjoyment of the game be impacted by a rude comment in response to what you posted?

In short, emerging media technologies are only making the sport entertainment reception experience more complicated. One goal of entertainment psychology in the future will be to make better sense of that complexity.

Emerging technologies also provide researchers with new tools for analyzing audiences. Traditionally and most commonly, studies in this area have relied upon post-hoc evaluations of the entertainment experience, often within a laboratory setting. However, mobile and wearable devices may soon provide researchers with the ability to (somewhat) unobtrusively and continually collect enjoyment-related data (e.g., psychophysiological, continuous response) *in situ* to better understand the roller-coaster of emotional and cognitive experiences viewers encounter during sport reception.

Secondly, and on a related note, today we have more information about sport, teams, and athletes than ever before: stadium deal negotiations, advanced performance statistics, arrest records, political opinions, trade rumors, offensive comments made in the boardroom and locker room. It seems reasonable to assume that some (if not all) of this information impacts the dispositions we form toward teams and athletes, and possibly even the fanship we hold toward a particular sport. We know that the strength and valence of those dispositions impact our enjoyment. Thus, scholars are also encouraged to explore how the glut of personal and professional information about sport teams and athletes impacts our dispositions and ultimately our enjoyment of the games they play.

Thirdly, the past decade has witnessed a flurry of intellectual activity in entertainment psychology and theory, moving the field beyond a pleasure-centric model of enjoyment to issues including cognitive enjoyment, appreciation, eudaimonic motivations, intrinsic need satisfaction, morality, and adaptive play, to name just a few.[5] Many of these approaches can further illuminate the complexity of the sport entertainment reception experience. For instance, a few years ago I proposed how moral considerations might be explored in sport viewing (Raney, 2011); Hall (2015) recently contemplated the relationship between sport and appreciation. More of this work must be accomplished.

From my perspective, all of the 'low hanging intellectual fruit' associated with sport entertainment studies has been picked. We must now move on to examining more complex relationships and interactions in our scholarship. This will require new and mixed methods (e.g., integrating the type of work described herein with audience-centered cultural studies, committing to longitudinal examinations, pursing cross-cultural comparisons), advanced analytic tools, and cross-disciplinary collaboration. This work will be difficult. But completing it is necessary if examinations of sport are to keep up with intellectual advances across entertainment studies specifically, and the communication discipline and academia in general. Such work is also necessary to ensure that studies of sport media maintain a credible and critical voice in broader social and cultural conversations.

Notes

1 In this chapter, the term *entertainment* refers to *media entertainment*. Social and cognitive psychologists study sport in a manner similar to media/entertainment psychologists, relying upon the same empirical methods to evaluate responses from sport spectators/ audiences. However, the resulting work differs in that media/entertainment psychology acknowledges, appreciates, and seeks to better understand how sport broadcasts/ coverage are constructed versions of reality shaped by the delivery system, commentary, advertising, camera-angle selection, technological enhancements, and a host of viewer factors. Thus, although conceptual overlap exists between entertainment experiences with mediated and nonmediated (or spectated) sport, this chapter will focus on scholarship examining encounters with mediated sport entertainment.

2 For brevity's sake, I will use the term *team* to refer to all participants, though the same reception processes are applicable to the viewing of individual sports.

3 The term *sport violence* is a contentious one in both academic and fan conversations. The nature of this chapter precludes a full discussion of this issue. For more on the topic, see Raney and Ellis (2014).

4 It seems reasonable to expect that such differences may have changed or no longer exist, as access to sport programming has greatly increased and as youth sport participation—continually evolving as a result of Title IX legislation—has possibly changed sport viewing habits over the past two decades. As such, a replication and updating of these studies may be in order.

5 For recent examples of such work, see the 2014 special issue of *Journal of Communication* (volume 64, issue 3) titled "Expanding the Boundaries of Entertainment Research."

References

Beentjes, J.W., Van Oordt, M., & Van Der Voort, T.H.A. (2002). How television commentary affects children's judgments of soccer fouls. *Communication Research, 29*(1), 31–45.

Bellamy, Jr., R.V. (2006). Sports media: A modern institution. In A.A. Raney & J. Bryant (Eds.), *Handbook of sports and media* (pp. 66–79). Mahwah, NJ: Erlbaum.

Bernhardt, P.C., Dabbs, J.M., Fielden, J.A., & Lutter, C.D. (1998). Testosterone changes during vicarious experiences of winning and losing among fans at sporting events. *Physiology and Behaviors, 65*(1), 59–62.

Blumler, J.G., & Katz, E. (1974). *The uses of mass communications: Current perspectives on gratifications research.* Beverly Hills, CA: Sage.

Bosshart, L., & Macconi, I. (1998). Media entertainment. *Communication Research Trends, 18*(3), 3–38.

Bryant, J. (1989). Viewers' enjoyment of televised sports violence. In L.A. Wenner (Ed.), *Media, sports, and society* (pp. 270–289). Newbury Park, CA: Sage.

Bryant, J., Brown, D., Comisky, P.W., & Zillmann, D. (1982). Sports and spectators: Commentary and appreciation. *Journal of Communication, 32*(1), 109–119.

Bryant, J., Comisky, P., & Zillmann, D. (1981). The appeal of rough-and-tumble play in televised professional football. *Communication Quarterly, 29*(4), 256–262.

Bryant, J., Rockwell, S.C., & Owens, J.W. (1994). "Buzzer beaters" and "barn burners": The effects on enjoyment of watching the game go "down to the wire." *Journal of Sport & Social Issues, 18*(4), 326–339.

Bryant, J., Zillmann, D., & Raney, A.A. (1998). Violence and the enjoyment of mediated sport. In L.A. Wenner (Ed.), *MediaSport* (pp. 252–265). London: Routledge.

Busselle, R., & Bilandzic, H. (2008). Fictionality and perceived realism in experiencing stories: A model of narrative comprehension and engagement. *Communication Theory, 18*, 255–280.

Cohen, J. (2001). Defining identification: A theoretical look at the identification of audiences with media characters. *Mass Communication & Society, 4*, 245–264.

Comisky, P., Bryant, J., & Zillmann, D. (1977). Commentary as a substitute for action. *Journal of Communication, 27*(3), 150–153.

Csikszentmihalyi, M., & Csikszentmihalyi, I.S. (1988). *Optimal experience: Psychological studies of flow in consciousness.* New York: Cambridge University Press.

DeNeui, D.L., & Sachau, D.A. (1996). Spectator enjoyment of aggression in intercollegiate hockey games. *Journal of Sport and Social Issues, 20*(1), 69–77.

Eastman, S.T., & Riggs, K.E. (1994). Televised sports and ritual: Fan experiences. *Sociology of Sport Journal, 11*(3), 149–174.

Gan, S-L., Tuggle, C.A., Mitrook, M.A., Coussement, S.H., & Zillmann, D. (1997). The thrill of a close game: Who enjoys it and who doesn't? *Journal of Sport & Social Issues, 21*(1), 53–64.

Gantz, W. (1981). An exploration of viewing motives and behaviors associated with television sports. *Journal of Broadcasting, 25*(3), 263–275.

Gantz, W., & Wenner, L.A. (1995). Fanship and the television sports viewing experience. *Sociology of Sport Journal, 12*, 56–74.

Giles, D.C. (2002). Parasocial interaction: A review of the literature and a model for future research. *Media Psychology, 4*, 279–205.

Goldstein, J.H., & Arms, R.L. (1971). Effects of observing athletic contests on hostility. *Sociometry, 34*, 83–90.

Green, M.C., & Brock, T.C. (2000). The role of transportation in the persuasiveness of public narratives. *Journal of Personality and Social Psychology, 79*, 701.

Green, M.C., Brock, T.C., & Kaufman, G.F. (2004). Understanding media enjoyment: The role of transportation into narrative worlds. *Communication Theory, 14*, 311–327.

Hall, A.E. (2015). Entertainment-oriented gratifications of sports media: Contributors to suspense, hedonic enjoyment, and appreciation. *Journal of Broadcasting & Electronic Media, 59*(2), 259–277.

Hartmann, T., Stuke, D., & Daschmann, G. (2008). Positive parasocial relationships with drivers affect suspense in racing sport spectators. *Journal of Media Psychology, 20*(1), 24–34.

Hillmann, C., Cuthbert, B., Bradley, M., & Lang, P. (2004). Motivated engagement to appetitive and aversive fanship cues: Psychophysiological responses of rival sports fans. *Journal of Sports & Exercise Psychology, 26*(2), 338–351.

Horton, D., & Wohl, R.R. (1956). Mass communication and para-social interaction. *Psychiatry, 19*, 215–229.

Kim, T., & Biocca, F. (1997). Telepresence via television: Two dimensions of telepresence may have different connections to memory and persuasion. *Journal of Computer Mediated Communication, 3*(2). Retrieved June 30, 2016, from http://onlinelibrary. wiley.com/doi/10.1111/j.1083-6101.1997.tb00073.x/full.

Kinnally, W. (2012). Examining the role of anticipation in outcome expectations and enjoyment of televised sports contests. *Media Psychology Review, 4*. Retrieved June 30, 2016, from http://mprcenter.org/review/expectations-sports-enjoyment/.

Knobloch-Westerwick, S., David, P., Eastin, M., Tamborini, R., & Greenwood, D. (2009). Sports spectators' suspense: Affect and uncertainty in sports entertainment. *Journal of Communication, 59*(4), 750–767.

Knoll, J., Schramm, H., & Schallhorn, C. (2014). Mood effects of televised sports events: The impact of FIFA World Cups on viewers' mood and judgments. *Communication & Sport, 2*(3), 242–260.

Krcmar, M., & Greene, K. (1999). Predicting exposure to and uses of violent television. *Journal of Communication, 49*(3), 25–45.

Lachlan, K., & Tamborini, R. (2008). The effect of perpetrator motive and dispositional attributes on enjoyment of television violence and attitudes toward victims. *Journal of Broadcasting & Electronic Media, 51*(1), 136–152.

Maccoby, E.E., & Wilson, W.C. (1957). Identification and observational learning from films. *Journal of Abnormal Social Psychology, 55*, 76–87.

McDaniel, S.R. (2003). Reconsidering the relationship between sensation seeking and audience preferences for viewing televised sports. *Journal of Sport Management, 17*(1), 13–36.

McDaniel, S.R., Lim, C., & Mahan III, J.E. (2007). The role of gender and personality traits in response to ads using violent images to promote consumption of sports entertainment. *Journal of Business Research, 60*(6), 606–612.

Melnick, M.J. (1993). Searching for sociability in the stands: A theory of sports spectating. *Journal of Sports Management, 7*(1), 44–60.

Moyer-Gusé, E. (2008). Toward a theory of entertainment persuasion: Explaining the persuasive effects of entertainment-education messages. *Communication Theory, 18*, 407–425.

Nolan, L.L., & Patterson, S.J. (1990). The active audience: Personality type as an indicator of TV program preference. *Journal of Social Behavior and Personality, 5*(6), 697–710.

Owens, J.B., & Bryant, J. (July 1998). *The effects of a hometeam ("homer") announcer and color commentator on audience perceptions and enjoyment of a sports contest.* Paper presented at the annual meeting of the International Communication Association, Jerusalem, Israel.

Peterson, E., & Raney, A.A. (2008). Exploring the complexity of suspense as a predictor of mediated sports enjoyment. *Journal of Broadcasting & Electronic Media, 52*(4), 544–562.

Rainey, D.W., Larsen, J., & Yost, J.H. (2009). Disappointment theory and disappointment among baseball fans. *Journal of Sport Behavior, 32*(3), 339–356.

Rainey, D.W., Yost, J.H., & Larsen, J. (2011). Disappointment theory and disappointment among football fans. *Journal of Sport Behavior, 34*(2), 175–187.

Raney, A.A. (2004). Expanding disposition theory: Reconsidering character liking, moral evaluations, and enjoyment. *Communication Theory, 14*, 348–369.

Raney, A.A. (2011). Fair ball: Exploring the relationship between media sports and viewer morality. In A.C. Billings (Ed.), *Sports media: Transformation, integration, consumption* (pp. 77–93). London: Routledge.

Raney, A.A., & Depalma, A. (2006). The effect of viewing varying levels of aggressive sports programming on enjoyment, mood, and perceived violence. *Mass Communication and Society, 9*, 321–338.

Raney, A.A., & Ellis, A. (2014). The enjoyment, appeal, and effects of mediated sports violence. In A.C. Billings & M. Hardin (Eds.), *Routledge handbook of sport and new media* (pp. 259–270). London: Routledge.

Raney, A.A. Ellis, A.J., & Janicke, S.H. (2012). The future of sports television? 3D TV and the sports reception experience. *Journal of Chengdu Sport University, 38*, 26–33.

Raney, A.A., & Kinnally, W. (2009). Examining perceived violence in and enjoyment of televised rivalry sports contests. *Mass Communication and Society, 12*(3), 311–331.

Reichart Smith, L.M. (2012). Winning isn't everything: The effect on nationalism bias on enjoyment of a mediated sporting event. *International Journal of Spot Communication,* *5*(2), 176–192.

Sargent, S.L., Zillmann, D., & Weaver, J.B. (1998). The gender gap in the enjoyment of televised sports. *Journal of Sports & Social Issues, 22*(1), 46–64.

Scheele, B., & DuBois, F. (2006). Catharsis as a moral form of entertainment. In J. Bryant & P. Vorderer (Eds.), *Psychology of entertainment* (pp. 405–422). Mahwah, NJ: Lawrence Erlbaum Associates.

Schwarz, N., Strack, F., Kommer, D., & Wagner, D. (1987). Soccer, rooms, and the quality of your life: Mood effects on judgments of satisfaction with life in general and with specific domains. *European Journal of Social Psychology, 17*(1), 69–79.

Sherry, J.L. (2004). Flow and media enjoyment. *Communication Theory, 14,* 328–347.

Slater, M.D., & Rouner, D. (2002). Entertainment-education and elaboration likelihood: Understanding the processing of narrative persuasion. *Communication Theory, 12,* 173–191.

Smith, G.J. (1988). The noble sports fan. *Journal of Sport & Social Issues, 12*(1), 54–65.

Sports: Gallup Historical Trends (n.d.). *Gallup, Inc.* Retrieved June 30, 2016, from http://www.gallup.com/poll/4735/sports.aspx.

Sullivan, D.B. (1991). Commentary and viewer perception of player hostility: Adding punch to televised sport. *Journal of Broadcasting & Electronic Media, 35*(4), 487–504.

Tüzünkan, F. (2007). *The role of morality and physical attractiveness of athletes on disposition formation* (Unpublished doctoral dissertation). Florida State University.

Vorderer, P. (2001). It's all entertainment—sure. But what exactly is entertainment? Communication research, media psychology, and the explanation of entertainment experiences. *Poetics, 29,* 247–261.

Vorderer, P., Klimmt, C., & Ritterfeld, U. (2004). Enjoyment: At the heart of media entertainment. *Communication Theory, 14*(4), 388–408.

Vorderer, P., Wulff, H.J., & Friedrichsen, M. (1996). *Suspense: Conceptualizations, theoretical analyses, and empirical explorations.* Mahwah, NJ: Lawrence Erlbaum Associates.

Wann, D.L., Schrader, M.P., & Adamson, D.R. (1998). The cognitive and somatic anxiety of sport spectators. *Journal of Sport Behavior, 21*(3), 322–337.

Westerman, D., & Tamborini, R. (2010). Scriptedness and televised sports: Violent consumption and viewer enjoyment. *Journal of Language and Social Psychology, 29*(3), 321–337.

Yu, Y., & Wang, X. (2015). World Cup 2014 in the Twitter world: A big data analysis of sentiments in U.S. sports fans' tweets. *Computers in Human Behavior, 48,* 392–400.

Zillmann, D. (1971). Excitation transfer in communication-mediated aggressive behavior. *Journal of Experimental Social Psychology, 7,* 419–434.

Zillmann, D. (1988). Mood management: Using entertainment to full advantage. In L. Donohew, H.E. Sypher, & E.T. Higgins (Eds.), *Communication, social cognition, and affect* (pp. 147–171). Hillsdale, NJ: Lawrence Erlbaum Associates.

Zillmann, D. (1994). Mechanisms of emotional involvement with drama. *Poetics, 23*(1), 33–51.

Zillmann, D. (1995). Sports and the media. In J. Mester (Ed.), *Images of sport in the world* (pp. 423–444). Cologne: German Sports University.

Zillmann, D. (1996). Sequential dependencies in emotional experience and behavior. In R.D. Kavanaugh, B. Zimmerberg, & S. Fein (Eds.), *Emotion: Interdisciplinary perspectives* (pp. 243–272). Mahwah, NJ: Erlbaum.

Zillmann, D., & Bryant, J. (Eds.) (1985). *Selective exposure to communication*. Hillsdale, NJ: Erlbaum.

Zillmann, D., & Bryant, J. (1994). Entertainment as media effect. In J. Bryant & D. Zillmann (Eds.), *Media effects: Advances in theory and research* (pp. 437–461). Hillsdale, NJ: Lawrence Erlbaum Associates.

Zillmann, D., Bryant, J., & Sapolsky, B. (1989). Enjoyment from sports spectatorship. In J.H. Goldstein (Ed.), *Sports, games, and play: Social and psychological viewpoints* (2nd ed., pp. 241–278). Hillsdale, NJ: Lawrence Erlbaum Associates.

Zillmann, D., & Cantor, J. (1976). A disposition theory of humor and mirth. In A.J. Chapman & H.C. Foot (Eds.), *Humour and laughter: Theory, research and applications* (pp. 93–115). London: John Wiley & Sons.

Zillmann, D., & Paulus, P.B. (1993). Spectators: Reactions to sports events and effects on athletic performance. In R.N. Singer, M. Murphey, & L.K. Tennant (Eds.), *Handbook of research on sports psychology* (pp. 600–619). New York: Macmillan.

18

SPORT AS BROADCAST STUDIES

R. Glenn Cummins

TEXAS TECH UNIVERSITY

It would seem obvious to note that consuming broadcast sport is vastly different from viewing competition in person. Contextual differences create unique viewing experiences for the sport spectator watching alone at home, listening from the road, watching with friends at a crowded bar, or standing alongside thousands in a packed stadium (Eastman & Land, 1997; Hocking, 1982; Wenner & Gantz, 1998). Even those watching in identical environments seemingly witness different events as they form conflicting perceptions of competition (e.g., Hastorf & Cantril, 1954). As such, sport spectatorship—in person or mediated—is an act of objective competition monitoring, yet perception of game events is influenced by context and filtered through biases (e.g., Plessner & Haar, 2006; Wann & Branscombe, 1995).

That said, what distinguishes broadcast sport from in-person spectatorship is that competition is filtered through more than just personal biases. Sport programming is the result of countless production decisions made by a "team of professional gatekeepers and embellishers" (Comisky, Bryant, & Zillmann, 1977, p. 150). Consider Morris and Nydahl's (1985) contrast between two spectators—one watching in person versus one watching from home. Whereas the in-person spectator sees the competition from a single vantage point, the at-home spectator sees events via a variety of perspectives: wide shots that provide viewers with an encompassing perspective of the stadium environment and field of play, medium shots that bring the viewer closer to the action, and close-ups that portray athletes' exertion in graphic detail. Broadcasts are further enhanced by onscreen graphics providing insight or context, attention-grabbing sound effects, game sounds captured in high fidelity, and the constant accompaniment of on-air commentators. Finally, competition is often witnessed repeatedly through instant replays. Based on this, they conclude, "the dramatic experience of watching the game on television is so different from the dramatic experience of being present in the arena that they are almost incomparable" (p. 105).

Careful review of the specific and meaningful ways sport is captured for broadcast consumption is a useful means of illuminating how broadcast sport is "capable of intensifying the dramatic tension in an assortment of ways" (Barnfield, 2013, p. 326). The purpose of this chapter is to identify key elements employed in the production of sport broadcasts and review scholarship exploring how these production practices alter the at-home spectator's experience of athletic competition.

Differentiating Sport as Broadcast Studies

A useful starting point for examining sport as broadcast studies is to differentiate this vein of inquiry from other chapters within this volume, placing emphasis on the actions of production personnel involved in the translation of athletic competition into a product consumed by the remotely located spectator. As Clarke and Clarke (1982) noted, "The presentation of sport through the media involves an active process of re-presentation: what we see is not the event, but the event transformed into something else—a media event" (pp. 70–71). Sport as broadcasting studies emphasizes this active process of transformation, with the focus resting squarely on broadcasters' efforts in packaging competition and less on the nature of competition itself.

One means of exploring this transformation is to briefly acknowledge how broadcasts of athletic competition have evolved, focusing on two themes: first, the paucity of resources formerly employed in mediation of action in contrast to the wealth of resources used today; and second, a corresponding evolution of the philosophy undergirding the production of televised sport. With respect to the former, the one camera used to broadcast the first televised sporting event in the United States—a single camera positioned along the third-base line in NBC's coverage of a Columbia-Princeton college baseball game in 1939—stands in stark contrast to the 46 cameras the network employed in its coverage of NFL's 2015 Super Bowl (Bryant & Holt, 1996; "Super Bowl XLIX," 2015). Technology employed in the mediation of sport continues to advance, and broadcasters increasingly rely on more innovative production techniques to combat viewer boredom because of the repetitive nature of sport broadcasts (Clarke & Clarke, 1982; Mullen & Mazzocco, 2000).

With respect to the philosophy embedded within the production of broadcast sport, tension between transparency versus the deliberate construction of media events is a natural outgrowth of this technical evolution (Rowe, 1999; Whannel, 1992). Early broadcasts placed primary emphasis on efficient presentation of competition to avoid confusion and capture action in a transparent manner:

> the television camera was thought of as an unseen eye, its "sweeping" of what was before it from a single, static position simulating the experience of the spectator watching from a particular vantage point. The key to this

form of television, as in all forms of realism, was to make the infrastructure of communication invisible.

(Rowe, 1999, p. 155)

However, Barnfield (2013) argued that any notion that contemporary sport broadcasts serve as mere chronicles of on-field action is an illusion. Instead, sport broadcasts now represent orchestrated media events characterized by added narrative emphasis and visual distortions of time and space (Clarke & Clarke, 1982; Gruneau, 1989; Morris & Nydahl, 1985).

Sport Broadcasts as Spectacle

In dissecting the nature of these media events, scholars have invoked the notion of 'spectacle' to illuminate the constituent components of the broadcasts, the production decisions involved in their creation, and the broader historical, political, or social context surrounding the broadcasts (e.g., Farrell, 1989; Gruneau, 1989; Morris & Nydahl, 1985; Real, 1975; White, Silk, & Andrews, 2008). Although the concept has been widely applied to describe many aspects of sport broadcasting, review of its historical origins reveals its specific utility here. Farrell (1989) noted that the concept of spectacle can be traced to Aristotle's *Poetics*, where he employed it as a means of differentiating between genuine drama resulting from narrative elements versus the technical embellishment of that narrative through the work of the "stage machinist" (Aristotle, 1961, p. 159). Aristotle defined spectacle as a "weak hybrid form of drama, a theatrical concoction that relied upon external factors . . . as a substitute for intrinsic aesthetic integrity" (p. 159). By this definition, sport production personnel serve as modern-day 'stage machinists' with great control over the production resources brought to bear in the creation of sport broadcasts—yet with little control over the nature of the competition itself and, therefore, work largely to supplement the competition.

Although this seminal definition of spectacle differentiates genuine drama from its embellishment through production efforts, the interdependent relationship between the two embodies the aforementioned tension between transparent presentation of competition rather than its enhancement. Farrell (1989) argued that contemporary spectacle involves the "appropriation of 'real' objects, even persons, for the purposes of visual display" (p. 160). He later added, "In every case, the quality of performance is interwoven with the quality of presentation" (p. 164). Thus, sport broadcasting as spectacle provides room for both (relatively unaltered) depictions of competition aided by spectacular adornment that builds upon displays of athleticism. This relationship is tacitly acknowledged by production personnel, the focus of Silk, Slack and Amis's (2000) case study exploring sport production routines. They observed a dichotomy such that "bread and butter shots" were employed to document or chronicle game events. When opportunities arose, the director would use "gravy shots" (e.g., close-ups, replays, etc.) to enhance the telecast (p. 10).

Implicit within this discussion of the production of sport spectacles is the primary motive to infuse competition with added drama or excitement (Barnfield, 2013; Silk et al., 2000). Acknowledgment of this motivation begs the question of whether broadcasters can create excitement or dramatic tension not inherent to competition. Perspectives on this issue are conflicting. Clarke and Clarke (1982) succinctly argued, "Even where the drama does not intrinsically exist in the event, it can be constructed through the media presentation and build up of the event" (p. 71). Additional observations about the generally dull nature of the majority of organized sport make broadcaster efforts to instill drama through spectacular adornment increasingly salient. Barnett (1990) argued, "Many sports, perhaps the majority of sporting events are not intrinsically or even consistently exciting" (pp. 156–157). Likewise, Gruneau's (1989) case study examining sport production routines quotes a program director with a similar observation:

> In most sports, sports are boring. There are only a few moments that are really exciting, and the trick, I guess, is to bridge from one exciting moment to another with something that is entertaining . . . so we keep the interest by doing the features, doing the extras.
>
> *(p. 144)*

Empirical evidence supports this assertion. Real's (1975) analysis of the 1974 Super Bowl noted that only a tiny portion of the broadcast, 3%, showed actual competition, and more recent observations echo this finding. Biderman's (2010) nonscientific breakdown of an NFL broadcast observed that the program featured only 11 minutes of live competition. In this light, the efforts of sport broadcasters to instill entertainment value have obvious merit. Nonetheless, Barnett (1990) argued the efforts to instill excitement via production techniques have limits: "If a match is tedious, or a race is all but won with fifteen laps still to go, even the most sophisticated camerawork cannot instill drama where none exists" (p. 156). In sum, a fair assessment may be that efforts to generate interest and excitement may work in conjunction with intrinsic qualities of an event in an additive fashion, creating a sense of excitement when it is absent or intensifying this excitement when it is intrinsically present (Fortunato, 2001).

'Visual Excitement' in Sport Broadcasts

A useful means of dissecting the efforts applied by production personnel in the mediation of on-field action involves differentiating between the visual and aural dimensions of sport broadcasts. Although evidence can be found to suggest the primacy of both, Greer, Hardin, and Homan (2009) argued, "the power of visuals in a medium defined and remembered for its images . . . cannot be overstated" (p. 174). To return to the earlier discussion regarding whether perceived excitement could be created when it was intrinsically absent, Rowe (1999) argued that visual production techniques were particularly adept at fulfilling this function, asserting that visual coverage "relies on capitalizing on the visual drama of movement when it is readily accessible and producing a sense of rapid momentum when it is not" (p. 154).

This sense of momentum is achieved through a constellation of visual production techniques. Williams (1977) undertook one of the earliest systematic analyses of visual aspects of sport television, chronicling the number and placement of cameras, number and duration of shots, added visual graphics, and more, concluding that the coverage was "kaleidoscopic and visually dynamic" (p. 136), adding, "coverage, even during lulls in action, maintained a high energy level" (p. 137). Decades later Greer et al. (2009) employed the phrase *visual excitement* to collectively refer to such efforts. They defined the concept as "the result of the production of events using techniques that can enhance viewers' emotional engagement and visual stimulation" (p. 174).

Despite these eloquent assertions regarding the strategic use of visuals within broadcast sport to create a sense of excitement, Krein and Martin (2006) lamented that relatively few studies have probed such techniques, as such studies would demonstrate effects on the at-home spectator. Indeed, qualitative studies of sport broadcasts speak of "incredible transformations" created through visual production techniques but fail to explore audience response (Morris & Nydahl, 1985, p. 103). Furthermore, an additional critique of much scholarship examining visual characteristics of sport content is the frequent failure to specify a theoretical mechanism relating visual production techniques with specific aspects of audience response.

To this end, one vein of research has systematically probed how varied perspectives of play can impact evaluation of—or emotional response to—competition. Cummins, Keene, and Nutting (2012) invoked the theoretical framework of (tele)presence, examining how presentation of game play via overhead, subjective cameras creates a sense of immersion, heightening enjoyment and emotional response relative to presentations of events from an objective, sideline perspective. Response to this novel perspective was dependent upon the nature of game play, as the use of subjective cameras only enhanced perception of play in response to events lacking an intrinsic sense of excitement. They argued that emotional responses elicited through production techniques have the practical benefit of sustaining stimulation during periods of dull play and elevating subsequent emotional response to more stimulating competition through excitation transfer (Cummins, Wise, & Nutting, 2012).

The argument that sport producers work to instill excitement through visual production techniques also provides a vehicle for scholars using the theoretical lens of hegemonic masculinity to examine gender differences in the production of men's versus women's sport. Although other chapters in this volume address these issues more fully, the emphasis on production resources merits brief discussion here. Clarke and Clarke (1982) argued that broadcast sport texts are uniquely suited to reinforce patriarchal values because of the 'natural' character of athletic competition, thereby squelching debate about gender hierarchies. They argued, "Sport provides apparently incontrovertible evidence, decisive testimony, for the inevitable superiority of the male over the female. Men beating women at tennis, women playing football, men running faster, throwing things further than women, are all added to this natural catalogue of male dominance" (pp. 66–67). However, studies demonstrating differences in coverage and the production resources employed in production of broadcast sport highlights how these mediated depictions of sport are not natural but instead a result of deliberate decisions throughout the production process: "What is 'shown' on television is always the result of a complex process of selection: what items to report, what to leave out, what to replay, and what to downplay" (Gruneau, 1989, p. 134).

Production personnel have finite resources at their disposal, and the varied resources brought to bear in the mediation of any given sport can convey implicit statements about its perceived importance (Barnett, 1990; Brookes, 2002; Morris & Nydahl, 1985). Based on this argument, studies have examined the resources reflected in broadcasts of men's versus women's sport. For example, Hallmark and Armstrong (1999) examined differences in visual characteristics in television broadcasts of the men's versus women's college basketball championship tournaments, finding that telecasts of women's games featured fewer production resources (e.g., cameras and graphics). Moreover, they also reported differences in the nature of coverage in terms of shot duration, which they argued had implications for the perceived excitement or intensity of competition. Similar results were produced by Greer et al. (2009) in their study of the visual excitement generated through television coverage of men's versus women's track and field in the 2004 Olympic Games. Subsequent studies of the production resources or visual framing devices used in men's versus women's sport have continued to probe such differences with varied outcomes (e.g., Smith, 2014; Smith & Bissell, 2012).

In addition to studies of specific visual properties of sport broadcasts, an additional concern is the broader significance of coverage itself. Fortunato (2001) invoked agenda-setting (McCombs & Reynolds, 2009) as a theoretical framework to argue that the selection of what events to cover and what events to ignore represents a first step in crafting audience perceptions of sport. By this logic, systematic differences in the coverage and exclusion of some sport can carry implications for their perceived importance. Examining disparities in mere time allocated to coverage of select sports has provided fertile ground for the discussion of gender and race issues in sport (e.g., Angelini, MacArthur, & Billings, 2012; Billings, 2008b; see Chapters 9–10). For example, Billings (2008a) provided a longitudinal study examining time allocated to coverage of men's versus women's events in Olympic telecasts, as well as more nuanced measures of the specific sport and the subjective versus objective nature of the competition. Although the findings globally demonstrate a focus on male athletes, examination of longitudinal trends as well as review of time allocated to specific sports suggests important implications for the nature of coverage.

One final component of visual excitement is the skilled use of editing— instant replay in particular—to enhance athletic competition. Gamache (2010) called instant replay the most important technological innovation brought to bear in the production of broadcast sport. On the one hand, replay provides the obvious pragmatic benefit of aiding game officials in making accurate judgments (Bordner, 2015). However, Vannatta's (2011) analysis illustrates how re-presentation can yield readings of competition that contrast with that formed through real-time viewing. In their discussion of television production techniques applied in the mediation of sport, Morris and Nydahl (1985) argued that replay "enables a director to present insights that not only alter our understanding of the original event, but also allow us to be recipients of entirely new events outside of real time and space" (p. 102). This lofty assertion is corroborated by others who argue that replay may be strategically used to enhance dramatic tension and suspense associated with game events (Barnett, 1990; Clarke & Clarke, 1982) and enhance visual coverage to bridge the periodized nature of competition (Silk et al., 2000).

These assertions were the subject of one recent study probing how viewing dull or exciting segments of college football followed by instant replay impacts perceptions of play. Cummins and Hahn (2013) employed exemplification theory as a theoretical framework to argue that selective re-presentation of game events from varied perspectives represent competing exemplars of a singular event that can alter viewer perceptions of competition. They argued that sport directors do not randomly select from multiple perspectives of play provided by numerous cameras but instead intuitively select perspectives that bring viewers closer to the action and reveal game events in more graphic detail. Their results partially supported this argument, as the use of replay enhanced the perceived violence of dull events.

Aural Dimensions of Sport Broadcasters

The second dimension of sport telecasts used to bolster excitement or drama is the aural component, chiefly the work of commentators. Barnfield (2013) called commentary a performative act in that production personnel aid in the creation of a unique media event that differentiates the event seen by in-person spectators. With respect to its functions within sport broadcasts, commentary uniquely embodies the aforementioned tension between merely describing competition for at-home spectators versus adding entertainment value in the form of historical context, personal experience, or other insight (Brookes, 2002; Morris & Nydahl, 1985; Rowe, 1999; Whannel, 1992).

One way that commentators can add this entertainment value is through the active, ongoing construction of a narrative surrounding the event (Rowe, 1999; Sullivan, 1991). As a case in point, White et al. (2008) noted that program producers explicitly specified four narrative themes or devices emphasized through coverage of the 2003 Little League World Series. Similarly, Bryant, Comisky, and Zillmann (1977) provided a quantitative examination of the commentary employed in professional football telecasts assessing whether commentary served a descriptive, dramatic, or humorous function. They report that one-quarter of on-air commentary served to provide "dramatic embellishment" (p. 149), with particular emphasis on intrapersonal struggles of athletes seeking to overcome personal challenge. Relatedly, Bryant and his collaborators (1982) later demonstrated that the creation of a narrative portraying competitors as fierce rivals versus neutral opponents or friends yielded maximal enjoyment of the broadcast. Such emphasis on the context surrounding on-field events is typically provided through "color commentary," which stands in contrast to "play-by-play commentary" that describes competition (Sullivan, 2006, p. 139).

In addition to the construction of narrative, commentators work to enhance perceptions of game events to make them appear more exciting or entertaining analogous to visual production techniques. Barnett (1990) argued for the power of the commentator as one who expertly crafts the audience perception of athletic competition, offering the occasional "embellishment which the game itself may lack" (p. 157). One specific outcome of commentary is the potential illusion that athletic competition is more violent than it appears. For example, Comisky et al.'s (1977) seminal study demonstrated how the manipulation of commentary can impact audience perception of play. In their study, research participants witnessed television recordings of hockey that systematically varied both the intrinsic violence of play as well as the accompanying commentary that stressed the roughness of play. Unlike previous research that asserted the primacy of visuals (Greer et al., 2009), their results suggested the opposite, with normal play stressing aggression generating highest evaluations of the perceived roughness of competition. Sullivan (1991) presented similar results, suggesting the superior influence of commentary over visuals. In his study, viewers watched a brief excerpt from a college basketball competition depicting a fight between players. The excerpt was paired with commentary that systematically varied its emphasis on aggression and assignment of blame. Sullivan reported that participants viewing the competition with the dramatic commentary judged the team that was assigned blame within that commentary as more hostile, contradicting visual evidence.

Thus far, the discussion of commentary has focused on deliberate actions designed to craft narrative or embellish game events, but a considerable body of scholarship has examined commentary as an implicit force that both reflects and reinforces cultural values or dominant ideology, particularly regarding gender and race (e.g., Billings, 2008b; see Chapters 6–7). Scholars examining these issues have invoked Goffman's (1974) concept of framing as a theoretical lens explaining how such language can influence spectator perception of athletes. For example, Billings, Halone, and Denham (2002) examined the nature of descriptors applied to male versus female athletes in collegiate basketball, finding not only disparity in the frequency of descriptors that favored male athletes but also differences in the specific ways that athletes were described or framed. Whereas male athletes were more often described based on athletic skill, comments concerning female athletes more frequently denoted characteristics unrelated to athletic performance, such as appearance, personality, or the athlete's background.

The Olympic Games have provided fertile ground for explorations of how commentary differs as a function of athlete gender and nationality because of both its coverage of men's and women's sport as well as its recurrent nature, which permits longitudinal assessment of how commentary can change over time (e.g., Billings, 2008a). Furthermore, the Olympic Games represent one of the few events that showcases female athletes in great volume. Indeed, longitudinal content analysis of sport highlight programming consistently demonstrates the paucity of coverage of women's competition in other sports (Cooky, Messner, & Musto, 2015).

Examples of research providing systematic study of Olympic coverage abound. One recent investigation examined commentary accompanying select events at the 2012 Olympic Games for differential references to athletes as a function of gender and sport (Billings et al., 2014). Similar studies have provided analogous comparisons focused on coverage of specific sports (e.g., beach volleyball, Smith & Bissell, 2012) or textual examinations of commentary surrounding women's sport without direct comparison to male sport (e.g., women's ice hockey, Poniatowski & Hardin, 2012). Although a simple summary belies the wealth of specific insights offered by this scholarship, these studies demonstrate collective acknowledgment of the power of commentators to propel stereotyped perception of athletes.

One last facet of the aural component of sport broadcasts oft-employed by production personnel to enhance sport broadcasts is what the audience hears in addition to commentary. Williams (1977) acknowledged the presence of aural enhancements in NFL broadcasts, noting that "sound mixtures and levels were highly manipulated, particularly when crowd noise and sounds from the field were used literally to 'orchestrate' live action, thus inducing notions of excitement as well as aurally communicating the force of physical contact" (p. 138). Although limited evidence has explored how such enhancements can aid sport broadcasts, one recent study demonstrated the influence of crowd response within sport radio. Cummins and Gong (2015) report a study where listeners heard excerpts from radio broadcasts of college soccer that included artificially enhanced crowd response. Compared with those hearing the unedited versions, listeners hearing the enhanced broadcasts reported game action to be more exciting. Notably, this effect was only evident for game events that were not as intrinsically exciting. Thus, the authors argue that this form of spectacular embellishment only served to generate excitement when it was otherwise absent.

The Future of Sport as Broadcast Studies

Despite widespread agreement regarding how visual and aural components of sport broadcasts can be employed to enhance sport broadcasts, robust opportunities to advance this literature remain. Perhaps the most obvious avenue for continued study is the examination of novel production techniques. As previously noted, sport broadcasters continually work to adopt new production technologies (Mullen & Mazzocco, 2000), and exploration of the nature and impact of these developments will provide fodder for continued broadcast sport studies. In addition, changes in the electronic media landscape create new models for distribution and consumption of broadcast sport (Hutchins & Rowe, 2009), some of which empower the at-home spectator in ways previously not possible

However, more substantive questions regarding the production of broadcast sport remain. One such question is whether at-home spectators occupy a privileged or diminished position relative to those watching in person. Whereas some scholars stress the unique vantage point afforded through mediation (e.g., Morris & Nydahl, 1985; Rowe, 1999), others rightly note that remote audiences receive an incomplete and filtered perspective of the event. Clarke and Clarke (1982) argued that the perceived transparency created through live coverage of an event is illusory: "We can never see the whole event, we see those parts which are filtered through this process of presentation to us" (p. 73). Barnett (1990) offers an equally dour perspective on mediated spectatorship: "The television viewer is a prisoner to sports producers, directors, and commentators, with sound and vision subject both to technological and to resource limitations as well as to the whims of one person in the control van" (p. 155). Thus, novel perspectives afforded the at-home spectator come at a cost in that the viewer's perspective of competition is still dictated by content producers.

Advances in sport broadcasting technology may present a partial solution to these concerns. Availability of customizable viewing experiences permits an unprecedented level of viewer agency in the creation of sport broadcasts that are uniquely suited to individual needs (e.g., Sandomir, 2010). In his insightful glimpse into the future of broadcast sport, Brookes (2002) described viewing scenarios where passionate, invested fans use advanced technology to customize the viewing experience through selection of camera angles, audio channels, and so on. Such scenarios are increasingly available through subscription-based portals such as MLB.tv or NASCAR RaceView. Thus, despite Barnett's (1990) earlier assertion that the at-home viewer is 'prisoner' to decisions by content producers, the increased agency afforded by these novel platforms partially frees them from the decisions made by production personnel (Barnett, 1990).

Lastly, the merging of television and online technology as well as the growing ubiquity of mobile technology holds implications for not only the at-home spectator but also those viewing competition in person. Screens large and small have increasingly become a part of the in-stadium experience. One outcome of the adoption of mobile smart phone technology is that spectators—both in-person and mediated—are transforming from content consumers to producers as well. As one example, sport leagues and television networks have expressed concerns over the use of new software applications that permit live streaming of content from within sport arenas as well as from home (Sandomir, 2015). Such technology facilitates piracy of copyrighted content via streaming of telecasts, threatening economic models of distribution that support sport broadcasting. In addition, in-person spectators can also employ mobile technology to record and distribute content, and media entrepreneurs have begun to develop models for the monetization of such user-generated sport content (Quintana, 2014).

Another outcome of the growing presence of screens in the stadium environment is that even nonmediated game consumption is increasingly mediated. Sport executives are working to provide infrastructure to support mobile technology to accommodate fans as a means of competing against the convenience of at-home spectatorship (Hammond, 2014). Furthermore, arenas are equipped with larger-than-life high-definition displays that can replay game events analogous to the at-home viewing experience (Branch, 2009). Thus, the constellation of production techniques, visual embellishments, and other means of enhancing athletic competition discussed here are not restricted to at-home viewing. Contrary to the opening refrain stressing a seemingly obvious distinction between mediated and in-person spectatorship, the two are increasingly similar.

References

Angelini, J.R., MacArthur, P.J., & Billings, A.C. (2012). What's the gendered story? Vancouver's prime time Olympic glory on NBC. *Journal of Broadcasting & Electronic Media, 56*, 261–279.

Aristotle. (1961). *Poetics* (F. Fergusson, Trans.). New York: Dramabooks.

Barnett, S. (1990). *Games and sets: The changing face of sport on television*. London: BFI Publishing.

Barnfield, A. (2013). Soccer, broadcasting, and narrative: On televising a live soccer match. *Communication & Sport, 1*, 326–341.

Biderman, D. (January 15, 2010). 11 minutes of action. *Wall Street Journal*. Retrieved July 1, 2016, from http://www.wsj.com/articles/SB10001424052748704281204575002852055561406.

Billings, A.C. (2008a). Clocking gender differences: Televised Olympic clock time in the 1996–2006 Summer and Winter Olympics. *Television & New Media, 9*, 429–441.

Billings, A.C. (2008b). *Olympic media: Inside the biggest show on television*. London: Routledge.

Billings, A.C., Angelini, J.R., MacArthur, P.J., Bissell, K., Smith, L.R., & Brown, N.A. (2014). Where the gender differences really reside: The "big five" sports featured in NBC's 2012 London primetime Olympic broadcast. *Communication Research Reports, 31*, 141–153.

Billings, A.C., Halone, K.K., & Denham, B.E. (2002). "Man, that was a pretty shot": An analysis of gendered broadcast commentary surrounding the 2000 men's and women's NCAA Final Four basketball championships. *Mass Communication & Society, 5*, 295–315.

Bordner, S.S. (2015). Call 'em as they are: What's wrong with blown calls and what to do about them. *Journal of the Philosophy of Sport, 42*, 101–120.

Branch, J. (January 29, 2009). Promising fans in seats a view from the couch. *New York Times*. Retrieved July 1, 2016, from http://www.nytimes.com/2009/01/29/sports/football/29view.html?_r=0.

Brookes, R. (2002). *Representing sport*. London: Arnold.

Bryant, J., Brown, D., Comisky, P.W., & Zillmann, D. (1982). Sports and spectators: Commentary and appreciation. *Journal of Communication, 32*(1), 109–119.

Bryant, J., Comisky, P., & Zillmann, D. (1977). Drama in sports commentary. *Journal of Communication, 27*(3), 140–149.

Bryant, J., & Holt, A. (2006). A historical overview of sports and media in the United States. In A.A. Raney & J. Bryant (Eds.), *Handbook of sports and media* (pp. 21–43). Mahwah, NJ: Erlbaum.

Clarke, A., & Clarke, J. (1982). "Highlights and action replays": Ideology, sport and the media. In J. Hargreaves (Ed.), *Sport, culture and ideology* (pp. 62–88). London: Routledge.

Comisky, P., Bryant, J., & Zillmann, D. (1977). Commentary as a substitute for action. *Journal of Communication, 27*(3), 150–153.

Cooky, C., Messner, M.A., & Musto, M. (2015). "It's dude time!": A quarter century of excluding women's sports in televised news and highlight shows. *Communication & Sport*. Advance online publication.

Cummins, R.G., & Gong, Z. (2015). Mediated intra-audience effects in the appreciation of broadcast sports. *Communication & Sport*. Advanced online publication.

Cummins, R.G., & Hahn, D. (2013). Re-presenting sport: How instant replay and perceived violence impact enjoyment of mediated sports. *Mass Communication & Society, 16*, 787–807.

Cummins, R.G., Keene, J.R., & Nutting, B.H. (2012). Sports spectatorship, emotional arousal, and presence: The role of camera angle and fanship. *Mass Communication & Society, 15*, 74–97.

Cummins, R.G., Wise, W.T., & Nutting, B.H. (2012). Excitation transfer between semantically related and temporally adjacent stimuli. *Media Psychology, 15*, 420–442.

Eastman, S.T., & Land, A.M. (1997). The best of both worlds: Sports fans find good seats at the bar. *Journal of Sport & Social Issues, 21*, 156–178.

Farrell, T.B. (1989). Media rhetoric as social drama: The Winter Olympics of 1984. *Critical Studies in Mass Communication, 6*, 158–182.

Fortunato, J.A. (2001). The television framing methods of the National Basketball Association: An agenda-setting application. New *Jersey Journal of Communication, 9*, 166–181.

Gamache, R. (2010). *A history of sports highlights: Replayed plays from Edison to ESPN*. Jefferson, NC: MacFarland.

Goffman, E. (1974). *Frame analysis: An essay on the organization of experience*. New York: Harper & Row.

Greer, J.D., Hardin, M., & Homan, C. (2009). "Naturally" less exciting? Visual production of men's and women's track and field coverage during the 2004 Olympics. *Journal of Broadcasting & Electronic Media, 53*, 173–189.

Gruneau, R. (1989). Making spectacle: A case study in television sports production. In L. Wenner (Ed.), *Media, sports, & society* (pp. 134–154). London: Sage.

Hallmark, J.R., & Armstrong, R.N. (1999). Gender equity in televised sports: A comparative analysis of men's and women's NCAA Division I basketball championship broadcasts, 1991–1995. *Journal of Broadcasting & Electronic Media, 43*, 222–235.

Hammond, T. (April 11, 2014). Sports stadiums go digital. *TechRepublic*. Retrieved July 1, 2016, from http://www.techrepublic.com/pictures/photos-sports-stadiums-go-digital/.

Hastorf, A.H., & Cantril, H. (1954). They saw a game: A case study. *Journal of Abnormal and Social Psychology, 2*, 195–134.

Hocking, J.E. (1982). Sports and spectators: Intra-audience effects. *Journal of Communication, 32*, 100–108.

Hutchins, B., & Rowe, D. (2009). From broadcast scarcity to digital plentitude: The changing dynamics of the media sport content economy. *Television & New Media, 4*, 354–370.

Krein, M.A., & Martin, S. (2006). 60 seconds to air: Television sports production basics and research review. In A.A. Raney & J. Bryant (Eds.), *Handbook of sports and media* (pp. 265–276). Mahwah, NJ: Erlbaum.

McCombs, M., & Reynolds, A. (2009). How the news shapes our civic agenda. In J. Bryant & M.B. Oliver (Eds.), *Media effects: Advances in theory and research* (3rd ed., pp. 1–16). London: Routledge.

Morris, B.S., & Nydahl, J. (1985). Sports spectacle as drama: Image, language, and technology. *Journal of Popular Culture, 18*, 101–110.

Mullen, L.J., & Mazzocco, D.W. (2000). Coaches, drama, and technology: Mediation of Super Bowl broadcasts from 1969 to 1997. *Critical Studies in Mass Communication, 17*, 347–363.

Plessner, H., & Haar, T. (2006). Sports performance judgements from a social cognitive perspective. *Psychology of Sport and Exercise, 7*, 555–575.

Poniatowski, K., & Hardin, M. (2012). "The more things change, the more they . . . ": Commentary during women's ice hockey at the 2010 Olympic Games. *Mass Communication & Society, 15*, 622–641.

Quintana, C. (December 2, 2014). Santa Fe startup's app makes taking sports video easy. *Santa Fe New Mexican*. Retrieved July 1, 2016, from http://www.santafenewmexican.com/news/business/santa-fe-startup-s-app-makes-taking-sports-video-easy/article_9658b7bf-f283-54b3-aa30-de2d277647de.html.

Real, M. (1975). Super Bowl: Mythic spectacle. *Journal of Communication, 25*, 31–43.

Rowe, D. (1999). *Sport, culture and the media: The unruly trinity*. Buckingham: Open University Press.

Sandomir, R. (October 30, 2010). Online World Series is no stand-in for broadcast. *New York Times*. Retrieved July 1, 2016, from http://www.nytimes.com/2010/10/30/sports/baseball/30sandomir.html.

Sandomir, R. (May 5, 2015). Periscope, a streaming Twitter app, steals the show on boxing's big night. *New York Times*. Retrieved July 1, 2016, from http://www.nytimes.com/2015/05/05/sports/periscope-a-streaming-twitter-app-steals-the-show-on-boxings-big-night.html.

Silk, M., Slack, T., & Amis, J. (2000). Bread, butter, and gravy: An institutional approach to televised sport production. *Culture, Sport, Society, 3*, 1–21.

Smith, L.R. (2014). Up against the boards: An analysis of the visual production of the 2010 Olympic ice hockey games. *Communication & Sport, 4*(1), 62–81.

Smith, L.R., & Bissell, K.L. (2012). Nice dig! An analysis of the verbal and visual coverage of men's and women's beach volleyball during the 2008 Olympic Games. *Communication & Sport, 2*, 48–64.

Sullivan, D.B. (1991). Commentary and viewer perception of player hostility: Adding punch to televised sports. *Journal of Broadcasting & Electronic Media, 35*, 487–504.

Sullivan, D.B. (2006). Broadcast television and the game of packaging sports. In A. Raney & J. Bryant (Eds.), *Handbook of sports and media* (pp. 131–145). Mahwah, NJ: Erlbaum.

Super Bowl XLIX Media Guide (August 1, 2015). Retrieved July 1, 2016, from http://nbcsportsgrouppressbox.com/super-bowl/.

Vannatta, S. (2011). Phenomenology and the question of instant replay: A crisis of the sciences? *Sport, Ethics, and Philosophy, 5*, 331–342.

Wann, D.L., & Branscombe, N.R. (1995). Influence of identification with a team on objective knowledge and subjective beliefs. *International Journal of Sport Psychology, 26*, 551–567.

Wenner, L.A., & Gantz, W. (1998). Watching sports on television: Audience experience, gender, fanship, and marriage. In L.A. Wenner (Ed.), *MediaSport* (pp. 233–251). London: Routledge.

Whannel, G. (1992). *Fields in vision: Television sport and cultural transformation*. London: Routledge.

White, R.E., Silk, M.E., & Andrews, D.L. (2008). Revisiting the networked production of the 2003 Little League World Series: Narrative of American innocence. *International Journal of Media and Cultural Politics, 4*, 183–202.

Williams, B.R. (1977). The structure of televised football. *Journal of Communication, 27*(3), 133–139.

19

SPORT AS SOCIAL MEDIA NETWORKING STUDIES

Jimmy Sanderson

CLEMSON UNIVERSITY

Social media, or social networking platforms such as Facebook, Twitter, Instagram, Pinterest, and Snapchat, have quickly proliferated across sport (Billings, Qiao, Conlin, & Nie, 2015; Sanderson, 2011a; Smith & Sanderson, 2015), and are predicated by design to promote community, collaboration, and sharing (Meraz, 2009). Considering that sport is a popular talking point in many interpersonal settings (see Turman, and Giles & Stohl, this volume) it is not altogether surprising that social media technologies have rapidly been adopted by a variety of sport stakeholders, including team personnel (e.g., coaches, public relations professionals), athletes, sport media personalities, and fans. As these various stakeholders have expanded their social media usage, a variety of implications have been created—both positive and negative for the sport industry—and it is not uncommon to find stories about social media and sport percolating daily sport headlines. For example, in July 2015, Ohio State University quarterback Cardale Jones used Twitter to provide commentary about #BlackLivesMatter, a hashtag created to respond to several noteworthy cases of African-American males killed in police brutality cases in the previous year (Rosenthal, 2015). Similarly, in March 2015, a high school wrestler in Montana was arrested and charged with sexual abuse of children for requesting a 15-year-old girl send him nude pictures over Snapchat (Devlin, 2015).

At the organizational level, sport teams often create public relations concerns resulting from social media campaigns. For instance, in May 2014, the Baltimore Ravens held a press conference where player Ray Rice addressed domestic violence and assault allegations toward his fiancé. During the conference, Rice made several unfortunate speaking missteps, such as life being about "not getting knocked down, but getting back up" which the team's Twitter account tweeted verbatim. Consequently, the organization received scathing criticism in the press (Yoder, 2014) as some fans equated the tweets with condoning domestic violence and assault (Sanderson & Freberg, 2016). Although social media can generate negative press, it also can provide opportunities for enhanced fan engagement; some teams are integrating social media into their facilities, such as the San Francisco Giants, who, in 2013, offered a social media café at AT&T Park. The café includes six 55-inch televisions where fans can view their social media content and view content curated by Giants employees and charge their mobile device—all while watching baseball (Heitner, 2013).

The aforementioned examples represent just a small fraction of the ways social media is influencing sport. While these incidents are at the micro-level, the larger macro-level shifts provide communication scholars with a plethora of opportunities to investigate this changing sport landscape. Scholars have examined topics ranging from athletes taking more control of their self-presentation through social media (Kassing & Sanderson, 2010; Lebel & Danylchuk, 2012); messaging student-athletes receive about social media and social media monitoring (Browning & Sanderson, 2012; Sanderson & Browning, 2013); how fans use social media to frame and shape narratives about sport stories (Burch, Frederick, & Pegoraro, 2015) and to manage social identity threats (Sanderson, 2013a); and ways that organizations are using social media to engage with fans (Armstrong, Delia, & Giardina, 2014; Conlin, McLemore, & Rush, 2014).

This chapter explores social media and sport communication research by (a) examining several prominent theories used in the literature; (b) reviewing some of the integral studies that have built the social media and sport communication literature; and (c) providing directions for future research at the intersection of these two areas. Social media and sport communication research is a vibrant area of study, yet the quickly changing landscape of social media provides some issues in making sure the literature keeps pace with technological evolution. Additionally, this literature is not without its flaws (Wenner, 2014) and it is hoped that this chapter will assist scholars working in this intersection to continue to build the literature using strong theoretical foundations (Hardin, 2014) and diversifying beyond content to look at the implications that social media creates for sport stakeholders (Sanderson, 2014a).

Relevant Theories to Sport Communication and Social Media

Scholars have used a variety of theories to examine the intersection of social media and sport communication. However, several theories appear to have pre-eminence and, accordingly, are addressed here: (a) parasocial interaction; (b) framing; and (c) self-presentation.

Parasocial Interaction

Parasocial interaction (PSI) occurs when an audience member behaves toward a mediated figure in a way that resembles actual, social interaction, but differs because it is mediated and one-sided (Horton & Wohl, 1956). Everyone from fictional characters to celebrities have been subjects of PSI—including athletes (Brown, Basil, & Bocarnea, 2003). Historically, PSI has occurred in more private settings, such as fans directing comments to an athlete while watching a sporting event, or writing a letter to an athlete hoping he/she will respond. However, with the advent of social media, PSI has become more overt and encompasses a variety of behaviors. In one of the earlier studies, Kassing and Sanderson (2009) examined how fans expressed PSI to cyclist Floyd Landis via his blog as he chronicled his experiences capturing the 2006 Tour de France, being stripped of the title because of doping allegations, and then fighting these allegations. Fans ascribed to Landis the emotional investments they were making (e.g., getting text updates on Landis's performance while driving) as well as giving Landis advice on how he could improve his performance, shifting PSI from a passive to more active phenomenon. Additionally, as athletes have become more active on social media platforms, PSI has shifted to a social–parasocial continuum, which Kassing and Sanderson (2015) reference as circum-social interaction because athletes do, at times, respond back to fans, shifting the interaction into a more social nature. Frederick, Lim, Clavio, Pedersen, and Burch (2014) discussed how athletes, through their messaging on social media, can cultivate either parasocial or social interaction. That is, some athletes may be more social by asking fans questions or responding to questions that fans ask of them, whereas other athletes may use social media as more one-way communication. For example, Sanderson (2013c) examined how rookie athletes in Major League Baseball (MLB), the National Basketball Association (NBA), National Football League (NFL), and National Hockey League (NHL) used Twitter to ask questions to the audience. Sanderson noted that athletes' questions ranged from restaurant recommendations to product feedback and posited that these overtures strengthened identification and subsequently PSI between the audience and athletes.

The ability for athletes to engage fans via social media is generally championed (Sanderson, 2011a); yet it inevitably yields some negative outcomes. Kassing and Sanderson (2015) observed the presence of hateful and vitriolic commentary expressed by fans toward athletes via social media, conceptualizing this behavior as "maladaptive parasocial interaction" (p. 10). This work extended PSI, which is generally conceived as a positive, supportive behavior. Building on this line of inquiry, Sanderson and Truax (2014) examined maladaptive PSI through tweets that were sent to University of Alabama placekicker Cade Foster after he missed three field goals during a rivalry game against Auburn in 2013. They found that maladaptive PSI manifested through: (a) belittling, (b) mocking, (c) sarcasm, and (d) threats. The threats included death threats along with insinuations of sexual violence toward Foster and his family, leading the researchers to suggest that athletic departments and sport organization personnel may need to monitor social media for maladaptive PSI to mitigate mental health consequences. Nevertheless, fans continue to engage in this troubling behavior, which seems to be particularly targeted to college football players, including high school recruits. Whereas athletes are subjected to negative reactions from fans via social media, they also can employ social media to 'turn the tables' when they are subjected to unfavorable press coverage. For example, *The Players Tribune*, a website where athletes generate their own articles on a wide range of topics, is a highly cultivated site where audiences can hear directly from athletes. As athletes put their point of view and perspective on topics, they frame stories and issues in ways that are meaningful to them. This capability also extends to fans, who can initiate their own framing of sport news. For instance, in 2014, after Florida State University (FSU) quarterback Jameis Winston was accused of raping an FSU student, fans went to Twitter to defend Winston against these allegations (Levin, 2014). Similarly, fans also engage in this behavior by personally attacking reporters who appear to be putting athletes in a negative light. As one example, in 2015, female reporters covering rape allegations against NHL player Patrick Kane were subjected to fans sending messages to their personal Twitter accounts that defended Kane, which included death threats (Spies-Gans, 2015).

Framing

As observed by Entman (1993), to frame is "to select some aspects of a perceived reality and make them more salient in a communicating text, in such a way to promote a particular problem definition, causal interpretation, moral evaluation, and/or treatment recommendation for the item described" (p. 52). Framing is a powerful influence in mass media (Stefanik-Sidener, 2013) and athletes have often been subjected to unfavorable framings from sport reporters (Sanderson, 2010) with little ability to counteract those perceived slights, as they were dependent on those media personnel for their public presentation. With the emergence of social media, athletes are now endowed with capability to introduce alternative narratives. For example, Sanderson (2008) investigated how Boston Red Sox pitcher Curt Schilling used his blog to counteract press reports that he faked an injury during the 2004 American League Championship Series (ALCS). Schilling was able to attack the sport journalists and proclaim the authenticity of his injury, all in a manner of his choosing. Whereas athletes can engage in this behavior, they also benefit from fans taking on this task. Sanderson (2010) investigated how fans of professional golfer Tiger Woods used his Facebook page to introduce alternative narratives about Woods' infidelity, countering how this incident was being portrayed in the mainstream media. Specifically, fans framed Woods' behavior as a private matter that reflected a human tendency to "make mistakes," while the mainstream media portrayed Woods as a flawed individual, magnifying the salacious details surrounding Woods' affairs. Thus, athletes may experience a public relations benefit as fans, unsolicited, introduce alternative narratives to counteract perceived negative framing.

In addition to defending athletes, fans can also use social media to counter-frame when larger fan identity is threatened. For instance, Burch, Frederick, and Pegoraro (2015) investigated how fans framed the 2011 Vancouver riots (which occurred after the Vancouver Canucks lost the Stanley Cup Finals to the Boston Bruins) via Twitter. They noted how Twitter became both an information source for fans, as well as a mechanism to shape public perceptions. Fans were able to use Twitter to distance themselves from the rioters and express regret and remorse for the rioters' behavior, which countered framings occurring in the mainstream media. Thus, when fans disagree with media coverage taking place, social media platforms offer the ability to counter press portrayals and to emphasize positive aspects of the collective fan base. Along these lines, work by Brown, Brown, and Billings (2015) and Brown and Billings (2013) analyzed how sport fans of collegiate athletic programs facing scandal used Twitter to engage in fan-enacted crisis communication, seeking to mitigate negative perceptions about the athletic programs. Through social media, fans now have a participatory role in shaping public dialogue about sport news and issues, which introduces a polyvocality of voices on a multitude of sport stories (Chewning, 2015). The capabilities social media provide to counteract perceived negative media framing also extend to self-presentation. Via social media, athletes take more control of their public portrayal and express aspects of their identity that are rarely shown in the mass media. In some cases, this self-presentation is part of a larger sport media process, such as collegiate recruiting. In that vein, Frederick and Clavio (2015) examined the self-presentation of the top 10 high-school athletes in the ESPN 300 football rankings, and found that these athletes communicated in a very personal and candid style. While such an approach can resonate with some fans, it can also cause recruits to lose scholarship offers, thus, Frederick and Clavio emphasized the need for proactive social media education for high-school athletes.

Self-Presentation

One of the capabilities social media affords athletes is the ability to take more control over their public personae. Drawing on the work of Goffman (1959), self-presentation involves an identity performance that is adaptive, depending on whether one is performing 'on stage' or 'off stage.' With the development of social media, athletes in particular have been able to take a more active role in presenting their identity to the public. Whereas prominent athletes are still dependent on mainstream media organizations to some degree for coverage, the ability to highlight certain aspects of their identity that may not appear in the mainstream media has been noted in the sport and social media literature (Lebel & Danylchuk, 2014; Sanderson, 2014b; Smith & Sanderson, 2015; Weathers et al., 2014). Indeed, whereas some athletes are going to always receive significant media coverage (e.g., Tiger Woods, LeBron James, Ronda Rousey), other athletes who see less media interest can use social media to elevate their awareness with audiences (Sanderson, 2014b). Certainly, some athletes will receive a large amount of media coverage regionally based on their sport (e.g., college football players in markets with no professional sport team), but even so, social media enables these athletes to connect with fans and other audiences in ways they may be unable to do so with traditional media outlets.

In one of the earlier studies, Sanderson (2008) explored how Boston Red Sox pitcher Curt Schilling used his blog to counteract how he was being portrayed in the media, stressing his positive characteristics, such as being a good teammate and being accountable for his decisions. Lebel and Danylchuk (2012) examined how self-presentation differed by gender through an examination of professional male and female tennis players' Twitter accounts, discovering that males tended to present more as sport fans, while female players presented more as brand managers. In other work, Lebel and Danylchuk (2014) discovered that audiences rated athletes more favorably who highlighted their athletic identity in their Twitter profiles.

Much self-presentation work has focused on Twitter, yet other research has examined self-presentation on other platforms. Smith and Sanderson (2015) explored how male and female athletes self-presented via Instagram, discovering that self-presentation tended to align with gender norms (e.g., female athletes were engaged in more physical touch than males), yet with noteworthy differences (e.g., more female athletes shown in action poses related to their sport). As a result, they contended that social media may enable athletes to break out of 'scripts' often present in mass media depictions; and the ability for athletes to show more of their likes and interests away from sport could help foster greater identification with fans, leading to enhanced parasocial interaction between athletes and fans.

The aforementioned theories have assisted sport and social media scholars to investigate some of the implications arising from social media. Nevertheless, these are far from the only theories that have been and should be utilized (see Sanderson, 2013b); scholars doing work in this area should be encouraged to not only test theory, but create theory as well. In addition to the studies previously discussed, there are several other studies that address implications and shifts in sport arising from social media that warrant inclusion.

Studies Connecting Sport Communication and Social Media

As noted earlier, social media has affected many different facets of sport. One in particular that warrants mention here is sport media. Specifically, social media have changed both the sport production and consumption processes. As Twitter was gaining traction in sport, Schultz and Sheffer (2010) and Sheffer and Schultz (2010) investigated how sport journalists perceived Twitter's impact on the profession, finding that journalists at that time were primarily using Twitter to offer commentary and opinion, and that there were differences in age as younger journalists viewed Twitter as having more value than older journalists, who saw Twitter as a complementary tool to promote their work on other platforms. Since that time, Twitter has become quite prominent in sport reporting, and this acceleration of sport news on Twitter (Hutchins, 2011) has fueled Twitter to be viewed by many sport reporters as a necessity for their job (Reed, 2013). Interestingly, other research has noted that sport journalists may behave differently on social media than they do in other mainstream media platforms (Sanderson & Hambrick, 2012). Sanderson and Hambrick (2012) examined sport media members' use of Twitter after the Jerry Sandusky scandal at Penn State University, observing that these individuals engaged in behavior, such as cursing, belittling Twitter users, and promoting competitors, that would be unlikely to occur via a newspaper column or television newscast. At some level, this behavior is not altogether surprising as the Sandusky case was very emotionally charged. Sandusky, a long-time assistant coach under legendary head football coach Joe Paterno, was accused of sexually abusing children, in some instances on Penn State grounds. This case sparked large controversy, as students rallied to defend Paterno, who was ultimately fired, and passed away shortly thereafter. Moreover, given the nature of Sandusky's actions, many of the reporters felt personally invested in the topic, specifically mentioning that their status as a parent was influencing their attitudes towards the case (Sanderson & Hambrick, 2012). Nevertheless, there appears to be some inconsistencies in journalism standards when social media enters the equation. More specifically, certain behaviors may be more 'acceptable' on social media than in traditional media (e.g., ridiculing fans, referring readers to an article by a competitor). Along those lines, many reporters include a disclaimer in their profile biography indicating that opinions are their own, and do not reflect their employer. Yet, many of these individuals also clearly list their affiliation in their profile as well, and the legitimacy of such disavowals seems suspect. Additionally, sourcing appears to be less rigorous and yet more territorial on social media. This has led to a conflict between the need to 'be first' or striving to 'be right.' How the sport media industry (and the journalism industry at large) navigates these issues in the future will be an important area to which sport communication and social media scholars should attend.

Whereas social media has impacted the work routines and professional ethics of sport media members, it also has placed them in direct competition with athletes and sport teams. For example, some sport organizations restrict what reporters can disseminate via social media during game broadcasts, which has caused some reporters to question whether they have the necessary access to do their job (Suggs Jr., 2015). Suggs Jr. (2016) investigated college sport journalists' perceptions of legitimacy in their work as a result of teams now bypassing the media and releasing content via their websites and social media platforms, finding that reporters indicated that their access had decreased and that, while the relationship between reporters and team personnel does not appear to be immediately threatened, some team communication employees are testing limits with granting access. Whereas Suggs found no immediate threat to the reporter–team relationship, there are concerns that as teams generate more media, they will simultaneously reduce access to mainstream media, particularly when negative press is expected.

While sport teams may be renegotiating boundaries with sport media members and taking a more active role in media production, they are concurrently trying to manage ways that athletes use social media. This is particularly evident in college athletics, where some student-athletes are prohibited from using social media during the season and/or are subjected to monitoring and surveillance by internal personnel or outside vendors. Sanderson and Browning (2013) investigated messages student-athletes received about Twitter and found that the athletes received overwhelmingly negative messages. Often athletes were only told about problematic uses after incidents occurred. Sanderson and Browning argued that collegiate athletic departments needed to be more proactive in educating student-athletes about both the positives and negatives of social media, rather than solely focusing on monitoring of social media accounts. Additionally, other research (Sanderson, 2011b; Sanderson, Snyder, Hull, & Gramlich, 2015) has discovered that social media policies for student-athletes are heavily skewed to discussing the negative outcomes arising from social media, with very little mention of positive applications of social media. These researchers have argued that policies should be more balanced, providing more discussion of positive uses for social media, as the tone of these policies is unlikely to change student-athletes' social media behavior. Interestingly, some student-athletes actually desire social media education so they can learn strategic and positive uses for social media (Sanderson, Browning, & Schmittel, 2015) and this area represents an important conversation in which sport and social media scholars can intervene. In particular, when student-athletes are restricted from using social media, concerns about first amendment implications arise (Paulson, 2012). While the risk may be greater for public universities who enact these bans, researchers can provide important contributions about social media, privacy, and organizational control to shape and influence public conversations and, potentially, policy on this topic.

As sport organization personnel grapple with internal and external issues with social media, for sports that have historically been marginalized or relegated to minimal media coverage from traditional media outlets, social media provides an opportunity for athletes and organizations in these contexts to amplify media coverage. For example, Vann (2014) observed how social media enabled women's professional netball in Australia to exceed the limits offered by traditional sport media coverage. Similarly, McCarthy (2011) examined how fans of gymnastics used blogs, video, and other online technology to enhance the coverage of the sport, and created a body of collective intelligence around gymnastics. Thus, via social media, fans, athletes, and sport organization personnel can create information repositories that can help underserved sports to gain more traction. Certainly, there are challenges here, as many of the top sports (such as football) are firmly entrenched atop the sport consumption hierarchy. Nevertheless, social media provides an outlet for underrepresented sports and their fans to take an active role in generating content and disseminating information and coverage around the sport (McCarthy, 2011).

The previously discussed studies have helped shape an emergent body of literature on sport communication and social media. While there have been notable advancements, much work remains—part of which involves becoming more focused and selective in sport and social media scholarship.

Future Research Directions

As social media technologies have enveloped the sport world, a corresponding increase in sport communication and social media research has occurred. Although the literature is still in what might be considered its infancy, fair critiques have been raised about this literature, some of which will be addressed here. Probably the foremost critique has been the presence of research devoted to Twitter (Wenner, 2014). On one hand, popular sport figures such as Shaquille O'Neal and Lance Armstrong were early adopters of Twitter; thus, Twitter has been argued to be the social media platform of choice for sport stakeholders (Browning & Sanderson, 2012; Kassing & Sanderson, 2015). In that sense, it is not surprising that Twitter research has been predominant in sport communication and social media scholarship. On the other hand, the literature has less frequently studied Facebook, which is surprising given that Facebook dwarfs all other social media platforms with over 1 billion monthly active users (Company Info, 2015). Additionally, scholars have not devoted much attention to emerging platforms such as Instagram, Snapchat, and Pinterest, which are growing in popularity with both general and sport audiences. In other words, analysis of work on Twitter should still be welcomed, yet much recent work largely replicates preexisting findings with only the given circumstance altered, doing little to advance the body of literature. In the June 2014 issue of *Communication & Sport*, editor Lawrence Wenner organized a forum where leading scholars provided critiques and direction for the future of Twitter research; readers are encouraged to review these essays, as space does not allow for an extensive review here. Essentially, researchers should look beyond the platform, and look more at the constructs and the issues to making meaningful contributions. As one example, rather than arguing that a study on baseball pitchers' self-presentation on Twitter is needed because "no studies have examined" the topic, it will be more fruitful to look at the larger function of athlete self-presentation on social media. Researchers in this scenario might examine self-presentation through economic factors (e.g., the presence of athletes drives users to these sites, which increases use numbers that sites can use to sell advertising) or how self-presentation on social media enables athletes to engage in topics that challenge power structures in sport, or which enable athletes to engage in conversations that question sport cultural ideology (see Hutchins, 2014; Rowe, 2014).

Accordingly, this chapter concludes by offering suggestions on topics that sport and social media researchers can undertake to reinvigorate and bolster the literature. One very compelling area centers on athlete activism and advocacy and organizational and audience response to such action. Schmittel and Sanderson (2015) investigated tweets from NFL players after the George Zimmerman verdict was announced and observed how the players used Twitter to express contempt for the verdict and convey thoughts about social justice for minorities in the United States. This advocacy seems more likely to come from social media than mainstream media interviews (consider the Miami Heat team posting a picture on LeBron James' social media accounts wearing hoodies in memory of Trayvon Martin, the victim in the Zimmerman case) ("Heat don hoodies," 2012). Certainly athletes can and do engage in advocacy and activism through mainstream media, but perhaps they feel more empowered to do so via social media.

Yet, engaging in activism via social media is likely to spawn extreme reactions from fans, who may disagree with athletes engaging in social justice, causing angst from team personnel who consider these statements to constitute a public relations incident. Thus, sport communication and social media scholars could pursue what is 'at stake' with this kind of advocacy, and how the intersection of free speech, employer rules, and the increasing commodification of sport intersect through this behavior. As one example, Sanderson, Frederick, and Stocz (2016) explored Facebook and Twitter responses from fans after five St. Louis Rams players displayed a 'hands up' gesture as they walked out during pregame warm-ups for a game on November 30, 2014. This gesture was in response to the slaying of African-American teen Michael Brown, by Darren Wilson, a white police officer in Ferguson, Missouri. The researchers found that fans used Facebook and Twitter to alert sponsors to the fans' displeasure with the athletes' actions, and to circulate calls for censure and boycott of the organization. In this case, neither the Rams nor the NFL took action against the players, but exploring the discourse that occurs in response to athletes' engaging in activism and advocacy is a rich area for future inquiry.

Additionally, in critiquing new media and sport research, Butterworth (2014) noted that there was a need for scholars to explore how sport stakeholders might engage in active citizenry and critical discussion about sport culture. Indeed, social media platforms may be ideal places to hold these discussions, as traditionally, mainstream media may be resistant to engage in these discussions.

How discussions about topics such as head injuries in football and the increase in women obtaining prominent positions in male-dominated North American sport (e.g., Becky Hammon being hired as an assistant coach by the NBA's San Antonio Spurs, and the Arizona Cardinals hiring the first female assistant coach in NFL history—Jen Welter) could shed important light on sport culture and ideology and perhaps introduce narratives that could challenge dominant discourses.

Another fruitful direction that scholars could pursue with sport communication and social media centers on youth sport. Messner and Musto (2014) noted the lack of research on children and sport, and this is one area where social media and sport communication scholarship can contribute. Consider that in February 2015, Rivals (a high school recruiting ranking service) began ranking sixth-grade football prospects. One of the two prospects, Daron Bryden, immediately announced this on his Twitter profile, which was amplified by major news outlets (Smith, 2015). Returning to the question, "what is at stake?": What are the implications of sixth-graders being ranked by recruiting services and being accessible to fans via social media? There is no shortage of fans who bombard high school athletes with messages persuading them to attend the fan's school (Steinberg, 2015), and having this attention directed at sixth-graders seems problematic and an area of research warranting attention.

In conclusion, the future of sport communication and social media is bright. While platforms may come and go, the underlying features of social media (e.g., content creation, connection, and collaboration) seem too powerful and alluring to evaporate en masse, at least in a short duration. As scholars investigate more of the effects of social media and address the implications and effects, the sport communication and social media literature will thrive to become a valuable resource for the scholarly community and the public.

References

Armstrong, C.G., Delia, E.B., & Giardina, M. (2014). Embracing the social in social media: An analysis of the social media marketing strategies of the Los Angeles Kings. *Communication & Sport*. Advance online publication. doi: 10.1177/2167479514532914.

Billings, A.C., Qiao, F., Conlin, L., & Nie, T. (2015). Permanently desiring the temporary? Snapchat, social media, and the shifting motivations of sports fans. *Communication & Sport*. Advance online publication. doi 10.11/2167479515588760.

Brown, N.A., & Billings, A.C. (2013). Sports fans as crisis communicators on social media websites. *Public Relations Review, 39*, 74–81.

Brown, N.A., Brown, K.A., & Billings, A.C. (2015). "May no act of ours bring shame": Fan-enacted crisis communication surrounding the Penn State sex abuse scandal. *Communication & Sport, 3*, 288–311.

Brown, W.J., Basil, M.D., & Bocarnea, M.C. (2003). The influence of famous athletes on health beliefs and practices: Mark McGwire, child abuse prevention, and androstenedione. *Journal of Health Communication, 8*(1), 41–57.

Browning, B., & Sanderson, J. (2012). The positives and negatives of Twitter: Exploring how student-athletes use Twitter and respond to critical tweets. *International Journal of Sport Communication, 5*(4), 503–521.

Burch, L.M., Frederick, E.L., & Pegoraro, A. (2015). Kissing in the carnage: An examination of framing on Twitter during the Vancouver riots. *Journal of Broadcasting & Electronic Media, 59*(3), 399–415.

Butterworth, M.L. (2014). Social media, sport, and democratic discourse. In A.C. Billings & M. Hardin (Eds.), *Routledge handbook of sport and new media* (pp. 32–42). New York: Routledge.

Chewning, L.V. (2015). Multiple voices and multiple media: Co-constructing BP's crisis response. *Public Relations Review, 41*, 72–79.

Company Info (September 30, 2015). Retrieved July 1, 2016, from http://newsroom. fb.com/company-info/.

Conlin, L., McLemore, D.M., & Rush, R.A. (2014). Pinterest and female sport fans: Gaining a foothold in the male-dominated sport world. *International Journal of Sport Communication, 7*, 357–376.

Devlin, V. (March 31, 2015). Documents detail drug, sex charges against Ronan wrestler. *Missoulian*. Retrieved July 1, 2016, from http://missoulian.com/news/local/documents-detail-drug-sex-charges-against-ronan-wrestler/article_9854b98d-f8b1-530a-8a90-2e3df6004fdb.html.

Entman, R.M. (1993). Framing: Toward clarification of a fractured paradigm. *Journal of Communication, 43*, 51–58.

Frederick, E.L., & Clavio, G. (2015). Blurred lines: An examination of high school football recruits' self-presentation on Twitter. *International Journal of Sport Communication, 8*, 330–344.

Frederick, E., Lim, C.H., Clavio, G., Pedersen, P.M., & Burch, L.M. (2014). Choosing between the one-way or two-way street: An exploration of relationship promotion by professional athletes on Twitter. *Communication & Sport, 2*, 80–99.

Goffman, E. (1959). *The presentation of self in everyday life*. New York: Doubleday.

Hardin, M. (2014). Moving beyond description: Putting Twitter in (theoretical) context. *Communication & Sport, 2*, 113–116.

Heat don hoodies after teen's death (March 24, 2012). *ESPN*. Retrieved July 1, 2016, from http://espn.go.com//nba/truehoop/miamiheat/story/_/id/7728618/miami-heat-don-hoodies-response-death-teen-trayvon-martin.

Heitner, D. (June 30, 2013). San Francisco Giants enhance reputation as digital leader with creation of social media café. *Forbes*. Retrieved July 1, 2016, from http://www.forbes/com/sites/darrenheitner/2013/06/30/san-francisco-giants-enhance-reputation-as-digital-leader-with-creation-of-social-media-cafe/.

Horton, D., & Wohl, R.R. (1956). Mass communication and para-social interaction. *Psychiatry, 19*, 215–229.

Hutchins, B. (2011). The acceleration of sport media culture: Twitter, telepresence and online messaging. *Information, Communication & Society, 14*, 237–257.

Hutchins, B. (2014). Twitter: Follow the money and look beyond sports. *Communication & Sport, 2*, 122–126.

Kassing, J.W., & Sanderson, J. (2009). "You're the kind of guy that we all want for a drinking buddy": Expressions of parasocial interaction on Floydlandis.com. *Western Journal of Communication, 73*, 182–203.

Kassing, J.W., & Sanderson, J. (2010). Tweeting through the Giro: A case study of fan-athlete interaction on Twitter. *International Journal of Sport Communication, 3*, 113–128.

Kassing, J.W., & Sanderson, J. (2015). Playing in the new media game or riding the virtual bench: Confirming and disconfirming membership in the community of sport. *Journal of Sport & Social Issues, 39,* 3–18.

Lebel, K., & Danylchuk, K. (2012). How tweet it is: A gendered analysis of professional tennis players' self-presentation on Twitter. *International Journal of Sport Communication, 5*(4), 461–480.

Lebel, K., & Danylchuk, K.E. (2014). Facing off on Twitter: A generation Y interpretation of professional athlete profile pictures. *International Journal of Sport Communication, 7,* 317–336.

Levin, J. (December 6, 2014). It's about ethics in sports journalism: Florida State football fans are the new gamergate. *Slate.* Retrieved July 1, 2016, from http://www.slate. com/articles/sports/sports_nut//2014/12/fsutwitter_florida_state_football_fans_are_ the_new_gamergate.html.

McCarthy, B. (2011). From shanfan to gymnastlike: How online fan texts are affecting access to gymnastics media coverage. *International Journal of Sport Communication, 4*(3), 265–283.

Meraz, S. (2009). Is there an elite hold? Traditional media to social media agenda setting influence in blog networks. *Journal of Computer-Mediated Communication, 14*(3), 682–707.

Messner, M.A., & Musto, M. (2014). Where are the kids? *Sociology of Sport Journal, 31,* 102–122.

Paulson, K. (April 15, 2012). Column: Free speech sacks ban on college-athlete tweets. *USA Today.* Retrieved July 1, 2016, from http://usatoday30.usatoday.com/news/ opinion/forum/story/2012-04-15/twitter-social-media-college-sports-coaches-ban/54301178/1.

Reed, S. (2013). Social media's influence on American sport journalists' perception of gatekeeping. *International Journal of Sport Communication, 6*(4), 373–383.

Rosenthal, S. (July 23, 2015). Cardale Jones gave an obnoxious Ohio State fan the Twitter knockout punch. [Web log post]. Retrieved July 1, 2016, from http://www. sbnation.com/lookit/2015/7/23/9025119/do-not-tell-cardale-jones-to-stick-to-sports-ohio-state-fans.

Rowe, D. (2014). Following the followers: Sport researchers' labour lost in the Twittersphere? *Communication & Sport, 2,* 117–121.

Sanderson, J. (2008). The blog is serving its purpose: Self-presentation strategies on 38pitches.com. *Journal of Computer-Mediated Communication, 13*(4), 912–936.

Sanderson, J. (2010). Framing Tiger's troubles: Comparing traditional and social media. *International Journal of Sport Communication, 3*(4), 438–453.

Sanderson, J. (2011a). *It's a whole new ball game: How social media is changing sports.* New York: Hampton Press.

Sanderson, J. (2011b). To tweet or not to tweet . . . : Exploring Division I athletic departments social media policies. *International Journal of Sport Communication, 4,* 492–513.

Sanderson, J. (2013a). From loving the hero to despising the villain: Exploring sports fans social identity management on Facebook. *Mass Communication and Society, 16*(4), 487–509.

Sanderson, J. (2013b). Social media and sport communication: Abundant theoretical opportunities. In P.M. Pedersen (Ed.), *The Routledge handbook of sport communication* (pp. 56–65). New York: Routledge.

Sanderson, J. (2013c). Stepping into the (social media) game: Building athlete identity via Twitter. In R. Luppicini (Ed.), *Handbook of research on technoself: Identity in a technological society* (pp. 419–438). New York: IGI Global.

Sanderson, J. (2014a). What do we do with Twitter? *Communication and Sport, 2*, 127–131.

Sanderson, J. (2014b). Just warming up: Logan Morrison, Twitter, athlete identity, and building the brand. In B. Brummett & A.W. Ishak (Eds.), *Sport and identity: New agendas in communication* (pp. 208–223) New York: Routledge.

Sanderson, J., & Browning, B. (2013). Training versus monitoring: A qualitative examination of athletic department practices regarding student-athletes and Twitter. *Qualitative Research Reports in Communication, 14*(1), 105–111.

Sanderson, J., Browning, B., & Schmittel, A. (2015). Education on the digital terrain: A case study exploring college athletes' perceptions of social media education. *International Journal of Sport Communication, 8*, 103–124.

Sanderson, J., & Freberg, K. (2016). When going silent may be more productive: Exploring fan resistance on Twitter to the Baltimore Ravens live-tweeting the Ray Rice press conference. In A. Hutchins & N.T.J. Tindall (Eds.), *Public relations and participatory culture: Fandom, social media, and community engagement* (pp. 230–242). New York: Routledge.

Sanderson, J., Frederick, E., & Stocz, M. (2016). When athlete activism clashes with group values: The "Boycott the St. Louis Rams" Facebook page and social identity threat management. *Mass Communication and Society, 19*, 301–322.

Sanderson, J., & Hambrick M.E. (2012). Covering the scandal in 140 characters: A case study of Twitter's role in coverage of the Penn State saga. *International Journal of Sport Communication, 5*, 384–402.

Sanderson, J., Snyder, E., Hull, D., & Gramlich, K. (2015). Social media policies within NCAA member institutions: Evolving technology and its impact on policy. *Journal of Issues in Intercollegiate Athletics, 8*, 50–73.

Sanderson, J., & Truax, C. (2014). "I hate you man!": Exploring maladaptive parasocial interaction expressions to college athletes via Twitter. *Journal of Issues in Intercollegiate Athletics, 7*, 333–351.

Schmittel, A., & Sanderson, J. (2015). Talking about Trayvon in 140 characters: Exploring NFL players' tweets about the George Zimmerman verdict. *Journal of Sport & Social Issues, 39*, 332–345.

Schultz, B., & Sheffer, M.L. (2010). An exploratory study of how Twitter is affecting sports journalism. *International Journal of Sport Communication, 3*(2), 226–239.

Sheffer, M.L., & Schultz, B. (2010). Paradigm shift of passing fad? Twitter and sports journalism. *International Journal of Sport Communication, 3*(4), 472–484.

Smith, C. (February 18, 2015). What do Rivals.com's 6th grade profiles mean for the recruiting industry? *USA Today*. Retrieved July 1, 2016, from http://usatodayhss. com/2015/rivals-com-is-now-officially-tracking-6th-grade-football-prospects.

Smith, L.R., & Sanderson, J. (2015). I'm going to Instagram it! An analysis of athlete self-presentation on Instagram. *Journal of Broadcasting & Electronic Media, 59*(2), 342–358.

Spies-Gans, J. (September 25, 2015). Female reporters threatened with violence for reporting on Patrick Kane allegations. *Huffington Post*. Retrieved July 1, 2016, from http://www.huffingtonpost.com/entry/julie-dicaro-twitter-threats-patrick-kane_5605b532e4b0af3706dc5210.

Stefanik-Sidener, K. (2013). Nature, nurture, or that fast food hamburger: Media framing of diabetes in the *New York Times* from 2000–2010. *Health Communication, 28*(4), 351–358.

Steinberg, D. (April 7, 2015). Wisconsin fans hurl insults at Maryland recruit Diamond Stone. *Washington Post*. Retrieved July 1, 2016, from https://www.washingtonpost. com/news/dc-sports-bog/wp/2015/04/07/wisconsin-fans-hurl-insults-at-maryland-recruit-diamond-stone/.

Suggs Jr., D.W. (2015). Valuing the media: Access and autonomy as functions of legitimacy for journalists. *International Journal of Sport Communication, 8*(1), 46–67.

Suggs, Jr., D.W. (2016). Tensions in the press box: Understanding relationships among sports media and source organizations. *Communication & Sport, 4*, 261–281.

Vann, P. (2014) Changing the game: The role of social media in overcoming old media's attention deficit toward women's sport. *Journal of Broadcasting & Electronic Media, 58*, 438–455.

Weathers, M., Sanderson, J., Matthey, P., Grevious, A., Tehan, M., & Warren, S. (2014). The tweet life of Erin and Kirk: A gendered analysis of sports broadcasters' self-presentation on Twitter. *Journal of Sports Media, 9*(2), 1–24.

Wenner, L.A. (2014). Much ado (or not) about Twitter? Assessing an emergent communication and sport research agenda. *Communication & Sport, 2*, 103–106.

Yoder, M. (May 23, 2014). It was not a good idea for the Ravens to live tweet Ray Rice's press conference. Retrieved July 1, 2016, from http://awfulannouncing.com/2014/it-was-not-a-good-idea-for-the-ravens-to-live-tweet-ray-rices-press-conference.html.

20

SPORT AND GAMING STUDIES

Video Games as an Arena for Sport Communication Scholarship

Nicholas D. Bowman

WEST VIRGINIA UNIVERSITY

Andy Boyan

ALBION COLLEGE

Sport media has always been primarily aimed toward closing the distance between the spectator and the on-screen action (cf. Bowman & Cranmer, 2014). From the first-wired reports of prizefights in London for an eager (and still British) American Colonial population to KDKA Pittsburgh's first live radio broadcast of Major League Baseball (a 1921 contest between the Pittsburgh Pirates and the Philadelphia Phillies) to the online streaming of the 2008 Beijing Games via NBCOlympics.com, sport media have substantially advanced in providing spectators with seemingly unprecedented access to the field of play. Social media technologies have extended this access to the locker room (Pegoraro, 2010; Frederick, Lim, Clavio, & Walsh, 2012; Bowman, 2013), and fantasy sport play (Bowman, Spinda, & Sanderson, 2016) have given fans some modicum of involvement into their favorite players and teams—albeit indirectly (i.e. no action control).

However, in all of these forms, spectator involvement has been inherently passive: no amount of exertion or exaltation on behalf of the fan has impacted the on-field action or performance of their favorite (or despised) athletes and teams. It is here that *sport video games*—video games simulating organized sport—provide a unique space among sport media, as they provide a space for intense agency, immersion, and involvement with on-screen sport action.

Sport video games are incredibly popular—games in the sport genre made up over 13% of the $15.4 billion dollars in digital game sales in 2014 (Entertainment Software Association, 2015)—but neither games scholars nor sport communication scholars have devoted much attention to studying this genre and its audience. In the face of this scholarship dearth, it seems many relationships that fans develop with teams or sport have ties to their sport gameplay—and vice versa. While exact relationships are unclear, it seems that sport video games offer a useful platform for investigating a number of sport communication research questions. Thus, we offer guidance on the intersection of gaming studies and sport communication by (a) offering a typology of sport games, (b) providing an overview of the player demographics of these games, and (c) suggesting points of departure for studying games as sport communication.

Video Games as Inherent (Sporting) Competition

Before exploring the different types of sport video games, we suggest that video games align nicely with the core competition and challenge/skill elements of sport. Video games are best understood as ludic interfaces (cf. Huizinga, 1938): human–computer interactions involving a human player engaging a computer input bound by a logic and rules system. In this way, video games and sporting contents are nearly isomorphic. Just as Super Mario Bros. requires players to advance from left to right while avoiding contact with enemies, an American football contest requires players to advance an inflated leather bladder from 'north' to 'south' while avoiding a determined defense; neither Mario nor Richard Sherman are allowed to leave the field of play, and, at critical junctures, both 'characters' are required to either avoid or encounter their enemies. In this way, the primary gratifications sought when playing video games are challenge and competition (Sherry, Lucas, Greenberg, & Lachlan, 2006) and that video games foster a sense of autonomy and competence (Tamborini, Bowman, Eden, Grizzard, & Organ, 2010).

One of the earliest commercially successful video games was also the first sport video game: PONG. Released in late 1972 in public venues such as bars and other adult recreational areas, PONG was a table-tennis simulation. With the success of PONG—which also became one of the very first home video game consoles—other sport-themed video games began to enter the market. Fast forward to 2014, and we see a video game industry generating $15.4 billion in sales worldwide. Of this, over 13% of these sales were spawned from sport video games (Entertainment Software Association, 2015), and three sport titles— Madden NFL 15, NBA 2K15, and FIFA 15—ranked numbers 2, 7, and 9 in total platform sales, respectively (Te, 2015).

A Typology of Sport Video Games

Understanding video games as inherently sporting pursuits helps highlight semantically common elements between games and sport, but it also explains why many video games are built around simulating many popular (and not-so-popular) sports. A few of the more popular types of sport video games are discussed below.

Racing and Driving Games

Building from the popularity of PONG, some of the first sport simulation video games attempted to replicate familiar sports and behaviors, such as driving. Such games benefitted from tapping into existing mental models individuals already had for competitions (similar rules, goals, etc.; Boyan & Sherry, 2011). The release of Speed Race in 1974 by Japanese manufacturer Taito introduced several innovative technologies, including the use of an authentic racing steering wheel, gas and brake pedals, gearshift, and a tachometer to help immerse players in the racing experience. Such naturally mapped controllers (McGloin, Farrar, & Krcmar, 2011; McGloin, Farrar, & Fishlock, 2015) take advantage of the mental models players associate with driving, which, when combined with their innate knowledge of racing rules and goals (to finish first, to not wreck one's car, etc.) result in easily accessible gaming experiences. The basic components of Speed Race have been emulated and evolved in 40-plus years since the game's release, with modern-day racing games including more realistic graphics, more sophisticated control interfaces (including some games with working manual transmission systems), and a variety of vehicles. Racing games continue to be among the staples of sport games—including a number of NASCAR and related sport licenses.

Madden and the 'Big Four' (+FIFA)

In June 1988, Electronic Arts founder Trip Hawkins released what would become one of the most influential video games in the history of the medium. Simply called *Madden* by fans, John Madden Football was initially released as the first American football simulation to feature 11 players on each side of the ball (a remarkable feat, given limitations on computer processing at the time). Madden's 11-on-11 play featured authentic plays (based on Madden's personal playbooks during his tenure as head coach of the NFL's Oakland Raiders) and set standards for realism and representation among the genre. While Madden represents perhaps the most successful video game franchise originating from the 'Big Four' U.S. sports—football, baseball, basketball, and hockey—Electronic Arts, under the EA Sports label, replicated the success of Madden with the Triple Play baseball series (1996–2002, replaced by MVP Baseball until a licensing agreement halted the franchise in 2005), the NBA Live basketball games (1995 to present, including a series of NBA games as far back as 1989), and the NHL Hockey series (1991 to present). Other titles based on 'Big Four' leagues have also had critical acclaim and sales success, such as games based on collegiate sport. However, in recent years the National Collegiate Athletic Association (NCAA) licensed games have been suspended because of litigation between the NCAA and former players who claim that those games unfairly used players' names and likenesses without compensation (Rovell, 2013)—litigation that resulted in the tentative approval of a $60 million settlement between college athletes and both the NCAA and EA (McGuire, 2015).

Outside the Big Four is the most popular sport entity in the world—the Fédération Internationale de Football Association, or FIFA. Perhaps unsurprisingly given the worldwide popularity of soccer, the FIFA franchise is also the most popular sport video game franchise of all time; surpassing the 100 million sales mark in the sales period from 1993 to 2010 (Business Wire, 2010) and some (Badenhausen, 2014) claim that the franchise's unexpected success in the United States is partly responsible for increased U.S. interest in soccer.

'Alternative' Sport Video Game Titles

Perhaps fitting for the Generation X movement that embraced alternative rock music and flannel fashion (Pickert, 2009), 1995 saw ESPN offering financial and media support for the first X Games. Parallel to this, the 1990s saw a number of sport video games embracing snowboarding (Coolboarders for the Sony PlayStation) and skateboarding (Tony Hawk's Pro Skater, released on several platforms) among other 'extreme sports.' Tony Hawk games are known for capturing the essence of street skateboarding, allowing players to skate various venues—from shopping malls to skateparks—as one of several professional skaters. The original Tony Hawk game was among the highest-rated on the Sony PlayStation One, lauded for capturing "the pure grit and radical feel of skateboarding" (Perry, 1999).

Career and Management Simulations

Although some of the above-listed games often have developed career modes in which players can take charge of their favorite athletes and teams over multiple seasons of play, the core of these games is the action of the sport itself. That is, most sport video games are chiefly concerned with replicating on-field action. However, some franchises have merged elements of popular sports with elements of other video game genres, such as simulation and role play. Regarding simulation video games, some of the more popular video game simulation franchises include Sid Meier's Civilization and EA's Sim City. In both games (and countless clones), players take charge as the 'head' of an entity—and make strategic decisions to grow it.

One of the earliest sport simulation games was Football Manager (McFerran, 2015). Football Manager started as a board game before migrating to a computer environment to outsource the more complicated calculations and probability models to a machine. Unlike action sport games, players do not actually control on-field play. Rather, players immerse themselves in the role of general manager, making lineup decisions and developing game plans before adapting these during 'live' action—possibly making changes to both (including trading and releasing players) between matches. In this way, the game automatically generates gameplay results, with earlier versions scrolling 'live' text printouts of match results and later versions allowing players to watch the matches in real-time using photo-realistic graphics. Such simulations allow players an unprecedented amount of control over the professional sport being managed, providing players control of everything from player salaries and training to concession prices and contract negotiations (cf. Spinda, 2016).

Simulation elements have found their way into more action and on-field oriented video games, such as the Madden series as well as Sony Entertainment's MLB: The Show franchise. The allure of these games is thought to be in part their faithful replication of on-screen gameplay combined with fantasy role-play elements similar to famous role-playing video games, such as The Legend of Zelda and the Final Fantasy series: players take control of their own avatar to vicariously experience a simulated fantasy environment—in this case, the road to professional athletics by way of training their player, earning a starting roster spot, and securing a place in sport history through their own Hall of Fame-worthy performances, albeit digitally.

Arcade Sport Games

While the first two types of games tend to attempt a good deal of authenticity in representing the sport, for many players video games are meant to be an accessible diversion. That is, partly what makes video games attractive is that they can provide flavors of an experience without completely replicating all of mundane elements of that experience—the attraction of the classic Windows-based Solitaire game is that the computer shuffles, deals, organizes, and counts the cards for the player, and the attractiveness of many sport-themed video games is that one can play or simulate a hockey or curling game without having to suit up, stretch, and take the ice. Game designers such as Posey (2013) explain that a core element of successful video games is they offer authentic in-game experiences by highlighting the more entertaining aspects of an activity while filtering out elements that might be less exciting.

To sport purists, games such as Arch-Rivals (a basketball game loosely inspired by the 1988–90 Detroit Pistons teams, in which players are allowed to punch each other in order to defend their goal) and NFL Blitz (a passing-oriented football game in which 30 yards were required for a first down and defenders would commonly elbow and leg drop onto turbo-boosted ball-carriers), might be seen as aberrations, showcasing only the basic (and even controversial) elements of sport. For example, the NBA Jam franchise—first released in arcades by Midway in 1993 before being emulated on several home console systems—featured a particular brand of two-on-two basketball play in which players used NBA licenses and teams (as well as former presidents—if they knew the code) while slam-dunking from half-court, hitting consecutive three-pointers until the basketball nets literally caught fire (to the announcer's scream of "He's on fire!"), and sinking bonus shots from colored areas of the court worth as much as nine points. Such games were immensely popular; by 1994, NBA Jam had earned over $1 billion in revenues from the arcade units alone (Leone, n.d.).

Sport-Inspired Fantasy Games

Many video games borrow from the traditions of science fiction and fantasy (not statistics-based fantasy sport)—indeed, elves, dragons, aliens, and teleportation are mainstays in contemporary video game culture. Notably for sport video games, many of these fantastical concepts can also be found in those games that borrow 'flavors' of popular sport, and often create wildly fantastic narratives and scenarios around common sport content. Important for this discussion, games in the fantasy theme tend to invent their own teams, league, and sport entities (even inventing their own sports) rather than borrowing from established sport brands.

In September 1993, EA Sports released a version of their Madden 93 game with the title Mutant League Football, and substituted monsters and goblins for the more popular NFL faces of the time—for example "Bones Jackson" in place of multi-sport Oakland Raiders running back Bo Jackson and "Scary Ice" in place of Hall of Fame San Francisco 49ers receiver Jerry Rice. Gameplay largely follows standard rules of professional NFL football, but with several fantasy elements, such as landmines and fire pits scattered across the playing field. These games could be won in a more traditional way (scoring more points than one's opponent) or a more gruesome one (murdering enough of the other players' teammates to force them to forfeit the game).

While the impetus for many sport-fantasy games may have been to sidestep formal licensing agreements with professional leagues and/or embellish or expand upon the rigid rules of recognizable organized sport, such agreements were not as important for other types of fantasy contests, such as racing games. Games such as F-Zero featured futuristic space races in which opponents literally rocketed around closed-circuit tracks, nudging each other into explosive fields to claim the top podium, and Rock & Roll Racing, which featured ghouls and goblins racing to the tune of popular 1970s and 1980s rock music. Finally, Nintendo and the characters from the Super Mario Bros. franchise have been featured racing (Mario Kart) as well as playing tennis (Mario Tennis), basketball (Mario Hoops 3-on-3), baseball (Mario Super Baseball), and even challenging rival video game properties and characters in a simulation of the Olympic Games (Mario & Sonic at the Olympic Games for the 2008 Summer Olympics in Beijing).

Natural Mapping and Virtual Reality Sport Games

Advances in user-interface technology such as naturally mapped and sensory-immersive technologies have resulted in video game experiences designed to invoke strong feelings of presence in gamers (Skalski, Tamborini, Shelton, Buncher, & Lindmark, 2011; McGloin, Farrar, & Krcmar, 2010). Natural mapping has been part of sport video games almost from the beginning, as a good example of such an interface would be the steering wheel and brake/gas pedal combination in Speed Race. Here, the control system shared a near-perfect correspondence with the analogous real-world activity. However, advancements in control systems that take advantage of the natural human perceptual system (Biocca, 1997) have allowed gamers to engage in a number of physically simulated sports from the comfort of their homes. Although not the first to take advantage of such technology, Nintendo's Wii Sports was one of the most commercially and critically successful games that engaged this technology. First released in November 2006, the game utilized Nintendo Wii's motion-sensor controllers so players could go bowling, play tennis, play baseball (pitching and hitting), try a golf course, or box each other all while mimicking the physical actions of each of these sports.

However, many self-identified sport gamers might not consider games such as Wii Sports (the number one selling videogame of all time, VGChartz.com) to be bona fide sport games, as they only tangentially model the action of sport and they do not have licenses or partnerships with known sport brands (Stein, Mitgutsch, & Consalvo, 2012). Research into motion-sensor and virtual reality type sport games (Pasch, Bianchi-Berthouze, van Dijk, & Nijholt, 2009) found that two main motivators for playing movement-based sport video games were for challenge and competition reasons (achievement) and for relaxation. The authors also reported that elements of natural control, movement mimicry, proprioceptive feedback (information about neighboring parts of the body), and physical challenge were most related to increased immersion in these games. Notably, none of these motivations are particularly aligned with the sport content of these games—lending credence to Stein et al.'s (2012) findings that many sport gamers disregard movement-based sport games as being 'legitimate' sport games.

Natural mapping and virtual reality sport games with brand partnerships have gained popularity. EA Sports partnered with Tiger Woods as part of their PGA Tour franchise, and the 2012 release of this game for the Sony PlayStation 3 was bundled with the PlayStation Move system—a motion-tracking controller system operating similarly to the Wiimote; the 2013 release for the Microsoft X-Box featured similar motion-tracking compatibility with that system's Kinect peripheral. Notably, motion-capture and other kinesic natural mapped devices (Skalski et al., 2011) were not new to the Wii: in the 1990s, the SEGA Genesis had both a motion-sensor golf controller (the TeeV, essentially a 26-inch golf club with an infrared sensor at the base) and baseball bat (the BatterUP, a 24-inch foam-and-plastic bat wired to the Genesis console) for home sport fans, and both were compatible with many popular game titles.

Advances in gaming technology have largely been followed with advances in virtual immersion—and sport video games are often viewed as a proving ground for these technologies, in large part (and as referenced earlier in this chapter) because they deal with familiar activities. As part of the 2015 US Open tennis tournament, headline sponsor American Express developed a head-mounted display allowing fans to experience a 100-mile-per-hour serve from the racket of Maria Sharapova—offering them a chance to virtually return the serve (Zaldivar, 2015).

Who Plays Sport Video Games?

As highlighted earlier in this chapter, sport-themed video games continue to be important to the video game market: they are among the highest-grossing video game titles, just over one in ten video game titles released is sport-related, and (while not the focus of this chapter) video games have become spectator sports with the rise of professional e-sports. Yet, one observation made by Stein et al. (2012) is that sport gamers tend to be younger, less racially diverse (largely Caucasian), and predominantly male as compared with the larger population of gamers as reported by the Entertainment Software Association (ESA, 2015), which reports the average gamer age to be 35 years old, with 56% of game players being male. One reason offered for this discrepancy is that the ESA numbers as reported do not consider genre-specific demographics. For example, Nielsen (2009) reports that players of casual games tend to be female players who self-identify as light video game players, while players of other genres such as shooters and role-playing games tend to be more male and play for longer periods of time. These genre-specific demographic breakdowns are somewhat replicated in some of the conventions of these games, such as casual games featuring more female main characters and protagonists (Wohn, 2011), contrasted with the majority of sport video games, which often share licenses with male athletes and leagues. Notably, these breakdowns seem to be changing as more men enter the casual games market (Casual Games Association, 2015) and famous franchises such as EA Sports' FIFA 16 have begun to include prominent professional and amateur female athletes (Eisenband, 2015).

However, the way the players engage with the game should be of interest to sport communication scholarship. Stein et al.'s (2012) survey reveals that 93.5% of respondents self-identified as general sport fans, and 76.4% of respondents were able to indicate what professional or amateur team they support. Such data suggests that sport fans are extending their sport fandom into the video game realm, suggesting that sport gamers are a desirable target for fandom scholars. The study also found that sport gamers are also audiences of a variety of sport entertainment content: 95% watch sport on television regularly, 81.4% of respondents attended a live sporting event as a spectator in the past year, and 74.6% participate in athletic sport activities. Many of these behaviors are considered behavioral indicators of strong fan avidity (DeSarbo & Madrigal, 2011), suggesting sport gaming to be an important feature of fandom. Conway (2010) found such evidence with players of Pro Evolution Soccer 2008 (a management simulation-style game), finding that players see the interactions and play time of the game as one part of a larger fan identity in their passion for soccer.

Examining the uses and gratifications of sport games, Kim and Ross (2006) found seven primary motivations for playing: knowledge application, identification with sport, fantasy, competition, entertainment, social interaction, and diversion—notably this list offers a number of unique gratifications associated with sport gaming not part of Sherry et al.'s (2006). In a later study, Kim, Walsh, and Ross (2008) confirmed that sport gamers consumed other sport media and tended to have stronger connections with favorite teams, but the data also suggested that sport gamers over the age of 40 played with their children and families as a bonding experience, providing a unique segment of video game players more in line with traditional cross-generation sport fandom.

Sport Games Applied to Sport Communication Scholarship

While studying video games requires some knowledge of their intricacies and specific functions to be able to utilize them properly in research, using games in sport communication research could provide a fertile and friendly ground for examining questions related to variables common to sport communication. A few such examples are offered below.

Fandom, Identity, and Narrative

As found by Kim and Ross (2006) and Kim et al. (2008), at least one reason players engage with sport video games is as an expression of identity. Playing sport games gives fans the opportunity to intensely identify with their favorite players and teams by allowing gamers to take complete control of the athletes/ teams, whether it be for a single gaming session played alone or as part of a season- or career-long gaming simulation (Conway, 2010). Sport gamers can also take their contests online, engaging other players (and, ostensibly, their favorite players and teams) while representing their fandom in a public digital space—newer games even allow the opportunity to share the results of these contests via social media. Sport games often offer players a variety of customizable options—such as creating players and editing existing teams, as well as configuring games to display a favorite player or team's likeness. Kwak, Clavio, Eagleman, and Kim (2010) found that players engaging in this customization spent more time playing, were more satisfied with, and enjoyed video games more. The extent to which these effects might transfer to actual sport properties would be a potentially profitable line of inquiry for marketers and scholars alike.

Identity and fandom could also be examined through the lens of player-avatar interactions (Banks & Bowman, 2016) to understand the different types of orientations that players might take with their on-screen athletes. For example, avid sport fans might approach these avatars with an 'Avatar-as-Me' orientation (if striving for a sense of personal connection with the sport) or an 'Avatar-as-Other' orientation (if striving for a sense of kinship with the on-screen players). Taken further, we might connect these different identification scenarios with elements of the well-known basking in reflected glory/cutting off reflected failure paradigm—the BIRGing and CORFing phenomena (Cialdini et al., 1976) by which fans (notably, sport fans) attach themselves to successful events and detach from unsuccessful ones. A compelling line of research might be the extent to which video game players—especially those playing to fulfill a high sense of identity with their favorite sports—might react to their own video game performance, such as winning or losing with their favorite athletes and teams, both in terms of short-term and long-term effects on fandom.

Fandom and identity can also include a sociocultural understanding of sporting events and other contexts. Crawford and Gosling (2009) argue that the interactive narrative arc of sport-themed video games provides players with a sense of identity and social understanding in their own lives, even beyond that of the video game. While on the surface sport games seem to be about representing simulations of sport, Crawford and Gosling (2009) argue that the open interpretation of narrative in games makes them a useful place for a different type of narrative, such as one in which the player is living out a social fantasy. The research provides an audience use-centered approach to examining the role of gratifications of playing sport video games. Another way of looking at games as sport narratives comes from Baerg (2012), who conducted a textual analysis of NBA 2K12 examining how the game represents a relationship with history, finding that the game represents history as a space of interpretive possibility rather than established factual occurrences—for example, the game allows players to play as past NBA legends and teams as a way to relive (and possibly rewrite) NBA history.

Sport video games might also be a useful tool for introducing audiences to newer sports. As alluded to earlier, games such as FIFA might be particularly useful at teaching gamers about sports that they might not be intimately familiar with, which could in turn drive potential interest in these sports. Reflecting on work by Billings (2008) and the Olympic Games, one approach taken by broadcasters attempting to fuel interest is to borrow from conventions of Hollywood drama—for example, framing athletes as protagonists and antagonists in order to model contests as entertainment media rather than sport media. Given that video games are inherently learning environments (Gee, 2007), one could learn a great deal about the complexities of a given sport by playing video games based on the same.

Social and Minority Media Portrayals

Sport video games present the same unique context as real sport when it comes to examining underrepresented populations in the mass media. Sport video games are one of the few places in media where racial minorities constitute the majority of the main characters (Williams, Consalvo, Caplan, & Yee, 2009). Race and gender representations have commonly been studied within the contexts of sport, given the social implications of how minority athletes have been traditionally portrayed through the mass media. For example, research has shown that newspaper coverage of Heisman trophy candidates tends to frame black athletes in terms of their athleticism (regardless of their intelligence) and white athletes in terms of their perceived leadership (regardless of their athletic ability; Cranmer, Bowman, Chory, & Weber, 2014). This work was replicated using a sport video game (NCAA Football, 2013); results showed that when players were given a news article about a black student-athlete, they were significantly more likely to run with the football than when reading about white student-athletes (Cranmer, Bowman, & Goldman, in press). Future work might consider using video games as observational measures of the retention or re-enactment of themes common to sport coverage framing, but might also more generally consider how exposure to interactive minority portrayals might alter how audiences take up and are influenced by these issues. Regarding gender, video games are already a medium lambasted for its negatively stereotypical portrayals of women (e.g. Sarkeesian, 2013); it is unlikely that sport video games contain many female portrayals at all—at least, not as on-field participants. Given evidence that women are often sexualized in sport media broadly (Bernstein, 2002), understanding these representations in video games could prove insightful.

Sport Video Games and Communication Theory

There are a number of areas of theory development that sport video games offer to sport communication scholarship, beyond those areas already discussed to this point in the chapter. Perhaps at the broadest level, scholars should aim to understand where sport video games fit into Wenner's (1989) transactional model of media sport and society relationships. Sport video games offer a particularly unique opportunity for scholars to study a form of sport media that is interactive: by design, video games actively and directly involve the player in co-creating and experiencing the on-screen content (Bowman, 2016). This element of co-created interactive content has a number of implications for how sport video games might be examined through the lens of sport communication.

Extending on their interactive nature, video games bring a unique aspect to the transactional nature of sport media in that the audience/player is effectively an on-field participant, able to manifest themselves within the digital competition (Tamborini & Skalski, 2006). Such a shift from passive audience to active player is somewhat addressed in literature on fantasy sport (Bowman et al., 2016), but even in fantasy sport contests fans are still observing rather than engaging on-field action. This shift from viewer to (inter)active player invites future research into areas such as fandom and fan identity, including both how players might use games as an expression of fandom (DeSarbo & Madrigal, 2011) and how gameplay impacts identity formation as a fan (Wann, 2006). Notably, many video game players report playing for fantasy is a motivation for gameplay (Sherry et al., 2006). In sport video games this comes in the form of playing as one's favorite team and winning, even when one's team in reality is not in a position to win consistently. On the other hand, when the player is responsible for a team's performance, classic sport media theories of basking in reflected glory and cutting off reflected failure may take on new meanings (Cialdini et al., 1976; Wann, 2006).

One particularly interesting element of video games is that they allow players to control teams and players not of their own culture, and for substantial amounts of time (Gee, 2007). Applied for example to playing as (or against) foreign teams, one might examine how nationalistic identity formations are impacted when players engage in active play compared with watching (Billings et al., 2013). For example, the fact that the U.S. women's national soccer team is among the 30 most popular teams selected among the 600-plus licensed franchises in FIFA 16 (Eisenband, 2015) suggests that the 100 million-plus FIFA players are more accepting towards female sport than might be assumed on first blush.

Discourse analyses among sport gamers playing online could reveal compelling patterns of interaction between sport fans (Boyan, Westerman, & Daniel, 2016), such as the emergence of gender as a salient and often toxic social identity cue (Ivory, Fox, Waddell, & Ivory, 2014)—especially given the central role that gender and sex roles have played in sport communication research (cf. Lavelle, 2015). Work focused on the sport entities themselves—athletes, teams, leagues, and other organizations—might look to see the role that sport video games play as part of the presentation of sport, both as a marketing device as well as a fan experience. Finally, as seen in the case of the NCAA and associated video games, issues of economic, political, and social capital can also be analyzed in terms of representation and labor.

Conclusions and Future Research Perspectives

The prominence and popularity of sport video games has not been reflected in current scholarship in either game studies or sport communication. We suggest that (a) game scholars tend to consider sport games as nonrepresentative of the sort of action and fantasy games that typify the medium and (b) sport communication scholars tend to classify video games as an entertainment technology rather than a bona fide part of the sport media landscape. With this in mind, the current chapter was designed to merge perspectives by defining sport video games as representative of sport media, identifying the different types of sport video games common to the genre, and offering a few points of practical and theoretical departure for sport communication scholars. It is clear that for some individuals, sport games are an integral part of sport fandom, sport media, and effects commonly associated with sport content—and we look forward to sport video games being promoted to the 'big leagues' of sport communication scholarship.

References

Badenhausen, K. (June 13, 2014). EA Sports' FIFA video game helps fuel interest in the World Cup. *Forbes.com*. Retrieved July 5, 2016, from http://www.forbes.com/sites/kurtbadenhausen/2014/07/13/ea-sports-fifa-video-game-helps-fuel-interest-in-the-world-cup/.

Baerg, A. (2012). Digital hoops history: NBA 2K12 and remediating basketball's past. *Communication and Sport, 1*, 365–381.

Banks, N.D., & Bowman, N.D. (2016). Emotion, anthropomorphism, realism, control: Validation of a merged metric for player-avatar interaction (PAX). *Computers in Human Behavior, 54*, 215–223. doi: 10.1016/j.chb.2015.07.030.

Bernstein, A. (2002). Is it time for a victory lap? Changes in the media coverage of women in sport. *International Review for the Sociology of Sport, 37*(3–4), 415–428. doi: 10.1177/101269020203700301.

Billings, A.C. (2008). *Olympic media: Inside the biggest show on television*. New York: Routledge.

Biocca, F. (1997). The cyborg's dilemma: Progressive embodiment in virtual environments. *Journal of Computer-Mediated Communication, 3*(2). doi: 10.1111/j.1083-6101.1997.tb00070.x. Retrieved July 5, 2016, from http://onlinelibrary.wiley.com/doi/10.1111/j.1083-6101.1997.tb00070.x/abstract.

Bowman, N.D. (2013). Social media, spaghetti westerns, and modern spectator sports. In D. Coombs & B. Batchelor (Eds.), *American history through American sports* (Vol. 3, pp. 31–48). Santa Barbara, CA: Praeger.

Bowman, N.D. (2016). Video gaming as co-production. In R. Lind (Ed.), *Produsing 2.0: The intersection of audiences and production in a digital world* (Vol. 2, pp. 107–123). New York: Peter Lang.

Bowman, N.D., & Cranmer, G. (2014). SocialMediaSport: Theoretical implications for the reified relationship between spectator and performer. In A. Billings and M. Hardin (Eds.), *Handbook of sport and new media* (pp. 213–234). London: Routledge.

Bowman, N.D., Spinda, J.S., & Sanderson, J. (2016). *Fantasy sports and the changing sports media industry*. Lanham, MD: Rowman & Littlefield.

Boyan, A., & Sherry, J.L. (2011). The challenge in creating games for education: Aligning mental models with game models. *Child Development Perspectives, 5*(2), 82–87.

Boyan, A., Westerman, D.K., & Daniel, S.E. (2016). Rooting with your rivals: Social presence in fantasy sports. In N.D. Bowman, J.S.W. Spinda, & J. Sanderson (Eds.), *Fantasy sports: Perspectives from the fields*. Lanham, MD: Rowman & Littlefield.

Business Wire. (November 4, 2010). *EA Sports FIFA soccer franchise sales top 100 million units lifetime*. Retrieved July 5, 2016, from http://www.businesswire.com/news/home/20101104006782/en#.VeOS-PZViko.

Casual Games Association. (2015). *Smartphone & table gaming 2013: Games market segment report*. Retrieved July 5, 2016, from http://issuu.com/casualconnect/docs/cga_market_report_fall2013/5?e=2336319/6014071.

Cialdini, R.B., Borden, R.J., Thorne, A., Walker, M.R., Freeman, S., & Sloan, L.R. (1976). Basking in reflected glory: Three (football) field studies. *Journal of Personality and Social Psychology, 34*, 366–375.

Conway, S. (2010). "It's in the game" and above the game: An analysis of the users of sports videogames. *Convergence, 16*, 334–354.

Cranmer, G., Bowman, N.D., Chory, R., & Weber. K. (2014). Race as an antecedent condition in the framing of Heisman finalists. *Howard Journal of Communication, 25*(2), 171–191.

Cranmer, G. A., Bowman, N.D., & Goldman, Z.W. (In press). *A preliminary study of racialized brawn and brain framing effects.* Communication Research Reports.

Crawford, G., & Gosling, V.K. (2009). More than a game: Sports-themed video games and player narratives. *Sociology of Sport Journal, 26*, 50–66.

DeSarbo, W.S., & Madrigal, R. (2011). Examining the behavioral manifestations of fan avidity in sports marketing. *Journal of Modelling in Management, 6*(1), 79–99. doi: 10.1108/17465661111112511.

Eisenband, J. (November 25, 2015). U.S. women's team is big hit on "FIFA 16". *The Postgame.com.* Retrieved July 5, 2016, from http://www.thepostgame.com/futures port/201511/uswnt-ea-sports-fifa-16-alex-morgan-heather-oreilly-becky-sauerbrunn.

Entertainment Software Association. (2015). Essential facts about the computer and video game industry. *ESA.com.* Retrieved September 1, 2015, from http://www. theesa.com/wp-content/uploads/2015/04/ESA-Essential-Facts-2015.pdf.

Frederick, E.L., Lim, C.H., Clavio, G., & Walsh, P. (2012). Why we follow: An examination of parasocial interaction and fan motivations for following athlete archetypes on Twitter. *International Journal of Sport Communication, 5*, 481–502.

Gee, J. (2007). *What video games have to teach us about learning and literacy.* New York: Palgrave Macmillan.

Huizinga, J. (1938). *Homo ludens: Vom ursprung der kultur im spiel. [Homo ludens: From the origin of culture in play].* Reinbek, Germany: Rowohlt Verlag.

Ivory, A.H., Fox, J., Waddell, T., & Ivory, J.D. (2014). Sex role stereotyping is hard to kill: A field experiment measuring social responses to user characteristics and behavior in an online multiplayer first-person shooter game. *Computers in Human Behavior, 35*, 148–156. doi: 10.1016/j.chb.2014.02.026.

Kim, Y., & Ross, S.D. (2006). An exploration of motives in sport video gaming. *International Journal of Sports Marketing & Sponsorship, 8*(1), 34.

Kim, Y., Walsh, P., & Ross, S.D. (2008). An examination of the psychological and consumptive behaviors of sport video gamers. *Sport Marketing Quarterly, 17*, 44–53.

Kwak, D.H., Clavio, G.E., Eagleman, A.N., & Kim, K.T. (2010). Exploring the antecedents and consequences of personalizing sport video game experiences. *Sport Marketing Quarterly, 19*, 217–225.

Lavelle, K.L. (2015). As Venus turns: A feminist soap opera analysis of *Venus Vs. Journal of Sports Media, 10*(2), 1–16. doi: 10.1353/jsm.2015.0010.

Leone, M. (n.d.). The rise, fall, and return of NBA Jam. *1up.com.* Retrieved July 5, 2016, from http://www.1up.com/features/rise-fall-return-nba-jam.

McFerran, D. (18 February, 2015). The great history of the football manager sim. *Redbull.com.* Retrieved July 5, 2016, from http://www.redbull.com/us/en/games/ stories/1331705823377/the-history-of-the-football-manager-sim.

McGloin, R., Farrar K., & Fishlock, J. (2015). Violent games and violent controllers: Investigating the use of realistic gun controllers on perceptions of realism, immersion, and outcome aggression. *Journal of Communication.* doi: 10.1111/jcom.12148.

McGloin, R., Farrar, K., & Krcmar, M. (2011). The impact of controller naturalness on spatial presence, gamer enjoyment, and perceived realism in a tennis simulation video game. *Presence: Teleoperators and Virtual Environments, 20*(4), 1–16.

McGuire, K. (July 17, 2015). Judge approves $60 million settlement in NCAA, EA Sports lawsuit. *NBCSports.com*. Retrieved July 5, 2016, from http://college footballtalk.nbcsports.com/2015/07/17/judge-approves-60-million-settlement-in-ncaa-ea-sports-lawsuit/

Nielsen. (August 2009). *Insights on casual games: Analysis of casual games for the PC.* Retrieved July 5, 2016, from http://www.nielsen.com/content/dam/corporate/us/en/newswire/uploads/2009/09/GamerReport.pdf

Pasch, M., Bianchi-Berthouze, N., van Dijk, B., & Nijholt, A. (2009). Movement-based sports video games: Investigating motivation and game experience. *Entertainment Computing, 1*, 49–61. doi: 10.1016/j.entcom.2009.09.004.

Pegoraro, A. (2010). Look who's talking—athletes on Twitter: A case study. *International Journal of Sport Communication, 3*, 501–514.

Perry, D. (1999, October 19). Tony Hawk's Pro Skater. *IGN.com*. Retrieved July 5, 2016, from http://www.ign.com/articles/1999/10/20/tony-hawks-pro-skater-10

Pickert, K. (2009, January 22). A brief history of the X Games. *Time.com*. Retrieved July 5, 2016, from http://content.time.com/time/nation/article/0,8599,1873166,00. html

Posey, J. (2013, March). *Tastes like chicken: Authenticity in a totally fake world.* Presentation at the Game Developers Conference, San Francisco.

Rovell, D. (2013, September 26). EA Sports settles with ex-players. *ESPN.com*. Retrieved July 5, 2016, from http://espn.go.com/college-football/story/_/id/9728042/ea-sports-stop-producing-college-football-game

Sarkeesian, A. (2013, March 7). Damsel in Distress: Part 1. *Tropes vs. Women in Video Games. [YouTube video series]*. Retrieved July 5, 2016, from https://www.youtube. com/watch?v=X6p5AZp7r_Q

Sherry, J., Lucas, K., Greenberg, B., & Lachlan, K. (2006). Video game uses and gratifications as predictors of use and game preference. In P. Vorderer & J. Bryant (Eds.), *Playing video games: Motives, responses, and consequences* (pp. 213–224). Mahwah, NJ: Lawrence Erlbaum Associates Publishers.

Skalski, P., Tamborini, R., Shelton, A., Buncher, M., & Lindmark, P. (2011). Mapping the road to fun: Natural video game controllers, presence, and game enjoyment. *New Media & Society, 13*(2), 224–242. doi: 10.1177/1461444810370949.

Spinda, J.S.W. (2016). Simulations as fantasy sports. In Bowman, N.D., Spinda, J.S.W., & Sanderson, J. (Eds.), *Fantasy sports: Perspectives from the fields*. Lanham, MD: Rowman & Littlefield.

Stein, A., Mitgutsch, K., & Consalvo, M. (2012). Who are sports gamers? A large scale study of sports video game players. *Convergence: The International Journal of Research Into New Media Technologies*, 1–19. doi: 10.1177/1354856512459840.

Tamborini, R., Bowman, N.D., Eden, A., Grizzard, M., & Organ, A. (2010). Defining media enjoyment as the satisfaction of intrinsic needs. *Journal of Communication, 60*(4), 758–777.

Tamborini, R., & Skalski, P. (2006). The role of presence in the experience of electronic games. In P. Vorderer & J. Bryant (Eds.), *Playing video games: Motives, responses, and consequences* (pp. 225–240). Mahwah, NJ: Lawrence Erlbaum Associates Publishers.

Te, Z. (January 15, 2015). Most-sold games of 2014 include GTA V, Call of Duty, and Super Smash Bros. *Gamespot.com*. Retrieved July 5, 2016, from www.gamespot.com/articles/most-sold-games-of-2014-include-gta-v-call-of-duty/1100-6424680.

VGChartz.com. (n.d.). Game database, best selling video games, game sales, million sellers, top selling—VGChartz. *VGChartz.com*. Retrieved September 1, 2015, from http://www.vgchartz.com/gamedb/.

Wann, D.L. (2006). The causes and consequences of sport team identification. In A.A. Raney & J. Bryant (Eds.), *Handbook of sports and media* (pp. 331–352). New York: Routledge.

Wenner, L.A. (1989). Media, sports, and society: The research agenda. In L.A. Wenner (Ed.), *Media, sports, and society* (pp. 13–48). Newbury Park, CA: Sage.

Williams, D., Consalvo, M., Caplan, S., & Yee, N. (2009). Looking for gender: Gender roles and behavior among online gamers. *Journal of Communication, 59*, 700–725.

Wohn, D.Y. (2011). Gender and race representation in casual games. *Sex Roles, 65*(3), 198–207.

Zaldivar, G. (August 18, 2015). Amazing technology allows fans to play tennis with Maria Sharapova at 2015 US Open. *Forbes.com*. Retrieved July 5, 2016, from http://www.forbes.com/sites/gabezaldivar/2015/08/18/amazing-technology-allows-fans-to-play-tennis-with-maria-sharapova-at-2015-us-open/.

21

SPORT AND ADVERTISING

Michael B. Devlin

DEPAUL UNIVERSITY

Sport is an expanding commodity, consumed in larger amounts each year—evident by revolving record-breaking television ratings (i.e., Women's World Cup finals in 2015, 2015 NBA finals, Super Bowl XLIX) and revenue generated by sport organizations and leagues (Badenhausen, 2015; Berkowitz, 2015). This increasing rate of sport consumption epitomizes an unprecedented form of capitalism, and sport's economic impact should not be underestimated, particularly as it relates to advertising. The value of sport is uniquely distinguished from other commodities because of its duality in relation to advertising. Sport utilizes advertising to promote its product while simultaneously offering an extension for other commodities to market themselves. Sport's multifaceted offerings provide unparalleled opportunities for advertising through traditional media (television and radio), digital media (online and social), as well as in-game sponsorships, team/player endorsements, and even stadium/event naming rights. Arguably, major televised sporting events offer DVR-proof television audiences, making sport an attractive draw for advertisers. Additionally, second-screen usage provides a new channel for advertisers to engage with audiences, thus new relationships between advertising and sport.

Wenner's 1989 seminal book, *Media, Sport, and Society*, discusses the transactional value of sport, and invites examination between dominant and emerging paradigms. As marketing practices continuously develop, and the relationship between sport, media, and society increasingly intertwine, gaining interest and acceptance into academic communities, so too should the study of advertising and sport. Maturing from antiquated transactional paradigms, relationship marketing theory acknowledges the existence of a deeper relationship between organizations and consumers, which influences loyalty, increases sales, and decreases costs (Kim & Trail, 2011; Mullin, Hardy, & Sutton, 2007). Building relationships rests on an organization's ability to segment audiences in ways that transcend age, race, and gender through psychographics providing deeper insights. Understanding the antecedents and effects of fan identification theory relative to relationship marketing may provide key insights that could help organizations build a deeper relationship with fans. Advertising research in both relationship marketing and fan identity has been conducted, providing a substantial framework to advance theory and practice for sport and advertising.

How Advertising Ties to Sport

Sport marketing encompasses an array of strategic marketing communication strategies, including—but not limited to—promotion, publicity, selling, public relations, *and* advertising. Advertising's role is limited to any paid, nonpersonal, clearly sponsored message conveyed through a media channel (Mullin et al., 2007) to create awareness, communicate benefits, develop brand reputation, change attitudes, and encourage behaviors (Batra, Myers, & Aaker, 1996). Advertising is an integral part of American capitalism, and "acknowledging the uniqueness of sport is necessary in order to understand how and why it is configured, and plays a role in configuring global consumer capitalism" (Jackson, 2015, p. 491). Sport as a commodity relies on advertising to promote the product, and its ability to concurrently serve advertising's needs undoubtedly makes sport "a powerful vehicle for transnational corporations and their allied advertising and promotional armatures" (Jackson & Andrews, 2005, p. 8).

Advertising the Sport Commodity

The division between sport as a game and sport as a business has not always been so indistinct. Early Olympic Games dating back to 776 BC were competitive displays between aristocrats and city-states, conducted as a dedication to the Olympic gods in ancient Greece (Kyle, 2014). However, modern times have witnessed the transformation of sport as a game to sport as a commodity, where homage is paid more to brands than gods. As Phil Schaaf (2004) writes in *Sports Inc.*:

> The main revenue streams for the Yankees in Babe Ruth's hey-day were simply tickets and concessions. Today the primary sources are tickets, national television contracts, local television contracts, cable television packages, radio rights, premium seating options, concessions, parking, licensing revenue, team sponsorships, global marketing agreements, and online revenue.
>
> *(p. 33)*

The approximate value of the entire sport industry in 2014 was $498.4 billion (Plunket Research, 2015). The National Football League (NFL) posted $11.2 billion in revenue in 2014 (Kaplan, 2015), Major League Baseball (MLB) reported approximately $9 billion in gross revenue (Brown, 2014), the National

Basketball Association (NBA) earned $4.8 billion in revenue, and the National Collegiate Athletic Association (NCAA) made nearly $1 billion in revenue in 2014 (Berkowitz, 2015). Revenues are combined through broadcast rights, tickets, licensing and merchandise, and sponsorship agreements, supporting the notion that sport has transitioned to a bundled product benefiting participants, spectators, sponsors, and media companies in order to fulfill business objectives (Shank, 1999).

Strategic marketing efforts have elevated sports from recreational pastime to the financial behemoth it is today, making advertising an integral fixture within the sports media and the sport promotional culture (Jackson, 2015). Each league and team attempts to separates themselves from competitors by identifying with traits appealing to audience segments and creating emotional bonds with fans in an effort to generate revenue through tickets, merchandise sales, and media fees (Mullin et al., 2007). Sport and society then capitalizes on the audience by using sport to promote other goods and services.

Sport as a Vehicle

Sport serves advertising's needs by providing space for lucrative television time, sponsorship integration, and impressionable endorsements; not only do these advertising opportunities yield financial revenue for media broadcasters, leagues, teams, and athletes, but advertising also yields abundant power in sport's decision-making process, such as scheduling broadcast times (integral to television advertising), dictating what city players will play in, and changing laws to financially support sponsor contracts.

Televised Promotion

Television networks pay high-dollar amounts for the broadcast rights for sporting events because of their ability to attract large audiences and key demographics appealing to advertisers. Advertisers are routinely charged, and pay, higher ad rates during televised sporting events because of the highly reliable audiences sport provides, creating a mutually beneficial relationship between television networks and advertisers. For example, the Super Bowl alone has generated a cumulative total of $2.19 billion worth of network advertising sales from 2005 through 2014 (Kantar Media, 2015). A brief examination of national TV ad spending during the 2014 post-season (playoffs) reveals approximately $3.8 billion was spent on advertising between the NFL, NCAA March Madness, NBA, MLB, NCAA Bowl Games, and NHL (Kondolojy, 2015). Bi-annual mega events such as the Olympics also garner lucrative advertising opportunities. The 2010 Vancouver Olympics generated $809 million in ad revenue across broadcast and cable networks by providing 4,288 advertising ad minutes (excluding network promotional advertising) (Kantar Media, 2014).

Television networks also look to secure broadcast rights for sporting events largely because of the opportunity to promote the television network's lineup. The relationship between sport and television network promotion is limited for the sake of brevity for this chapter, but a complete comprehensive synthesis of sport and television promotion is provided by Billings (2006).

Sponsorships

Sponsorships can be defined as "the provision of assistance by a commercial organization, in cash or kind, to a sports property, in exchange for the rights to be associated with the sports property for the purpose of gaining commercial and economic advantage" (Tripodi, 2001, p. 96). *Global* spending for sponsorships in 1990 was a mere $3.6 billion, but by 2014, that value has significantly increased to $21.4 billion—in North America alone. Sport-only sponsorship spending acquired nearly 70% of the market share, earning $14.4 billion in 2014 (IEG, 2015). There has been an average of 4% growth in sport sponsorship spending year-over-year since 2010 (IEG, 2015), demonstrating a practice unlikely to cease.

Unlike traditional advertising, sport sponsorship "allows brands to be presented to a vast array of audiences" (Tripodi, 2001, p. 110) that marketers would not normally reach, because "sport as a corporate marketing tool provides increased flexibility, broad reach, and high levels of brand and corporate exposure" (Pegoraro, Ayer, & O'Reilly, 2010, p. 1454). Research suggests that sponsorship may be more effective than traditional advertising because of the combination of cognitive processes involved with sport (Harvey, Gray, & Despain, 2006) and the variety of market factors, such as sponsor–event congruency and brand prominence which positively influence recall and brand evaluations (Johar & Pham, 1999; Pham & Johar, 2001). Sponsorships engage the consumer at an emotional level, creating a link between the sponsor and the event that the consumer already values (Crimmins & Horn, 1996). Ultimately, research has concluded a positive correlation between firms' sponsorship announcement and their shareholder wealth, adding to the financial validity of this practice (Clark, Cornwell, & Pruitt, 2009).

Sponsorship not only impacts the business of sport, but may also impact players' and organizations' decision-making because of the financial opportunities tied to them. In 2012, Dwight Howard, sponsored by Adidas, would not consider a trade to the Chicago Bulls largely because Chicago Bulls star Derrick Rose was also sponsored by Adidas, compromising Howard's existing deal with Adidas. When asked about the decision, an Adidas executive stated:

> Adidas simply cannot have its two signature players on the same team in the same market . . . Derrick is the face of that market, and Adidas can't possibly have maximum bang for its buck with Dwight there. It serves Adidas no purpose. They need them as rivals in competing markets.
>
> *(Wojnarowski, 2011)*

More recently, sponsorship's role influenced the 2014 FIFA World Cup and Brazil's anti-alcohol policy in soccer stadiums. Beer sales had been illegal at football matches in Brazil since 2003; however, a bill was signed by the Brazilian legislature—under pressure from FIFA—permitting Budweiser beer to sell its products in stadiums during the World Cup. This of course allowed Budweiser to maintain its sponsorship as the "Official Beer of the FIFA World Cup." Anheuser-Busch purchased a World Cup sponsor package with annual fees ranging from $10 to $25 million (IEG Press Release, 2010), leading many to believe this lucrative contract was the foundation of FIFA's pressure on the Brazilian government to change their policy.

In sum, sport and advertising conjointly benefit by promoting the bundled sport product, subsequently providing space to promote other brands. Sport and advertising's relationship fulfills the assertion that we are "a developed world with few concerns for immediate needs towards survival, consumerism appears to have become an end in itself . . . an abstract escape from the predetermined, and the means to build an identity for themselves" (Thrassou, Vrontis, Kartakoullis, & Kriemadis, 2012, p. 290). In a time of hyper-mediation, increased market competition, and plentiful consumerism, the duality of sport *and* advertising, as well as sport *as* advertising, offers an opportunity for research and further theoretical development.

Theories Relevant to Sport

Sport is consumed in stadiums, arenas, mass media, and—to an extent—social media. The proliferation of mediated sport offerings increases competition for viewer attention, suggesting the need for holistic, value-based approaches to marketing communication encompassing traditional and contemporary marketing theories to reach specialized audiences (Thrassou et al., 2012). Advertising strategies focusing on relationships and consumer insights may yield effective outcomes for attracting audiences and maintaining fans.

Antiquated marketing theories, such as the four Ps (price, product, promotion, and place; Stanton, Etzel, & Walker, 1994), are important to consider but fail to address the complexity of the sport bundle. The bundled sport product is somewhat abstract because of the convening of tangibles and intangibles together, making it difficult to define what is actually being provided and by whom. Secondly, products are typically developed in one area and disseminated at another (Masteralexis, Barr, & Hums, 2008); however, with sport, the product is assembled simultaneously while being consumed, and then recycled through mass media channels offering reviews and highlights. Place also presents a conundrum, because sport takes place in one area, yet can be simultaneously consumed by live audiences and through several mediated outlets. Lastly, fans have become disconnected, largely stemming from ballooning prices for entry into many stadiums (Mullin et al., 2007), making the study of sport promotion increasingly significant, particularly as to how transactions can be mutually beneficial to consumers and organizations to ensure continuous reciprocity. It is because of these outlying variables that relationship-based and identification-centric theories should be used when examining sport advertising and its ability in "establishing, developing, and maintaining successful relationship exchanges" (Morgan & Hunt, 1994, p. 22).

Relationship Marketing Theory

Scholars have advocated a shift from a transactional paradigm towards a consumer-relationship paradigm focusing on cooperation and interaction based on shared values and interests (Bee & Kahle, 2006; Gladden & Sutton, 2009). Relationship marketing offers benefits that outweigh transactional models because "it can: a) render a platform to organize a wide-ranging relational construct; b) provide insight into evaluating relationship marketing effectiveness; and c) diagnose and address problems in the relationship" (Kim & Trail, 2011, p. 57). Acknowledging the complexity and the opportunities of the sport bundle because of ancillary product offerings promotes the need for relationship-focused approaches opposed to a transactional-focused approach to fully augment profits.

Addressing the complexities of the sport product requires building a two-way relationship between the brand and potential consumer that surpasses superficial transactional relationships by "attracting, maintaining, and in in-multi-service organizations, enhancing customer relationships" (Berry, 1983, p. 25). Relationship marketing does not discount the importance of financial exchanges, but rather accentuates long-term customer retention and influences repeat purchases through the development of psychological attachment, increased product familiarity, and decreased risk-reduction for consumers (Dwyer, Schurr, & Oh, 1987; Bee & Kahle, 2006; Kim & Trail, 2011; Sheth & Parvatiyar, 2000). Researchers suggest "[s]ports organizations should strive to develop this deeper level of relationship with their target consumers" (Bee & Kahle, 2006, p. 103) to decrease marketing costs and increase sales for the organization by building brand and team loyalty (Gladden & Funk, 2001).

Both brand loyalty and fandom can start at an early age within the context of sport, unlikely to later shift in support of a competitor (Beech & Chadwick, 2007). Research suggests psychological effects may precede consumption (Hoyer & MacInnis, 2007), and "the prediction and explanation of consumer behavior is critical to understanding relationship marketing, and attitudes provide some insight into this phenomenon" (Bee & Kahle, 2006, p. 104). Bee and Kahle's framework (2006) posits a model beginning with consumer compliance, then advancing towards identification, and ultimately arriving at internalization. Compliance is superficial, and is mostly transactional, whereas identification is pivotal in establishing a relationship, most likely through attractiveness to a team or player. Lastly, internalization occurs when an individual's behaviors are ingrained through shared values with the organization. Using Bee and Kahle's framework as a guide permits integration of underpinning identity-centric theories to better understand, predict, and manipulate behaviors of sport fans.

Fan Identification Theory

Fan identification theory can be utilized as an underlying theory for relationship marketing by providing valuable insights for segmenting audiences and creating strategic communication material. Organizations should endeavor to match the values of their organization to their customers' values through strategic and integrated marketing strategies (Bee & Kahle, 2006; Morgan & Hunt, 1994), and fan identification theory provides a useful heuristic for accomplishing that task. Fan identity has successfully been used as a predictor for sport consumption (Devlin, Billings, & Brown, 2015) and to understand subsequent behavior outcomes, which provides useful insights for creating messages to attract audiences and target consumers through sport (Madrigal, 2001; Wann, Dolan, McGeorge, & Allison, 1994).

Fan identification is defined as "the extent to which a fan feels a psychological connection to a team and the team's performances are viewed as self-relevant" (Wann, 2006, p. 332), ultimately providing fans with a sense of belonging and attachment to a larger social structure (Wann & Branscombe, 1993). This results in the development of an emotional ownership of the team, leading to internalization of their team's performance (Donavan, Carlson, & Zimmerman, 2005). The individual emphasizes which categories are important and relevant to their identity, which leads to their organizational commitment (Spears, Doosje, & Ellemers, 1999), willingness to exert effort on behalf of the group, and their desire to maintain membership (Reichers, 1985). Two factors associated with influencing organizational commitment are the perceived prestige of the group (Chatman, Bell, & Staw, 1986) and distinctiveness of the group (Turner, 1985). Together, these two factors may be instrumental in building fan identification by producing the strongest long-term effects (Sutton, McDonald, Milne, & Cimperman, 1997), thus adding useful insights for crafting advertising messages, and exemplifying an audience that can be appropriated through sport.

Fan identification is also fostered through interactions with others as a result of exposure to the sport (Funk & James, 2001), explaining why companionship is a common motivation for consuming mediated sport (Gantz & Wenner, 1991; Wann, Royalty, & Roberts, 2000), and why repeated exposure fosters the socialization process. Understanding the importance of fostering interaction subsequently becomes an important underlying principle for those practicing relationship marketing. Lastly, highlighting similarities between the fans and players nurtures fan identification because the athlete and team is seen as part of the individual's own social identity (Wann, 1994). This may also be a useful heuristic for understanding *why* sponsorships and endorsements are not only attractive for marketers, but also why fans are more likely to purchase their team sponsors' products, even if they report lower affective responses towards the product (see Madrigal, 2000, 2001).

Significant Theoretical Findings in Sport

Scholars have outlined fundamental aspects of relationship marketing theory as it pertains to sport and advertising. Sheth and Parvatiyar (2000) outlined three aspects for entering in and maintaining a mutually beneficial relationship—process, purpose, and participation; Underwood, Bond, and Baer (2001) indicated that sport organizations should develop strategies that permit for interaction between organizations and their fans, and highlight values such as history, heritage, rituals, and traditions; Bee and Kahle (2006) examined how and why consumers develop and enter into relationships with sport, presenting three levels for understanding fan formation: (a) compliance, (b) identification, and (c) internalization. Additionally, Bee and Kahle presented factors affecting sport–consumer relationship formation, identifying involvement, trust, and having shared values as moderating factors. Lastly, Kim and Trail (2011) developed a conceptual framework with general constructs for the sport consumer–organization relationship, outcomes, and moderators affecting the relationship. Kim and Trail's (2011) framework proposes five distinct relational constructs—trust, commitment, intimacy, self-connection, and reciprocity— suggesting relationship marketing influences likelihood of word-of-mouth marketing, media consumption, game attendance, and merchandise purchases.

Other studies examining marketing sport properties and existing sponsors have proposed a framework to assist partners in meeting organizational linkages through the association of three broad elements—context of the relationship, mutually derived benefits for both parties, and the strength of relationship (Cousens, Babiak, & Bradish, 2006). Similarly, Tower, Jago, and Deery (2006) examined relationships between venues and partnering associations in the not-for-profit sport sector, finding that effective relationships focus on achieving goals the individual partners could not achieve individually, foster innovation, and share resources (knowledge and expertise). They also found that factors contributing to a beneficial partnership were commitment, communication, and shared cultural styles.

In sum, organizations could achieve advantages over competitors using relationship marketing strategies focusing on creating bonds rather than focusing on short-term ticket sales and immediate profits (Gladden & Sutton, 2009). The conclusive work provides an overwhelming amount of evidence to support a paradigm shift. This suggests that as sport and advertising continues to advance, organizations should focus on building relationships while the academy continues to test theory via measurement of the effectiveness of relationship marketing.

Additionally, findings in fan identification reveal highly identified fans' reactions as being more intense than those of a less-identified fan (Branscombe &

Wann, 1992; Bizman & Yinon, 2002), leading to predictive behaviors that can guide advertisers' planning and provide much-needed insights. Studies show game attendance (Fisher & Wakefield, 1998; Wann & Branscombe, 1993) and merchandise purchases (Andrew, Kim, O'Neal, Greenwell, & James, 2009; Fisher & Wakefield, 1998) are more prevalent among highly identified fans than low-identified fans. Fan identity has been shown to impact sponsorship recognition, attitude, satisfaction, and knowledge of sponsors (Gwinner & Swanson, 2003; Madrigal, 2000, 2001). Highly identified fans perceive higher levels of *normative pressure* from other members, resulting in higher intentions to engage in in-group behaviors. Madrigal (2001) used this rationale to explain why highly identified fans report higher intent to purchase sponsors' products despite reporting lower affective responses. Research has also proposed models accounting for existing variables in the sport bundle (see Cornwell, Weeks, & Roy, 2005), outlining strategies for marketing professionals to consider when considering participating, such as congruency to the event and the brand's prominence in the market (Johar & Pham, 1999; Pham & Johar, 2001). For a comprehensive review of sport sponsorship, see Kinney (2006).

Future Research

Highlighting the importance of relationship marketing theories and fan identification theory within sport and advertising may be useful in guiding future research—particularly research that investigates the needs and wants of contemporary consumers of the sport commodity. It is imperative that market research grows by segmenting and targeting a distinct group—the highly identified fan. Understanding the antecedents and effects of fandom should guide account planners in developing insights for promoting sport or using sport as a vehicle for advertisers.

A plethora of research opportunities in various contexts—using both relationship theory and fan identification theory—exist. One of the most pertinent areas exists in digital and social media. The power of this multifunctional channel was recognized by Knoda CEO, Kyle Rogers, who reported, "[w]e were able to put together a high impact athlete endorsement campaign for the Super Bowl in nine days, and since athletes have a powerful emotional connection with their audience, our campaign exceeded our expectations by delivering thousands of new leads and followers" (Fidelman, 2014, p. 1). Social media marketing enables influential athletes and organizations in sport to sell products directly to fans following them on digital platforms while providing precise digital analytics to increase the effectiveness and efficiency of strategic messages. From a theoretical perspective, this provides an opportunity to examine fan identification, relationship marketing, in conjunction with social exchange theory (Homans, 1958), to better understand how economic outcomes can be improved through increased social interaction between brands, fans, and organizations.

Additionally, social media research provides an opportunity to collect quantifiable data regarding sport-related networks. Work using social network analysis (Clavio, Burch, & Frederick, 2012) revealed the formation of networks and subnetworks were largely built between fans and traditional media. Examining opportunities for third-party sponsors to engage with a network can extend this line of inquiry. Additionally, the relationship marketing approach can benefit by identifying and learning the psychological needs and social behaviors of these network to create strategic marketing materials for the organization.

While the importance of quantifiable, big data is undeniable in marketing research, critical analysis of the relationship between sport and advertising also exists—predominantly pertaining to the commodification of sport and its impact on sport ranging from amateur athletes (NCAA), youth programs such as the America Youth Soccer Organization (AYSO), and global organizations such as the International Olympic Committee (IOC) and the Federal International Football Association (FIFA). The work cited throughout this chapter focuses on the direct and indirect methods of increasing advertising efficiency and effectiveness within sport, but does little to address problematic practices and socially undesirable outcomes resulting from the increased commodification of sport.

It is worthwhile to continue evaluating and critiquing how the consumer culture impacts amateur events such as the NCAA, and global events such as the Olympics and the World Cup—not only how these affect consumers, but how they influence the organization's decision-making. Slack and Amis seemingly forewarn scholars, stating, "sport sponsorship is best described in the same way as some of the more critical management scholars have described research in mainstream marketing—devoid of social and historical context, staunchly positivistic, exhibiting a low level of theory development, and lacking in self-reflectivity" (2004, p. 259), underscoring the importance of examining antecedents and consequences associated with the transition of sport from a game to a business. The need for critical examination includes the gamut of corporate sponsorship's ability to change laws, as in the case of the 2014 FIFA World Cup, to the exploitation of sexual attractiveness being valued over athleticism in women's sport to sell ratings and secure sponsorships (Hargreaves, 1994).

Conclusion

For the most part, sport is viewed as a form of entertainment, but its ancillary offerings provide resources enabling sport to act as a transferable service, making the advertising and sport relationship compelling. Sport provides "a statement of culture, lifestyle, locality, social group, nationality, socio-economic class, political orientation, history and much more" (Thrassou et al., 2012, p. 295), all of which are mirrored in advertising. This chapter attempts to demonstrate that sport and advertising are conjoined: one, sport is an economically valuable commodity that deserves increasing attention on effective marketing practices, and two, sport is an appealing service that is prime for opportunities to engage in partnerships seeking to advertise goods or services, by using sponsorships, endorsements, or traditional television commercial spots.

Two theories were offered to guide both research and practice. Relationship marketing theories undoubtedly focus on building a relationship between the firm and the fan, thus making advertised messages increasingly effective and efficient. This theory can also be used to study sport's role as a service provider, and examine how relationships between a venue, team, or even player can be mutually beneficial to organizations looking to reach fans. Fan identification theory, when viewed as an underpinning for relationship marketing, is useful for segmenting audiences and identifying core values and insights to guide account planners in advertising; however, more research on the construction of effective message formation is necessary. Insights provided by understanding this audience segment are valuable to sport organizations and their ancillary partners wishing to build lasting relationships with consumers.

References

Andrew, D.S., Kim, S., O'Neal, N., Greenwell, C., & James, J.D. (2009). The relationship between spectator motivations and media and merchandise consumption at a professional mixed martial arts event. *Sport Marketing Quarterly, 18,* 199–209.

Badenhausen, K. (July 15, 2015). The world's 50 most valuable sports teams, 2015. *Forbes.* Retrieved July 5, 2016, from http://www.forbes.com/sites/kurtbadenhausen/2015/07/15/the-worlds-50-most-valuable-sports-teams-2015/.

Batra, R., Myers, J.G., & Aaker, D.A. (1996). *Advertising management* (5th ed.). Englewood Cliffs, NJ: Prentice Hall.

Bee, C.C., & Kahle, L.R. (2006). Relationship marketing in sports: A functional approach. *Sport Marketing Quarterly, 15,* 102–110.

Beech, J., & Chadwick, S. (2007). *The marketing of sport.* London: Pearson Education.

Berkowitz. S. (March 15, 2015). NCAA nearly topped $1 billion in revenue in 2014. *USA Today.* Retrieved July 5, 2016, from http://www.usatoday.com/story/sports/college/2015/03/11/ncaa-financial-statement-2014-1-billion-revenue/70161386/.

Berry, L.L. (1983). Relationship marketing. In L.L. Berry, L.K. Shostack, & G.D. Upah (Eds.), *Emerging perspectives on service marketing* (pp. 25–58). Chicago, IL: American Marketing Association.

Billings, A. (2006). Utilizing televised sport to benefit prime-time lineups: Examining the effectiveness of sports promotion. In A.A. Raney & J. Bryant (Eds.), *Handbook of sports and media* (pp. 253–263). New York: Routledge.

Bizman, A., & Yinon, Y. (2002). Engaging in distance tactics among sports fans: Effects on self-esteem and emotional response. *Journal of Social Psychology, 142,* 381–392.

Branscombe, N.R., & Wann, D.L. (1992). Physiological arousal and reactions to outgroup members during competitions that implicate an important social identity. *Aggressive Behavior, 18,* 85–93.

Brown, M. (December 10, 2014). Major league baseball sees record $9 billion in revenues for 2014. *Forbes.* Retrieved July 5, 2016, from http://www.forbes.com/sites/maurybrown/2014/12/10/major-league-baseball-sees-record-9-billion-in-revenues-for-2014/.

Chatman, J.A., Bell, N.E., & Staw, B.M. (1986). The managed thought: The role of self-justification and impression management in organizational settings. In D. Giola & H. Sims (Eds.), *The thinking organization* (pp. 191–214). San Franciso, CA: Jossey Bass.

Clark, J.M., Cornwell, B.T., & Pruitt, S.W. (2009). The impact of title event sponsorship announcements on shareholder wealth. *Market Lett, 20*, 169–182.

Clavio, G., Burch, L.M., & Frederick, E.L. (2012). Networked fandom: Applying systems theory to sport Twitter analysis. *International Journal of Sport Communication, 5*, 522–538.

Cornwell, T.B., Weeks, C.S., & Roy, D. (2005). Sponsorship-linked marketing: Opening the Black Box. *Journal of Advertising, 34*(2), 21–42.

Cousens, L., Babiak, K., & Bradish, C.H. (2006). Beyond sponsorship: Re-framing corporate-sport relationships. *Sport Management Review, 9*, 1–23.

Crimmins, J., & Horn, M. (1996). Sponsorship: From managment ego trip to marketing success. *Journal of Advertising Research, 36*(4), 11–20.

Devlin, M., Billings, A., & Brown K. (July 26, 2015). Interwoven statesmanship and sports fandom: World Cup consumption antecedents through joint lenses of nationalism and fanship. *Communication & Sport.*

Donavan, D., Carlson, B.D., & Zimmerman, M. (2005). The influence of personality traits on sports fan identification. *Sport Marketing Quarterly, 14*(1), 31–42.

Dwyer, F.R., Schurr, P.H., & Oh, S. (1987). Developing buyer-seller relationships. *Journal of Marketing, 51*(2), 11–27.

Fidelman, M. (March 10, 2014). 5 ways the sports marketing industry is about to change forever. *Forbes.* Retrieved July 5, 2016, from http://www.forbes.com/sites/markfidelman/2014/03/11/5-ways-the-sports-marketing-industry-is-about-to-change-forever/.

Fisher, R.J., & Wakefield, K. (1998). Factors leading to group identification: A field study of winners and losers. *Psychology & Marketing, 15*, 23–40.

Funk, D.C., & James, J.D. (2001). The psychological continuum model: A conceptual framework for understanding an individual's psychological connection to sport. *Sport Management Review, 4*(2), 119–150.

Gantz, W., & Wenner, L.A. (1991). Men, women, and sports: Audience experiences and effects. *Journal of Broadcasting and Electronic Media, 35*, 233–242.

Gladden, J.M., & Funk, D.C. (2001). Understanding brand loyalty in professional sport: Examining the link between brand associations and brand loyalty. *International Journal of Sports Marketing and Sponsorship, 3*(1), 67–94.

Gladden, J.M., & Sutton, W.A. (2009). Marketing princioles applied to sport management. In H.P. Masteralexis, C.A. Barr, & M.A. Hums (Eds.), *Principles and practices of sport management* (pp. 42–59). Sudbury, MA: Jones and Barlett Publishers.

Gwinner, K.P., & Swanson, S. (2003). A model of fan identification: Antecedents and sponsorship outcomes. *Journal of Services Marketing, 17*(3), 275–292.

Hargreaves, J. (1994). *Sporting females.* London: Routledge.

Harvey, B., Gray, S., & Despain, G. (2006). Measuring the effectiveness of true sponsorship. *Journal of Advertising Research, 46*(4), 398–409.

Homans, G.C. (1958). Social behavior as exchange. *American Journal of Sociology, 63*(6), 597–606.

Hoyer, W.D., & MacInnis, D.J. (2007). *Consumer behavior* (4th ed.). Boston, MA: Houghton Mifflin Company.

IEG Press Release. (June 3, 2010). FIFA secures $1.6 billion in World Cup sponsorship revenue. *IEG.* Retrieved July 5, 2016, from http://www.sponsorship.com/About-IEG/Press-Room/FIFA-Secures-$1-6-Billion-in-World-Cup-Sponsorship.aspx.

IEG. (2015). Sponsorship spending report: Where the dollars are going and trends for 2015. *IEG Sponsorship Report*, 1–10.

Jackson, S.J. (2015). Assessing the sociology of sport: On media, advertising and the commodification of culture. *International Review for the Sociology of Sport, 50*(4–5), 490–495.

Jackson, S.J., & Andrews, D.L. (2005). *Sport, culture, and advertising: Identities, commodities, and the politics of representation.* New York: Routledge.

Johar, G.V., & Pham, M.T. (1999). Relatedness, prominence, and constructive sponsor identification. *Journal of Marketing Research, 36*(3), 299–312.

Kantar Media (January 14, 2015). Kantar Media report the Super Bowl Scores with $2.19 billion of ad spending during a decade of growing revenues. Retrieved July 5, 2016, from http://kantarmedia.us/press/super-bowl-scores-during-decade-growing-revenues.

Kantar Media (January 22, 2014). Kantar Media takes a historical look at winter Olympics ad spending. Retrieved July 5, 2016, from http://kantarmedia.us/press/kantar-media-takes-historical-look-winter-olympics-ad-spending.

Kaplan, D. (March 9, 2015). NFL projecting revenue increase of $1B over 2014. *Sports Business Journal.* Retrieved July 5, 2016, from http://www.sportsbusinessdaily.com/Journal/Issues/2015/03/09/Leagues-and-Governing-Bodies/NFL-revenue.aspx.

Kim, Y.K., & Trail, G. (2011). A conceptual framework for understanding relationships between sport consumers and sport organizations: A relationship quality approach. *Journal of Sport Management, 25,* 57–69.

Kinney, L. (2006). Sports sponsorship. In A.A. Raney and B. Jennings (Eds.), *Handbook of sports and media* (pp. 295–310). New York: Routledge.

Kondolojy, A. (March 9, 2015). March madness generates $7.5 billion in TV advertising since 2005. *TV by the Numbers.* Retrieved July 5, 2016, from http://tvbythenumbers.zap2it.com/2015/03/09/march-madness-generates-7-5-billion-in-tv-advertising-since-2005/372813/.

Kyle, D.G. (2014). *Sport and spectacle in the ancient world.* London: John Wiley and Sons.

Madrigal, R. (2000). The influence of social alliances with sports teams on intentions to purchase corporate sponsors' products. *Journal of Advertising, 29*(4), 13–24.

Madrigal, R. (2001). Social identity effects in a belief-attitude-intentions hierarchy: Implications for corporate sponsorship. *Psychology and Marketing, 8*(2), 145–165.

Masteralexis, L.P., Barr, C.A., & Hums, M.A. (2008). *Principles of practice of sport management* (3rd ed.). Sudbury, MA: Jones and Bartlett.

Morgan R.M., & Hunt, S.D. (1994). The commitment-trust theory of relationship marketing. *Journal of Marketing, 58*(July), 20–38.

Mullin, B.J., Hardy, S., & Sutton, W.A. (2007). *Sport marketing.* Champaign, IL: Human Kinetics.

Pegoraro, A.L., Ayer, S.M., & O'Reilly, N.J. (2010). Consumer consumption and advertising through sport. *American Behavioral Scientist, 53*(10), 1454–1475.

Pham, M.T., & Johar, G.V. (2001). Market prominence biases in sponsor identification: Processes and consequentiality. *Psychology & Marketing, 18*(2), 123–143.

Plunket Research. (2015). Industry statistics sports & recreation business statistics analysis. *Plunket Research, LTD.* Retrieved July 5, 2016, from https://www.plunkettresearch.com/statistics/sports-industry/.

Reichers, A.E. (1985). A review and reconceptualization of organizational commitment. *Academy of Management Review, 10,* 465–476.

Schaaf, P. (2004) *Sports, Inc.: 100 years of sports business.* Amherst, NY: Prometheus Books.

Shank, M.D. (1999). *Sports marketing: A strategic perspective.* Upper Saddle River, NJ: Prentice-Hall.

Sheth, J.N., & Parvatiyar, A. (2000). *Handbook of relationship marketing.* Thousand Oaks, CA: Sage.

Slack, T., & Amis, J. (2004). Money for nothing and your cheques for free? A critical perspective on sport sponsorship. In T. Slack (Ed.), *The commercialisation of sport* (pp. 259–276). New York: Routledge.

Spears, R., Doosje, B., & Ellemers, N. (1999). Commitment and the context of social perception. In R.S.N. Ellemers (Ed.), *Social identity* (pp. 59–83). Oxford: Blackwell.

Stanton, W.J., Etzel, M.J., & Walker, B.J. (1994). *Fundamentals of marketing* (10th ed.). New York: McGraw-Hill.

Sutton, W.A., McDonald, M.A., Milne, G.R., & Cimperman, J. (1997). Creating and fostering fan identification in professional sport. *Sport Marketing Quarterly, 6*(1), 15–22.

Thrassou, A., Vrontis, D., Kartakoullis, N.L., & Kriemadis, T. (2012). Contemporary marketing communications framework for football clubs. *Journal of Promotion Management, 18*, 278–305.

Tower, J., Jago, L., & Deery, M. (2006). Relationship marketing and partnerships in not-for-profit sport in Australia. *Sport Marketing Quarterly, 15*, 167–180.

Tripodi, J.A. (2001). Sponsorship: A confirmed weapon in the promotional armoury. *International Journal of Sports Marketing & Sponsorship, 3*(1), 95–114.

Turner, J.C. (1985). Social categorization and the self-concept: A social cognitive theory of group behavior. In E.J. Lawler (Ed.), *Advances in group processes* (Vol. II, pp. 77–122). Greenwich, CT: JAI Press.

Underwood, R., Bond, E., & Baer, R. (2001). Building service brands via social identity: Lessons from the sports marketplace. *Journal of Marketing Theory and Practice, 9*(1), 1–13.

Wann, D.L. (1994). The "noble" sports fan: The relationships between team identification, self-esteem, and aggression. *Perceptual & Motor Skills, 78*(3), 864–866.

Wann, D.L. (2006). The cause and consequences of sport team identification. In A.A. Raney & J. Bryant (Eds.), *Handbook of sports and media* (pp. 331–352). Mahwah, NJ: Routledge.

Wann, D.L., & Branscombe, N.R. (1993). Sports fans: Measuring degree of identification with their team. *International Journal of Sport Psychology, 24*(1), 1–17.

Wann, D.L., Dolan, T.J., McGeorge, K.K., & Allison, J.A. (1994). Relationships between spectator identification and spectators' perceptions of influence, spectators' emotions, and competition outcome. *Journal of Sport & Exercise Psychology, 16*(4), 347–364.

Wann, D.L., Royalty, J., & Roberts, A. (2000). The self-presentation of sport fans: Investigating the importance of team identification and self-esteem. *Journal of Sport Behavior, 23*, 198–206.

Wenner, L.A. (1989). Media, sport, and society: The research agenda. In L.A. Wenner (Ed.), *Media, sport, and society* (pp. 13–48). Minneapolis, MN: Sage.

Wojnarowski, A. (December 11, 2011). Jordan's shadow hangs over new NBA season. *Yahoo Sports.* Retrieved July 5, 2016, from http://sports.yahoo.com/nba/news;_ylt=ApkZ3Hyk6_dMEeUjkBME6KG8vLYF?slug=aw-wojnarowski_michael_jordan_nba_2011-12_season_122411.

22

SPORT AND PUBLIC RELATIONS

Kenon A. Brown

UNIVERSITY OF ALABAMA

Thomas E. Isaacson

NORTHERN MICHIGAN UNIVERSITY

The attention paid to sport and, subsequently, the topic of sport public relations is increasing. A recent article in *The Economist* shared the attendance figures of the world's most popular sports ("The Spectacle of Sports," 2014). Based on average fans attending a game in 2013, the National Football League attracts more fans than any other sport in the world at 68,401. If total attendance over the course of a season is used as the metric, Major League Baseball earns the top spot with 74 million. On television in the US, the Super Bowl is regularly the most-watched TV event in history (Brown, 2014). When Forbes announced the world's most valuable 50 sport teams in 2015, the average value of a team on the list is $1.75 billion (Badenhausen, 2015). Regardless of the metric, the attention to sport in the US—and worldwide—remains high.

In this environment, the volume of sport research by scholars in public relations and related fields, not surprisingly, is increasing. Earlier book chapters dealing with the topic have either noted the lack of research as a significant problem (Neupauer, 2001) or chronicled the relative limitations in overall volume (Isaacson, 2010). This is finally changing, as researchers explore a variety of topics ranging from new contributions to traditional topics such as media relations (e.g., Clavio & Miloch, 2008; Zhang et al., 2011), expanded applications of PR crisis communication theory to sport issues (e.g., Brown & Billings, 2013; Glantz, 2013; Hambrick, Fredrick, & Sanderson, 2013), and nationally trending topics that are also relevant in sport, such as corporate social responsibility (e.g., Babiak & Wolfe, 2009; Walker & Kent, 2009). At the same time, sport public relations research has been featured in sports-specific outlets, such as *Communication and Sport* (e.g., Brown, Brown, & Billings, 2013; Hambrick et al., 2013) and *International Journal of Sport Communication* (e.g., Meng & Pan, 2013), and is becoming more prominent in public relations and mass communication journals as well (e.g. Brown, Billings, Mastro, & Devlin, 2015; Coombs & Osborne, 2012). In fact, *Public Relations Review* featured a "public relations and sport" special issue in 2008. The increase in production and outlets over the last ten years provides new avenues for future research explorations.

Despite this production increase, research devoted to sport public relations is still meager when compared with other areas of sport communication. An accepted challenge related to sport public relations research topics involves lack of widespread access to the sport organizations and their relevant internal and external stakeholders. Consequently, a high number of case studies and the use of convenience samples have become commonplace for data collection; use of empirical research is rare. However, as the overall number of related published studies increases, some themes emerge from the work that become the crux of this chapter: (1) the role of public relations in sport, (2) the role, function, and issues surrounding sport information in collegiate sports, (3) image repair and crisis communication, and (4) corporate social responsibility.

The Role of Public Relations in Sport

The majority of research addressing the role of public relations in the sport arena specifically pertains to connections between public relations and mass media. Typically, these studies look at public relations through two lenses: (1) the mutually dependent relationship between practitioners and journalists, and (2) the role of agenda-setter. While the role of public relations in society has been examined through PR-specific theories, such as excellence theory (Grunig, 1992) and contingency theory (Cancel, Cameron, Sallot, & Mitrook, 1997), these theories have seldom been used when addressing PR's role in sport.

Despite the variety of goals stated by sport public relations professionals, Stoldt, Miller, and Vermillion (2009) found that a strong commonality among those interviewed was the importance of relationships with the media. Hall, Nichols, Moynahan, and Taylor (2007) also stress media relations as a core function of public relations in sport, emphasizing four roles: (a) writing print media relations tactics, (b) producing visual media relations tactics, (c) preparing and delivering media publicity tactics (e.g., press conferences, media tours), and (d) managing the relationship with media gatekeepers.

From a media relations standpoint, agenda-setting is the predominant theoretical approach for examining this relationship. For instance, Fortunato's (2001) study on the role of media relations within the NBA discussed an industry focus on the mutual dependency of the media and public relations representatives. Through interviews with key executives, Fortunato found that a continuous relationship between mass media, NBA public relations practitioners, and the league's stakeholders caused public relations personnel to become key influencers in setting and framing league agendas. Further, he posited that the coverage of the league would be vastly different without the league's PR activities.

Zhang et al. (2011) explored the agenda-setting role of PR from a quantitative approach pertaining to audience effects of media relations efforts by the Women's National Basketball Association (WNBA) public relations' representatives. Through their research efforts, a supported link was found between media relations efforts and game consumption, providing evidence that agenda-setting efforts of PR practitioners are essential in driving fan product consumption. Clavio and Miloch (2008) also examined the media–PR–stakeholder relationship through agenda-setting, further explicating the role of public relations activities in building a positive perception for a sport organization, which leads to team support. Their findings from the study of the efforts of a minor league hockey team stressed the 'win-win situation' for the team and the media, illustrating media dependency on PR practitioners who provide stories for coverage, and the practitioners' dependency on the media to provide credible coverage about their teams through established media outlets (Clavio & Miloch, 2008).

Stemming from the aforementioned findings of Clavio and Miloch (2008), several scholars have studied the role of public relations in building a positive reputation for an organization. Through communication efforts, studies have addressed the need for public relations to facilitate the relationship between a sport organization—including its athletes—and fans (e.g., Batchelor & Formentin, 2008; Summers & Morgan, 2008) or the community (e.g., Mitrook, Parish, & Seltzer, 2008). Scholars have also found that public relations practitioners are neglecting basic publicity tactics in favor of more strategic (Ruihley & Fall, 2009; Summers & Morgan, 2008) and integrated approaches with marketing and advertising (Batchelor & Formentin, 2008; Summers & Morgan, 2008).

Although there has been an abundance of research dedicated to examining the role of public relations in sport, one weakness of this research is that it does not adapt PR-specific theories to examine this role. There are two notable exceptions. Mitrook et al. (2008) used contingency theory of accommodation (Cancel et al., 1997) to examine the push by the Orlando Magic to garner a new arena in 2001. Through 10 interviews with team personnel, the researchers uncovered nine common themes during the negotiations between the team and government personnel that illustrated the Magic's struggle with framing the need for a new arena. These themes highlighted shifts between accommodation and advocacy when there was conflict between the team and its stakeholders.

Coombs and Osborne (2012) focused on the public relations efforts of Aston Villa Football Club (AVFC) after the purchase of the club by Randy Lerner, former New York-based owner of both Aston Villa and the Cleveland Browns, through the lenses of relationship management (Ledingham, 2003) and excellence theory (Grunig, 1992). Considered a 'gold standard' effort in public relations management, the authors used a multimethod case study that included participant-observation among fans, depth interviews with a variety of internal and external stakeholders, and monitoring fan websites, to gain a deeper understanding of the club's efforts to remove the stigma of American ownership of a

European soccer club. From a relationship management perspective, they noted that AVFC took successful steps to strengthen community ties by cultivating trust through transparency and engagement. From an excellence theory perspective, the researchers illustrated the club's efforts as a strategic and managerial function, compared with more common publicity tactics often used in sport public relations.

Sport Information

Within the realm of sport public relations, sport information—the term commonly used to describe sport public relations work at a university level (Davis, 1998)—has attracted the attention of scholars over an extended period of time. Much of the earlier published work is descriptive in nature (e.g., Hardin & McClung, 2002; Stoldt, Miller, & Comfort, 2001) and has been summarized elsewhere (Isaacson, 2010); consequently, this commentary will focus on more recent work. In addition, much of the work is grounded in PR theory or related theoretical frameworks that can be applied to issues in sport public relations (e.g., Hardin & Whiteside, 2012; Pratt, 2013; Stoldt et al., 2009).

Both Pratt (2013) and Stoldt et al. (2009) conducted qualitative research contributing to an improved understanding of a practitioner profile. Pratt (2013) interviewed athletic directors of NCAA Division I universities with major basketball programs about their perceptions of public relations. Results showed themes related to conducting PR as integrated marketing communications, an approach toward interacting with publics consistent with the two-way symmetrical model of public relations, and the management of impressions as the essence of PR, an assumption theoretically linked to work by Grunig (1992) and Goffman (1959).

Finding indications of the practice of two-way symmetrical PR is noteworthy for two reasons. First, it is a contradiction of earlier descriptions of the type of PR practiced in sport where it has more commonly been linked to press agentry/publicity. Follow-up quantitative research should test this further in an effort to produce more generalizable results; if confirmed, it would be a positive indication of progress in sport PR work. Second, these results are gleaned from the sport PR practitioners' bosses. Again, if confirmed in follow-up research, it would show a higher level of respect for sport PR work from a key member of the dominant coalition.

Two published articles by the same authors explore issues impacting women working in the male-dominated sport information field (Whiteside & Hardin, 2012; Hardin & Whiteside, 2012). The first used survey research and a small number of follow-up interviews to determine impacts of the glass ceiling and a method for understanding women's responses to it using the concept of negotiated resignation, the psychological strategies women use to accept its existence (Wrigley, 2002). The second article applied Frohlich's

(2004) friendliness trap—"a term used to describe the faulty belief that women, by virtue of their feminine qualities, possess an advantage in communication-related fields" (Hardin & Whiteside, 2012, p. 309)—in the analysis of focus group results to gain a better understanding of women's experiences in the field.

Image Repair and Crisis Communication

A substantial amount of research has been devoted to the study of the image repair and crisis communication efforts of athletes and sport organizations. Sport image repair and crisis communication has taken on a greater importance because of the global reach of sport, the major economic, and sometimes even political, impact of sport, increased coverage and conversations about troubled athletes and organizations, and the increased activism of sport fans (Hopwood, 2005; Brazeal, 2008). The vast majority of research devoted to image repair and crisis communication in sport has been discussed through the lens of Benoit's (1995) image repair theory (IRT). There have been two overarching findings from athlete image repair research: (1) the mortification (apology) strategy is typically 'successful' (usually operationalized by (a) generating positive news coverage, (b) producing positive ratings from public opinion polls in rhetorical studies and content analyses, or (c) producing a higher image scale score in empirical studies) by itself or in combination with other strategies, and (2) strategies seeking to reduce the offensiveness of the act in question tend to be unsuccessful.

Most studies examining the mortification strategy, whether rhetorical (Glantz, 2013; Kennedy, 2010; Meng & Pan, 2013; Utsler & Epp, 2013; Walsh & McAllister-Spooner, 2011) or empirical (Brown, 2016; Brown, Dickhaus, & Long, 2012), show that the strategy is largely successful. In rarer instances when studies find the strategy to be unsuccessful, a rationale regarding the timeliness of the response is typically the culprit (Brazeal, 2013), along with the honesty (or lack thereof) behind the response (Smith, 2013), or the sincerity (or lack thereof) behind the response (Brazeal, 2008). Brown (2016) and Brown et al. (2012) found empirical evidence that the mortification strategy is more successful as a standalone strategy compared with other strategies, based on audience's perceptions after an athlete provides a statement in response to a transgression.

In some cases, the mortification strategy even supports strategies used to reduce the amount of responsibility the athlete faces. For example, Glantz (2013) studies Plaxico Burress's successful image repair attempts after accidentally shooting himself in the thigh at a nightclub. Burress used a combination of mortification, accident, and provocation (painting himself as a target of criminals because of his celebrity status). Michael Phelps successfully used a combination of mortification and defeasibility, by framing the act as a "youthful indiscretion," after a photograph surfaced of him smoking marijuana (Walsh & McAllister-Spooner, 2011).

Previous rhetorical studies have also provided evidence that strategies used to reduce the offensiveness of the actions of an athlete or team were largely unsuccessful, typically when evidence or previous statements contradict claims. For example, Benoit and Hanczor (1994) studied the image repair attempts of figure skater Tonya Harding after associates attacked competitor Nancy Kerrigan before the Winter Olympics. Harding unsuccessfully used several bolstering strategies, which stressed her family values and contributions to the Special Olympics, and attacked her accuser, ex-husband Jeff Gillooly. In a similar vein, baseball pitcher Roger Clemens also unsuccessfully attempted to attack his accusers, particularly his former trainer Brian McNamee, in response to allegations of performance-enhancing drug use (Sanderson, 2008). However, when an accuser's credibility is in question, reducing offensiveness strategies can be successful, as in the case of Duke University's lacrosse scandal (Fortunato, 2008) and Kobe Bryant's sexual assault scandal (Kennedy, 2010).

An abundance of rhetorical analysis of IRT strategies have been employed, including, but not limited to, the ones discussed previously in this section; however, image repair and crisis communication has less often been examined empirically. Brown (2016), Brown et al. (2012) and Brown et al. (2015) are examples of audience-oriented approaches to image repair research, experimentally examining audience reaction and perceptions of the accused after image repair strategies have been employed. Also, some content analyses have been conducted to examine image repair strategies through traditional (Len-Ríos, 2010) and social (Brown & Billings, 2013; Hambrick et al., 2013) media channels. Studies by Brown and Billings (2013) and Brown et al. (2013) have illustrated a new approach to crisis communication research by examining how sport fans can become an arm of crisis communication, specifically through social media usage. Brown and Billings (2013) used Coombs' (2007) reputation repair strategies to examine strategies used by fans of the University of Miami in response to NCAA allegations in 2011. Results found that most fans used ingratiation (by stressing the need for Miami fans to bond and unite) and reminder (by praising Miami's previous successes) as responses to the accusations. Brown et al. (2013) examined fan-enacted crisis communication during the Penn State scandal and found similar results, using ingratiation and reminding strategies, but vastly using scapegoating strategies to place blame on anyone other than beloved head coach Joe Paterno.

Corporate Social Responsibility

The increase in research examining the role of corporate social responsibility (CSR) in sport is hardly surprising, given its increased attention across disciplines. Specifically in professional sport organizations in the United States, the pace at which they are entering into CSR-related initiatives is prolific. Babiak and Wolfe (2009) describe how, prior to 1990, five or fewer professional sport organizations among each of the four major sport leagues—NFL, MLB, NHL, NBA—had individual foundations. Less than 20 years later nearly all organizations have established charitable foundations to manage involvement in a wide variety of community initiatives, and all of the primary sport leagues have management of league-wide initiatives orchestrated from the league offices. Further, numerous examples exist of charitable foundations established by individual players (e.g., Derek Jeter's Turn 2 Foundation, LeBron James Family Foundation).

The basic premise of CSR for sport organizations is not altogether different from traditional businesses. Bradish and Cronin (2009) offer the following definition:

> CSR can be broadly understood as the responsibility of organizations to be ethical and accountable to the needs of their society as well as to their stakeholders. CSR is not pure philanthropy, but rather, a holistic business mindset, much like a corporate culture, where the "socially responsible" obligations of a firm could and indeed, should incorporate both social and economic interests.
>
> *(p. 692)*

Within sport, however, it is noteworthy that many teams across leagues engage in similar CSR activities with a primary focus on youth, education, health, and community (Sheth & Babiak, 2010).

The CSR research with ties to public relations practice generally fits two categories: (1) published research focusing on the motivations of sport organizations to engage in CSR activities (e.g., Babiak & Wolfe, 2009; Heinze, Soderstrom, & Zdroik, 2014) and (2) a much smaller number of studies focusing on fan reactions to CSR activities (Walker, Kent, & Jordan, 2011; Walker & Kent, 2009).

Babiak and Wolfe (2009) conducted qualitative research through in-depth interviews and a review of organizational materials related to four different professional sport organizations, hoping to better understand the external pressures influencing CSR activities and unique internal resources available that can raise awareness for CSR causes. Results provided possibilities for future research ideas (e.g., CSR activities between sponsors and sport organizations, impact of CSR on a team's brand and image, ability to promote causes via internal and external media outlets).

A case study approach of the Detroit Lions by Heinze et al. (2014) explored how the organization changed its CSR strategy in an effort to improve perceived authenticity and to better link its activities to community needs. Future quantitative work exploring the effects of such changes with relevant stakeholders, grounded in theories of persuasion, provides a logical extension.

Walker et al. (2011) sought to determine if differences related to the impact of CSR on reputation, purchase decisions, and patronage varied among fans attending NASCAR, PGA, and NHL events. Predictions based on a specific theory are not included; instead a basic conceptual model helped to explore effects of CSR on the three outcome variables. CSR beliefs were found to have statistically significant effects on all three variables. Further analysis revealed that a higher percentage of variance on the outcomes was explained with NHL consumers than NASCAR or PGA Tour consumers.

Walker and Kent (2009) explored the impact of CSR on corporate reputation and patronage intentions by surveying NFL fans at two different game locations. Team identification was included as a potential moderating variable. While team identification has commonly been used in sport-related research related to fan involvement, PR scholars may be more familiar with these distinctions using the situational theory of publics (Grunig & Hunt, 1984). The results found significant main effects of CSR on reputation, word of mouth intentions, and merchandise consumption, with team identification as a moderating variable. The research contributes to a better understanding of the influences of CSR activities on fans.

The important contributions of the two previous studies are the focus on consumers. In sport public relations, additional research focused on this key target audience is necessary for an improved understanding of the impact of PR and community relations activities on an organization's finances and long-term success. Extensions of these studies should explore the effects on community members and casual fans that may support a team without attendance at games. Since convenience samples at games were used, generalizability is limited.

Future Research

Although the amount of published research in sport public relations has increased over the last decade, the area still lags behind other strategic communication areas, such as marketing and advertising (see Chapter 21), in terms of the depth and the breadth of the research. It is evident from this synthesis of sport public relations research that the field is becoming legitimate in the eyes of public relations scholars, yet there are areas and approaches ripe for analysis with the potential to further strengthen the field.

One of the obvious needs for sport public relations research—and a need for public relations research, in general—is the use of more empirical research. While the case study approach is necessary for examining phenomena in a real-world setting, it is difficult to generalize the findings to a holistic sport setting (Yin, 2003). While empirical, and specifically experimental, research loses the advantage of a realistic setting, the findings are not isolated to one incident, potentially explaining phenomena across the intersection of sport and public relations.

Another general issue with sport public relations research is the lack of use of existing public relations theories. Excellence theory (Grunig, 1992), relationship management (Ledingham, 2003), contingency theory (Cancel et al., 1997), and situational crisis communication theory (Coombs, 2007), while prevalent in general public relations theoretical research, have not been used regularly in sport public relations research. Applying these theories can help bolster the acceptance of sport public relations research. This application of mainstream PR theories could also lead to the revelation that sport public relations could benefit from its own theoretical approaches.

When investigating the role of public relations in sport, related to Grunig and Hunt's (1984) four models of public relations, it is clear that scholars are finding a shift from the press agentry/publicity and one-way asymmetrical model of public relations to more strategic, integrated, two-way symmetrical approaches. Although this shift occurs largely with practitioners and, in some cases management, research should be conducted to examine if this approach truly exists by examining the effectiveness of outputs created by sport public relations practitioners. If the goal of excellent public relations is to build meaningful, mutually beneficial relationships (Grunig, 1992; Ledingham, 2003), future research should ascertain the effectiveness of public relations strategies and tactics in building successful relationships among fans, communities, and media. This measure of effectiveness cannot be determined by conducting interviews with practitioners and management alone; future research must sample stakeholder groups to determine if the relationships that exist in the minds of practitioners also exist in the minds of stakeholders. Coombs and Osborne (2012) provide a great example of the type of research needed for future work investigating the role of public relations in sport, using a multimethod approach to examine the organization–stakeholder relationship from both sides.

There is an obvious lack of research devoted to investigating the fan as a stakeholder group. While fan involvement, identification, and loyalty have been examined in other scholarly areas abundantly, there is a need for public relations scholars to examine the team/athlete–fan relationship from the fan's point of view—particularly regarding crisis communication research. Most research in this area approaches image repair from a source-oriented point of view (Benoit, 2000). Adding a focus on an audience-oriented point of view would allow for better analysis of audience reactions and outcomes. This can be approached in two ways. First, while empirical image repair studies have measured changes in perceived image as a one-dimensional variable (e.g., Brown, 2016; Brown et al., 2015; Brown et al., 2012), future research should study image as multidimensional, incorporating measures addressing the trustworthiness of the accused, acceptance of the response, wrongfulness of the act, and perceived responsibility for the act. Other behavioral outcomes, such as behavioral intentions and negative word-of-mouth, should be measured as well. Second, more scholars should follow the lead of Brown and Billings (2013) by investigating fans as an extension of crisis communication. This area could be translated to other sectors of public relations by observing the role of customers and other stakeholders as advocates for an organization in times of crisis, providing an opportunity for sport public relations scholars to assert leadership in a necessary area of inquiry.

The role of social media has been investigated in public relations research, but has, somewhat surprisingly, not been the focus of much sport public relations research. Most research devoted to the use of social media in sport has been used to examine how fans, journalists, and athletes use outlets to communicate in specific situations (see Chapter 19). Because social media has dramatically changed the way organizations communicate to their stakeholders, particularly in terms of speed and volume of information, future research should examine this dialogue created on social media between teams (and athletes) and stakeholders for outcome-driven results. The use of social media in sport organizations should also be examined, hopefully leading to the development of a practical-theory approach to using social media effectively to build relationships.

A final area that could be expanded pertains to the influence of CSR activities on the organization–fan and organization–community relationships. While the majority of CSR research in sport has examined the motivations for organizations to engage in CSR activities, more research should be devoted to examining the effectiveness of these activities in improving or maintaining team image, increasing positive media coverage, and sustaining the organization–fan relationship.

Conclusion

Since Isaacson (2010) summarized the research devoted to the then-fledgling field of sport public relations, many scholars have answered his initial call for more research in the field. Since then, the amount of public relations research conducted in a sport context has dramatically increased. However, most of this work has focused on public relations activities from the organization's (or in rare cases, the athlete's) perspective, developing metrics for determining public relations tactical effectiveness. This is typical of the start of a research stream, where case studies, rhetorical analysis, and anecdotal evidence—in addition to some qualitative research—are used to build theory and establish best practices from the side of the source. For sport public relations as a research stream to ascend, scholars in this field must build empirical research to investigate the relationships between the organization and its various stakeholder groups. This should lead to studying the effectiveness of the public relations practices that practitioners are using. Whether it is media relations, community relations, crisis communication, or corporate social responsibility, there needs to be a shift in focus to comprehensively investigate the outcomes of public relations' efforts to truly see if practitioners are practicing what they are preaching.

References

Babiak, K., & Wolfe, R. (2009). Determinants of corporate social responsibility in professional sport: Internal and external factors. *Journal of Sport Management, 23*, 717–742.

Badenhausen, K. (July 15, 2015). The world's 50 most valuable sports teams 2015. *Forbes.* Retrieved August 15, 2015, from http://www.forbes.com/sites/kurtbadenhausen/2015/07/15/the-worlds-50-most-valuable-sports-teams-2015/#2715e4857a0b4a979e7b57fd.

Batchelor, B., & Formentin, M. (2008). Re-branding the NHL: Building the league through the "My NHL" integrated marketing campaign. *Public Relations Review, 34*(2), 156–160.

Benoit, W. (1995). *Accounts, excuses, and apologies: A theory of image restoration strategies.* Albany, NY: State University of New York Press.

Benoit, W. (2000). Another visit to the theory of image restoration strategies. *Communication Quarterly, 48*, 40–43.

Benoit, W., & Hanczor, R. (1994). The Tonya Harding controversy: An analysis of image restoration strategies. *Communication Quarterly, 42*, 416–433.

Bradish, C., & Cronin, J.J. (2009). Corporate social responsibility in sport. *Journal of Sport Management, 23*, 691–697.

Brazeal, L. (2008). The image repair strategies of Terrell Owens. *Public Relations Review, 34*, 145–150.

Brazeal, L. (2013). Belated remorse: Serena Williams's image repair rhetoric at the 2009 U.S. Open. In J.R. Blaney, L.R. Lippert, & J.S. Smith (Eds.), *Repairing the athlete's image: Studies in sports image restoration* (pp. 239–252). Lanham, MD: Lexington.

Brown, K. (2016). Is apology the best policy? An experimental examination of the effectiveness of image repair strategies during criminal and non-criminal athlete transgressions. *Communication and Sport, 4*(1), 23–42.

Brown, K.A., Billings, A.C., Mastro, D., & Devlin, N. (2015). Changing the image repair equation: Impact of race and gender on sport-related transgressions. *Journalism & Mass Communication Quarterly, 92*(2), 487–506.

Brown, K., Dickhaus, J., & Long, M. (2012). "The Decision" and LeBron James: An empirical examination of image repair in sports. *Journal of Sports Media, 7*, 149–167.

Brown, M. (February 3, 2014). Super Bowl most-watched U.S. TV event of all time with 111.5 million viewers. *Forbes.* Retrieved August 15, 2015, from http://www.forbes.com/sites/maurybrown/2014/02/03/super-bowl-most-watched-tv-event-of-all-time-with-111-5-million-viewers/#2715e4857a0b14499ef06f7d.

Brown, N.A., & Billings, A.C. (2013). Sports fans as crisis communicators on social media websites. *Public Relations Review, 39*(1), 74–81.

Brown, N.A., Brown, K.A., & Billings, A.C. (2013). "May No Act of Ours Bring Shame": Fan-enacted crisis communication surrounding the Penn State sex abuse scandal. *Communication & Sport.* doi: 10.1177/2167479513514387.

Cancel, A., Cameron, G., Sallot, L., & Mitrook, M. (1997). It depends: A contingency theory of accommodation in public relations. *Journal of Public Relations Research, 9*, 31–63.

Clavio, G., & Miloch, K. (2008). Agenda-setting in minor league hockey: A strategic justification and practical guide. *International Journal of Sport Management and Marketing, 5*, 151–161.

Coombs, W. (2007). *Ongoing crisis communication: Planning, managing and responding.* Thousand Oaks, CA: Sage.

Coombs, D.S., & Osborne, A. (2012). A case study of Aston Villa Football Club. *Journal of Public Relations Research, 24*(3), 201–221.

Davis, H.M. (1998). Media relations. In L.P. Masteralexis, C.A. Barr, & M.A. Hums (Eds.), *Principles and practice of sport management* (pp. 356–379). Gaithersburg, MD: Aspen.

Fortunato, J.A. (2001). Public relations strategies for creating mass media content: A case study of the National Basketball Association. *Public Relations Review, 26*(4), 481–497.

Fortunato, J.A. (2008). Restoring a reputation: The Duke University lacrosse scandal. *Public Relations Review, 34*(2), 116–123.

Frohlich, R. (2004). Feminine and feminist values in communication professions: Exceptional skills and expertise or 'friendliness trap'? In M. de Bruin & K. Ross (Eds.), *Gender and newsroom cultures: Identities at work* (pp. 67–80). Cresskill, NJ: Hampton Press.

Glantz, M. (2013). Plaxico Burress takes his best shot. In J.R. Blaney, L.R. Lippert, & J.S. Smith (Eds.), *Repairing the athlete's image: Studies in sports image restoration* (pp. 187–202). Lanham, MD: Lexington.

Goffman, E. (1959). *The presentation of self in everyday life.* Garden City, NY: Doubleday.

Grunig, J.E. (1992). Communication, public relations and effective organizations: An overview of the book. In J.E. Grunig (Ed.), *Excellence in public relations and communication management* (pp. 1–28). Hillsdale, NJ: Lawrence Erlbaum Associates.

Grunig, J.E., & Hunt, T. (1984). *Managing public relations.* New York: Holt, Rinehart, & Winston.

Hall, A., Nichols, W., Moynahan, P., & Taylor, J. (2007). *Media relations in sport.* Morgantown, WV: Fitness Information Technology.

Hambrick, M.E., Frederick, E.L., & Sanderson, J. (2013). From yellow to blue: Exploring Lance Armstrong's image repair strategies across traditional and social media. *Communication & Sport.* doi: 2167479513506982.

Hardin, R., & McClung, S. (2002). Collegiate sports information: A profile of the profession. *Public Relations Quarterly, 47*(2), 35–39.

Hardin, M., & Whiteside, E. (2012). Consequences of being the "team mom": Women in sports information and the friendliness trap. *Journal of Sport Management, 26*, 309–321.

Heinze, K.L., Soderstrom, S., & Zdroik, J. (2014). Toward strategic and authentic corporate social responsibility in professional sport: A case study of the Detroit Lions. *Journal of Sport Management, 28*, 672–686.

Hopwood, M.K. (2005). Applying the public relations function to the business of sport. *International Journal of Sports Marketing & Sponsorship, 6*(3), 174.

Isaacson, T. (2010). Sports public relations. In R. Heath (Ed.), *The SAGE handbook of public relations* (pp. 599–609). Thousand Oaks, CA: Sage.

Kennedy, J. (2010). Image reparation strategies in sports: Media analysis of Kobe Bryant and Barry Bonds. *The Elon Journal of Undergraduate Research in Communications, 1*, 95–103.

Ledingham, J. (2003). Explicating relationship management as a general theory of public relations. *Journal of Public Relations Research, 15*, 181–198.

Len-Ríos, M.E. (2010). Image repair strategies, local news portrayals and crisis stage: A case study of Duke University's lacrosse team crisis. *International Journal of Strategic Communication, 4*(4), 267–287.

Meng, J., & Pan, P.L. (2013). Revisiting image-restoration strategies: An integrated case study of three athlete sex scandals in sports news. *International Journal of Sport Communication, 6*(1), 87–100.

Mitrook, M.A., Parish, N.B., & Seltzer, T. (2008). From advocacy to accommodation: A case study of the Orlando Magic's public relations efforts to secure a new arena. *Public Relations Review, 34*(2), 161–168.

Neupauer, N. (2001). Sports information directing: A plea for helping an unknown field. In R.L. Heath (Ed.), *Handbook of public relations* (pp. 551–555). Thousand Oaks, CA: Sage.

Pratt, A. (2013). Integrated impression management in athletics: A qualitative study of how NCAA Division I athletic directors understand public relations. *International Journal of Sport Communication, 6*, 42–65.

Ruihley, B.J., & Fall, L.T. (2009). Assessment on and off the field: Examining athletic directors' perceptions of public relations in college athletics. *International Journal of Sport Communication, 2*(4), 398–410.

Sanderson, J. (2008). How do you prove a negative? Roger Clemens's image-repair strategies in response to the Mitchell Report. *International Journal of Sport Communication, 1*, 246–262.

Sheth, H., & Babiak, K.M. (2010). Beyond the game: Perceptions and practices of corporate social responsibility in the professional sport industry. *Journal of Business Ethics, 91*, 433–450.

Smith, J. (2013). Bad Newz Kennels: Michael Vick and dogfighting. In J.R. Blaney, L.R. Lippert, & J.S. Smith (Eds.), *Repairing the athlete's image: Studies in sports image restoration* (pp. 151–168). Lanham, MD: Lexington.

Stoldt, G., Miller, L., & Comfort, P. (September 2001). Through the eyes of athletics directors: Perceptions of sports information directors, and other public relations issues. *Sport Marketing Quarterly, 10*(3), 164–172.

Stoldt, G.C., Miller, L.K., & Vermillion, M. (2009). Public relations evaluation in sport: Views from the field. *International Journal of Sport Communication, 2*, 223–239.

Summers, J., & Morgan, M.J. (2008). More than just the media: Considering the role of public relations in the creation of sporting celebrity and the management of fan expectations. *Public Relations Review, 34*(2), 176–182.

The spectacle of sports. (June 5, 2014). *The Economist.* Retrieved August 15, 2015, from http://www.economist.com/blogs/graphicdetail/2014/06/daily-chart-2.

Utsler, M., & Epp, S. (2013). Image repair through TV: The strategies of McGwire, Rodriguez and Bonds. *Journal of Sports Media, 8*(1), 139–161.

Walker, M., & Kent, A. (2009). Do fans care? Assessing the influence of corporate social responsibility on consumer attitudes in the sport industry. *Journal of Sport Management, 23*, 743–769.

Walker, M., Kent, A., & Jordan, J.S. (2011). An inter-sport comparison of fan reactions to CSR initiatives. *Journal of Contemporary Athletics, 1*(5), 1–20.

Walsh, J., & McAllister-Spooner, S. (2011). Analysis of the image repair discourse in the Michael Phelps controversy. *Public Relations Review, 37*, 157–162.

Whiteside, E., & Hardin, M. (2012). On being a "good sport" in the workplace: Women, the glass ceiling, and negotiated resignation in sports information. *International Journal of Sport Communication, 5*, 51–68.

Wrigley, B. (2002). Glass ceiling? What glass ceiling? A qualitative study of how women view the glass ceiling in public relations and communications management. *Journal of Public Relations Research, 14*(1), 27–55.

Yin, R. (2003). *Case study research: Design and methods.* Thousand Oaks, CA: Sage.

Zhang, J.J., Lam, E.T., Cianfrone, B.A., Zapalac, R.K., Holland, S., & Williamson, D.P. (2011). An importance–performance analysis of media activities associated with WNBA game consumption. *Sport Management Review, 14*(1), 64–78.

INDEX